AML

D1426891

RED
ROSES

RED
ROSES

BLANCHE
OF GAUNT
TO
MARGARET
BEAUFORT

AMY LICENCE

The
History
Press

For Tom, Rufus and Robin

—

There in the flower garden
I will die.
Among the rose bushes
They will kill me.
I was on my way,
Mother, to cut some roses;
There in the flower garden
I found my love,
There in the flower garden
They will kill me.

Anonymous, Spain, *c.* 1400

First published 2016

The History Press
The Mill, Brimscombe Port
Stroud, Gloucestershire, GL5 2QG
www.thehistorypress.co.uk

© Amy Licence, 2016

British Library Cataloguing in Publication Data.
A catalogue record for this book is available from the British Library.

ISBN 978 0 7509 6400 5

Typesetting and origination by The History Press
Printed in Great Britain

CONTENTS

ACKNOWLEDGEMENTS

Thanks go to Sophie Bradshaw, Naomi Reynolds and the team at The History Press for their encouragement and support, but to Sophie in particular for encouraging me to write this book and for being flexible when I overran my deadline. I have been particularly blessed to have some wonderful friends: thank you to Jonathan Howell, Magdalen Pitt, Anne Marie Bouchard, Neville Brett, Tim Byard-Jones, Geanine Teramani-Cruz, Sharon Bennett Connolly, Kyra Kramer, Karen Stone and Harry and Sara Basnett for keeping me sane during the writing of this book. There have been others. Thanks also to all my family, to my husband Tom for his love and support, to Paul Fairbrass and also the Hunts – for Sue's generosity and John's supply of interesting and unusual books. Most of all, thanks to my mother for her invaluable proofreading skills and to my father for his enthusiasm and open mind: this is the result of the books they read me, the museums they took me to as a child, and the love and imagination with which they encouraged me.

INTRODUCTION

TIME HONOUR'D LANCASTER

A nybody who was anybody in medieval England had an impressive array of heraldic devices at their disposal. Animals and plants, colours and patterns, objects and astrological symbols; all formed a visual shorthand for the identification of rank and family, for loyalty, allegiance and service. The Lancastrian dynasty is a prime example of this: through the fourteenth and fifteenth centuries, it was represented by the red rose, the crowned eagle or panther, the ermine (gennet) flanked by yellow broom flowers for the Plantagenet name, the columbine or aquilegia flower, the antelope, tree trunk, fox's tail or the plume of ostrich feathers adopted by the Black Prince. Marriages and alliances brought a swathe of further connections, traceable through their banners and coats of arms, embroidered upon their liveries or carved above their hearths, trickling through the branches of the family tree. The Lancastrians were patrons of poets, knights in battle, riding the wheel of fortune through its full compass, and immortalised in the plays of William Shakespeare.

The most famous of all these Lancastrian symbols is the red rose, associated with the county itself and reputedly adopted by Edmund Crouchback, the first earl, following his marriage to Blanche of Artois in 1276. This was the genus of the dynasty, although the rose symbol lay fallow for a century until John of Gaunt adopted it again on his marriage to Blanche, Edmund's great-granddaughter. Today, the red rose of Lancaster has come to possess an inviolable quality, a metonymic for an entire dynasty and its struggles to gain and retain the throne, taking on a life of its own centuries after its use. It is a cultural shorthand, an historian's handle, a neat visual juxtaposition with the white rose of York. It represents the interface of fact and fiction, history and romance. Nowhere is this more clearly represented than in Henry Payne's painting *Choosing the Red and White Roses in the Old Temple Gardens*, now displayed in the Commons East Corridor of the Palace of Westminster and familiar from the front cover of many books dedicated to what we now refer to, anachronistically, as the Wars of the Roses. Completed around 1908–10 in the Arts and Crafts style, *Choosing the Red and White Roses in the Old Temple Gardens* infuses the flowers with a profound political significance, representing the moment hostilities broke out and allegiances were declared. But this scene comes from fiction; more specifically, from drama. It is an illustration of Act II, Scene IV in Shakespeare's *Henry VI Part I*, in which the characters of Richard of York (Richard Plantagenet) and Edmund Beaufort, Duke of Somerset select their colours. Yet this gentle symbol, the red damask rose, is essentially martial and masculine. While writing this book, I was searching for another symbol that could stand for the collective biographies of dozens of women, very different in role, character and fate, overlapping across a span of 150 years. I wanted something that would represent the very different way in which women experienced life as members of this famous, much-defined dynasty.

It would not be easy. The range was vast. The women in this book were born into a variety of circumstances, in a number of different countries: England, France, Castile in modern Spain, The Hague in the Netherlands and what is now the Czech Republic. Nor were their destinies clear at birth; some, such as Blanche of Lancaster, Joan, Queen of Scots and Margaret Beaufort, were daughters of Lancastrian parents, destined to become ambassadors for the family, while others joined it through marriage. Some of those marriages seemed full of promise but were cut remarkably short by rapidly changing events. French princess Catherine of Valois was Henry V's queen for just over two years, while Margaret Beaufort's marriage to Edmund Tudor lasted a brief twelve months, though both were tied closely to Lancastrian fortunes by the life of a single, precious son. Others bore no children but contributed as consorts, wives or queens, though often their status was not enough to protect them when their enemies closed in, as Eleanor Cobham and Margaret of Anjou discovered. Some were happily married, even for love, while others were selected as brides for political reasons and, like Constance of Castile, won their husbands' respect if not their love. Cecily Neville was born to, and Jacquetta of Luxembourg married, a Lancastrian but both changed sides to follow the fortunes of their husbands and children. The primary contribution of a few was to reproduce, like Blanche of Gaunt and Mary de Bohun, but the distinct phases of the dynasty meant that they never saw their children live to claim the throne or reap the rewards of their labours. A handful of later Lancastrian wives did become queens. Joan of Navarre, Catherine of Valois and Margaret of Anjou all married kings, whilst one of the two Joan Beauforts gained a crown through marriage. A couple of women who were close to the throne came within a hair's breadth of becoming queen; Cecily Neville is considered by some to have been queen by rights, although such proximity proved to be the undoing of Eleanor Cobham. Later still, a few were forced to fight to defend their rights as the dynasty began to wane, taking far more political positions than they might have anticipated. Finding a suitable symbol for them all, to balance the masculine red rose, to demarcate their unique experiences from each other and from those of their men, would not be simple.

Room 40 of the British Museum is dedicated to items from medieval Europe. It houses a small white swan badge standing 3.3cm tall by 3.5cm wide, with additional length provided by a gold chain attached to a collar around the bird's neck. It was made in Paris at the end of the fourteenth century, from gold overlaid with opaque white enamel, and has minute traces of pink enamel on the beak and black on the legs and feet. Known as the Dunstable Swan Jewel since its discovery at the priory of that town in 1965, it was probably a livery badge made to represent Lancaster, either owned by a member of the family or someone who wished to display their allegiance. The swan sounds very much like the one listed in Richard II's treasure roll: 'item, i cigne d'or amiell blanc ove i petit cheine d'or pendant entour le cool, pois ii unc, pris xlvis viiid,' or 'item, a gold swan enamelled with white with a little gold chain hanging around the neck, weighing 2oz, value 46s 8d.'[1] It is very likely that it found its way into the royal treasury after the goods of Richard's uncle, Thomas, Duke of Gloucester, were seized in 1397, which included a book embroidered with swans from the family of his wife. The Dunstable jewel has become an important medieval symbol, a rare survival drawing the attention of the museum's visitors with its delicate beauty and its mysterious past.

The swan symbol came into the Lancastrian dynasty through the marriage of Henry IV, then Henry of Bolingbroke, to the heiress Mary de Bohun in the 1380s. Around the same time, Henry's uncle, the Duke of Gloucester, married Mary's elder sister Eleanor, her only surviving sibling, which transferred the entire de Bohun inheritance to the English royal family. Swans had been featured on the de Bohun family seal since earlier that century and may have come to them from their connection with the Mandeville family, the Earls of Essex, whose use of it may have been a reference to their descent from Adam Fitz Swanne. A contemporary of William the Conqueror, Swanne or Sweyn, owned a great deal of land in the north of England, including some properties in Hornby in Lancashire, and the swan device was also used by other families descended from him, including that of Cecily Neville, whose seal featured a swan with the shield of York upon its breast. Yet there may already have been a regal connection, given the daring motto Edward III had painted upon his shield: 'Hay, hay the white swan, by God's tout I am thy man.'[2]

As my research progressed, I found more evidence of the swan being used as a symbol in a way that highlighted the feminine contribution to the dynasty. The first Lancastrian king, Henry IV, married into the de Bohun family two decades before he claimed the throne and the swan forms the centrepiece of the seal used by his wife Mary: a white swan with wings raised but not fully outstretched, head bent forward and one eye visible, chained about the neck with a coronet collar. Her sister Eleanor, who married a son of Edward III, also used the swan, which features on her tomb in Westminster Abbey, while her will bequeathed to her son Humphrey a book and a psalter with white swans enamelled on the clasps, to be passed on from heir to heir. Her great-great-great-grandson, the Duke of Buckingham, was still using the swan well into the reign of Henry VIII.

As a result of this connection, the de Bohun swan became part of the visual culture of the Lancastrians; a constant reminder of the female contribution and what was owed to it: Henry IV rode a horse covered in cloth embroidered with swans and the seal of his son, the future Henry V, featured an ostrich feather in a scroll held by a swan. It was made into jewellery, such as the Dunstable Swan, which may or may not have been one of the New Year's gifts exchanged by Mary and Henry mentioned in family records. It found its way on to Henry V's banner, it was used by Humphrey, Duke of Gloucester and made into badges by Margaret of Anjou to distribute on behalf of her son. Not every woman associated with the Lancastrian dynasty employed the device of the swan, they often brought their own personal or family devices to an already crowded visual field, but the qualities embodied by the creature make it a fitting symbol of their varied endeavours.

Apart from the connection with Adam Fitz Swanne, the de Bohuns identified with the popular French story of 'the Swan Knight', known to us in its modern form of the myth of Lohengrin, the subject of Wagner's famous opera first performed in 1850. The story was treasured among the de Bohun family; it was the subject of the book decorated with swan clasps, which Eleanor passed down to her son. It is not possible to know which version of the verse romance the book contained, but it would have been derived from the Crusade Cycle of the *Chansons de Geste*, from which the Chevalier au Cygne appeared in 1192 and then the late fourteenth-century *Chevelere Assigne*. The various accounts include a mysterious woman bathing whilst clutching a gold necklace, who captivates a passing man and becomes his wife, and bears septuplets before the jealousy of others drives the family apart for years. The themes are those of beauty and truth, romantic and passionate love, motherhood and fertility, misunderstanding and rivalry, unjust punishment and avenging justice, just as swans are frequently the artistic symbols of elegance and power, poetry and harmony. Not every woman associated with the Lancastrian dynasty used the swan badge, but its qualities could be metonymic for all their contributions. In addition, the chain around the bird's neck speaks of a limited freedom, of the nature of women's existence as the possessions of men, bound by their gender, although many of the ladies in this book challenged and defied such restrictions.

I thus elected to use the de Bohun swan as the uniting factor for these women. It provides the perfect foil for the red Lancastrian rose, illustrating the layered nature of history and the human experience: the dominating political masculine sphere which dictated the course of their lives and which has created an overarching metanarrative of the period above the symbiotic quieter, more marginalised feminine strand, less well understood and less well defined by the processes of history, a function of the male world yet also in constant difference and emergence from it, both within and without. The stories of the Lancastrian men have been told many times. They are full of larger-than-life characters, the giants of history, so this book seeks to trace a series of *petits récits*, or small individual narratives, to illuminate the biographies of the women in their lives. These daughters, wives and mothers did not necessarily live on the margins but have been sidelined by the dominant narrative. In fact, even a cursory glance at their biographies shows that these women played influential roles. This book seeks to ascertain the nature of their contribution and the means by which they influenced their men and historical events. It was largely a question of personality and circumstances.

JUNE 1509

On a Saturday at the end of June 1509, the streets of London filled with people hoping to see the new King of England ride past on his way from the Tower to his coronation in Westminster Abbey. Banners fluttered in the breeze amid an air of expectation. From a house in Cheapside, members of the royal family had gathered to await the procession's arrival. The most imposing figure was that of the new king's 66-year-old grandmother, Margaret Beaufort, her tiny frame encased in a dress of tawny-brown damask and silk – a colourful change from her usual black and white attire and the headdress and wimple she wore as a vowess. Though she was three-times widowed and had resolved to live a religious life, this was not a day she intended to miss. She had hired the Cheapside house from a citizen for a daily rent of 2s 10d, though, for the sake of discretion, she was concealed from the crowds by a lattice.

It might have been the young Henry VIII who was about to be crowned, but it was Margaret's skill in organisation that ensured the day ran smoothly. Over the previous two decades she had gained such a reputation for her abilities that the Privy Council had appointed her regent during the transfer of power from one king to the next. Margaret had wasted no time in assembling the councillors in her chambers to ascertain the correct proceedings and etiquette for the occasion, just as twenty-three years earlier she had set in stone the arrangements for the births of Henry and his siblings. Since then, she had played a central role at the heart of the Tudor dynasty and, before that, had fought against the odds to survive when her family's very existence was threatened. There had been moments when her life was in danger, when she feared the only son she cherished, Henry VII, was dead and when he had spent years beyond her reach. The coronation of June 1509 was a bittersweet moment for Margaret, Countess of Richmond and Derby. It was a triumph, handing power seamlessly from one king to the next without the bloodshed or dispute that had marred recent decades, but it had only been possible because of the death of Margaret's son. Henry VII now lay beside his wife in the chapel he had built at Westminster Abbey.

But the pathos of the moment was lost amidst the sound of trumpets. Heralds had run ahead to announce the imminent arrival of the king. At the far end of Cheapside appeared the blue robes of the new Knights of the Garter, anointed in a secret ceremony held overnight at the Tower. Behind them came a figure riding on horseback, a horse dressed in cloth of gold, walking slowly under a gold canopy held aloft by the Barons of the Cinque Ports. Henry VIII was just 18, tall at over 6ft, athletic, broad-shouldered, strawberry blonde and handsome. He wore a gold jacket embroidered with gems: diamonds and pearls, rubies and emeralds, underneath long robes of crimson velvet and around his neck was a collar of rubies. Following behind was his new queen, the Spanish princess Catherine of Aragon, to whom he had been married for only two weeks: two exciting weeks filled with passion and plans. Catherine was a petite, curvaceous beauty, wearing her long red hair loose for the coronation and a gold coronet with oriental stones set upon her head. She was dressed in white embroidered satin and riding a horse trapped in white cloth of gold. They made a handsome couple, with the blood of the dynasties of York and Lancaster flowing in Henry's veins and Catherine's Spanish heritage tempered by her descent from Catherine of Lancaster, the daughter of John of Gaunt. Their marriage brought the Lancastrian dynasty full circle, tracing its path from its earliest days, with the children of Edward III, through 150 years of turbulent history. By marrying a direct descendant of the Lancastrian line, Henry was honouring his grandmother's family, herself a great-granddaughter of Gaunt. There was a pleasing symmetry to it, a sense of conclusion.

On the following day, Midsummer's Day, Margaret took her seat in Westminster Abbey to witness the coronation. She had been given a privileged position in the choir, so she would have been able to see everything as her grandson swore his oath and stepped forward to be anointed at the high altar, his body daubed with holy oil in nine different places. Then the crown of Edward the Confessor was raised above him before being gently placed upon his golden head. It was a moment that resonated down the centuries, of the coronations of kings and queens less fortunate than Henry, whose reigns had been cut short, or marred by dissent, or tainted by scandal or violence. Margaret's personal history, her family line, had been bound up with the lives of all of them: the Lancastrians Henry IV, Henry V, Henry VI, the Yorkists Edward IV and Richard III, and her own son Henry VII, the first king of the Tudor line. It was an intimidating legacy and Margaret knew it. The day also brought to the surface her particular blend of superstition and fatality: for her, happy events always contained a kernel of tragedy, of fear for the future, just as the wheel of fortune could be trusted to keep on turning. She wept tears of fear as well as tears of joy that day.

Such superstition was only to be expected. As she sat in the choir watching her grandson being crowned, Margaret was both central to the proceedings and marginal to them. As a woman, even such a strong one, the line of inheritance had passed through her but her sphere of influence was necessarily limited, her voice muted. Behind that long line of kings was an equally long line of women whose fortunes had been intimately associated with the Lancastrian dynasty, marrying its men and bearing its children, through peaks of success and terrible losses and failures, struggling to survive and enduring the unexpected, on both personal and national levels. Since the house of Lancaster had first claimed the English throne back in 1399, it had been a tumultuous ride and, for a while, the cause had almost seemed lost. Margaret had played a significant role in the final phase of the struggle, a wise and shrewd player for whom patience had reaped the ultimate reward.

The coronation of Margaret's grandson marked the end of her journey. Five days later, she died peacefully in the Deanery of Westminster Abbey and was given a state funeral. Many of her predecessors had not met with such a fortunate end. They had been deposed, exiled, lost their lives in childbirth or plague, endured violence or rejection, or outlived their loved ones and died alone. Each woman was a single piece of the family's picture, a branch on the tree that had finally blossomed. This book tells the story of Margaret and all the other women who helped build the Lancastrian dynasty.

PART ONE

I

BLANCHE OF LANCASTER, 1345–68

… the brightest lights and the darkest shadows meet.[1]

1

On the last day of December 1347, a ship limped into the harbour at Genoa in northern Italy. Its journey had been long and perilous, 'delayed by tragic accidents' as it brought survivors home from the siege that was taking place at Caffa, far away on the Baltic Sea. The Genoan citizens nervously watched it approach. After months of hearing terrible reports of atrocities inflicted by the Mongols on the Christians trapped behind Caffa's walls, news of the ship's arrival spread through the streets and people left their homes and businesses and hurried down to the docks. As Gabriele de' Mussis of Piacenza, who is thought to have been among those on board, recounted, 'relations, kinsmen and neighbours flocked … from all sides,' hoping to hear news of their loved ones. And yet, those staggering off the ship on to the quay had brought home more than they had bargained for. 'To our anguish,' says de' Mussis, 'we were carrying darts of death. When they hugged and kissed us, we were spreading poison from our lips even as we spoke.'[2] Within days the first ominous signs began to appear. Genoa's citizens fell ill with icy chills that developed into burning fevers, racking headaches and the glands in their armpits and groins swelled up, hard, painful and discoloured. The signs of plague were unmistakeable. Tragically, they were also unavoidable. Thus began one of the worst pandemics of the medieval era: the Black Death.

In the mid-1340s, the bubonic plague had crept slowly across Europe: a tiny bacterium, invisible to the naked eye, which thrived in the guts of fleas. Those fleas burrowed into the fur of rodents running through the city sewers, or crept into the folds of cloth brought by merchants from the east. It had devastated the Mongol army at Caffa, who loaded their trebuchets with piles of bodies and propelled them over the city walls and on to their enemies, in the belief that the stench of the dead would infect the very air the Christians breathed. De' Mussis believed that 'one infected man could carry the poison to another, and infect people and places with the disease by look alone.'[3] Genoa would prove to be its foothold in Europe. By the end of January, the disease had taken hold in Venice and Marseilles, the ports along the Ligurian Sea and the Côte d'Azur. Then it started to spread north.

By April, the first cases were being reported in Avignon. Its resident pope, Clement VI, was the fourth of seven to choose to base himself in the French city instead of Rome. Louis Heyligen of Beeringen, a musician at the papal court, in the service of Cardinal Colonna, wrote that 'when one infected person dies everyone who saw him during his illness, visited him, had any dealings with him, or carried him to burial, immediately follows him, without any remedy'.[4] He reported that people were afraid to drink from wells or to eat sea fish, in the belief that it could have been contaminated by bad humours, and no one dared eat spices less than a year old in case they came from infected Italian ships. The pope ordered anatomical examinations of the corpses, which were found to have infected lungs filled with blood; he also consulted astronomers, who blamed the conjunction of Jupiter, Mars and Saturn, while popular opinion conformed to type by pointing the finger at the Jews. Yet the true cause of the pestilence, and the cure, continued to elude them. Heyligen's employer, Cardinal Colonna, was among the casualties, dying on 3 July 1348. Another of Avignon's victims was Petrarch's beloved Laura.

By the summer, the pandemic was approaching the English Channel and the kingdom of Edward III, the seventh Plantagenet ruler. In Paris, Carmelite Friar Jean de Venette described how 'those who fell ill lasted little more than two or three days, but died suddenly, as if in the midst of health, for someone who was healthy one day could be dead and buried the next.' Five hundred bodies were being buried every day in the cemetery of the Holy Innocents.[5] At Tournai, just 80 miles from the port of Calais, Gilles il Muisis, Abbot of St Giles, wrote in his *Chronicle* that 'the mortality was so great that in many places a third of the population died, elsewhere a quarter or a half, and in several places only one or two people out of ten survived.'[6]

Its island nature could have been England's salvation. However, as the cause of the contagion was not understood, nothing was done to curb the flow of maritime activity that was usually the country's life-blood. The household accounts of Edward III from this period show that over 15,000 mariners were currently in the king's employ, divided among at least 700 ships, from Bristol in the west to Sandwich in the east, Southampton in the south, all along the coastline to Newcastle in the north and abroad in Spain, Ireland and Flanders.[7] In fact, on 6 May 1348, instructions were issued to the collectors of customs at the ports of Sandwich, Winchelsea, Southampton and Chichester, to allow freer export of wool to Flanders.[8] Additionally, towards the end of that month, free passage was given to Benedictine monks in England through Calais to St Mary's Abbey at Lire, 80 miles west of Paris, where the plague was raging. As late as 6 August, Edward III ordered that a group of Knights Hospitaller must be allowed to embark from Sandwich for Rhodes 'with their household and reasonable expenses in gold'.[9] By this point, it was already too late. England was infected.

It only took one ship. The unhappy vessel had landed at Melcombe in Dorset carrying sailors from Gascony, and the first deaths were recorded as taking place on 23 June. The plague arrived at Bristol a week later and the *Anonimalle Chronicle* recorded that it 'lasted in the south country around Bristol throughout August and all winter', before spreading north and west the following year, so that 'the living were hardly able to bury the dead.'[10] By Easter 1349, it was raging through East Anglia and July saw the first cases arrive in Lincolnshire, the Cistercian Abbey of St Louth recording the loss of its abbot and that 'so great a pestilence had not been seen, or heard, or written about, before this time'.[11] It did not help that constant rain fell 'from Midsummer to Christmas' or that the harvests failed and the lack of available fish meant that 'men were obliged to eat flesh on Wednesdays', the traditional Catholic day of fasting.[12] Rents went unpaid, lands went to seed, lying uncultivated, and prices soared. The *Rochester Cathedral Chronicle* reported that 'there were in those days, death without sorrow, marriage without affection, self-imposed penance, want without poverty and flight without escape.'[13] Worse still, most people believed that the plague was a punishment sent directly from God, a divine visitation upon the heads of a world that had somehow offended. In Oxford, John Wycliffe predicted that the world would end in the year 1400.

The plague claimed rich and poor alike. The family of Edward III, King of England for the last twenty years, were to discover that royal blood and thick castle walls would provide no safeguard against its terrible, irrepressible spread. With his wife Philippa of Hainault and their ten surviving children, Edward listened to the reports of the disease's devastating effects on his people and avoided some of the worst afflicted places. Having returned from laying siege to Calais only that October, he came home to a devastated realm and chose to pass the Christmas season of 1347 at Guildford Castle. Behind its stout closed doors, the royal family could forget for a moment that the world outside was disintegrating and throw themselves into celebrations. The court donned fantastic costumes for a masque, which included the heads and wings of fourteen peacocks, headpieces of silver angels and the heads of virgins and 'wodewose' or wildmen.[14] There was also a royal marriage to be planned. In the summer of 1348, Edward and Philippa's daughter, the 14-year-old Joan of England, left England to travel to Castile in order to be married. Her trousseau included a wedding dress of over 150yd of silk, a brown and gold silk dress embroidered with lions enclosed in circles, a gown of green silk sewn with wild men, animals and roses. Yet, as soon as her ship disembarked at Bordeaux, her party started falling ill and, despite fleeing the city, Joan died on 2 September. Two of her younger brothers, Thomas and William of Windsor, then aged about 1 year and 10 weeks respectively, were also lost during that summer.

In Lincolnshire, another family with small children were bracing themselves for the arrival of the plague. At Bolingbroke Castle, situated in the open countryside between the city of Lincoln and the North Sea coast, Henry of Grosmont, Earl of Lancaster, was hoping that his home was remote enough to shelter his family from the coming onslaught. It had been built in the 1230s, with five towers, walls 12ft thick and a moat almost eight times as wide. The ground rose to hills on three sides, which afforded them some natural protection. Animals were kept in the outer bailey and several fishponds would have kept the family supplied with fresh food. By the summer of 1349, it had passed into Lancaster's hands, and the earldom had been created for him, as a great-grandson of Henry III. Lancaster was a veteran of the Hundred Years' War and Scots Wars, having paid his own exorbitant ransom after spending a year in captivity in the Low Countries, on account of the king's debts. He had been married for twelve years to Isabella de Beaumont, the granddaughter of John of Brienne, King of Jerusalem, a French nobleman who had fought in the fifth and sixth crusades and ruled in Constantinople. The pair had at least two daughters: Maud, who was ten in 1349, and Blanche, whose age may have been anything between four and nine. The existence of another daughter, Isabel, is suggested by a gift of white wine made to her and her mother in 1338 by the Borough of Leicester, although she appears not to have survived infancy.[15]

As the plague spread closer, Lancaster was already aware that his best chance of survival was to stay away from London. Along with his peers, he had been due to attend a session of Parliament summoned to Westminster for that Easter but, in early March, letters were issued from the palace insisting that no 'magnates and other lieges' must attend 'until further order, as the king has prorogued that Parliament until a new summons because that mortal plague which caused the previous prorogation … is increasing' and their assembly would be 'too dangerous'.[16] Members of Parliament heeded this advice, fled their city homes and took refuge on their estates, hoarding provisions, shutting the gates and sitting the danger out. Through that summer, the plague swept up to the walls of Bolingbroke Castle and devastated the surrounding county. A mere 20 miles north, the chronicler of the Cistercian Abbey of Louth described what happened when the first cases appeared that July; many of the monks died, including the Abbot, Walter de Louth, with the illness killing 'confessor and penitent together'. So great a pestilence, wrote the monk, 'had not been seen, or heard, or written about before this time' and 'struck the whole world with immense terror.'[17] The Bishop of Lincoln consecrated new cemeteries to receive the victims of the plague, at Great Easton on 4 May and at Stragglethorpe on 9 June, a further 18 miles north of Bolingbroke.[18] The number of deaths among the Lincolnshire clergy rose from fifteen in June to sixty in July and eighty-nine in August, while the entire nunnery of Wothorpe was wiped out, save for a single nun. It has been estimated from vacant benefices that the Deanery of Bolingbroke lost about 39 per cent of its inhabitants before the plague finally went into decline with the onset of autumn.[19]

For the moment, Lancaster and his family were among the survivors. He received another summons from Westminster in November 1350, for Edward's twenty-ninth Parliament, once it was judged that the danger had passed. Then, with an estimated 1.5 million dead out of a population of 4 million, the magnates would meet between 9 February and 1 March. Five days later, Edward would elevate Henry's earldom to the duchy of Lancaster 'and grant to him all the royal rights pertaining to the county palatine, in that country, to hold for life, and that he should have executions by writs and ministers there'.[20] This might have been as a result of his swift bravery at the Battle of Winchelsea, otherwise known as the Battle of L'Espagnols sur Mer, that had taken place on 29 August 1350. A fleet of Castilian privateers mounted an unexpected attack upon Edward III's ships, which were anchored off what was then the busy port of Winchelsea in East Sussex. Lancaster's swift action saved the king's two sons from the sinking vessel: young John of Gaunt, then aged ten, and the all-important heir, Edward, the Black Prince. According to Froissart, 'during this danger of the prince, the Duke[21] of Lancaster … approached … and saw that his crew had too much on their hands, as they were bailing out water, so he drew his ship alongside for the prince to board'.[22]

According to his own memoirs *The Book of the Holy Doctors*, written in the medieval tradition as penance for a life of vice, Lancaster was tall, fair and slim in his youth, fond of fine clothes and jewels, hunting, jousting, dancing, feasting and the pleasures of the flesh.[23] One source suggests the existence of an illegitimate daughter by the name of Juliane, who was married to a William Dannet of Leicester at some point before 1380.[24] His various foreign crusades had resulted in campaigns, battles, treaties and a narrowly averted duel with the Duke of Brunswick, which was halted when King John II of France intervened. By his forties, Lancaster was ageing and suffering from gout, but his legitimate daughters were two of the most eligible young women in England.

II

As the daughters of the most senior peer of the realm, Maud and Blanche of Lancaster already had a connection with the household of Queen Philippa of Hainault before they entered it on a formal basis. With Blanche's birth occurring somewhere between 1340 and 1348, an earlier date might suggest that she may have been placed with the queen by 1349, while a later one would indicate her likely presence in Lincolnshire during the plague, followed by her entry to the court in the early 1350s. Lancaster's activities suggest that he was in England during the peak of the epidemic but his later foreign career might have led his duchess to seek the queen's company in his absence, along with the surgeons, alchemists, cures and other benefits of the royal establishment. They also suggest that the young Blanche came into contact with Philippa's third surviving son, John of Gaunt, whose ninth birthday fell three months before the plague ship arrived in Melcombe. Although confined within the domestic, female sphere, the queen's women would have attended formal occasions, religious observances and feast days, where there would be opportunities to talk and perhaps even dance with members of King Edward's household.

Philippa was reputed to be a 'virtuous loving wife' and 'affectionate mother',[25] described by Froissart as 'most liberal and most courteous'[26] and renowned for having pleaded for the lives of the Burghers of Calais in 1347. A description of a child princess of Hainault, which may refer to Philippa or one of her sisters, paints a picture of a girl of 8 with hair 'betwixt blue-black and brown', her head 'clean shaped, her forehead high and broad … the lower part of her face still more narrow and slender than the forehead. Her eyes are blackish brown and deep. Her nose is fairly smooth and even, save that it is somewhat broad at the tip and somewhat flattened yet it is no snub nose … her mouth fairly wide. Her lips somewhat full … she is brown of skin all over and much like her father … nought is amiss so far as a man may see.'[27] Even if this account, by Walter Stapledon, Bishop of Exeter, referred to Philippa's elder sister Margaret or the younger Joanna, only a couple of years separated the three, so the colouring and general sense may well be taken to describe Edward III's queen. Moreover, at the end of her life, Philippa insisted that her tomb represent a realistic, honest depiction of herself rather than an idealisation. Her effigy in Westminster Abbey, carved by Jean de Liège of Brabant, bears out Exeter's description of what might have been a family nose, smallish and even, with broad nostrils and flattened end.

Having spent her childhood at the sophisticated Hainault court, Philippa was a keen patron of the arts, gathering a collection of illustrated manuscripts and possessing an appreciation of poetry from an early age. On her marriage she gave her husband the gift of an enamelled ewer depicting characters from popular epics and romances of the day. Edward's present to her had been a French translation of Petrarch's dialogues the *Secretum*, an examination of his faith. In 1341, Philippa's chaplain, Robert de Eglesfield, founded Queen's College, Oxford, naming it in her honour, and the queen took a keen interest in the establishment, securing for it the revenues from a small hospital in Southampton.[28] Philippa was also the patron of the chronicler Jean Froissart, who gained her attention with a narrative poem praising Prince Edward's role at the Battle of Poitiers in 1356. She invited Froissart to England as her secretary in 1361, after which he described the queen as 'tall and upright, wise, gay, humble, pious, liberal and courteous'. Such was the woman under whose influence young Blanche spent her formative teenage years.

As part of Philippa's household, Maud and Blanche would have enjoyed even greater luxury than they had as the daughters of the premier peer of the realm, at the royal residences including Woodstock, Westminster, Eltham, Sheen, Windsor, Langley, Berkhamsted, Clarendon and Philippa's own palace of Havering atte Bowe in Essex. Edward's building programme of the 1350s also saw the development of castles at Hadleigh, Nottingham, Rotherhithe and the magnificent Queenborough, built by William of Wickham for £25,000. Among his innovations were roasting houses for his meat, glazed windows, tiled bathrooms and bronze taps with running hot and cold water.[29] An examination of the records for a few months in the middle of 1353 gives an indication of the provision for the queen's household. Her ferreter and fishmonger was to catch 'conies [rabbits] in warrens and fish in fisheries and stews [ponds]' for her table; the steward of her wardrobe was to bring timber; wine was ordered for the queen's buttery; stock for her buttery, bakery and bakehouse; her usher of the hall was to supply brushwood and coal for her bedchamber and rooms; her clerk to buy stockfish and other victuals.[30] A comparison between the daily food allowance made for an individual of ducal status and that of a mere knight in the late 1340s shows 13s and 4d for the former and only 2s for the latter.[31] The girls would also have accompanied the queen on royal progresses, like her trip into the West Country in August 1347, and may even have been with Philippa at the convent near Winchelsea in 1350, where they awaited news of the sea battle off Sandwich. The girls' arrival at court could well have been timed to fill the place of Philippa's maids in waiting who had married, such as Elizabeth Vaux, who became the wife of Ralph de Buxton in 1351 and was well taken care of by a royal annuity of 40 marks awarded for the duration of her life.[32] As such, Maud and Blanche could expect to be well looked after; then, and in the future.

In November 1351, Blanche, Maud and their mother were probably involved in the preparations for the marriage of Philippa's eldest daughter Isabella to Bernard d'Albert of Gascony. The princess was furnished with a costly mantle of Indian silk furred with ermine, 119 circlets of silk and pearls each decorated with a gold *agnus dei* set on green velvet, jewellery and dresses of gold and silver in preparation for her departure after Christmas.[33] It was set to be a fairy-tale wedding but, with only a week to go, the wilful Isabella refused to go through with the match and remained unmarried until the age of 33. The Lancaster girls would have felt the ripples of scandal run through the court and perhaps witnessed any public or private manifestations of the king and queen's displeasure: it set a standard for a royal marriage, but also perhaps the precedence of love or personal inclination over duty.

Lancaster's daughters grew to maturity in the 1340 and '50s. They received the education of aristocratic women, developing the practical and refined accomplishments, such as deportment, dancing and needlework, combined with religious devotion and the reading of saints' lives, which were designed to instil them with the virtues of nobility and humility, piety and duty. As soon as they became aware of their position, the girls knew that their futures would lie in the making of a successful marriage and the bearing of children. The elder sister, Maud, had followed the aristocratic custom of being wed in early childhood, her husband being the young Ralph of Stafford, eldest son of the first Earl of Stafford. Despite the example of Princess Isabella, Maud is unlikely to have had a say in this, probably spending very little time with the young boy to whom she had been contracted for the benefits of dynastic ties. The agreement was signed on 10 October 1344, with the wedding following on 1 November,[34] when Maud was 4 or 5. The couple's youth prevented this from being anything more than a match on paper and Ralph's early death in November 1347, when Maud was only 7 or 8 years old, put an end to her hopes. A similar match was planned for Blanche, the agreement being made on 4 May 1347 for her to marry John of Segrave, the son of the fourth Lord Segrave. No actual wedding took place though, and this potential union was abandoned before 1350.

It was probably Queen Philippa who suggested a more prestigious match for Maud. Her new husband was to be the queen's own nephew, William V, Count of Holland, Zeeland and Hainault, also known as William I, Duke of Bavaria, the son of Philippa's sister Margaret. The wedding took place in February 1352 in the King's Chapel[35] at Westminster before the couple departed for Bavaria, accompanied by Henry Grosmont. Maud was 13 or 14 at the time of the marriage and Blanche was between 7 and 12, perhaps old enough to be able to understand what it meant and anticipate a husband of her own.

Blanche was renowned for her beauty yet no reliable contemporary image of her survives. However, a vivid pen portrait does, thanks to the presence of one of John of Gaunt's most famous contemporaries. The poet Geoffrey Chaucer had been employed by the royal family from at least 1357, when he was listed in the household accounts of the wife of Edward III's second son Lionel; in 1366 he was married to Philippa de

Roet, a lady in waiting whose sister would later be employed as governess to Blanche's daughters. Chaucer was thus well positioned to write his description of her as the White Lady, a play on her name, which appeared in his dream-vision poem, *Book of the Duchess*. According to his praise, her hair was 'not red, ne nouther yelowe ne broun' but 'most lyk gold' and her complexion 'was whit, rody, fressh, and lyvely hewed'. He singled out her neck for particular praise, as 'whit, smothe, streght and pure flat', with a throat which seemed 'a round tour of yvoyre [ivory]'. Punning on her name, he added that 'goode faire White she het [was called]' and 'she hadde not hir name wrong', being 'bothe fair and bright'. Her shoulders were 'right faire' and her body was 'long', her breasts were 'round', her hips good and broad, and her back was straight and flat. Her white hands had 'nayles rede'.[36]

Chaucer's poem also gives some insight into the wooing of Blanche by the young John of Gaunt. Although it is likely, given their court connections, that the pair had known each other since their early days, the *Book of the Duchess* presents a formal, conventional courtship of romantic distance and idealised beauty. When invited to do so by the narrator, a young man in black (Gaunt) relates the circumstances under which he first saw his beloved. Coming into 'the fairest company of ladyes that evere man with eye had seen together in one place', he noticed one who was like none of the others, as bright as the summer sun, brighter 'than any other planet in heaven' or the moon and stars. She was accomplished, womanly and noble:

I sawgh hyr daunce so comlily,
Carole and synge so swetely,
Laughe and pleye so womanly,
And loke so debonairly,
So goodly speke and so frendly,
That certes y trowe that evermor
Nas seyn so blysful a tresor.[37]

Although the Gaunt protagonist observed that she 'loved as man may do his brother', he had little hope of winning her love, about as much as a man living in India. He lacked the language and wit to understand her and his spirits were too dull to 'comprehend her beauty'. Yet he recognised that her face lacked all 'wicked signs' and was 'simple and benign' and that she never spoke ill against any man or woman, but only truth and, although she knew the ways of the world, she never chided or flattered. Without her, the company was as naked as a crown without stones. In the best conventions of the courtly lover's complaint, she rendered him sorrowful, soft and quaking for dread, sometimes pale of face, sometimes red, hanging his head and fearful to speak. She refused him at first when at last he confessed his feelings, swearing to be true and faithful, loving her 'always freshly new', but took pity on him and gave him a ring.[38]

In reality, the marriage was probably arranged, or at least approved, by the king. John of Gaunt was the third surviving son of Edward III, born at the Abbey of St Bavo in Ghent on 6 March 1340. He had returned to England with his parents that November, where he entered the royal nursery with his siblings before embarking on the traditional programme of education for a king's son by entering the household of his eldest brother Edward, the Black Prince. That year, he witnessed the English victory against the fleet of Don Carlos de la Cerda at Winchelsea because, as Froissart states, he was 'too young to bear arms but [Edward III] had him with him in his ship, because he much loved him',[39] and was rescued by Lancaster. In 1351 he was granted the earldom of Richmond and in 1355, at the age of 15, took part in his brother's campaign to fight across France from Bordeaux to Toulouse, which concluded with the English victory at the Battle of Poitiers. He had also accompanied the Black Prince north to Scotland and, after the English recaptured Berwick, he witnessed the documents by which Edward Balliol surrendered his claim to the Scottish throne in return for an English pension. At Christmas 1357, Gaunt can be pinpointed at Hatfield in Yorkshire, staying with his elder brother Lionel, among whose household was Chaucer, whose acquaintance with Blanche's future husband probably dates from this period. The following April, the entire court was present at Windsor for the Feast of the Round Table, at which knights of the garter were created and lords tilted at the lists to amuse the captive kings of Scotland and France: no doubt Gaunt took the opportunity to impress Blanche with his fine armour and chivalric accomplishments.

One of the most persistent legends about John of Gaunt's appearance was his reputed great height. A suit of armour in the Tower of London measuring 6ft 8in is said to have been made for him, although this identification dates from the reign of James I and the armour is, in fact, only a little older. Yet Chaucer's depiction of him as a man of 'noble stature' might suggest that he was above average height. A description compiled by the Portuguese chronicler Fernão Lopes, who based his pen portrait on the descriptions of people who had seen him in life, claims that he had 'majestic features and piercing eyes' and was 'well-built and straight' but 'did not seem to have as much flesh as required by the height of his body'.[40] An illuminated miniature of 1380 in the *St Albans Abbey Benefactors' Book* shows a man with wavy red-brown hair to his jawline, ruddy cheeks and forked beard.

The most well-known portrait of Gaunt is not contemporary but based on a lost original that was painted during his life. Commissioned in the 1590s, it depicts a man in armour overlaid with a red and black tabard embroidered with heraldic devices, wearing a crown over his helmet. Whilst displaying the fourteenth-century context lifted from the original, the style of the portrait is still resonant of the late Elizabethan era, comparable with the features and stance of the queen's recently deceased favourite, Robert Dudley. In both cases, the face is shrewd and narrow with high cheek bones and red cheeks, eyes focused on the viewer under dark arched brows, thin pursed lips and the same style of moustache and slight beard. Both men have the lower part of their chins obscured, Gaunt by chain mail, Dudley by a ruff, but the similarities suggest that the process of copying Gaunt may have been affected more by contemporary fashions than veracity. One drawing of him as part of a fresco in St Stephen's Chapel, Westminster in 1355 has partly perished, so that the face is obliterated, and the effigy on the often-sketched tomb of Gaunt, from the north side of the high altar at St Paul's which perished in the Great Fire of London, was actually added in the reign of Henry VII.

Gaunt may have been captivated by Blanche's beauty but it was not his first love affair. In the late 1350s, perhaps even in the year of his marriage, one of his mother's ladies in waiting had borne him an illegitimate child, a daughter who was named Blanche, perhaps out of deference to his intended wife. According to Froissart, John's lover had been Marie de St Hilaire, who was also connected with Hainault, or was perhaps the daughter of a family that had arrived in England with the queen, or later, thanks to her patronage. Marie appears to have had a sister, Joan, in the royal service, as they were both granted annuities in 1360, although Marie would later receive a pension from Gaunt after their daughter had made a good marriage to Sir Thomas Morieux. If Blanche knew about her namesake, she would not have been shocked. Despite the church's teaching about lechery and fornication, such liaisons were considered as normal youthful discretions and indicate that Gaunt and his contemporaries found little difficulty in reconciling their spiritual and temporal selves. It also indicates the discrepancies in standards between aristocratic men and women of the day: Gaunt might father a bastard on a waiting woman but, for the sake of the royal inheritance, Blanche's chastity must be unquestionable.

On Sunday 19 May 1359, Blanche and John of Gaunt were married at Reading Abbey. A papal dispensation had been issued on 6 January as the couple were third and fourth cousins through their mutual descent from Henry III. Gaunt was 19, Blanche at least 14, perhaps a few years older. The age of consent for girls was 14, and it was common for such marriages to be consummated once the bride reached that significant age. Blanche's female relations do not set a consistent precedent though, her mother Isabel marrying at around 17, her sister becoming a wife at around 13, while her maternal grandmother Alice wed some time before her nineteenth birthday. When it came to the marriages of the royal family, where desirable heiresses were involved, average marital ages were fairly consistent with the age of consent. Blanche's new mother-in-law, Queen Philippa, was wed five months before her fourteenth birthday and became a mother days before she turned 16.

In 1359, the entire royal family were present at Blanche's wedding and her father-in-law, Edward III, gave her gifts worth £389 11s 6d including jewels: a ring with a ruby costing £20, a belt garnished with rubies, emeralds and pearls worth £18 and silver buckles worth £30.[41] Other members of his immediate family gave gifts amounting to an additional £300, while Gaunt himself gave his bride a diamond ring and a jewel set in gold and surrounded by pearls.[42] The ceremony was carried out by Thomas de Chynham, clerk of the Queen's Chapel, who was paid £10 for his services. Three days of celebrations were held at Reading, where jousting took place in honour of the 'new Diana', followed by a further three days in London from 27 to 29 May. There, according to tradition,[43] mysterious knights accepted the challenge to fight made by the city's mayor, wearing the colours of the city. To the delight of the crowd, they were later revealed to be the king and his four sons Edward, Lionel, John and Edmund.[44] The spirit of the wedding feasting may be suggested by Chaucer's description of the Franklin, 'the son of Epicurus', in the general prologue to *The Canterbury Tales*, but it no doubt surpassed it:

> His bread and ale were always fresh and fine,
> And no one had a better stock of wine.
> Baked meat was always in his house, the best
> Of fish and flesh, so much that to each guest
> It almost seemed to snow with meat and drink
> And all the dainties of which one could think.
> His meals would always vary, to adhere
> To all the changing seasons of the year.
> The coop was partridge-filled, birds fat as any,
> And in the pond the breams and pikes were many.

Blanche's marriage fulfilled exactly the expectations of her social position. With royal blood flowing through her veins, and as the daughter of the leading aristocrat of the land, as an intimate of the court and the possessor of great beauty, ability and nobility, if Chaucer is to be believed, she had easily attained her destined position by becoming Gaunt's wife. If there was also a genuine attraction and affection between them, as far as it is possible to discern across the centuries, it would seem that she had something of a charmed life. She quickly proved herself to be fruitful, falling pregnant in the weeks following her wedding. It may have been the announcement of her condition that prompted the king to award her an annual £100 towards the 'expenses of her chamber'.[45]

TTT

The marriage was five months old in October 1359 when John of Gaunt and Henry, Duke of Lancaster left England as part of Edward's invasion force in France. Blanche remained at court well into the New Year, as a letter from Edward III to his wife testifies. Being 'heavily pregnant', and 'because of the concern we feel for her condition', the king wished her to remain with Philippa until a month or two before her delivery,[46] which was anticipated at the end of March. Married aristocratic women often returned to their parents' home to give birth, especially when their husbands were abroad, retreating from the world at around the eighth month of pregnancy, so it would have been February when Blanche made the journey north to Leicester Castle, the traditional residence of the Earls of Lancaster. There, probably with her mother, she awaited the birth of her first child, in rooms specially prepared and equipped for the delivery, lined with carpets, piled high with sheets, and with religious texts, icons and artefacts close to hand on a 'cup-board'. Apart from the herbal concoctions and remedies prepared by her women, Blanche's faith and determination would be all the relief she could expect during the coming ordeal. A magnificent bed would have been prepared, perhaps with a spare alongside for her to rest in once the sheets had been soiled. Those sheets would have covered mattresses stuffed with feathers, under an embroidered counterpane and tester hung from the wooden frame. One bed recorded in the Close Rolls as being owned by Queen Philippa cost £3,000 and was made of green velvet embroidered with gold and bore the motif of sea sirens holding a shield with the arms of England and Hainault.[47] When Philippa had given birth in 1347, she had used twelve carpets at a cost of £60, probably lining the walls and ceiling as well as the floor. Blanche would have enjoyed a comparable luxury, but a greater degree of privacy, in her parents' home.

Blanche gave birth to a daughter, Philippa, on 31 March 1360. She was probably attended to by a local midwife who features in Gaunt's records, named Ilote or Elyot, who would have stayed with her through the entire proceedings, which might have lasted as little as a few hours or as long as a couple of days. Probably an experienced older woman with children of her own, and likely to have been a widow, Ilote's accumulated wisdom would have allowed her to spot potential dangers, advise Blanche on birthing positions, breathing and remedies, and actively assisted in the child's arrival. After her ordeal, Blanche would have remained in bed for up to four weeks, attended by her women while her baby slept in a cradle nearby. It was not the custom for aristocratic mothers to breast-feed, handing out their babies instead to carefully chosen wet nurses, which would allow their menstrual cycles, and hence their fertility, to resume more quickly. A letter written in 1376 gives a clue to the identity of Philippa of Lancaster's first nurse: in it, John of Gaunt is warned about potential treason by a woman named Maud, who was possibly the Maud Godegibbeswyf, the wife of a man named Godegibbe or good Gibbe, recorded in Gaunt's register as the beneficiary of his support until her death in 1381. She signs the letter 'your humble suppliant and servant, Maud, former nurse to your very dear daughter, the very honourable lady Philippa'.[48] The lack of reference to any of Blanche's subsequent children suggests that Maud served Philippa alone, so she may have been a wet nurse, chosen for her health and milk supply, rather than a long-term servant of the Lancastrian nursery. Philippa would have been christened within a few days, probably in the twelfth-century church of St Mary de Castro standing opposite the castle within the keep. Judging from her given name, it would appear that the queen was the child's godmother as well as her grandmother. A few weeks later, Blanche rose from her bed dressed in a veil and walked the short distance to the porch, where her churching ceremony began. Like the christening, this was an important rite of passage in the Catholic Church which marked the cleansing of sin and her return both to society and to her husband's bed. Gaunt departed from Honfleur on 18 May and presumably was reunited with his wife shortly afterwards.

Edward III, Gaunt and Lancaster had been lucky to survive an unprec-edented event in France which, to the fourteenth-century mind, was little less than a direct communication from God. On 13 April, subsequently known for centuries as 'Black Monday', the skies opened on Edward's armies, lying just south of Paris, and huge hailstones killed around 6,000 horses and an estimated 1,000 men. One chronicler wrote that it was 'a foule day full of myst and hayle, so that men dyed on horseback',[49] while Froissart's description emphasised divine disapproval: it was 'as if the heavens would crack and the earth open up and swallow everything'. Only days before, the English army had gone on a rampage around the outskirts of Paris, raping and killing villagers, which culminated in 900 locals being burned to death in the Benedictine Priory where they had taken refuge and the murder of 300 who attempted to escape. The terrible storm of Black Monday may well have been seen as retribution, but worse was still to come.

By the spring of 1361, the dreaded plague was sweeping through England again. In desperation, people resorted to a range of superstitious methods to try to stay healthy, refraining from eating strong-smelling food that could perish easily such as meat and cheese, washing themselves in vinegar and rose water and drinking warm mixtures of powdered egg shells, marigolds and treacle. Some resorted to drinking their own urine in the belief that it would offer them a degree of protection, whilst others clasped a live chicken to any afflicted areas of their body. If they did fall ill, those who could afford it were bled by a surgeon to rid themselves of infection, with a poultice of violets and clay applied to the wounds. If this failed and they developed the painful bubo swellings in armpit and groin, these were lanced and dressed with resin, white lily and human waste. Beyond this, there was little to do but pray to a God who many believed was visiting a pestilence of punishment upon the world. The unlucky ones were buried in pits, as far from the centre of town as possible, and their clothing was burned.

The 1361 outbreak reawakened memories of the horror twelve years before. Those memories counselled caution among the Cambridge colleges, where the students were dismissed and the Trinity term adjourned twice as 'great multitudes of people are suddenly smitten with the deadly plague now newly prevailing as well in the city of London as in neighbouring parts, and the plague is daily increasing.'[50] On 30 April, Edward forbade anyone to leave the kingdom except for merchants and on 10 May the law courts were prorogued until the end of June 'in consequence of a pestilence'.[51] The York *Anonimalle Chronicle* referred to the great 'mortality of infants', who seemed to be particularly susceptible on this occasion, with heavy child deaths reported around the country. On two days alone, 24 and 25 June, the plague killed 1,200 people in London, and a local chronicler noted that the disease was 'nothing near so dismal and universally fatal as the former [1348-49] but much more destructive of the nobility and prelacy'. It also proved particularly strong in Leicester, killing the dean and seven canons of the collegiate church of the Annunciation of the Blessed Virgin Mary in the Newarke, as well as almost all the brothers of St John's Hospital , both of which establishments had been founded by Lancaster. Forty-three parish priests also succumbed throughout the city. The plague also claimed two members of the Leicestershire aristocracy as its victims.

Henry, Duke of Lancaster had returned to England the previous November, following great success in the Rheims campaign, where he had negotiated the treaty of Brétigny. There is a chance that he was in London, but it is more likely that he was at Leicester Castle when he died on 23 March. Blanche's father was buried on 14 April in the church of the Newarke, on the south side of the High Altar. The building was only recently completed, intended as a mausoleum for the Lancaster family, which it became far earlier than Henry of Grosmont might have anticipated. The will he had made on 15 March requested the presence of Prince Edward and his brothers at his funeral and named Lancaster's wife, his sister and his cousin as beneficiaries. From this, it would appear that Isabel outlived her husband for a short while, but she soon fell ill and died on 6 July, and was laid to rest beside Lancaster at Newarke.[52] Their marble tombs were destroyed when the church was dissolved during the Reformation.

The plague may also have struck at the heart of the royal family, claiming two of Blanche's sisters-in-law. Around the same time that she and Gaunt had married in 1359, Princess Margaret had married John Hastings, second Earl of Pembroke, shortly before her thirteenth birthday. Gaunt's other sister, the 16-year-old Princess Mary, was married on 3 July 1361, to John V, Duke of Brittany. The deaths of both young women occurred relatively soon after their nuptials; Margaret after two years in 1361 and Mary the following year, which might indicate their loss in childbirth but is more likely to have been a result of the spreading pestilence. Both were buried in Abingdon Abbey. Some contemporary chroniclers compounded the theory that children were particularly vulnerable by adding that a high rate of mortality among women was also a feature of this outbreak. On hearing of her parents' deaths, Blanche's sister Maud returned to England from Bavaria, in order to claim her inheritance of the castle, honour and earldom of Leicester. However, she had not been back in the country long before she also succumbed to the plague, on 10 April 1362. At Westminster that November, Gaunt was granted Maud's titles, including the dukedom of Lancaster that had been intended to remain with the family only for the duration of Grosmont's lifetime. This made him one of the richest men in the land. Maud's body was returned to Bavaria, where she was interred at Rijnsburg Abbey.

During the worst of the plague in the summer of 1361, Edward's eldest son had turned 31. Ten years older than John of Gaunt, the Black Prince remained unmarried while John had already become a father, as had the brother that came between them, Lionel of Antwerp, although neither had yet produced a son. Now the Black Prince was determined to marry the woman of his choice, his cousin Joan Plantagenet, also known as Joan of Kent through marriage, a widow of 33 who had borne at least four children. Described by Froissart as 'the most beautiful lady in the whole of England and the most amorous', Joan's past was colourful enough to match that of her proposed husband, who had already fathered several illegitimate sons by at least two mistresses. In addition, the shadow of treason and execution hung over her branch of descent from Edward I. Before her second birthday, Joan's father, Edmund of Woodstock, had been executed by his nephew, the young Edward III, for attempting to overthrow him, so the young Joan had been brought up at Philippa's court, alongside the Black Prince. It was likely to have been at this point that the young man conceived a passion for his beautiful cousin.

But Joan's marital future was to prove complicated. When she was 12, Joan had made a secret marriage to Thomas Holland, Earl of Kent and Baron Holand,[53] without having obtained the necessary royal approval. It appears to have been a marriage of affection. Holland was seneschal to the Earl of Salisbury, responsible for organising his domestic household and overseeing his servants. A year later, in Holland's absence, Joan's family arranged her match to William Montacute, heir to the Earl of Salisbury against her wishes.[54] She lived with Montacute as his wife for several years until Holland returned from the crusades, but was only able to return to her first husband after the pope declared in his favour in 1349. Joan went on to bear Holland four or five children, remaining with him until his death in December 1360.

As a mature widow with a brood of children and tainted by marital scandal, Joan was less than ideal material for a future queen of England. Yet the Black Prince was determined to have her for his wife. They were betrothed six months later, and although King Edward and Queen Philippa were not consulted first, they permitted the match to go ahead. They had little choice: Edward and Joan went ahead and got married at Lambeth on 8 October. Four days later, John and Blanche attended a more formal ceremony at Windsor. Joan was to prove a friend to their family in the future.

There is a chance that Blanche was already pregnant for a second time by Joan and Edward's wedding in 1361. The next surviving child she bore would be conceived in May 1363, but there is a suggestion of another birth before that time. It may have been 1361 or 1362 when she was delivered of a son named John, who did not survive birth or infancy, a victim of the many hazards that might strike during pregnancy, labour or in the early weeks and months. Blanche's windows of conception, meaning the periods during which she conceived, can be established by examining the dates of Gaunt's absences in France. In this case, the dates suggest two approximate time frames for a second pregnancy. Firstly, John had returned to England in May 1360, by which time Blanche had already been churched. Philippa had been born at the end of March and, allowing for a couple of months to re-establish Blanche's menstrual cycle, she may have conceived between June and 24 August, when Gaunt left London for Calais. If this was the case, a full-term pregnancy would have resulted in John's birth falling between February and April 1362. However, this leaves an entire year before Blanche conceived for a third time, in May 1363. The other possibility is that she did not fall pregnant with John until after Gaunt returned from Calais in the first week of November 1360. At the very least, this allows a six-month conception interval between Philippa and John, although John still may not have been conceived until March 1362 to allow for him to have a birthdate of the same year. Gaunt was certainly recorded as being in England at various points during that time, including June 1362 at Leicester and touring his castles in the Midlands that summer and autumn. He was in Berkshire in January 1363, the Savoy Palace in London in May, Leicester in July and Bolingbroke in December.[55] Whatever the timings, Blanche bore a son named John who did not survive and a daughter named Elizabeth, who arrived on 21 February 1364.

If a birthdate of 1345 is correct for Blanche, she had borne three children by the age of 18. It was not uncommon for aristocratic women to start breeding young, but this was comparable with the record of Queen Philippa, who had delivered her third baby at around the age of 19, although the estimated birthdate of her own mother Isabel indicates that she may have been a couple of years older. If Blanche was born earlier, between 1340 and 1344, making her closer in age to her husband, she would have borne her third child in her early twenties. Her involvement in the daily running of the children's nursery would have been one of organisation and supervision, rather than the duties of changing, washing, rocking and feeding the children, which were left to female servants. The letter sent by Philippa's nurse Maud suggests that each child had its own separate staff, although the two girls may have been reared together as they grew older. This left Blanche free to accompany her husband on ceremonial occasions, such as in June 1362 when he was first received as a Lord in Leicester[56] or the reception of King John of France at Eltham Palace in January 1364.

Blanche fell pregnant again in the second half of 1364 and a son, Edward, arrived in 1365, possibly at Bolingbroke Castle, where Gaunt signed a letter in April. However, the child did not live and was buried at the church of the Newarke in Leicester, perhaps coinciding with Gaunt's stay in the castle there on 12 June. That August, Blanche was pregnant again by the time Gaunt departed for a brief trip to Bruges and a second son, named John, arrived in May 1366. This child also died early and was presumably buried in the same location as his brother. To date, Blanche had carried five children to term and while both her daughters survived, all three of her sons had died. High rates of infant mortality were not uncommon, with miscarriages, still births, birthing injuries, cot deaths and infections accounting for losses which were often inexplicable to midwives at the time. The initial failure of any of Edward III's children to produce a legitimate surviving son had serious implications for the royal family, though. The king having passed his fiftieth birthday in 1362, it would be the Black Prince, not Gaunt, who provided him with a guarantee that his throne would remain in the family. Joan of Kent gave birth to a son, Edward of Angoulême, in January 1365. She wrote to the king, announcing the child's arrival in a letter dated 4 February. Edward was so pleased that he granted the lucky messenger an annuity of £40. Blanche's disappointments must have been all the more bitter as a result.

The year 1365 saw another happy event take place in the family of Edward III. The king's dark-eyed, spirited eldest daughter Isabella remained unmarried at the age of 33, a time when most of her peers were already mothers of a brood of children, perhaps even becoming grand-mothers. Having rejected her parents' choice of Pedro of Castile, she had become something of an uncertainty at the Plantagenet court, as the years passed and no husband was found for her. Exactly why Edward and Philippa were so lenient with her given her potential to make a powerful foreign alliance is unclear, but ultimately, she was permitted to choose her own partner for the sake of love. Her eye fell upon a young French prisoner named Enguerrand de Coucy, seven years her junior, who had been brought to England as a hostage in 1360 in exchange for the release of King John. Hostage he may have been, but he was treated as a guest by the English and impressed them all, according to Froissart, by shin-ing 'in dancing and carolling whenever it was his turn'. He particularly impressed Princess Isabella. The couple were married at Windsor Castle five years later on 27 July and Coucy was granted his freedom. Later that year, they travelled to France to live on the Coucy estate, where Isabella bore her first child, Marie, nine months after the wedding. They were frequent visitors to England and their second daughter, Philippa, arrived at Eltham Palace in 1367.

Another cousin was soon to arrive in the royal nursery. Just two months after the birth of the short-lived John in 1366, Blanche had fallen pregnant again. In September, Gaunt was received into the Fraternity of Benedictines at Northampton before departing in November to join his brother's campaign to intervene in the Castilian Civil War. As the dark December days drew in and she approached the end of her second trimester, Blanche based herself at Bolingbroke Castle, where she was visited by Edward III during the festivities. Given the king's concern over Blanche's first pregnancy, and her subsequent record, the duchess may also have spent some time at court during her husband's absence. The separate households of Edward and Philippa had been combined into one in 1360, partly as a result of the queen's increasing ill health. Philippa was now 52 and had borne fourteen children, six of whom were still alive in 1366, the youngest only 11. After suffering from a fall whilst riding in 1358, the increasingly stout queen suffered from a variety of complaints and anticipated death, even making specifications for her own tomb as early as 1362. Early in 1367, news came from abroad that Joan of Kent had borne another son, whom she had named Richard, known as Richard of Bordeaux, who would become the future Richard II. As with the birth of Philippa, Blanche returned home for her lying-in, and her son Henry, the future Henry IV, was born at Bolingbroke Castle on 15 April 1367. He was nursed by a Mary Taaf of Dublin, presumably a wet nurse, as Blanche recovered her strength and fertility. Only days before, Gaunt had fought alongside the Black Prince at the Battle of Najera in Castile, returning home to meet his son that August. The fates of these two boy cousins would be irrevocably entwined in the years to come.

As Queen Philippa's health deteriorated dramatically, her court was now mostly confined to Windsor, where she was increasingly forced to remain in bed. In the second half of 1367, Blanche fell pregnant for a final time, perhaps around the time that Gaunt was at Westminster to witness a Charter that October or whilst they kept Christmas at Windsor. The following 20 April 1368, Edward made an annuity of £40 paid to John of Florence, physician to the king and queen, who would have been in attendance upon Philippa and perhaps also observed the progress of Blanche's pregnancy. Her child may have been expected any time between May and September. The exact dates of its arrival and the timing and circumstances of Blanche's death have, until recently, been unclear. The problem was caused by Froissart, whose little elegy to Blanche was composed in 1369, leading to the assumption that this was the year of her death; in fact, she had already been dead for a year when the poet came to reflect on her life and beauty. While it was suggested that the plague had taken her in 1369, the proximity of her own death to the arrival of her last child suggests that she died in childbirth or as a result of fever or complications afterwards.

By September 1368, Blanche was resident at the Lancastrian stronghold of Tutbury Castle in Staffordshire. Originally a Norman castle, it had been extended and improved considerably since and overlooked the River Dove and distant Derbyshire hills. A plan of 1584–85 shows two main wings forming a right angle opposite John of Gaunt's gateway, while a surviving illustration from 1733 depicts a collection of chimneys, small buildings, a wide tower and an imposing gatehouse set amid wide castellated walls. Blanche may have intended to deliver her child there, or else she was taken by surprise en route elsewhere, or she may have travelled there after being churched, suggesting a period of recovery after the birth. We will never know. Where they are known, the birth places of her other children indicate that she scheduled her lying-in to take place in the seclusion of various castles belonging to her parents or husband, rather than at Edward's court. Her final child was a girl, Isabella, who did not survive. Blanche herself died on 12 September. Childbirth during the medieval period was an unpredictable process, claiming the lives of experienced and first-time mothers alike. Blanche may have already borne six babies, but the narrow window between the arrival of some and the conception of others must have taken its toll on her young body over the course of nine years. Gaunt was with Blanche at the end, writing to the Bishop of Carlisle from Tutbury to announce her loss and asking him to arrange masses to be said for her soul. This letter also firmly dates her death to 1368. Her body was carried south, alongside a life-sized wooden effigy, and spent the night in the Abbey at St Albans before being interred in St Paul's Cathedral.

According to Chaucer's *The Book of the Duchess*, Gaunt was overwhelmed by grief. In the poem's penultimate lines he confesses his loss to the incredulous narrator:

'Sir,' said I, 'where is she now?'
'Now!' said he, and stinte anoon [stopped at once].
There with he grew as dead as stone,
And said, 'alas! that I was borne,
That was the loss, that her-before
I tolde thee, that I had lorn [lost] …'
'Allas! sir, how? what may that be?'

'She is deed!' 'Nay!' 'Yis, by my trouthe!'

'Is that your los? By god, hit is routhe!'

And with that worde, right anoon,
They gan to strake forth; al was doon,
For that tyme, the hert-hunting.

Gaunt observed the anniversary of Blanche's death for the three decades
that he outlived her and would ultimately request to be buried beside
her. Their life together had been a happy and harmonious one, the result
of genuine affection and resulting in the conception of seven children.
Blanche left little political legacy in terms of a Lancastrian princess, but
her exemplary life, wifedom and maternity showed her daughters that
happiness could be combined with duty and sacrifice. Froissart recorded
the pain of her death twelve months later, perhaps on its first anniversary:

Help! Put a plaster
On my heart
For when I remember it
To be sure, I am overwhelmed with sighs
I am so full of melancholy
She as young and pretty when she died
About twenty-two years old
Gay, joyous, frolicksome, frisky
Sweet, simple, modest of mein
The excellent lady was called Blanche.

At her death, Blanche was survived by the 8-year-old Philippa, 4-year-old
Elizabeth and Henry, who was 18 months. By the time of Froissart's writing, they had also lost their grandmother, Queen Philippa. Their father
would need to find someone to oversee the running of their establishments and provide a steady maternal influence in their lives. The woman
he chose had been a familiar face for years and was already employed in
his household.

2

THE GIRLS' GOVERNESS,
1368–71

I suddenly saw a man in black
Reclining, seated with his back
Against an oak, a giant tree
'Oh Lord,' I thought, 'who can that be?'[1]

Katherine Swynford had also grown up at the court of Queen
Philippa, her fellow Hainaulter, and, being a few years younger
than Blanche, had seen the beautiful duchess blossom, win the
heart of Gaunt and become his wife. She had been present on
the outskirts of the charmed royal circle, properly clothed and fed according to her rank, her education and manners overseen, so that she became,
in Holinshed's words, 'a woman of such bringing up and honourable
demeanour' that she could command the respect of those who knew
and served her. When the court feasted at Christmas and saints' days, the

young Katherine was sitting in the same hall, only further down the lavish tables; she would have walked behind the queen and her children in stately procession, echoed their prayers and sat on cushions on the royal platform to watch the men joust. She probably even attended Blanche's wedding at Reading Abbey, a pretty girl of 8 or 10 admiring the bride's jewels and dreaming of her own future.

A favourite of popular novelists, Katherine's name has long been associated with scandal. She set tongues wagging during her lifetime by blurring the boundaries between the roles of servant and mistress, when the concept of service was broad enough to include devotion between members of the same class, and the notion of the household, or family unit, was a fluid and expandable concept that might include friends, allies and staff. By the time she became John of Gaunt's mistress, Katherine had already passed her formative years at the side of Queen Philippa, married one of Gaunt's knights and served in the nursery of Blanche of Lancaster. In fact, Gaunt had probably already noticed her but, like his father, he was devoted to his wife. The affair he conducted before his marriage with Marie de St Hilaire was no secret but no rumours of other relationships before 1368 have survived. Yet, just as Edward was to turn to Alice Perrers for comfort in the final years of the queen's infirmity, Gaunt's affair with Katherine followed in the wake of his grief.

Katherine's father was Gilles de Roet, or Roelt, later known as Pan, Paon or Payne, who was born around 1310, probably in the province of Hainault, in modern-day Belgium. Bisected by the River Haine, from which its name derived, the province's principal towns were Mons, Cambrai and Charleroi, set amid largely agricultural country. Pan's birthplace has been suggested as Le Roeulx, a district lying to the north-east of Mons, and the village of Guignies, lying to the south of Tournai, although the latter might be a confusion caused by the title 'Guyenne King of Arms' on his tomb. The confusion may be clarified by an official reference to him as 'Paganus de Rodio', which uses the Latinised form of Roeulx. Froissart suggests Pan was one of the young squires who came to England in Philippa's train on her marriage to Edward III and remained in her service after the majority returned home following the wedding in January 1328. This would confirm a birthdate of 1310 or shortly after, which would place the squire Pan in his late teens. He is unlikely to have been married at that point, so his wife or wives may have been drawn from the English court, or been brought there on Philippa's arrangement, though their identities and nationalities are unknown. Equally, there is uncertainty about the order of arrival of his four children, Walter, Katherine, Isabel (or Elizabeth) and Philippa, whose key life events suggest that they were born between the mid-1330s and late 1340s. The theory that Pan married twice, producing Isabel and Walter first, followed by Philippa and Katherine a decade later, is a plausible one.[2] Isabel was placed in the convent of Sainte Waudru in Mons during her adolescence, at some point after 1349, rising to become its canoness and dying around 1366, the year when her younger sisters were entering marriage. By 1355, Walter was a Yeoman of the Chamber to the Black Prince, also suggesting he had been born by at least 1340. Pan appears to have returned to Hainault for a time in 1350 and 1351, when he features on several occasions in the accounts of Philippa's sister Margaret.

The timing of this absence raises questions about the arrival of the sisters Katherine and Philippa de Roet. Either they were both born in England before 1350 or Pan entered a second marriage during his years of absence and fathered two girls in Hainault. It is even possible that the timing of Isabel's entry to the convent was prompted by this second marriage. With no references to any wife of Pan's, it may be that the second Mrs de Roet was a Hainaulter who died during or shortly after childbirth. They may even have met at Margaret's court. Equally, Philippa and Katherine might have been born in the late 1340s and left, along with Walter, in the household of the English Queen while their father travelled abroad with Isabel, his eldest child. Pan was back in England by the end of 1351 or early 1352, in the train of Countess Margaret, who was forced to flee after being defeated at the Battle of Vlaardingen. In time, each of Pan's children entered the service of a different member of the English royal family: Walter under the Black Prince, Katherine under the queen and Philippa into the Irish establishment of Elizabeth, Countess of Ulster, the wife of Gaunt's elder brother, Lionel of Antwerp. It was while she was in attendance on Elizabeth's daughter, born in 1355, that Philippa met her future husband, the poet-to-be Geoffrey Chaucer.

Philippa's marriage certainly took place before an annuity was granted to her by Edward III in September 1366. It may even have been a year or more before this. The date of Katherine's, however, is less certain and, for convenience, is estimated to have taken place around the same time. This is probably placing both marriages way too late and two entries in the Calendar of the Fine Rolls may shed some light upon Katherine's nuptials. In November 1361, the lands of Thomas de Swynford of Lincoln were taken into the king's hands following his death and the following January, a Walter de Kelby of Lincoln was ordered to 'deliver to Hugh, son and heir of Thomas de Swynford, knight, the lands late of his said father, as the king has taken his homage and fealty'.[3] Thus, on 31 January 1362, Hugh de Swynford came into his inheritance, which can only imply that he was also of age. Therefore, Hugh had been born before January 1341, making him a close, if not exact, contemporary of John of Gaunt, into whose service he may have transferred once his previous master, the Black Prince, left England. Katherine was being referred to by her married name by the start of 1365, along with her position in the ducal household, so it would seem that the marriage took place during this interval, probably soon after her fourteenth birthday. This may have fallen as early as 1362. Hugh was not a particularly good catch as a mere knight, but he and Katherine had the same status and they are likely to have been matched by Gaunt or the queen, rather than to have fallen in love, although this cannot be ruled out. It might even have been Blanche who suggested the loyal Swynford as a suitable husband.

Katherine's married home was Kettlethorpe Manor in Lincolnshire, a rather disappointing manor that Swynford leased from Gaunt and which was in need of much repair by the 1350s. As with all married women at court, Katherine had to balance the personal and public aspects of her life, engaging in periods of service that required her to accompany the duchess to the various Lancaster properties, and to run her manor and manage the needs of its dependents. The time she spent with her husband would have been intermittent and brief, as he was frequently abroad in Gaunt's service, spending an entire year in France in 1366–67. It would seem natural for the lives and concerns of wives to have been shared, following a similar relation of service to that established by the duke and his squire overseas.

Although the timing of Katherine's childbirths is uncertain, it would appear that she conceived quickly and her first daughter was born around 1363 and named after Blanche, with Gaunt standing as godfather. The little girl was raised alongside princesses Philippa and Elizabeth as a playmate and it is possible that the timing of her birth allowed her mother to act as wet nurse to the latter: the early life of Henry's cousin Richard shows it was common in the royal family for the wives of trusted retainers to fulfil this function.[4] Over the next couple of years, Katherine may have borne two more daughters, Margaret and Dorothy, before the arrival of her son Thomas in February 1367, at a time when Hugh and Gaunt were away fighting in Castile. Thomas might have arrived at Kettlethorpe, or possibly while Katherine was staying with Blanche at a house in central Lincoln, reputed to be owned by Gaunt in his capacity as Earl of Lincoln. On 25 February, Thomas was christened at the church of St Margaret, which used to stand within the cathedral close, a short walk from the site of Gaunt's house on the High Street. Katherine was probably still in Lincoln, or at Kettlethorpe, when Blanche bore Henry less than two months later; presumably, she returned to the duchess' service once she was churched and recovered. When not incapacitated by childbirth, Katherine's role, along with other women in Blanche's chamber, would have been to take care of the children and support the duchess through pregnancy and birth. No doubt her own experiences would have been considered valuable and she shared in the highs and lows of Blanche's various losses as well as the babies that thrived.

The three little girls, Elizabeth and Philippa of Lancaster and Blanche Swynford, would have been ready to establish their own chamber once they reached the age of 3 or 4. Having been weaned and encouraged to walk, their education in Christian virtues and good manners would have started as soon as they uttered their first words, long before their formal lessons began. Songs, music, prayers and stories would have played a significant part in their early lives, and many girls of the nobility were presented with their own Books of Hours at around the age of 5 or 6, progressing to the Bible and the Golden Legend. As they grew, Blanche and Katherine were their first teachers, encouraging them to learn their letters, to dance, embroider, to say their prayers and follow the example set by the female saints. They may have gone on to study Greek and Roman authors, as well as something of the natural sciences and theology. The ultimate goal of their education was to prepare them for marriage, with the accomplishments and virtues needed to secure a husband and the requisite skills to run their own future household. While this might, for Lancaster's daughters, be in the position of queen, it was more likely to have been as the wife of a knight for Blanche Swynford. While the 1371–72 text of the *Book of the Knight of La-Tour Landry*, or the Goodman of Paris, would offer advice suitable for a girl of Blanche's status, such as not travelling widely, eschewing vanity, gossip and not having her 'herte moch on the world,' her social milieu made it likely that she would make a more advantageous marriage than a mere knight. She could hardly match the £200 annual allowance for the Lancaster girls, which their father made in the year the Goodman of Paris wrote his book.

One of the poems often given to children to help them learn was an ABC. Set out in the form of an acrostic, each new stanza beginning with the next letter of the alphabet, these not only helped with reading and writing, but with imparting certain sets of beliefs, usually religious or cultural, regarding behaviour and manners. The ABC that Geoffrey Chaucer produced in the 1360s, *La Priere Nostre Dame*, might have been created at the request of Blanche of Lancaster or written and used after her death, expressing the core sentiments of her daughters' education. Based on a prayer by Guillaume de Deguileville, written in the 1330s and revised in 1355, it presents a vanquished sinner appealing to the Virgin Mary, to whose status as a bountiful, 'mighty, gracious lady' of 'unspotted maidenhead' Blanche's daughters might offer a secular parallel. Preparing to take roles as future wives, mothers and patrons, and to oversee their own household and perhaps even their own court, the girls would have learned that a great lady might replicate 'the generous giver of full felicity, the haven of refuge, quiet and rest', the comfort, sweetness and mercy of the 'bright lady', whose description echoes that of the duchess. The poem also mentions 'kalendars and illuminated texts' that are lit by the Virgin's name, reflecting other reading that formed part of the girls' education, along with reference to the stories of Isaac, Zachariah and Moses. Though the date of composition is not completely certain, it would seem likely that any existing copy of the ABC would have found its way into Gaunt's nursery in the late 1360s or early 1370s, once the poet's wife and sister-in-law were employed there. Katherine may well have read it to Blanche, Thomas and Margaret.

It appears that Katherine had borne her three children by Hugh Swynford by 1368, so she may have been with Blanche at Tutbury Castle when she died that September. It is almost certain that as an intimate member of her household, Katherine would have travelled to London to attend her mistress' funeral, perhaps being lodged in Gaunt's splendid Savoy Palace on the Thames. Over the following two years, she disappears from view as other women played more prominent roles in Lancaster's nursery: Blanche Lady Wake, their great aunt, was appointed as governess to their children in 1369 and in 1370 Alyne Gerberge, the wife of Gaunt's squire, was rewarded for her good service 'during the death of our beloved companion'. The nursery also expanded to include Arundel, Mowbray and Percy cousins, including young Henry Hotspur, occasionally bringing them into contact with the de Bohun girls, Eleanor and Mary, the latter of whom would marry Gaunt's eldest son. No doubt Henry of Derby grew up close to Katherine's son Thomas Swynford, as they were close in age and would remain staunch allies throughout their lives.

These arrangements were part of a necessary restructuring of Lancaster's establishment. There was no longer any need for a separate chamber and staff for the duchess, although some of those previously in her employ would have made the transition to the households of her children, while others might have found work under Gaunt in another capacity, or were simply retired from his service. Young Philippa and Elizabeth had lost a mother, but surely Gaunt would have thought carefully before depriving them of familiar faces who may have been something of a maternal substitute. Katherine's name might not have been listed among these transitional promotions and payments because her reward was her daughter's continuance in the chamber of the Lancaster girls, with all the advantages that brought. If she remained in service to them, providing some continuity with the past, she was balancing this with managing her own estate in Hugh's absence.

In August 1369, Queen Philippa died at Windsor Castle. Amid rumours of a resurgence of the dreaded plague, she had passed away from what her contemporaries considered to be dropsy. Orders were given for mourning garments to be supplied to her family and servants, and lengths of black cloth were issued to her grandchildren Philippa and Elizabeth, as well as Blanche Swynford, as a 'demoiselle of the daughters of the Duke of Lancaster'. It might have been fear of disease that delayed the queen's funeral until the following January, or perhaps Edward was awaiting his son John, who returned from France that November and observed Christmas with his father and children at King's Langley. Hugh Swynford also returned home and would have been reunited with Katherine and their offspring, probably at Kettlethorpe. At the end of December, they were rowed downriver to the capital. The queen's body left Windsor on 3 January and was interred on the south side of the chapel to Edward the Confessor, in a tomb topped with a life-sized effigy and thirty-two small figures. Edward had spent the equivalent of around £3,000 following his wife's request and commissioning a life-like memorial carved out of alabaster by Hennequin of Liège. Given her close connections with Philippa's court, Katherine Swynford is likely to have attended.

It would have been difficult for Katherine to avoid gossip about the woman who replaced the queen in Edward's affections. Alice Perrers was a similar age to Katherine and had served in Philippa's household in the early 1360s, becoming the ageing king's mistress at the age of 15, at around the time that Katherine wed Hugh. The rumours that she was the illegitimate daughter of a tavern whore are unlikely to have been true if Alice had been given a position as Philippa's maid-in-waiting. During the last years of the queen's life, the pair had been discreet enough, Alice leaving court in 1364 in order to bear an illegitimate son in secrecy. It was not unexpected for a king or aristocrat to seek sexual satisfaction among women of a lower class, especially during periods when their wives were unavailable through illness or childbirth. Blanche's father Henry Grosmont had written in *The Book of Holy Medicines* of how he had loved and lost many women, preferring the embraces of common women to those of aristocrats, as they were 'less censorious' of his behaviour.[5]

Following the queen's death, though, and in the process of bearing Edward two more children, Perrers began to accrue lands, estates, grants of money and jewels, some of which had belonged to Philippa, and loose tongues began to wag about her influence over the king, who turned 60 in 1372. That year, she would take Edward's place on the marble throne of state to oversee the Court of the King's Bench at Westminster and preside over a Smithfield tournament dressed as the Lady of the Sun, sparkling in Philippa's jewels.[6] Thomas Walsingham would refer to her as 'a shameless woman and wanton harlot … being neither beautiful or fair, she knew how to conceal these defects with her flattering tongue'.[7] It was an important lesson to Katherine about the sexual power a woman might yield over a man outside the usual rules of matrimony, about the degree of licence that a willing mistress might enjoy, or exploit, in providing for herself. It was also a reminder that although criticism was to be expected, the king's protection was more than enough to silence it, keeping Alice safe for the duration of Edward's lifetime. Or rather, of Edward's sanity.

In June 1370, Gaunt sailed for France, to join the Black Prince and help him defend Aquitaine against a joint attack from Charles V of France and Enrique II of Castile. Hugh Swynford departed with him, unaware that he would never set foot on English soil again. He was little more than 30 when he died of unknown causes in Aquitaine on 13 November 1371. The last military action either had seen was the siege of Limoges a full fourteen months before and the fact that Gaunt had already returned to England, leaving Swynford behind, suggests that he was suffering from an illness that prevented him travelling. The news of Swynford's death would have reached England later the same month, or in early December. A young widow with four children and a crumbling estate to run, Katherine's future looked uncertain. However, Gaunt was mindful of her and Hugh's service to his family and quickly stepped up to protect her, more than doubling her annuity and breaking custom to restore ownership of Kettlethorpe to her during her son's minority. Dressed in her black widow's weeds, she was invited to Hertford Castle to attend upon the new Duchess of Lancaster. Gaunt had taken a new wife while he was abroad but this time, the dynamic between duke, the duchess and Katherine was to prove very different. Within weeks, she and Gaunt had become lovers.

3

CONSTANCE OF CASTILE, 1371–94

It hath and schal ben evermore
That love is maister wher he wille.[1]

1

Gaunt's second wife was born amid the parched brown hills, flat wide landscapes and cream-grey stonework of Castrojeriz in Castile, northern Spain. Two hours' drive (today) south of the Bay of Biscay, it sat along the popular pilgrim route the Camino to Santiago de Compostela, which leads to the Galician cathedral of St James. Particularly popular with English pilgrims, the devout had trod its path since the eleventh century, finding shelter in the hospitals and hostels along the route and pausing to pray in the Romanesque churches. As they approached Castrojeriz, still almost 500 kilometres from their destination, the pilgrims of the 1350s would have seen two imposing sights. Stumbling up the road, under the stone archway and into the ancient monastery of San Antón, where monks of the Hospital Brothers of St Anthony bathed their weary feet, they could not help but notice the palace of King Pedro of Castile. 'O noble, O worthy Petro, glorie of Spayne, whom fortune held so high in majesty, well ought me thy piteous death complain', effused Chaucer in *The Monk's Tale*. Yet Pedro also earned the epithet of 'Pedro the Cruel' and his two daughters found themselves exiled from their homeland as a result of his wars.

Pedro had been the intended bridegroom of Edward III's daughter Joan of England, who had embarked full of hopes with coffers packed full of dresses of red and green silk, embroidered with stars and diamonds, roses and animals, but she died from the plague before reaching Castile. Five years later, the tall, fair-haired 'muscular' Pedro fell in love with a Spanish noblewoman named Maria de Padilla and married her in secret. Although he was forced soon afterwards to make a dynastic marriage, Pedro abandoned his new wife, Blanche of Bourbon, on the grounds of her reputed adultery with his brother, and imprisoned her. He returned to Maria, who went on to bear him four children, of whom three daughters survived to adulthood: Beatrice, born in 1353; Constance, in 1354; and Isabella, in 1355. Maria died in 1361, possibly during the outbreak of plague that killed the parents of Blanche of Lancaster. The rejected Blanche of Bourbon also died that year, but her death came at the end of eight years of imprisonment and the suggestions that Pedro ordered her execution have never been satisfactorily proven or disproven.

On 18 November 1362, Pedro made a will declaring his children by Maria to be legitimate and produced witnesses to the effect that their marriage had been valid. He then entered a prolonged war with Aragon and lost his throne, sending his daughters into exile. Pedro appealed to the Black Prince, as the ruler of Aquitaine, to help him regain it in 1367, but his reputation clearly preceded him. As a guarantee for Pedro's good behaviour, the Black Prince required that his two daughters be sent as honourable hostages in Aquitaine, under the hospitality of the English. Pedro agreed to the demand and the young Constance and Isabella were dispatched north to Bordeaux, where they would have been supervised by Edward's wife Joan of Kent. They probably stayed in the Archbishop's

Palace, on the site of the current Palais Rohan, where Joan had given birth to her second son that January. On 3 April, Edward and Gaunt accomplished a victory for Pedro at the Battle of Najera, despite their army being vastly outnumbered by the combined forces of France and Castile.

However, Najera proved to be something of a pyrrhic victory. Pedro did not repay his friends, even though his daughters were in English custody. It was whilst waiting at Burgos for Pedro to reimburse his expenses that the Black Prince fell ill with dysentery. With symptoms of terrible stomach cramps, vomiting and diarrhoea, the disease swept through the English camp, wiping out 80 per cent of the surviving soldiers.[2] The English heir would never fully recover his health. Pedro would not enjoy his kingdom for long either. He was murdered in 1369 and although his second daughter Constance inherited his title of Queen of Castile, the throne was immediately seized by Pedro's half-brother and killer, Henry of Trastamara. Ruling Aquitaine in his brother's absence, John of Gaunt was struck by a plan. He would take Constance as his second wife, and his younger brother, Edmund of Langley, would marry Isabella. Between them, they would retake Castile and its throne would then pass into Gaunt's eager hands.

On 21 September 1371, Gaunt married the 17-year-old Constance at Roquefort near Mont-de-Marsan in Aquitaine. The ceremony probably took place at the church of Santa Maria, which was attached to the twelfth-century Benedictine Abbey. The couple presented each other with the gift of a gold cup, Constance's bearing the decoration of a double rose and dove. Little is known about Constance's appearance, but a manuscript produced over a century later depicts her with dark hair. Her daughter Catherine was described on several occasions as tall, with blue eyes and fair, reddish-blonde hair, so it is likely these genes were inherited from the English royal family or from her Castilian grandfather Pedro. Constance was pious and serious, focused on restoring her father's memory and lands, but this was about all she had in common with John of Gaunt. With Edward III ageing, the Black Prince severely ill and the second brother, Lionel of Antwerp, dead since 1368, Gaunt had become the most powerful man in England; following his marriage, he adopted the coat of arms of Castile and León and took the title of king, addressed as 'My Lord of Spain' or 'Yo el Roy'. After a couple of days of celebrations in Bordeaux, the newly-weds requisitioned a merchant ship at La Rochelle on 25 September and arrived in Fowey, Cornwall, on 4 November.

Even given the terrible conditions sometimes experienced in the Celtic Sea and Bay of Biscay, their return journey was a long one. As the crow flies, it is little more than 430 miles. If she had not already conceived in Bordeaux, Constance would do so on board the *Gaynpayn* and would probably experience her first symptoms of pregnancy, although it is likely that she may have confused these with seasickness. Fowey was just a small fishing village, so after their initial recovery, they left it and travelled to the Augustinian Priory of St Peter and St Paul at Plympton in Devon. The party had covered the 40 miles across Bodmin Moor by 10 November, followed by a similar distance again, along the edge of Dartmoor to Exeter. Constance's first experiences of her adopted country were of wide skies and sweeping landscape dotted by crops of stone, which were not so unlike the plains of Castile. Exeter was her first experience of an English city, with its tall, narrow medieval buildings clustered around the green on which the imposing cathedral stood. Constance would have approached its impressive West Front, begun as recently as 1340 from Purbeck marble, with its row of stone angels and kings of Judah looking down disapprovingly. Deeply devout, she would have welcomed the opportunity for silent prayer and, despite being short of money, the couple made an offering of 20s.[3]

Constance's next stop was the thirteenth-century hunting lodge of Kingston Lacy. Gaunt's main home in the west, it was an impressive building on the site of the present seventeenth-century mansion, which lay forgotten until a storm in 1990 uprooted trees that exposed some of the foundations of the house that Constance stayed in, as well as marble roof tiles, ceramic tiles and pottery.[4] In 1371, the property was at the height of its glory, before going into decline in the fifteenth century, with three gates, a central courtyard surrounded by a thatched cob wall, outside which were a hedge and ditch. Within it stood the house topped with marble tiles, a chapel, kitchen, dairy, bakehouse, granary, dove cot, stable, workshop, cattleshed and garden. Inside the house, the plastered walls were painted ochre and the glazed floor tiles were yellow, brown and green.[5] It appears that Constance remained at Kingston Lacy for a while, perhaps to rest and recover, while Gaunt returned briefly to London. Her sister Isabella would have been with her but it is unclear whether any Spanish or French ladies were included in her retinue. Gaunt may have recruited local women to support his wife, assisted by Kingston Lacy staff, to watch over her in his absence. After a brief stay at the Savoy, perhaps to see his children, Gaunt travelled back to Dorset, where he celebrated Christmas with Constance, Isabella and his father, who were all named in an order to the clerk of the wardrobe for the distribution of Christmas presents.[6] The festivities did not last long though, as Gaunt was back at Hertford Castle by 3 January and was there again, or still there, a week later. It is not impossible that Constance had travelled there with him as the final stop on her journey to the capital, although being positioned to the north of London it would have taken her considerably out of her way. On 30 January, Gaunt had returned to the capital to oversee the final arrangements.

On 10 February, Constance made her ceremonial entrance into London, where she was greeted by the Black Prince, who had risen from his sick bed for the occasion. The crowds gathered in Cheapside to see her progress to the Strand, where Gaunt had ridden ahead to welcome her. He then conducted her back to the Savoy, the palace he had inherited from the Duchy of Lancaster, which Constance now saw for the first time. Built of stone around two courtyards, it included a great hall, chapel, cloister and private apartments, and was catered for by its own stables, smithy, bakehouse, brewery, laundry and fishpond, as well as a fruit and vegetable garden surrounded by a hedge.[7] Constance would have entered through the large street gate that led to the Strand and been settled into her private rooms, which faced inward, rather than out on to the river. She would have prayed in the chapel and given thanks for her safe arrival, then rested in the palace for a while with her husband, as arrangements were made for her own household to be set up at Hertford Castle. Gaunt's presence there between 1 and 3 March suggests that they set out from London at the end of February.

Hertford Castle was 30 miles north of the Savoy, on the River Lea. Behind an impressive gatehouse frontage, it contained timber-framed apartments on the east side, a chapel and an aisled hall which dated from the thirteenth century. The property also had a sizeable park that was renowned for good hunting. In early March, Gaunt introduced Constance to her new home and, perhaps, to her stepchildren, who were to form part of her household, returning on 4 April to see how they had settled in. Among these new surroundings, these strange English customs and ways, and speaking little of the language, Constance would have sought comfort in her faith and ambition. She had already been displaced from home and Gaunt was, in effect, her saviour; their marriage does not appear to have developed into a love match but it gave her status, stability and hope. As a dynastic match, it was a prestigious and important alliance that benefitted both husband and wife.

In April, Constance was benefitting from the ducal wardrobe, when Gaunt's clerk received the request to deliver jewels for her personal use, including 1,808 large pearls and 2,000 smaller ones, a string with four rubies, a gold circlet set with emeralds and rubies and twenty-one pearls set in gold. She also received from her husband a reliquary in the shape of a barrel, decorated with gold and precious stones, perhaps specially chosen for her in recognition of her piety. Such reliquaries were fairly uncommon: one similarly barrel-shaped survivor in the Walters Art Museum, Baltimore contains a central crystal section, bored through the centre to create a chamber that would preserve and magnify a relic. Constance may already have had an object she wished to house in the barrel, perhaps a finger bone or fragment of the clothing of a favoured saint, or else the sacred item was already preserved within. Given the timing, it is likely that the relic may have had some significance for her approaching confinement, as expectant mothers would cling to religious objects and wear the girdles of saints in the belief that this would ease their suffering.

Constance had fallen pregnant very soon after her marriage. In the summer of 1372, just nine months after the ceremony, she retreated to Hertford Castle to await the child's arrival. From around 1360, it had been one of Gaunt's chief country residences, conveniently located just 30 miles north of the Savoy, where the duke was awaiting news. From there on 6 June, he issued an order to the receiver of Leicester to send Ilote, or Elyot, the wise woman to Constance 'with all the haste in any manner that you can'.[8] Katherine Swynford also received instructions to attend on Constance, as her experience of the practices of childbirth were clearly valued, and her own sister Philippa Chaucer and Constance's sister Isabella of Castile may have been present too. Although the baby would have been christened by that point, it is not certain whether her name, Catherine, or Catalina in Castilian, was chosen by her mother or father. Gaunt's movements may suggest an approximate date for the baby's arrival. According to the *Register of John of Gaunt*, he was in London on 25, 26, 27 and 30 June, conducting business from the Savoy and Westminster, and is also recorded there on dates through the early and middle part of July, being in residence on the 19th, before showing up in the records at Hertford Castle on 20 July.[9] It was a fleeting visit though, as he was back at the Savoy again two days later. The suggestion that he was also present on 7 July is unlikely, as he was conducting business on the other side of London at Reigate Castle.

There is a chance, though, that Constance's baby arrived at a later date, or that a second child arrived some nine months after she had delivered her first. A reward is recorded as being made to Katherine Swynford on 31 March 1373, for bringing Gaunt news of his child's birth. Gaunt was then at Hertford on 20 April. It may simply be that there was a delay in the issuing of the reward and its record in the accounts, but if this was in fact Constance's first child, it must have been conceived when Gaunt visited Hertford on 20 July 1372. The other possibility is that Constance gave birth to a first child early in June, soon after the midwife Elyot was summoned, and had risen from her bed and been churched by the time Gaunt arrived six weeks later. She may have conceived again on that occasion and borne a second infant the following March. If this is the case, the chances are that the second child did not survive, perhaps having been conceived so soon after the process of giving birth. So far as can be ascertained, Constance did not bear another baby. She and Gaunt may have been disappointed, as Catherine was the sole inheritor of their claim to Castile and her gender no doubt made this more problematic. At some point, there would be her future marriage to consider, as the title of King of Castile would transfer to her husband. It is possible that Gaunt and his wife continued to sleep together in the anticipation of more children, especially a son, but his burgeoning romance with Katherine Swynford may have kept him from Constance's side. It was around this time that Katherine conceived the first of four children she would bear him.

On 11 July, Edmund of Langley married Isabella of Castile at Wallingford Castle in Oxfordshire.[10] If Gaunt attended, he must have covered the 50 miles between there and the Savoy at great speed, since he was recorded as being in London on both 10 and 13 July.[11] The imposing Wallingford was once a major royal residence which had been considerably refurbished in the thirteenth century and had belonged to Gaunt's grandmother, Isabella of France. There, the 31-year-old Edmund married the 17-year-old Isabella, ensuring that the Anglo-Castilian claim would be preserved, even in the unfortunate eventuality of Constance dying in childbirth. Gaunt's gifts to the newly married couple were singularly unusual, including cups and ewers decorated with grotesque figures and a three-legged silver gilt vessel shaped like a monster. In comparison with Constance's rose-lidded cup, jewels and reliquary, they might indicate a difference between the sisters' characters or tastes. With the Castilian connection secured, Gaunt could return to London to plan his campaign to claim the Iberian throne: increasingly driven by the desire to be a king in reality, he hoped to fulfil his ambition and the intention behind his marriage in one go.

¶

Katherine Swynford must have become Gaunt's lover early in 1372, almost as soon as they had become reacquainted. Due to his absence in Aquitaine, the last time they could have seen each other was before Gaunt's departure in the summer of 1370, although the dissolution of Blanche's household may have made it even earlier than this. If Katherine had retired to Kettlethorpe after the loss of her mistress, the pair may not even have seen each other since the autumn of 1368. A lot had changed since then. Their marital positions were now reversed: Katherine was in her widow's weeds and Gaunt was once again a married man. The deaths of Duchess Blanche and Queen Philippa, followed by the dominance of Alice Perrers, made for a different atmosphere at court and Katherine was associated with earlier, happier days, as well as having proved a loyal and valued servant. Perhaps there was also an element of chivalric protection towards the widow of a man who had fought at Gaunt's side and lost his life while in his service. Their reunion would have stirred memories of their shared past and, perhaps, reawakened feelings of attraction that the

RED ROSES

pair had not been in a position to act upon before. No doubt Katherine was also attractive, perhaps with the similar fair hair and pale skin that evoked memories of the lost duchess.

Did their eyes meet with 'subtil looking' over the cradle waiting by Constance's bed, or as Katherine read to Elizabeth and Philippa? Were there 'dissymulyngs' at the dinner table? The monk of the *Evesham Chronicle* related that Gaunt knew Katherine carnally 'for a long time, during the lifetime of his wife Constance', and the *Chronicon Angliae* suggests that it was a fresh scandal in 1378, which may be the point at which the affair became public news, but it is clear their connection began long before this point. There is little doubt that the relationship would have been initiated by Gaunt as Katherine's position and degree of dependency would have prevented her making any overt approach or suggestion that could be taken as an affront to his status. The ducal household was a microcosm of the court, with its mixture of familiarity and formality. By necessity, members of the royal family lived in close proximity to the minor gentry, who served them, and while this meant that daily life used ritual and service as means of preserving social distance, it also created a degree of familiarity. This social mixing also created opportunities for mobility in the careers of those who proved their worth and, sometimes, on a personal level.

The precise point at which any woman's relationship became sexual with a social superior, let alone a prince, can be difficult to ascertain. For those at the top and bottom of the structure, expectations were clearly defined: queens and princesses were legally wedded and expected to yield up the marital debt as soon as their age made it legitimate to do so. Likewise, the transaction between a nobleman and a prostitute, or woman of lower class, was unambiguous. But Gaunt and Katherine's attachment was based in affection, which would endure for the rest of his life: whatever John's methods of seduction, Katherine was responsive. There was much in Gaunt to attract her, but the protection of such a powerful figure would also have been invaluable to the widow of a knight. His attention would have been flattering, especially once it became clear to Katherine that it was not just to be a passing fancy. Sizeable grants made to 'our very dear demoiselle' that May, and the settlement of her lands in June, might suggest that the relationship had already become physical. Gifts of venison for her table and oaks to rebuild her house soon followed.

There is also the question of the plague. By 1373, Katherine and Gaunt's world had been shaken by two devastating outbreaks of the disease and several lesser ones, the impact of which is impossible to measure. Not only had around a third of the population died in 1348, but the outbreak of 1361–62 in particular had proved devastating for Blanche's family and Gaunt's sisters. Besides the practical problems, such as the harvest not being gathered, the empty clerical posts, the closed universities and courts, the businesses and homes abandoned, and the rise of wages, survivors cannot have escaped a certain impact of this onslaught, an alteration of their approaches to life, a reawakening of the underlying medieval certainty that life was 'nasty, brutish and short'.[12] Although it is impossible to generalise, considering that almost the entire memory of a generation was overshadowed by the plague, any periods of abeyance along with the human highs of success, love, marriage and childbearing, may have seemed like affirmations of life and worth pursuing. This is not to suggest that their lives were hedonistic, although some of the chroniclers feared this consequence, but a shared sense of survival against the odds may have united those who had witnessed loss. As Katherine's brother-in-law wrote, 'all too little … lasteth such joy, ythanked be Fortune, that seemeth truest when she will beguile'. The sense that Dame Fortune had turned her wheel, or that God had spoken through the pestilence, or the sincere religious devotion of men like Gaunt did not prevent them from seeking pleasure. The king in Chaucer's *The Knight's Tale* speaks philosophically about death, advocating the need to accept its inevitability, and the importance of making a virtue of necessity. In Katherine, Gaunt found a woman with whom he was able to connect in a way that he did not with his wife. The usual expectation that equality of status was most desirable in marriage was overridden by more personal concerns.

Having assisted with the delivery of baby Catherine, Katherine soon became aware that she had conceived Gaunt's child. Based at Hertford Castle, her pregnancy would have become visible by the autumn, so it is likely that she retired to Kettlethorpe in order to be out of Constance's sight, though perhaps not out of mind. There is no way of knowing when Gaunt's wife became aware of her husband's infidelity, whether she cared, or if the lovers were discreet. Gaunt's banishment of a group of Constance's Castilian ladies to Nuneaton Abbey between 1373 and 1375 was a punishment for their gossip about his affair, so it would seem that Constance probably knew about Katherine then, although her husband's harsh response might have counselled her to remain aloof, considering the mistress a necessary evil, rather than a threat to her status as duchess. Ultimately, Constance needed Gaunt to recover Castile, so, though conscious of her position, she was unlikely to initiate any sort of breach with him.

When Gaunt sailed from Sandwich on 31 August, the pregnant Katherine was probably left behind. Suggestions that she bore her child abroad run contrary to Gaunt's usual practice of leaving his women safely behind at home, as well as his knowledge of the terrible conditions he had encountered at sea and in the army camps. It was a lucky escape for Katherine. The ships were buffeted by storms, blown off course and some were smashed to pieces with great loss of life. Forced to admit defeat before setting foot on French soil, John returned home. He spent that Christmas with Constance and his children at Hertford.

Katherine gave birth to a son early in 1373. He was acknowledged by Gaunt and given the name John Beaufort. He was her fourth child, perhaps a full decade younger than her daughter Blanche. The name bestowed on the boy has given rise to much speculation. He was not born in the Chateau de Beaufort, which had been lost to the French, nor, probably, in the English Beaufort Castle, which John had previously owned and sold. The title might have been an acknowledgement of the lordship of Beaufort that Gaunt had once held, and to which he still felt entitled, but it may equally have been descriptive, combining the French words for 'handsome' and 'strong', as a tribute to the newborn's appearance. The likeliest locations for his birth are Kettlethorpe or Gaunt's house in Lincoln.

Katherine's sister Philippa had probably embarked on bearing her family too: having been married for seven years and served the queen and Constance in succession, she is thought to have borne between two and four children. It has been proposed that, with Chaucer in the separate establishment of the king, she might also have been the object of Gaunt's affections and that he fathered at least one of her children. The evidence suggests otherwise though, as Gaunt did not deny his paternity of Katherine's son but never acknowledged any child of her sister.

Additionally, any connection between Gaunt and Philippa would have created a bond of affinity that would have served as a barrier in later years, when he wished to make Katherine his wife. The Chaucers must have found ample opportunity for privacy during the periods that the royal households overlapped and all contemporary evidence points to the conclusion that all Philippa's children were Geoffrey's.

In the summer of 1373, Gaunt was planning a second attempt at the invasion of France that had been defeated by the weather. He equipped and repaired Tutbury Castle as the residence of his wife and children during his absence, but for Katherine he had a different plan entirely. On his way south to join his armies, he paused for around three weeks at Northbourne Manor near Deal in Kent, which was owned by St Augustine's Abbey in Canterbury. The present Jacobean house and gardens on the site probably sits on the medieval foundations of Gaunt's property, close to which stood a chapel dating from the twelfth century. The house was conveniently close to the post of Sandwich, just 6 miles along the coast, easily accessible once the tides and winds decided to co-operate. Katherine was with him for part, or all, of his sojourn in Kent, before his departure for Aquitaine at the end of July. After that, Katherine may have returned to Constance's household at Tutbury to resume her intermittent role as governess and to await Gaunt's return the following April. In the autumn of 1374, Katherine conceived her second child by Gaunt, a boy she delivered the following summer, probably at Kenilworth Castle. Gaunt had inherited the property from Blanche of Lancaster, who had received it on her father's death, and in 1373 he began an extensive building programme that would include new state apartments, a great hall, kitchens and towers. With his wife based at Hertford, Katherine might have been the first to benefit from Gaunt's improvements. Her lover may have been with her, or at least waiting nearby until she gave birth, as the *Register* places him 30 miles to the north-east, at Leicester Castle on 4, 12 and 18 August, before his arrival at Kenilworth on 30 August 1375. Their son was given the name Henry Beaufort.

With the arrival of her children by Gaunt, Katherine was also considering her eldest daughter's future. Assuming that Blanche had been born soon after her mother's first marriage, she would have been approaching her twelfth birthday by the arrival of 1375. Although she had been educated alongside the duke's children, young Blanche was still the daughter of a knight and her proposed husband was of a similar rank. As a New Year's gift, Gaunt granted Katherine the wardship and marriage of the son of Sir Robert Deyncourt, deceased, who might have had connections to Kenilworth Castle. On 13 January, instructions were given to Gaunt's steward to guard Robert's son until such time as Katherine sent for him to be married to her daughter. However, no more references to young Blanche survive and her fiancé lived on into the 1440s, suggesting that Katherine's daughter died before she came of age. Given that she would have reached maturity at the age of 14, this would mean that Blanche died at some point between 1375 and 1377. Little is known about the life of this elusive child, who was given an education above her station and whose life was probably spent entirely within a female, domestic sphere, in which Katherine and her sister Philippa, Blanche of Lancaster and Constance of Castile were the most significant figures, before succumbing to some childhood illness. The year 1375 also saw another outbreak of the plague in England, which offers another potential reason for Blanche's loss, not that much reason is required to explain the consistently high levels of childhood and early adult mortality in the fourteenth century. No doubt the loss of her eldest child, so close to the threshold of her adult life, would have been a terrible personal blow to Katherine. Yet these years were also to witness political upheaval and change.

As Edward III became increasingly infirm in body and mind, the political influence of his mistress Alice Perrers had created resentment at court and by April 1376, Parliament was ready to move against her. Known as the 'Good Parliament', it refused the king's demands until, as Thomas Walsingham put it, 'certain abuses and defects had been corrected, and until certain persons who seemed to have impoverished the king and the kingdom, to have vilely tarnished his fame and to have greatly diminished his power, should have been eliminated, and their excesses properly punished according to their kind'.[13] Parliament was aiming at no less than the removal of Alice Perrers, perhaps even her execution. Edward certainly believed so. That final word of Walsingham's account is most ominous, as Alice was considered to be of a base 'kind', rumoured to be illegitimate, who posed a threat to the good kingship and laws Edward had previously come to represent. Having already borne Edward at least one illegitimate child, Alice was then discovered to have been married in secret, to a William Windsor, and to have successfully petitioned the king for his release from charges of bribery and extortion. This meant that she had put the unwitting Edward in the position of committing adultery. Although Alice was temporarily removed, on condition that she stayed away from him, he summoned her that September in the belief that he was dying.

The double blows of Parliament's attack and Alice's marriage paled into insignificance when it became apparent that the Black Prince's life was ebbing away. Having endured ill health that often confined him to a stretcher for a decade, Prince Edward died at Westminster Palace at the age of 45. He was survived by his wife, Joan, and their second son, Richard of Bordeaux, then aged 9. In his final hours, the Black Prince requested that his father should protect their inheritance. That September, the king's eldest son was laid to rest in Canterbury Cathedral in a tomb of his own design, carved from Purbeck marble by Henry Yevele and featuring his coat of arms and the motif of three ostrich feathers used by the Prince of Wales. That title was quickly conferred upon his son Richard, in the face of Parliamentary concerns that Gaunt might attempt to seize power.[14] The king did not last long enough to see his new heir reach adulthood. Almost exactly a year after the death of his eldest son, on 21 June 1377, he suffered a stroke and passed away at Richmond Palace.

By the terms of his will, written at Havering atte Bowe the previous October, Edward left his heir, young Richard, 'an entire bed, marked with the arms of France and England, now in our Palace at Westminster', 1,000 marks to Joan of Kent and appointed John 'King of Castile and León and Duke of Lancaster' as one of ten executors. Edward's body was carried through the streets to Westminster Abbey, followed by great processions including his sons, nobles and prelates, before he was laid to rest beside his queen. Nine years later, a monument was erected to him, featuring carvings of all his children. It was of great significance that his will named Richard as his heir, followed by Gaunt and his sons, bypassing the claim of Lionel of Antwerp's daughter Philippa and her 2-year-old son Roger, Earl of Mortimer. This was the line from which the Yorkist kings would later descend, arguing their precedence over the heirs of Lionel's younger brother John of Gaunt.

England's new king was only 10 years old in 1377. If there was any foundation to the rumours that Gaunt was considering usurping his nephew, he did not act upon it. To the contrary, he protested in Parliament, refusing to serve on a committee until he was 'excused of the things which the Commons [common people] had evilly said about him'.[15] In fact, Gaunt scarcely needed to act upon his ambition: a Continual Council was appointed to guide King Richard during his youth but, in effect, Gaunt was now the most powerful man in the land. Yet that land was in crisis. Gaunt's failed expeditions to France had resulted in the imposition of new taxes but the financial situation remained desperate and there had been a collapse in trade, so an even higher rate was imposed in 1380. This proved deeply unpopular and Gaunt was held responsible in the popular imagination; his coat of arms was defaced in London and scandalous rumours were spread about his foreign birth. He also came in for criticism for his support of John Wycliffe, a religious reformer who led the Lollards and advocated the translation of the Bible into English and favoured a personal approach to God rather than following the dictates of a corrupt church. On one occasion, as Adam of Usk relates, Gaunt had to flee a London mob along the Thames in a boat 'hastily provided'. Yet Usk was wrong to claim that Gaunt fled from the rebels in 1381; he was already campaigning in Scotland when the Peasants' Revolt broke out in Essex and Kent.

Gaunt was an easy target. His foreign campaigning and high status put him out of touch with the common people in a way that was only exaggerated by his chivalric code; his aspirations for the Castilian crown and extensive power and lands created fear and suspicion that England was being ruled by two masters. Led by three figures, a subversive priest named John Ball, the speaker Jack Straw and their figurehead Wat Tyler, the rebels declared they would accept no king called John and marched on London. At Blackheath, they sent a petition to King Richard demanding the deaths of the men they perceived to be his enemies and theirs, including Gaunt. It is not clear where Katherine was at this point, but it is likely that she was not in London when anarchy broke out. Initially, she may have been with Constance at Hertford, or at Kettlethorpe, or perhaps at Leicester when the rebels went on their spree of killing and looting. According to the *Anonimalle Chronicle*, once the news reached her, she 'went into hiding where no one knew where to find her for a long time',[16] as 'savage hoards' attacked prominent figures and properties. The Savoy was looted and burned to the ground, the wine casks in the cellar smashed, furnishings torn down and Gaunt's treasure thrown into the Thames. Five wagon loads of treasures were destroyed, along with court rolls and duchy records: Gaunt's 'lodging unrivalled in splendour and nobility within the kingdom' was left a ruin. Constance fled north to Pontefract Castle as a mob attacked Hertford Castle, looting and inflicting further damage. Their absence from the capital certainly saved the lives of Gaunt and his women. Terrifying reports must have reached them of the damage, although by that time, the bravery of the young king in confronting them had already brought the rioting to a standstill. For a while, Gaunt remained in Scotland, fearful for his life and the rumours that Parliament had declared him a traitor, until Richard made a clear denial of this and summoned him south.

Gaunt must have viewed the wreck of his beautiful palace on the Thames with horror. The Savoy had been a symbol of his power, his government, but also of every privilege that his rank brought in terms of luxury, beauty and the arts. All that had been desecrated by the rampant mob, and it must have become something of an emblem for him, a warning against the follies of the flesh and his own powerlessness in the face of fortune. For twenty years it had been his London base but he had no inclination to repair it. Lead was taken from the roof and sent to make repairs at Hertford Castle and damaged timbers were sold.[17] The palace gates were rebuilt to repel intruders but inside them, the Savoy remained a ruin. Gaunt would not even mention it in his will eighteen years later.

The attacks upon Gaunt may have come as a shock to Katherine. The last few years had been full of personal happiness and success. She had borne a son, Thomas, around 1377 and a daughter, Joan, in 1379, both probably at Kettlethorpe. Two successful marriages had also been arranged: Blanche and Gaunt's second daughter, the 17-year-old Elizabeth of Lancaster, became Countess of Pembroke through her marriage to the young John Hastings at Kenilworth Castle in June 1380. The following March, Gaunt's illegitimate daughter Blanche, by Marie de St Hilaire, was married to Sir Thomas Morieux, one of Gaunt's knights, and received gifts of silver spoons, ewers, saucers and basins, plus an annual £100 drawn from the estates of Fakenham and Snettisham in Norfolk. The scandalous reports of Gaunt riding brazenly about the countryside with Katherine sharing his horse also date from this period. Yet if the reports of the revolt were not bad enough, a worse shock was about to reach Katherine. Gaunt was devastated by the news. Although he had initially tried to conceal his horror at the evident depths of the hatred directed at him, which certainly would have claimed his life, these events sent him into a deep contemplation of his life. Dwelling on how he might have caused such offence, he sought advice from his household and various men of the cloth, reaching the conclusion that 'he had paid no attention to what was said to him, because he was blinded by desire, fearing neither God nor shame amongst men'.[18] Deeply shaken, he needed someone to blame for having taken the wrong direction.

Gaunt now vowed to 'remove that lady from his household, so that there could be no further offence'; in the confessional he 'blamed himself for the deaths … and reproached himself for his liaison with Katherine Swynford, or rather renounced it'. Summoning Constance north to meet him, he asked her forgiveness 'for his misdeeds to her'.[19] Determined to lead a new, blameless life, he dismissed Katherine from his service – as a reference to her in February 1382 as 'recently governess of our daughters' confirms – and increased her annuity to 200 marks for life, to enable her to live independently of him. Gaunt did not forget her children either. He granted Katherine's son Thomas Swynford an annuity of 100 marks on his marriage to Jane Crophill, which took place in March 1383; three years later, he knighted Thomas along with Robert Ferrers, who was betrothed to Katherine and Gaunt's young daughter Joan. Katherine retreated to Lincoln, where she took a house in Minster Yard called The Chancery. Here, inside the first-floor chapel, she must have also prayed for guidance, now that it seemed her liaison with Gaunt was over and an uncertain future stretched ahead.

III

Constance willingly accepted her husband's apology. If the first decade of her marriage had been less than successful, in terms of personal relations, childbearing and the pursuit of the Castilian throne, the coming years would bring her some comfort. Constance was now in her early thirties and although she may have borne a short-lived son, she and Gaunt had only the one daughter, Catalina, whose thirteenth birthday fell somewhere between summer 1385 and spring 1386. She was approaching marriageable age when relations between England and Portugal changed for the better. After years of struggle against the Spanish, the Battle of Aljubarrota had confirmed King John I as Portugal's ruler in August 1385. John then made friendly approaches to Gaunt, to forge an alliance against their mutual enemies, offering safe passage and an escort for English ships across the Bay of Biscay. With the recent turmoil in England and his narrow escape, Gaunt was ready to shift his focus elsewhere, to press his advantage and recapture his wife's inheritance. With the signing of the Treaty of Windsor, Constance could finally feel confident that her long-held ambitions were on the verge of being realised. Then, to their great encouragement, Pope Urban VI recognised Gaunt as the legitimate king of Castile and León. It was the spur he needed.

While Gaunt's standard was raised in St Paul's Cathedral and prayers were conducted for his campaign, Constance responded by embarking on a pilgrimage. It was common for all ranks of society to undertake such devotions to ask the saints for intercession in their lives. Pre-Reformation England was a network of religious sites, from the popular and fairly commercial shrine of St Thomas at Canterbury and the Virgin's Chapel at Walsingham, to holy wells, local churches and shrines to obscure saints. Hundreds of thousands journeyed relatively long distances to ask for forgiveness or guidance on matters of health, wealth, marriage and fortune: whatever question might be troubling them, there was an appropriate saint to whom they might offer thanks, or ask questions, and leave a gift of whatever amount they were able. Constance headed to the Abbey at St Albans in Hertfordshire, then a particularly important Benedictine community, centre of the arts and home to the chronicler Thomas Walsingham. She would have prayed for success in the Castilian campaign at the exquisite Lady Chapel, completed in 1327 in Purbeck marble carved with painted figures, angels and foliage. Located just 14 miles to the west of her usual residence of Hertford Castle, it was a community she would have known well and they would have enjoyed her patronage since the early days of her marriage. She was greatly admired there for her piety and during her visit was received into the confraternity of the abbey. More secular confirmations also took place, with a ceremony at Westminster, where Richard II placed gold coronets on the heads of Gaunt and Constance. Then, on 9 July 1386, Constance, Gaunt and Catalina set sail from Plymouth, along with Philippa and Elizabeth of Lancaster, accompanied by more than ninety ships and thousands of men. Constance was going home.

The English fleet arrived at the port of La Coruña on 25 July, the feast day of St James the Apostle. Since it was a day of devotion and celebration, the citizens put up little resistance and Gaunt's armies were able to enter the undefended town. According to Froissart, they remained there a month before proceeding south to Santiago de Compostela, where Gaunt was immediately recognised as king. An illustration in Froissart's chronicle depicts the surrender of the city to Gaunt and Constance, who appear on horseback. It is a generic enough portrait, with Constance riding side-saddle, demure enough for a conquering claimant to the throne, dressed in a golden gown with blue trim, her hair scraped back under a cone-shaped hennin with a gauzy veil. A coronation may even have been staged, using a crown of Spanish gold that had been brought specially from England for the purpose. Gaunt set up court for the winter of 1386–87 at Ourense, 100km to the south-east; a Roman town that sat at the junction of four rivers. Perhaps he and his family took over the twelfth-century episcopal palace with its courtyards, cloisters, lodgings and defensive walls. As word spread, the Galician nobles came to submit to Gaunt and pledge to help his campaign; this might have been prudence, given his position of occupation, but it gave him the support he needed. Constance was back in her homeland for the first time since her exile. With her husband and daughter at her side, this first part of the campaign was a great success, and as she moved within reach of her birthright, it must have been a happy time for the long-neglected wife.

That November, Gaunt met with John of Portugal to discuss their joint invasion, which was confirmed by a treaty of marriage between Blanche's eldest daughter Philippa and the Portuguese king. Catalina was initially suggested as the bride, but the hostility between Castile and Portugal led John to choose Philippa instead of her Castilian half sister.

She was then 26 and though various offers had been made for her hand, none had come close to fruition. An illustration from Jean de Waurin's fifteenth-century *Chronique d'Angleterre* depicts Gaunt and John, along with various prelates, debating the marriage over dinner. Although produced long after the event and therefore unhelpful as an actual portrait, it is remarkable as a depiction of their setting, with its tiled floor, red and gold walls, blue hangings and the formal table, draped in white and set with plates, bread and knives, as a chain of servants bring out the dishes. Gaunt himself is solid and grey-haired, with furs around his neck and lining his hat. Most significantly though, the ladies are not present as their futures are decided. Before the middle of November, Philippa had said her goodbyes and departed for Portugal. Her marriage took place the following February, at the Cathedral of the Assumption of Our Lady in Porto, also depicted in an illustration accompanying Jean de Waurin's work, in which the magnificently dressed couple stand before a golden altar flanked by marble pillars. In reality, the service was performed in the couple's absence, by proxy. They did not meet until they were already man and wife.

In March, Gaunt and John of Portugal prepared to invade Castile and crossed the River Douro to engage with the armies of Constance's cousin, John I of Castile, son of the man who had killed her father. Constance, Catalina and Elizabeth of Lancaster went with them. They travelled south, taking the towns of Valderas and Villalobos, although their arrival had been anticipated and defences were ready in most other major towns, reinforced by French mercenaries. The campaign proved disastrous: 'they found the country all laid waste and the English suffered much from the climate.'[20] As they ran out of supplies, terrible sickness spread through the troops; a number of leading knights died, including Gaunt's son-in-law Sir Thomas Morieux, and he was forced to abandon his plans. By May, after quarrelling fiercely, John and Gaunt agreed to come to terms with Castile. Walsingham recounts that the Portuguese king urged Gaunt to kill a number of English deserters but Gaunt wept and replied that they were driven to it out of desperation, not treason.[21] Perhaps the presence of his wife and daughters is the reason for his easy capitulation, or else his personal epiphany following the Peasants' Revolt made him less willing to push his men to the limit in impossible conditions, as he had on previous campaigns. It is also not impossible, as the single chronicler of St Denys suggests, that Constance was pregnant during this time and lost a child. Having returned to his wife and repudiated his mistress, Gaunt may well have seen his duty extending to fathering a new son, an heir to Castile who would be born on Spanish soil. Such a loss might have underpinned Gaunt's despair in the early summer of 1387.

Gaunt may also have been considering the situation of his daughter Elizabeth. Her marriage to John Hastings, concluded in 1380, had been annulled when it emerged, shortly before their departure for Spain, that Elizabeth had been seduced by her cousin, John Holland, Duke of Exeter. Holland was the son of Joan of Kent, Princess of Wales, from her first marriage, and was then in his mid-thirties. John Hastings was still only 14 and it seems unlikely that their union had been consummated. The royal party was already at Plymouth, waiting to embark, when the scandal broke. Elizabeth was pregnant and she and Holland were married just two weeks before they set sail. Her daughter, Constance, must have been delivered in Spain, probably early in 1387 at Ourense, and Elizabeth was nursing an infant of 3 or 4 months during the campaign. At the end of May, Holland and Elizabeth left the army and were granted safe conduct through Castile back on to Portuguese soil. Negotiations for a truce were made at the end of June and early July, at Trancoso, where Gaunt had stopped on his way to visit his newly-wed daughter Philippa. These led to the Treaty of Bayonne, which was concluded in 1388.

However, Constance's point had been made. Although she and Gaunt renounced their claim to the throne of Castile and agreed to return their conquests in Galicia, they were compensated with a payment of 600,000 gold francs, followed by an annual income of 40,000. Nor was Constance's right forgotten: her daughter Catalina was to marry the King of Castile's son, the 9-year-old Henry, and one day become queen by his side. Although some historians have considered the campaign to be a disaster, Walsingham thought the settlement was favourable, as it was the result of Gaunt's prayers and conveyed divine favour.[22] Their final weeks in Portugal were not easy. King John fell gravely ill and it was believed that he would soon die; the pregnant Philippa miscarried; and a plot was hatched by a Castilian knight to poison Gaunt. Around this time, he wept in public in repentance of his many sins and made a vow to the Virgin

Mary not to return to his dissolute ways. Perhaps this was in anticipation of his return to England, or a response to his recent misfortune.

The peace proved decisive for another daughter of Lancaster. Catalina married the 9-year-old Henry of Castile at Palencia Cathedral on 17 September 1388. The union neatly tied together the English and Castilian claims and it must have been a moment of triumph for Constance to attend this legal union with the title that her father had held. She must have relinquished the possibility of ever reigning Castile herself, but this was the next best thing, knowing that the line would continue through her daughter. Henry would inherit the throne in 1390 and Catalina would go on to bear him three children. Constance also took the opportunity to visit them in Castile that October, where she arranged for the reburial of her father's remains in the tomb of his ancestors. At the end of the month, Gaunt set sail for Bayonne, where he insisted that English pilgrims should keep their right of access to visit the shrine of St James at Santiago de Compostela even if he was handing over his Galician conquests.[23] A considerable period of negotiation followed. Gaunt, Constance and the remaining members of his family finally set sail and landed back in England on 19 November 1389, after an absence of over three years.

Gaunt returned to a scene of political drama. During his absence, certain reputedly 'evil' counsellors of the young Richard II had been challenged by a group known as the Lords Appellant. Led by Gaunt's younger brother Thomas of Woodstock, Duke of Gloucester and including Gaunt's son Henry of Bolingbroke, then aged 21, they launched an attack in the Merciless Parliament of 1388, forcing the young king to come to terms with them after a number of his favourites were impeached and executed. It was largely due to Gaunt's influence after his return from Castile that the king and the Lords Appellant were reconciled, although the problem was alleviated rather than solved. Political tension continued to simmer at court.

During Gaunt's absence, Katherine received an unprecedented honour. In April 1387, Richard II appointed her a Lady of the Garter, for which she attended a lavish ceremony of investiture at Windsor Castle, dressed in robes of red and blue embroidered with gold. This was a remarkable step for the king and Richard's motivation is not transparent.

Following Gaunt's repudiation of his relationship with Katherine, it must have been satisfying for her to receive this recognition, which was the highest honour available to her as an English woman. It may even have been a reward for her recent chaste living, although this was more the result of, rather than the catalyst for, Gaunt's return to his wife. The true nature of their affair, though, is not clear and Richard's action may have been intended to honour Katherine for her new-found morality, for her service to the family or her position as Gaunt's mistress. Whatever moved Richard to honour her in this way, it was a significant step considering Katherine's birth. She now divided her time between her estate at Kettlethorpe and the house in Lincoln, but would have continued to visit London in a ceremonial role. It was also a mark of the respect in which Katherine's experience was held within the family, that she was called upon to assist on at least one occasion at the lying-in of Mary de Bohun, Gaunt's young daughter-in-law. As a result of these connections, or perhaps even by letter from Gaunt himself, she would have learned that he was heading back to England.

On her return to England, Constance retired to her castles of Tutbury and Hertford. Her main aims in Castile had been achieved and her daughter was well married, so she lived out a quiet, pious existence with regular contact with the nearby Benedictine community at St Albans. Gaunt had commissioned a new chapel to be built at Hertford in 1380 and the work had been completed around three years later, providing Constance with a new location for her devotions. By this point, there was little purpose in maintaining relations with Gaunt on a personal level and the pair lived apart for the remainder of their marriage. This separation was also reflected by Katherine and Gaunt's reunion, and Katherine's presence in the ducal household is indicated by the 12*d* a day that was spent on the maintenance of the dozen horses she kept in his stables. However, she was a visitor rather than a permanent resident. The majority of the time, until 1393, Katherine appears to have been living at The Chancery in Lincoln. By 1391, Gaunt's household records show that his four children by Katherine were also involved in his life to some degree, being allotted 6*d* a day for their lodgings and given stabling for their horses. In March 1391, he sent wine to Katherine at Lincoln and that Christmas she was invited to Hertford Castle, along with their daughter Joan and Gaunt's son Henry and his family. Gaunt's gift to his mistress was a gold ring set with a diamond. In her final years, Constance is likely to have turned a blind eye to her husband's relationship and, given that chroniclers date a public awareness of his affair to after Constance's death, Gaunt most likely behaved discreetly out of respect for her. They would have come together mainly on ceremonial occasions, the last time being at Hertford for Christmas 1393. Gaunt was sent to France to conclude a four-year truce early in 1394, so he was far from home when Constance died at Leicester Castle on 24 March.

Constance, Duchess of Lancaster was 40, or not far off it, when she died. The cause of her death is not known. Her loss did not affect Gaunt to the degree that Blanche's had, back in 1368. That death had caused him a deep, almost inconsolable grief following their union of affection. There was never any suggestion that Constance was a replacement for Blanche in that sense, but she had proven herself to be a perfect model wife: regal, devout and serious, a suitable consort and partner for the pursuit of his Castilian ambition. She had set a standard of serious piety, given him a daughter and lived quietly without scandal. On a personal level, there was clearly little attraction between them, but the match had been made for dynastic, not personal reasons. Gaunt would have mourned his wife as befitted her character and status as the daughter of a king, but he was not heartbroken. Constance was laid to rest as she had lived: with honour and dignity alongside Henry, the first Duke Lancaster and his duchess Isabel at the church of the Newarke in Leicester. She had played her part in Lancastrian history, but ultimately left a limited mark in terms of its future. In the year of her death, 1394, the dynasty was about to enter a period of great trial. Its impending change in fortunes would threaten the Lancastrian inheritance, its reputation, even its very existence.

PART TWO

4

MARY DE BOHUN, 1380–94

1

The Essex village of Pleshey lies 5 miles to the north of Chelmsford. Its main street, dotted with weatherboarded house fronts and thatched roofs, gives little indication of the importance of the location back in the fourteenth century. Behind the houses, it is possible to glimpse a stretch of water and, rising up behind it, a large mound of earth. This is the first sign that the quiet village was once clustered around a bailey, the enclosure of a large Norman castle which boasted a motte over 50ft high, topped by a large rectangular keep nearly 70ft wide. Around it, on the site of the present houses, were kitchens, bakehouses, breweries, smithies, stables, the original church and more accommodation; everything to allow the inhabitants to be self-sufficient. It was all enclosed by a high wall of timber or stone and a deep moat, the typical rampart and ditch of which the earthworks can still be found today. It was here, during the

1380s, that a group of friars created a series of illuminated manuscripts to celebrate an important royal marriage.

The groom was Henry, Earl of Derby, the only surviving son of John of Gaunt and Blanche of Lancaster. Having been raised in the household of his stepmother Constance, with Katherine Swynford as his governess, he was taught by Hugh Herle and Thomas Burton, Burton having served in the household of Henry's maternal grandfather, the Duke of Lancaster. This established his connection with the title that would be his inheritance. The young man already knew Latin, French and English, and showed early promise in riding, hunting and the other sports that were to lead to his later reputation as a champion jouster. At the age of 10, he had been knighted alongside his cousin Richard, son of the Black Prince, at a Garter ceremony at Windsor Castle and, three years later, when Richard had become king, he attended the wedding of his half-sister Maud Holland to the Count of Saint-Pol. Henry reached the age of 13 in April 1380, after which Gaunt sought a marriage for him with a wealthy heiress who would bring land, estates and titles into Lancastrian hands.

The bride he found was even younger. Mary de Bohun was only 10 on her wedding day, which fell on, or shortly before, 5 February 1381. Their union may have been engineered by Gaunt, Mary's relatives or even come at Henry's suggestion. Perhaps, as dutiful children, they had no difficulty allying their personal preference with the dynastic advantages each could bring the other. Yet Mary and Henry had known each other since they were infants, so there is a chance, suggested by the frequency of her later pregnancies and records of them exchanging gifts and their shared interests, that this was a match inspired by mutual affection. It may have been that the two children were already fond of each other and went willingly into the match, as later events might imply. After all, a grandson of Edward III would have a good chance of securing an important international match, so Henry would not have lacked potential brides elsewhere. There is no doubt though that marriage to Mary brought him lucrative titles: all the affection in the world could not have facilitated the marriage, had her breeding and inheritance been lacking.

The de Bohuns were a Norman family who had come over with William the Conqueror in 1066. Initially they settled in Wiltshire and served at the court of subsequent kings Henry I and Stephen. Through judicious marriages, they inherited the earldoms of Hereford and Essex and by the mid-thirteenth century, members of this line of the de Bohun family were resident at Pleshey Castle, having taken it over from the disgraced Mandeville family. Mary was certainly well connected. Her father was Humphrey de Bohun, seventh Earl of Hereford, sixth Earl of Essex, second Earl of Northampton and her paternal grandmother was the widow of Edmund Mortimer, from which marriage the future Yorkist kings were descended. Mary's mother was Joan FitzAlan, the fourth child of a second marriage, who arrived in 1347 or '48, probably at the seat of the Earls of Arundel at Arundel Castle in West Sussex. Her brothers were to play a key role in the life of her future son-in-law. Joan's parents were Richard FitzAlan, tenth Earl of Arundel and Eleanor of Lancaster, a great-granddaughter of Henry III: theirs is the touching monument in Chichester Cathedral made famous by Philip Larkin's poem 'An Arundel Tomb', which describes them lying side by side, hand in hand. Joan and Humphrey were married at some point after September 1359, when Joan was 12, though they probably waited a couple of years to consummate the match. Joan bore two surviving children, Eleanor in 1366 and Mary, who arrived four years later, in 1370.

Life at Pleshey Castle in the 1360s and '70s would have been privileged and cultured. Duke Humphrey inherited the property from his childless uncle in 1361, along with the group of Augustinian friars working there to produce a collection of illuminated manuscripts for the glory and use of the de Bohun family. Humphrey was also a patron and collector of books: around 1350 he ordered a translation of the romance of *William and the Werwolf* or *The Romance of William of Palerne*, an early thirteenth-century story of a baby prince raised by a werewolf. Later, under the lead of Friar John de Teye, a total of eleven books were created at Pleshey for Humphrey's family, including some celebrating Mary's marriage. Mary's psalter now resides in the Fitzwilliam Museum, illustrated with thirty-five scenes from the life of David, while another book, Egerton 3277 in the British Library, created between 1353 and '73, is so beautiful it can be described as 'virtually a royal manuscript',[1] perhaps produced for Humphrey, his wife and daughters. In total, four small manuscripts with illustrations were made solely for Mary, featuring appropriate biblical imagery for a girl of her age and heraldic illustrations coupling her arms with those of Henry.

One illustration depicts the Annunciation of the Virgin, featuring a golden-haired, crowned figure seated in a golden chair: a model of piety for a young girl.[2] Another image of two women kneeling before the Virgin, one adult, one a girl of about 10, is likely to depict Mary and her mother Joan, and stresses the child's piety and nobility through her posture of prayer and her ermine-lined clothing. Her mother has a hand protectively on her shoulder as both look up at the Virgin and child. A love of books was one quality Mary shared with her future husband.

Humphrey died young. He had been a commander in France during Gaunt's campaign of 1369 and an ambassador to the Duke of Brittany in 1372, but made his will at the end of that year and died the following January, aged only 31. His daughters, aged 6 and 2, were made wards of the king. With no brothers to inherit their titles, they were rich prizes for any husband who would assume the dukedoms of Hereford and Essex, besides much more when the girls came of age. Eleanor's future was arranged first. In 1376, at the age of 10, she was married to Gaunt's younger brother Thomas of Woodstock, later Duke of Gloucester, and the couple took over residence of Pleshey Castle, keeping the younger Mary in their care. Thomas was around eleven years older than his wife and they did not consummate the marriage until Eleanor had reached the legal age of 14. The young duchess celebrated her birthday some time in the first three weeks of June 1380. According to the Close Rolls, she was still underage on 28 May, when the Sheriff of Essex was given instructions to pay her husband her income 'until the lawful age of the said Eleanor whom he has taken to wife'. However, by 22 June, Eleanor had come of age, which had been 'proved before the escheator'[3] and the king granted her and her husband extensive manors in Essex, Hertfordshire, Lincolnshire, Nottinghamshire, Oxfordshire, Berkshire, Norfolk and Cambridgeshire. Within weeks, Eleanor was pregnant.

Mary and Henry were married soon after this, by the second week of February 1381 at the latest. According to Froissart, Thomas had originally been against the match, hoping to encourage Mary to enter a nunnery so that his wife Eleanor could inherit all of the Hereford estates and titles; the nineteenth-century historian Mary Anne Everett Green suggested they entrusted her education to the nuns of St Clare.[4] Froissart adds that Mary 'seemed inclined to their doctrine, and thought not of marriage'. It is unlikely that Mary's voice alone would have been enough to prevent this from happening; knowing that Thomas would oppose his son's match, John of Gaunt waited until his brother was out of the country, then purchased the right of Mary's marriage. Froissart suggests this was accomplished by a semi-abduction, during which Mary was lured to Arundel Castle by Henry's maternal aunt Mary FitzAlan, although Mary never repudiated her husband as some abducted brides did. Froissart adds that the union was 'instantly consummated', which may have been a way of ensuring that it was legally binding, after which the couple were parted until they came of age. However the union was made, it is likely to have caused tension between Gaunt and his brother, who lost the opportunity to inherit as he had planned. It was a relationship that was to become increasingly strained as the sisters' husbands were drawn further into the political turmoil of Richard II's reign.

Mary was still recognised as a child at the time of her wedding and this had implications for her married life, both personally and legally. On 26 October 1380, she was being referred to as underage in a petition to the Sheriff of Nottingham which stated that her inheritance was held in wardship by her brother-in-law 'until her lawful age'.[5] By 10 February 1381, 'Henry, Earl of Derby … [had] taken to wife Mary, daughter and one of the heirs of Humphrey, Earl of Hereford and Essex,' but Mary was still not 'of lawful age',[6] so the ceremony occurred at some point between these dates. It is likely to have taken place at Rochford Hall, Essex, a residence of the earls of Hertford, close to the River Roach near Southend-on-Sea. Little of the original house survives, but the present building is a mixture of the manor later owned by the Boleyn family and modern improvements, giving a sense of the scale of the site. Opposite it lies the fifteenth-century church of St Andrew, where the ceremony would have been conducted. The king sent minstrels to celebrate the occasion and Gaunt was probably present, having given his daughter-in-law a diamond and a ruby set in a newly made ring. No doubt a lavish feast at the hall followed, but there was to be no consummation yet. Mary returned to the protection of her family until she came of age. Gaunt made payments to her mother Joan to cover her expenses until such time as she was able to live with Henry as his wife: £26 13s 4d at Easter and Michaelmas 1382, as part of her 100 marks annuity.

And yet, but for a twist of fate, there would have been no married life at all. While John of Gaunt had headed north on campaign to Scotland, his 14-year-old son was in London. There is a fair chance he was at the family home of the Savoy Palace when news reached him of the specific threats that had been voiced against his father and his own life by the rebels. With a small group of trusted companions, including his guardian, tutors, clerk and friend Thomas Swynford, he fled to the protection of the Tower, where a number of the rebels' other targets had also sought refuge, including the king, his mother Joan of Kent, the Archbishop of Canterbury, the Treasurer and other officials and members of Gaunt's household. On 14 June, the 14-year-old King Richard left the Tower and bravely headed off to meet Wat Tyler at Greenwich. There, he made an ill-advised declaration to the rebels that he would bring traitors to justice, which was taken by some as an invitation to break through the Tower's defences. According to Froissart, they killed indiscriminately, pursuing personal grievances and targeting immigrants, as well as anyone associated with the king. Inside the Tower, they assaulted Joan of Kent with an irreverent kiss and beheaded Gaunt's physician, the archbishop and others. Then their attention turned to Henry. It must have been terrifying. Perhaps it was Henry's youth that saved him, but one of the guards somehow found the words to make the killers stop. Whatever John Ferrour said, Henry was unharmed, though the ordeal cannot but have left its mark upon him.

Even apart from his unpopular parentage, Henry would have drawn the attention of the rebels for his appearance. According to Froissart, one of rebel leader John Ball's grievances was Henry's clothing, and that of his peers: 'they are clothed in velvets and rich stuffs, ornamented with ermine and other furs, while we are forced to wear poor cloth.' Henry's account book for 1381–82, kept by his guardian Hugh Waterton, lists a dazzling amount of clothing and jewellery: damask, silk and satin robes in red, blue and gold, with regular payments to his goldsmiths for rings, pendants, buckles and other adornments. Yet this was entirely appropriate for a young man in his position, according to the Sumptuary Laws of 1363, passed by his own grandfather. The lifestyle and property of the nobility also came under attack from the rebels: 'they have wines, spices and fine bread, when we have only rye and the refuse of the straw; and if we drink, it must be water. They have handsome seats and manors while we must brave the wind and rain.'[7] Today, Ball's theories concerning class appear ahead of his time, almost proto-Marxist, as epitomised in his comment 'When Adam delft and Eve span, who then was the gentleman?' At the time, his ideas were anachronistic and unsupported against a wider tide of privilege and never had a realistic chance of being heard. For Mary, a product of her time, it was a simpler story. Waiting in the comfort of Pleshey, 40 miles north-east of the Tower, she finally received news that her young husband was safe.

The marriage ceremony did not change Mary's daily life significantly. Her legal status and her future were secure but, for the time being, she continued her education and polished the routine accomplishments that would prepare her for her future as a duchess. A manual for a young wife written by the Ménagier of Paris in the early 1390s outlines some of the expectations of women of the nobility at the head of their own household. He offered instruction in religious devotion and the behaviour necessary to 'win you the love of your husband and to give you in this world the peace which should be in marriage', as well as offering the biblical models of discreet service in Susanna, Sarah, Rachel, Rebecca and the folkloric patient Griselda. She was also expected to 'increase the profit of the house, gain friends and save one's possessions' and to 'aid oneself against the ill fortunes of ages to come'. This included diligence and perseverance in housework, cultivating a garden, choosing and managing suitable servants and ruling over her domestic domain as its 'sovereign'. She should know how to order meals, converse with tradesmen and know about spices and medicine, as well as pursuing amusements to give her 'something to talk about in company': playing dice and chess, feeding and flying falcons, and enjoying riddles.[8] Mary's status would have also given her position a political dimension, but Ménagier's guidelines give a good indicator of some of the accomplishments she would have pursued besides her love of books and music, particularly the harp, cither and singing, whilst she waited to come of age. One day these would be an adornment to her husband's position. She may have been the recipient of one of the twenty-nine gold rings Henry ordered in December 1381 as presents for New Year's Day.

The main expectation of a duchess was to bear heirs. In the spring of 1382, probably in April, Mary's elder sister Eleanor fulfilled her duty, having conceived in the weeks following her marriage. She was at Pleshey when she delivered a son to whom she gave her father's name of Humphrey. At a time when babies usually bore family Christian names, typically those of their grandparents, it is significant that the child was named after Eleanor's father, in acknowledgement of his Hereford inheritance, rather than Edward, after Thomas' father, or even Richard, in honour of his nephew, the new king. Humphrey's birth would have been an all-female affair, with Eleanor closeted in her chamber according to birthing traditions, attended by close female relatives, likely to have included her mother Joan and sister Mary, as well as the experienced women of their household. Gaunt's records of payments show that such women were valued in the Lancastrian family and it is possible that Katherine Swynford was also present, given that she would assist Mary's deliveries in years to come. Gaunt oversaw his 15-year-old son Henry's gifts to the baby's nurse and the bearer of the tidings of Humphrey's arrival. Observing the process at first hand, it would have been a powerful induction for Mary into the experience that was to dominate her short adult life.

Mary spent the following three years living quietly but, for Henry and the Lancastrian family, it was a time that marked their increasing separation from the king. Mary is unlikely to have taken up the duties of a duchess at this point, so she may not have accompanied her husband to the coronation of Anne of Bohemia in January 1382, where Henry wore a tabard of blue damask provided by his stepmother Constance, Duchess of Lancaster. He attended the tournament afterwards at Smithfield, where he jousted in magnificent armour decorated with silver spangles in the shape of roses. There is a chance that Mary joined him at the May Day jousts at Hertford, but it is more likely that she remained at Pleshey with her sister, who bore two more children during this time: Anne in 1383, named after the new queen, and Joan in 1384, after the girls' mother. It has been suggested that Mary herself bore a child during this time, which her seclusion would certainly have facilitated, but no evidence survives to support this and the proposed date, April 1382, indicates that it is more likely that one sister has been confused with the other.

As historian Ian Mortimer has established, this stems from a misreading of the Lancastrian account books, by which earlier historians mistook baby Humphrey for a child of Mary, based on the fact that Henry rewarded members of the infant's household. In fact, these payments were authorised on 18 April by Gaunt himself, who was also present. Henry was still living in his father's retinue and is unlikely to have consummated the marriage with Mary.

The contemporary *Book of Vices and Virtues* advised that man and wife should keep themselves 'clenliche and truliche' (clean and true) for each other and, according to the teaching of St Paul, women should be chaste and sober in eating and drinking, as greed could fuel the fires of lechery and temptation. The book describes how marriage was created as a 'state of innocence' in an earthly paradise, and that partners should respect it as holy and honest. This was easily achieved in Pleshey Castle for the young Mary, as she whiled away the days until she came of age. For Henry, who was mostly in his father's household during these years, the advice that he should never resort 'to another womman than to [his] own' was tempered by the relationship between Gaunt and Katherine, which had become public knowledge by this point. While the hostile chronicler Henry Knighton berated Gaunt for riding with his mistress in public and guiding her saddle in a thinly concealed metaphor for sexual dominance, the young Henry appears not to have succumbed to the advances of other women.

Mary disappears from the historical records while Henry accompanied his father to France in December 1383 to negotiate a peace treaty with Charles VI. He may also have gone north with Gaunt and Eleanor's husband Thomas to repel Scots invaders in the spring of 1384, and it was during this time that slanderous tongues at court convinced the young king that his uncle was plotting against him. Volatile and sensitive to criticism, Richard had gone as far as to order Gaunt's execution before his two uncles returned to protest their innocence. It was a time of national anxiety, with the newly appointed Archbishop of Canterbury drawing Richard's wrath by admonishing him for a lack of control and the Earl of Arundel, Mary's uncle, pronouncing that the realm was on the brink of destruction. At the end of 1384, a further breach occurred when Gaunt told the inexperienced king that war was unavoidable with France.

Richard's extreme response prompted Gaunt to walk out of the Council chamber and Richard again planned to have him killed the following February. Furious, Gaunt confronted him in armour and refused to attend him for fear of his life, at which the king backed down. They were formally reconciled at Westminster the following month but trust between the throne and the house of Lancaster had been irrevocably damaged.

It was around this point that Mary reached the age of consent. It was recorded on 22 December 1384 that her age had been proved before the escheator in Essex, allowing Henry to inherit her portion of the Hereford titles and estates.[9] It is likely that this also marked the moment when the pair began to share a bed. The arrangements were certainly not uniform for every woman in her position; she may have lived with Henry permanently in London, and in Gaunt's various properties, or been based at a particular location, such as Hertford or Leicester, or divided her time between Pleshey and wherever Henry happened to be. His political career took on a more formal aspect. He was included in the king's campaign against the Scots the following summer and, for the first time, was summoned to attend Richard's thirteenth Parliament, which sat in Westminster Hall between 20 October and 6 December. After the destruction of the Savoy, Gaunt and his family used Ely Palace as their residence in the capital, so Mary might have been there during the autumn of 1385. That Christmas, the households of Henry and Gaunt came together at Leicester and it was around this time that Mary became pregnant.

11

Monmouth Castle had been in the Lancaster family for a century, having been granted to Edmund Crouchback, a younger son of Henry III. He had added a large hall to the south of the original two-storey Norman buildings, before the castle passed to Henry Grosmont, who remodelled the Great Tower with large windows, a new entrance and roof, before it came into the hands of Gaunt, who made his own improvements. Standing at the meeting place of the rivers Wye and Monnow, right on the English-Welsh border, it overlooked the Forest of Dean to the east and the beginning of the Marcher hills to the west. Mary retreated there, into apartments in the castle gatehouse, to give birth to her first child, Henry, in the summer of 1386 or 1387.

Despite the existence of some powerful evidence, confusion has arisen among scholars about the exact day and year that Mary's confinement took place. Perhaps the most significant indication is an astrological chart drawn up for the king during his reign, which gives his birthdate as 19 September 1386, followed by the even more specific detail that he arrived at 11.22 a.m. It was not customary to record the exact timings and details of births, even among the aristocracy, before the introduction of parish records in the mid-sixteenth century. Birthdays were not always celebrated, or even known, among the lower classes, as evidenced in the contemporary court records when witnesses were frequently called upon to establish a year of birth. There was no indication in the 1380s that Henry would ever go on to become king, especially as the young Richard II was newly married and likely to produce a son. The details of Henry's arrival were recorded retrospectively, but this is not sufficient reason to reject them: the birthday of Richard III in 1452 was recorded in a similar manner, and is now widely accepted, and Joan de Bohun was clearly aware of the birthdates of both her daughters, in order to later prove that they had come of age. Although no surviving record of Henry's birth from the 1380s can be located, it does not follow that Henry himself was not informed of it by someone such as his grandmother Joan, who lived long enough to see him become king.

However, according to another document,[10] Henry was in his twenty-sixth year when he was crowned, in April 1413, which means he had not yet reached his twenty-sixth birthday, making him 25. This would suggest a birthdate of 1387, as would the statement that he died in his thirty-sixth year: so, when he was 35, working backwards from 31 August 1422. The day of his birth matters even more in this instance, as it is sometimes cited as falling either side of the end of the period he is thought to have died, 9 August to 16 September, altering his age at death. If we accept the birthdate of December 1370 for Mary, which her coming of age suggests, she would have been either 15 or 16 when she gave birth, depending on which year is correct. Additionally, it is known for certain that Mary and her husband Henry were at Monmouth in the summer of 1386, but not in 1387, along with Henry's companion Thomas Swynford and members of his household. The arrival of Mary's second child, whose nurse was referred to at Christmas 1387, makes it very unlikely that she had delivered two babies in one year, especially as her eldest son arrived in August or September. On balance, the weight of contemporary academic opinion favours the earlier date.

Despite the rumours, this was Mary's first child. In September 1386, she was 15 years and 9 months old, so her pregnancy had been commensurate with her sixteenth year thus far. Eleanor had been the same age when she bore her first child. Living at Pleshey, Mary would have seen her sister's three subsequent pregnancies develop and had probably been present at the births, giving her a fair understanding of what could be expected. Inside the duchess' all-female household, the inner circle who had the care of her body, linen and the provisioning of bedchamber, there would have been a similar patterning of familiar connections as in the establishments of Gaunt's wives. There was also considerable overlap, with wards and valued servants such as Katherine Swynford moving between satellites of the ducal households to offer support during childbirth and child rearing. With Gaunt and Constance embarking for Spain that July, Katherine was transferred to another branch of the family, dividing her time between her estates and children and Gaunt's young daughter-in-law during subsequent pregnancies until his return. When Mary moved to her own home at Monmouth, she took a wealth of experience and knowledge with her, from a female oral tradition that had been passed down through generations of families. Katherine and her daughter Joan were certainly present in Mary's household at Christmas 1386, when provision was made for them in Mary's chamber and wardrobe accounts record two lengths of silk brocade, white and blue, together with a number of miniver furs.[11]

However, having witnessed these events and actually experiencing them are two different things entirely. There is no doubt that a young woman of Mary's age and situation would be apprehensive about her approaching delivery, or that such an event, often stretching over several days, represented a very real danger to both mother and child. The author of the tract *Hali Meidenhad* warned young women that the process was one of 'sore sorrowful anguish, the strong piercing pang, the comfortless

94

ill, pain on pain … thou art in trouble herewith, in the dint of death'.[12] The possibility of a breech birth, or a baby presenting at an unusual angle, could prove problematic at best, fatal at worst, and doctors were called in to attend emergency cases, bringing with them a terrifying variety of knives and hooks to extract the child.[13] Contemporary tracts outlining methods for repairing a ruptured perineum indicate just how brutal birth could be, when the dimensions of a small-hipped mother were combined with a large, overdue child. Even if a delivery did follow the expected lines, there was precious little to be had in the way of pain relief, beyond herbal remedies, alcohol and prayers. The prospect must have been terrifying.

There has been some suggestion in recent scholarship that medieval mothers were more pragmatic about childbirth, that low rates of survival instilled in them some sort of disconnection from their child, or absence from the experience as they put their faith in God and the afterlife. Somehow, medieval mothers have come to be considered less than motherly. This is belied by the very real grief manifested by women in the face of loss, by their prayers and offerings on pilgrimage, by the all-female churching celebrations, by Catherine of Aragon's lamentations 'like a natural woman' on the loss of her baby.[14] It is also to deny the timeless strength of the maternal bond, as well as the odds of gynaecological injury, infection and the use of churching not just to cleanse a woman but to welcome her back from the brink of darkness, the brink of oblivion. Childbirth customs were established not just to ease the delivery; laces were untied and arrows loosened in order to smooth the child's passage, but prayers and charms, talismans and holy water were used to stave off the devils creeping into the breach before the child could be baptised and the mother blessed. Coupled with *Hali Meidenhad*, the depositions of midwives in Court Assizes records show there is no question that the process of giving birth was one of danger and uncertainty.[15] It was for this reason that birth was a rallying time for women, including a mix of family members, friends, professional nurses and midwives, and any female considered to be experienced. Mary would have been well provided for when she went into labour. She was fortunate that her child was healthy and that both survived the process. Her new son was named Henry, probably after his father.

It was customary for a mother to spend a month lying-in, recovering in her darkened chamber, before the gradual process of sitting up, ritual washing and the final act of churching, which signalled her return to her duties as a wife. Mary was only partway through this process when her husband left Monmouth to obey a summons to attend the Parliament at Westminster that had been called for 1 October. Later known as the 'Wonderful Parliament', it marked the beginning of significant conflicts between Henry and his king as the members pushed for reforms in the face of Richard's despotic rule. While this situation developed in London, Mary would have gradually grown stronger while her infant son was nursed by a Joan Waryn,[16] described as Henry's 'nutrix', and who received the annual salary of 40s for his care. Given that in the 1340s, archers and infantrymen received between 2s and 3s a day, besides her fee Joan would have received board and lodgings, and she may have had an additional allowance for clothing. The nursery at Monmouth would have been typical of an aristocratic household, overseen by Mary, with a separate space dedicated to the child, rockers employed to send him off to sleep and other staff to ensure the warmth, safety and cleanliness of the room and the baby's bedclothes and linen. Little Henry would have been swaddled for the first year of his life, living quietly in the castle while his father's world suddenly spiralled into drama and rebellion.

In November, when his son was 2 months old, Henry joined with his brother-in-law Thomas of Woodstock, now Duke of Gloucester, his father-in-law Richard FitzAlan and uncle-in-law Thomas FitzAlan, known as Thomas Arundel, to form the Lords Appellant, a group who sought to curb the king's nepotistic favour of certain influential friends. According to Adam of Usk, the intention was 'to bridle the wantoness [sic] and extravagance of his servants and flatterers and ... to reform the business of the realm'.[17] The main figure of contention was Robert de Vere, Earl of Oxford, the king's first cousin by marriage, who had been created Marquess of Dublin in 1385 and Duke of Ireland in 1386. Richard found their demands intolerable. He walked out and intended to turn his back on Parliament, but Gloucester and Arundel alluded to the deposition of his predecessor Edward II because of the belief that the realm was being mismanaged to the point of ruin. Richard capitulated and returned to Parliament, where he replaced his unpopular chancellor with Arundel. He also appeared to favour Henry by awarding him the dukedom of Hereford. The Lords Appellant then proposed a great council, which would sit for the term of a year, starting that November. His work done, Henry returned home to Mary and his son for the Christmas period. However, the king was never to forget this Parliament and would later seek to punish all the Lords Appellant for their efforts to rein in his excesses. Knighton, Walsingham and the Monk of Evesham all record that Richard secretly made plans to assassinate his enemies but, for the time being, these came to nothing.

During this time with her husband, either over Christmas or in the following spring, Mary fell pregnant again. The speed of her conceptions suggest that the pair were not only compatible in their musical and literary tastes but enjoyed a close physical relationship. Henry was obliged to attend the annual Garter ceremony at Windsor in April, but was soon back with his family, spending the summer with them at Kenilworth Castle. It is also likely that he retired from the public eye as he is known to have suffered from the pox in this year, requiring the attentions of Richard's physician John Middleton. The term 'the pox' has been used to describe a range of illnesses which include the sexually transmitted syphilis, but given his youth it seems unlikely that, by 1388, whatever it was had had sufficient time to develop beyond a primary level and require serious treatment. Nor is there any evidence of Henry having a mistress, or resorting to prostitutes, or abstaining from relations with his wife in order to protect her. Most historians agree that Henry is more likely to have been suffering from some form of smallpox, which could leave the face covered in rashes and blisters. Alternatively, 'the pox' may have been a misdiagnosis for a number of skin conditions including psoriasis. In 1405, Henry would experience an outbreak of red pustules on the face and believe himself to be suffering from leprosy, but this possibility has been disproved by analysis of his remains. If it was some form of smallpox, Henry would have spent much of this period resting, contemporary treatments advising that his bed and room be hung with scarlet-coloured cloth.

The impressive sandstone castle of Kenilworth had long been a favourite Lancastrian retreat, developed into a palace during the thirteenth century with a huge two-storey keep, solid stone walls, an enclosed garden and a great lake. Gaunt had transformed the buildings, adding his own great hall with its stone panelling, six fireplaces and bay and traceried windows. The state apartments were to the south, on the first floor, with their own oriel window; opposite them were more rooms and storage larders, alongside a generously sized kitchen. Started in 1371, Gaunt's alterations were nearing completion, employing some of the same craftsmen who also worked on Windsor Castle. However, Kenilworth also had a tradition of being a bastion of rebellion, being held by the de Montforts against Henry III in 1266, by Edmund, Duke of Lancaster, who rebelled against Edward II in 1322 and providing a prison for that king as he was forced to abdicate four years later. Within months of that happy family summer, whiled away at a favourite retreat, Henry was to continue that tradition, leading an army against troops loyal to his king.

While Henry was at Kenilworth, Richard summoned judges to Nottingham to examine the question of royal power and its exercise over Parliament. Reluctantly and even under duress in some cases, they upheld his right to dissolve Parliament and confirmed its inability to act independently to impeach his favourites. Richard then summoned Gloucester and Arundel but, afraid of his intentions, they refused, prompting the king to issued secret instructions for the murder of Arundel. The dukes were camped to the north of London, drawing in the support of some of the rebels of 1381, anticipating attack. But Henry was not with them; by this point, he and his family were in London, probably at their house in Bishopsgate. It was from there, on 25 November, that his wife and children were sent away to the safety of the countryside, suggesting that Mary had given birth to her second son, Thomas, during their stay at Kenilworth that summer or in the early autumn in London. The latter seems likely, as they were in the capital that November, when Henry rewarded the midwife who had brought Thomas into the world. Therefore, Mary made the journey north to Kenilworth with young Henry aged around 15 months, a babe in arms.

One cannot be certain about the nature of trust men placed in their wives, even those who were loved, due to the rigid separation of households which bred a sense of gendered spheres. Politics and government were the jurisdiction of men. Contemporary manuals advised against the lines being blurred, citing women's propensity to gossip as damaging to male business, and women who formally wielded power were relatively unknown. However, this must have varied as much as personal relationships did and, as Chaucer's writings make clear, intelligent women must have been influential where circumstances allowed, acting at the very minimum as listeners, advisors and encouragers. There is no doubt though that, waiting at Kenilworth, Mary was aware of the dangers of Henry's situation. Theirs seems to have been a close marriage and now she was not simply the bearer and protector of his heirs, but a vital source of communication, playing a critical part in the coming events.

The Lords Appellant had made a formidable enemy in de Vere, who gathered an army in response to a request from Richard and in retaliation to their calls to strip him of his power. In response, Henry rode north from London and met his fellow Lords at Huntingdon on 12 December, waiting to hear of de Vere's movements in order to be able to cut him off before he could reach London and the king. It was during this time that Mary was able to write to her husband, at Northampton, Daventry and other locations, giving him information about the route of de Vere's army which was then in the Midlands. Henry and his allies were able to keep pace with him as he headed south, and planned for Henry to push ahead to hold the bridges along the Thames while the other Lords chased him south into the trap. The armies of de Vere and Henry met on Radcot Bridge, one of three crossings in present-day Oxfordshire,[18] about 20 miles from Chipping Norton. The original bridge was almost 200 years old, built with pointed arches from Norman stone paid for by King John. De Vere now found that most of it had been rapidly destroyed, along with its two partners, halting him in his tracks.

Taken by surprise, the approaching troops had not expected such a determined show of force. Racing towards London, they had believed the danger lay behind them and, sandwiched between the forces of the Appellants, many began to desert. Watching his troops disappear and desperate to reach London, de Vere rode along the river bank, stripping himself of heavy armour and clothing, seeking a safe place to cross. That night, he slipped into the water. An illustration in Froissart's manuscript depicts him in a boat, but the danger was so grave that he probably swam his way across under the cover of darkness. From there he fled south to Kent, and then abroad; Henry and his men presumed him dead. It was a reasonable assumption: there had been one significant fatality already, of which de Vere may have been aware. Sir Thomas Molyneaux of Kuerdale, who had raised de Vere's armies in Cheshire, was killed as he had tried to climb out of the river. According to chronicler Henry Knighton, the blow had been struck by Thomas Mortimer, an illegitimate son of the Earl of March, who reacted brutally to Molyneaux's pleas for mercy. Like other events of this turbulent period, the implications of this action would resurface in the coming years.

Henry and the other Lords Appellant then marched to London and demanded the keys of the Tower. According to Adam of Usk, who had witnessed them pass through Oxford, 'they placed the king, who lay therein, under new governance, and delivered his fawning councillors into divers prisons until the next following Parliament.'[19] This Parliament, which sat from 3 February until June, was later christened by Knighton the Merciless Parliament, on account of the ruthlessness of the trials that resulted. A number of the king's inner circle of friends were condemned of 'living in vice' and misleading the king; for this they were hung, drawn and quartered without formal trial. The net then widened to include minor officials in Richard's household: chaplains and clerks, as well as the judges who had met the king at Nottingham and been forced to approve his actions. Their most significant and divisive victim was Simon Burley, the king's tutor, who was defended in vain by Edmund, Duke of York, which led to a breach with his brother Gloucester. This set Henry's uncles against each other. Henry may well have played a mediating role during this process, restraining Gloucester and Arundel, who were keen to restrict Richard's powers further and sympathised with York's defence.

An uneasy truce had been reached, but the rift between Richard and the Lords had only been patched over. That summer, Henry may have expected to be included among the armies sent north to repel the Scots, which resulted in the Battle of Otterburn. He set out from London that June but his name is not recorded in Froissart's accounts of the English defeat, led by the Earl of Northumberland with his sons Henry 'Hotspur' Percy and Ralph Percy. Perhaps personal reasons prevented him. Given that Gaunt's physician, a priest and scholar from Oxford named Geoffrey Melton, was summoned to Kenilworth that summer, it seems plausible that either Henry or Mary was ill. Henry appears to have suffered from serious illnesses throughout his life, often requiring medical attention, but it may well be the case that the patient on this occasion was Mary. Having given birth to Thomas in the late summer or early autumn of 1387, and given her history of rapid conceptions and short recuperations, it is possible that Mary was experiencing a difficult pregnancy or had miscarried. Usually, the care of an expectant mother was undertaken by women but, on occasions requiring medical intervention, male doctors performed the necessary surgery, which was considered a separate body of knowledge from gynaecological science. Melton is referred to by historian Nigel Saul as 'Gaunt's medical consultant', and identified as 'in attendance on the childbirth labours' of Mary,[20] although this may have been on the specific occasions when things went wrong, in 1388 and 1394. Otherwise, he would wait until his interventions were deemed necessary. Mary may well have miscarried or lost a child in the summer of 1388. Her gynaecological record and the presence of Melton would allow for it, although it cannot be established for a certainty.

III

True to her impressive fertility record, Mary fell pregnant again in early September. Where it is possible to discern the interval between her giving birth and conceiving again, on average Mary was usually pregnant again between three and nine months when it comes to her first five children. Henry attended the session of Parliament that sat at Cambridge from 9 September to 17 October. Given that this newly conceived child would arrive on 20 June the following year, a standard forty-week pregnancy gives a conception date of 13 September; a slightly overdue baby allows for a date just days before Henry departed for Cambridge. He probably learned of the news on his return in the second half of October. The family spent Christmas together at Kenilworth and, although Henry was in London in the spring to attend a council meeting, he had returned home by the time Mary delivered their third surviving son, John.

In November 1389, Mary's father-in-law John of Gaunt returned home from Spain after an absence of three years. The house of Lancaster was under threat during that time, but Gaunt would have appreciated that Mary had delivered three more healthy male heirs, especially given that

King Richard and his wife Anne were yet to have a child. The family were all together for Christmas at Hereford Castle, where the traditional celebrations, festivities and exchange of New Year gifts took place. Around that time, almost seven months after the arrival of baby John, Mary became pregnant again before Henry departed for Parliament in January. With her nursery of three small boys being overlooked by trusted women such as Joan Waryn, governess Mary Hervy and perhaps also Katherine Swynford, Mary probably spent the months of waiting quietly at Kenilworth. Between March and May, Henry attended the jousts at Saint-Inglevert in France, but no sooner had he returned than he was ready to depart again, having conceived the idea of undertaking a pilgrimage to Jerusalem. By mid-July, when she was six months pregnant, Mary was at Lincoln, perhaps in a property owned by Gaunt, to say goodbye to Henry, knowing that she would not be seeing him again for many months.

Mary retired to await the birth of her fourth child. Her return journey south took her close to Bytham Castle, home of her mother, so it is likely that she visited Joan there, before returning to Kenilworth. Wardrobe accounts for Mary at this time include the purchase of 'three dozen and four knots' of strings for instruments, and the following year, she also had foreign minstrels playing the lute and fiddle,[21] so she probably devoted herself to the quiet pursuits of music and literature in her husband's absence. At the start of October, her labour pains began and she was delivered of a son on the third of the month. She named him Humphrey, after her father. The news took a while to reach Henry; he received a letter from a sailor at Könisberg, probably written by Mary, on 1 November. Three days later, Henry laid siege to Vilnius and then proceeded to Danzig before arriving back in England the following spring, in late April or early May, when he was reunited with his wife and children.

For a while, the parliamentary upheaval of previous years gave way to a period of reconciliation, with Gaunt and Henry representing the interests of the house of Lancaster and the king ruling with the assistance of the Lords. Apart from taking place in a tournament at Kennington that July, Henry was with Mary at Kenilworth until November, when he was obliged to depart for the opening of Parliament at Westminster. By this time, Mary was midway through her next pregnancy, for which Henry sent her a gift of 100 apples and 150 pears from London. Parliament was dissolved on 2 December and Henry left London to spend Christmas with his family and Gaunt's at Hereford Castle. His gift to his wife was a golden hind with a white enamelled body and wearing a golden collar.[22] By this point, Mary is likely to have been about to enter her third trimester, or already in it. Payments in Henry's account book indicate that his next child arrived after Christmas, when is not listed, and clothing was provided for its nurse the following May. In the spring, Henry and Gaunt went to France to negotiate a peace, arriving in Calais on 11 March and leaving after the truce was agreed on 8 April, so it is likely that Henry was absent again when Mary went into labour.

The location of Mary's next lying-in is given by Victorian historian James Hamilton Wylie as Walmsford, now known as Wansford, a village to the west of Peterborough on the River Nene. Perhaps this was incorrectly recorded when Peterborough Castle was intended, which was the next location Mary would give birth. The distance of around 10 miles between the village and castle represented around a day's travel, based on estimates of Henry's movements in 1406–07,[23] perhaps more, considering that Mary was heavily pregnant. It may be that she went into labour on the way to Peterborough, perhaps her child arrived early, and she was forced to stop and deliver the baby in a manor house or hospital. Wansford was situated on the main road north, now the A1, and would have had provision for travellers, pilgrims and the infirm. This did happen to women travellers, as attested by the surviving accounts of monastic establishments that set aside a quota of beds as even aristocratic and royal women could be taken unawares, such as in the case of Elizabeth of York in 1503. Women sometimes did travel in the months preceding their due dates, particularly if a certain destination had been chosen for their lying-in, and they anticipated spending a month in confinement: Mary may have been travelling to reunite with the newly returned Henry. If her child did arrive early, the countess and her household would have commandeered whatever location was suitable and required the locals to support and supply her through her efforts. Her child arrived safely. This time, it was a girl. Mary named her Blanche, after her paternal grandmother.

Henry was back in England by May, but not for long. Having got the taste for travel, he planned an extended pilgrimage, which would take him through Prussia to Prague, Vienna, Venice and on to Jerusalem.

It is not recorded whether Mary had an opinion about his absence: there had been a political purpose to his recent trip to France, but the motivation now was religious. Perhaps this was even more compelling to the late fourteenth-century mind. Gaunt certainly backed his son, granting him additional income and advancing money to facilitate his provisions and journey. Despite their personal separation, it is likely that Mary was also supportive, understanding that the nature of medieval aristocratic marriage necessitated the endurance of absence. Henry departed in July and, almost surprisingly, Mary was not pregnant. He would be away for a year, a significant interval which allowed her body to recover from the frequent childbearing of the last few years. Mary was only 21 or 22 and she had already borne five surviving babies.

Mary disappears from the records again during Henry's absence. While he travelled, she would have remained with her household and children, perhaps at Kenilworth, or visiting her sister at Pleshey, her mother at Bytham or her mother-in-law at Hereford. As her eldest boys, Henry and Thomas, turned 6 and 5 that autumn, they would have been under the instruction of a tutor and possibly established at Bytham, under their grandmother's eye.[24] That November, news reached England of the death of Henry's adversary from Radcot Bridge: Robert de Vere had been killed hunting at Louvain, still in exile. Three years later, King Richard would have his former favourite's embalmed body brought back to England and would open the coffin to look at him, fuelling Walsingham's suggestion of homosexual love between them. However, this was standard practice to be certain of someone's demise. De Vere was given an impressive funeral at Colne Priory in Essex. The months passed until Henry returned, arriving at Dover on 30 June 1393.

Mary's reunion with her husband would have been brief, if it took place at all that summer. Henry had reached London by 5 July and, the following month, was marching north with Gaunt to fight a group of rebels who had gathered in Lancashire and Cheshire with the intent of attacking the leading Lancastrians, including Gaunt, Henry and Gloucester, as enemies of the king. Gaunt had reached Lancaster by 10 August and the insurgents were rapidly dealt with. After this, Henry would have ridden home to Mary. Within weeks, around early September, Mary was pregnant again for the sixth time. Henry remained with his family for the remainder of the year, passing Christmas as usual at Hertford for jesting and jousting, before departing for Parliament at the end of January. He sent his wife a gift of oysters, mussels and sprats. Perhaps these, along with his previous gift of apples and pears, might indicate the foods that Mary was craving as their child grew bigger.

Richard's twenty-first Parliament ran until 6 March. It was marked by increasing disagreement between Gaunt and Arundel about the northern rebellion and Lancaster's influence over the king. When Richard announced his intention to lead a campaign to Ireland, the natural figure to keep the realm safe in his absence would be Gaunt, but Gaunt had planned to visit Gascony, so suggested Henry instead. This was in line with the terms of Edward III's will, which had named Gaunt and his heirs as successors to the throne after Richard and his offspring. It provoked anger from Roger Mortimer, fourth Earl of March, a descendant of Gaunt's elder brother Lionel of Antwerp. This branch of the family had been excluded from the succession because it passed through the female line, which was confirmed by Richard in 1386. For now, the king commanded Mortimer's silence, but the fact that both Roger and Henry considered himself rightful heir to the throne remained unresolved.

By the end of the parliamentary session, Mary was six months pregnant. Henry may have gone to Leulinghen with his father and Gloucester or returned to be with Mary at Hertford or Peterborough, which had been chosen for her lying-in. If so, he would have been with her when the news arrived of the death of his stepmother Constance of Castile on 24 March, soon after Gaunt's departure. Mary went into labour in the first days of June. It was her sixth child, so she knew what to expect. Katherine Swynford, now Gaunt's acknowledged mistress, may have been in attendance, and Mary's mother Joan may have taken the older children to Bytham with her, as she would do later. On 4 June, Mary delivered a healthy baby girl, whom she named Philippa, after Henry's grandmother. Yet Mary did not recover as hoped, perhaps as a result of injury, blood loss or some post-partum infection. The exact date of her death is unclear. It may have occurred during the process of giving birth, or in the weeks that followed. She shared her burial with Constance, at the church of St Mary de Castro in Leicester: Constance was laid to rest on 5 July and Mary on 6 July. Curiously, Mary's death is recorded in the

Chronicle of the Grey Friars of London: 'thys yere dyde Mare the countes of Derby,' although the entry comes in the twentieth year of Richard's reign, 1396, two years late, and features alongside the death of John of Gaunt, which is recorded three years early. Gaunt's death is also entered a second time, which suggests the account was written retrospectively, carelessly or by multiple scribes. While Gaunt's death might be expected to appear, the inclusion of Mary's is unusual. The demise of a countess was not usually listed. This implies a later realisation of her importance. When Mary died, she could have hardly imagined that the turbulent years ahead would place her husband and eldest son on the throne of England.

5

RICHARD II'S QUEENS, 1382–97

A tiny scrap of humanity.[1]

1

The summer of 1394 was to claim the life of a third royal woman, that of Richard II's queen, Anne of Bohemia. Aged 28, she passed away, probably from the plague, at Sheen Palace, on the site of the later Tudor palace of Richmond. Having been at her side until the end, Richard was so grief-stricken that he ordered Sheen be torn down, for he never wanted to return to it. As the king's wife and a foreigner, Anne's life followed a different path from that of her cousin by marriage, Mary de Bohun, although they shared a love of literature and courtly entertainment. Elegant and cultured, she helped Richard establish a court where art and protocol were placed above war, and her story sheds a different light on the despotic figure with whom Henry and Gaunt came into conflict.

Anne of Bohemia was born in May 1366 in Prague, a city of 35,000 people. She was the eldest of six children from the fourth marriage of Charles IV, King of Bohemia and Holy Roman Emperor, whose reign was considered a golden age in the history of Prague in political, legal and cultural terms. He encouraged the first Humanist thinkers, corresponded with Petrarch and founded universities, acted as patron to manuscript painters and consolidated the imperial states. His previous wives had come from France, Bavaria and Poland, and he was 47 when he married the 16-year-old Elizabeth of Pomerania in 1363, who brought him a dowry of 100,000 gold florins. By this time, he had already spent years working to achieve his ambition: to make Prague the most beautiful city in the world, rebuilding the castle, the St Vitus Cathedral, municipal buildings and bridges in a high Gothic style known as the Bohemian School. It was a city influenced by the artistic traditions of Northern Italy and France, creating a culturally sophisticated court that led one historian to describe Anne as a member of a 'late-fourteenth-century international jet set'.[2]

Anne was raised in the Hradschin Palace, largely under the care of her elder half-brother Wenceslaus, especially after he became king following the death of their father in November 1378. The match had already been suggested by Charles the previous year, along with a host of other offers that Richard received on becoming king. Initially it was rejected as his mother, Joan of Kent, was keen on securing him a wealthy Milanese wife. By April 1379, three English envoys were negotiating with the Duke of Visconti, who had produced eleven daughters among seventeen legitimate children. There were already connections with the English royal family, Richard's uncle Lionel of Antwerp having been briefly married to Violante Visconti, who remarried after his death to the duke's son Ludovico. His younger sister Lucia was suggested as a candidate for the hand of Henry, Earl of Derby, following the death of Mary de Bohun, but she would later wed Mary's cousin, Edmund Holland. Possible brides for Richard included Caterina, Agnese and Antonina, who were of an age, and were all wed in 1380. Their five younger sisters meant there was no shortage of available Visconti girls but the English were encouraged to look elsewhere by Pope Urban VI, under whose influence negotiators were sent to Bohemia. In response, Anne's mother Elizabeth sent Duke Primislaus of Saxony, Anne's uncle, to investigate England and determine whether it was suitable for 'that excellent virgin, the damsel Anne', who herself wrote to the English Council, saying she would become Richard's wife 'with full and free will'.[3]

For all Prague's cultural status and enthusiastic building programme, there was little money left to furnish its daughters with dowries. Although a dowry was initially discussed, it was actually Richard who ended up paying Wenceslaus, in the form of a loan of £15,000, to wed Anne. Adam of Usk wrote respectfully of her, whilst stating that she had been 'bought for a great price'.[4] Richard must have been keen for the match to go ahead, as the loan made the marriage unpopular at his court and those councillors who had anticipated the arrival of a wealthy foreign queen. The English negotiators Simon Burley and Michael de la Pole had even been captured and ransomed, which set back talks until the summer of 1380. The following May, Gaunt received the Bohemian delegation at the Savoy: one of that palace's last official functions before its destruction at the hands of the rebels in mid-June. The Patent Rolls for May 1381 record payments made to the visitors: 250 marks to 'Peter de Wartemberg, knight, master of the chamber of the king's brother, the king of the romans and Bohemia'; and the same amount to Conrad Crayer, 'knight, master of the same king's household', and 50 marks to Crayer's son Leopold.[5] The marriage was to take place at once. Anne was 15, Richard 14.

Anne set out from Prague in September. She spent a month in Brussels as the guest of her paternal uncle Wenceslaus, before proceeding to Gravelines, accompanied by the Duke of Brabant and his duchess, Anne's aunt. They handed Anne over to the earls of Devon and Salisbury at Calais, who conducted her across the Channel to Dover on 18 December. Richard and Thomas, later Duke of Gloucester, were awaiting her at Dover in the formidable castle perched on the white cliffs overlooking the Channel. Anne would have met a tall, handsome, fair-haired young man, 'his face fair and rosy, rather round than long and sometimes flushed', according to the Monk of Evesham. She would have rested and been refreshed after her journey in the three-storied Great Tower, which had been rebuilt by Henry II, safe from the storm brewing outside, which dashed her ships to pieces in the harbour below. From Dover, the couple rode the 25 miles north and west, through Canterbury to the village of Ospringe outside Faversham, where they stayed at the royal lodge, allowing the young pair a chance to get to know each other away from the eyes of the court. Their next stop was Leeds Castle, the fairy-tale Norman stronghold set in the middle of a lake which had been bought by Richard's great-great-grandmother, Eleanor of Castile. Traditionally a location for royal honeymoons, it had been passed down through a string of English queens and Richard continued this line, granting it to Anne as a gift while they spent the Christmas season there.

Great celebrations and pageantry had been prepared to welcome Anne into London. The city dignitaries came out to meet her at Blackheath, where Richard had met Wat Tyler and the rebels the previous summer. At Cheapside, the Goldsmith's company had built a castle, a 'somer-castell'[6] suspended on cords, from which three virgins scattered leaves painted in a 'diaper' or lozenge pattern over the royal procession.[7] The Goldsmiths wore red and black particoloured clothes, decorated with silver bars and trefoils, gold and silk knots, and red powdered hats.[8] The total cost to the company was just over £35, an amount which would have bought seven horses for a knight in 1374 or been sufficient to feed his household for a year. No doubt the Londoners enjoyed the spectacle of foreign royalty: Anne and her entourage were to establish new fashions in horned headdresses, long-toed 'cracow' shoes and riding side-saddle: two centuries later, John Stow wrote that by Anne's 'example the English people had used piked shoes, tied to their knees with silken laces, or chains of silver or gilt'. Although she had not brought a dowry, Anne's trousseau was not entirely worthless; it included the silver gilt basins and plates bearing her father's arms which were listed in the treasure roll after her death.

In spite of the preparations, the atmosphere was uneasy; the people of London were aware that the Violante marriage would have brought greater wealth into the country and barely six months had passed since the rebels had gone on their killing spree through the streets, attacking the houses of wealthy immigrants. While the royal pair had been feasting at Leeds Castle, the city had been raising the funds required for Anne's reception and coronation, with all the commensurate expenses for robes, decoration and display. At Blackheath, part of the decorations featuring Anne's arms had been ripped off a fountain and destroyed by the people[9] and there was resentment about the rewards for her large entourage. Although there would be periods of peace and court culture would flourish, the tensions at the heart of her husband's reign would never dispel.

Anne and Richard were married in Westminster's St Stephen's Chapel on either 14 or 20 January 1382 and she was crowned shortly after, in the cathedral by Archbishop Courtenay on 22 January. She had at least two crowns, a gem-encrusted one which was made in Paris and required repairs in 1402 for the wedding of Henry's and Mary de Bohun's daughter Blanche, and a second, which had been held in security by the city of London, whose return Richard demanded on 1 January 1382.[10] After a week of celebrations, the court moved to Windsor; a month later, they were at the Black Prince's palace of Kennington; and later that year, Richard took Anne on progress to Bristol. The pair would have had plenty in common, with a shared appreciation of culture and court ritual, as well as devotion to their favourite saints. Richard had long been devoted to the cult of Edward the Confessor and in 1382 Anne appealed to the pope for permission to solemnly celebrate the feast day of her patron saint, St Anne, on 26 July.

Richard and Anne regularly went on pilgrimage, to give thanks and offer prayers. They began their marriage with a tour of East Anglia, visiting important shrines such as Ely, Bury St Edmunds and Walsingham, at the heart of the Marian cult, and ended their travels in spring 1394 with a visit to the shrine of St Thomas at Canterbury. They were patrons of religious and secular literature, and translations of the Gospels into English were made for Anne, a fact John Wycliffe would exploit when urging the widespread use of the Bible in the vernacular, although there is no evidence of Anne ever supporting him. This fact has also led to her being claimed rather anachronistically as one of the female founders of the Protestant Reformation. Chaucer dedicated his *Legend of Good Women* to Anne, as did the author of a treatise on heraldry in the 1390s, while Richard commissioned *Confessio Amantis* from John Gower after meeting him on the Thames around 1385 and inviting him on to the royal barge. Anne's emblem of the ostrich, bound and chained, began to appear in the margin of English manuscripts decorated in the Bohemian style and the style of divine art was imported into depictions of royalty, culminating in the Westminster Coronation portrait and the Wilton Diptych.

An illustrated initial in a royal charter to the city of Shrewsbury depicts Anne kneeling before Richard, wearing a cloak with ermine collar, a large crown that matches his, long hair streaming down her back and stylised features. She is presented as much smaller than her husband physically and, although the perspective and relative sizes and ages of illustrated figures was not consistent in such images, this is borne out by the comments of the Monk of Evesham who described her as a little 'scrap of humanity'. Anne is also depicted in fairly generic royal style in an altar piece in the English College of Rome, although her voluminous robes make her appear large and solid. Although it is possible that the artist never saw Anne in the flesh, the corresponding image of Richard gives the king the beard and moustache familiar from his portraits. John of Gaunt's confessor, Richard Maidstone, who saw Anne on at least one prolonged occasion, in 1392, described her as:

> A maiden too, her face enclosed by yellow hair
> Her tresses neatly set beneath a garland's gleam
> Her red dress shines in colour, brightened by the gold,
> Concealing underneath her very pretty limbs ...
> Her name is Anne; I pray she might be Anne in deed.
> She's beautiful, with other beauties all around;
> Led by such Amazon, New Troy is unsurpassed.
> Her dress is strewn and overspread with gleaming gems!
> Carbuncle, adamant and beryl, all are there
> Her head is overspread with every precious stone.[11]

The best visual image of Anne might be found in the *Liber Regalis*, which appears to have been complied, or at least updated, with details of her coronation, in 1382. Sitting on a throne facing her husband, she wears flowing blue and white robes to match his, her long golden hair loose beneath her crown, and even the cast of her features echoing his. A contemporary manuscript illustration[12] of her funeral shows the effigy placed on top of her coffin, dressed in pink and white, with her arms folded, but the hair showing under her gold coronet is of a light brown. This would have been a wig placed on the wooden sculpture that now survives in Westminster Abbey, but was chosen to create the closest possible likeness to her during life. Likewise, the features of the effigy would have been modelled on those of the real Anne, perhaps shortly after death. Her tomb was inscribed with the legend 'beauteous in body and her face was gentle and pretty', and there is some correlation between the oval face, high eyebrows and long nose of the effigy and the face of Anne on her gilt bronze tomb, cast in 1396–99 by London coppersmiths Nicholas Broker and Godfrey Prest, to top a design by Yevele.[13]

One of the most interesting books to be commissioned during Anne's queenship was *The Forme of Cury*, 'cury' being cooking, allowing a glimpse into the diet and cuisine of the royal pair. It was created by Richard's chef on the 'advice of masters of physic and philosophy for the health of the household'. The recipes contain typical English ingredients; vegetables such as beans, spinach, peas, onions, marrow, cabbage, mushrooms and leeks; fruits such as apples, pears and figs, along with the herbs garlic, mint, rosemary, parsley, sage and marjoram. Other, luxury, items were imported for the royal table, including whole or ground rice, sugar, saffron, cinnamon, mace, galingal, cloves, pepper, ginger, nutmeg, cardamom, caraway, raisins and dates, which would have been brought by Italian and Turkish merchants trading with Egypt and the Middle East. A few recipes indicate further foreign influence, such as Sawse Sarzyne (Saracen Sauce), which combined hops, fried almonds, red wine, sugar, rice flour, pomegranate and 'pouder douce' (sweet powder), Lumbard Mustard (from Lombardy in Italy) which mixed mustard seeds with honey, wine and vinegar, and Vyande Cypre of Samoun (Salmon meat of Cyprus), containing salmon, almonds, rice flour, sugar, salt and spices. The most popular flavours were sweet and strong, as testified by the frequent use of 'pouder douce' and 'pouder fort'. Many of the dishes were dyed, using saffron for yellow, sandalwood for red and alkalet root for purple; some were adorned with gilded or silvered tree leaves. The royal pair also requested the translation of a treatise on urine, the examination of which was then the most common diagnostic method used by doctors, into 'the mother tongue for the comprehension of laymen and for their governance'.[14]

Richard was keen to show off his bride, keeping her close to him at all times. Following the pilgrimage to East Anglia in 1383, they travelled to the south coast, through the New Forest, to Arundel, Beaulieu and Corfe. In fact, they were rarely apart.[15] The marriage appears to have been genuinely close, right from the start, and Chaucer used Anne as his model for Alceste, Queen of the God of Love, although the question of their sexual relations has long since puzzled historians, largely because of their childlessness. Infertility can affect couples in numerous ways, with either partner experiencing symptomless reproductive impediments: low fertility, such as poor sperm motility, could never have been suspected during the fourteenth century, let alone treated. The inability to produce an heir could have devastating effects on families of all ranks: for a king, it could be a matter of life or death. Richard's situation in 1399 may have been markedly different had he had a legitimate teenaged son waiting in the wings. Chronicler Walsingham's speculations about the king's sexuality, his choice of second wife and the chronicler's later propaganda emulating Edward the Confessor have led many historians to conclude that Richard's childlessness was elective, that he actually lived chastely with Anne, that they did not consummate their marriage at all, or else refrained from sex early on.

Yet Anne appears not to have given up hope of bearing a child. Apothecary bills dating from the end of her life include ingredients traditionally used to aid conception,[16] and conception could not have occurred unless the couple were sharing a bed. Given his awareness of the importance of an heir and the press of rival claims at his court, it would seem remarkable for Richard to deliberately choose a chaste union. It has been suggested that religious motives dictated such a move, a conscious elevation to the condition of purity, an aspiration to deity, but Richard had outlets enough for his faith and his position would have been strengthened, not weakened, by the appearance of an heir. It was what his contemporaries expected. Richard may have been ahead of them in many ways, seeking a form of absolute kingship and ceremony that many failed to appreciate, but ultimately he wished to preserve his position. The marriage to Anne was unpopular from the start: it brought little status and no wealth. The bride and groom had not met, so there was no prior attachment, while there had been financial advantages to the proposed alliance with Milan. The question arises as to why Richard married at all, had his intentions been to live a chaste life. Even if it was for the sake of appearances, to satisfy the council, there was still a danger that the marriage might be considered invalid. Richard would have been a remarkably unusual medieval king if he had taken steps to avoid sleeping with his wife and producing a son. Conclusive proof of a pregnancy emerges from a letter written by Anne to her brother Wenceslaus, now housed in the British Library, in which the queen shares her sadness over a miscarriage she had recently suffered.[17]

One of the few occasions when Anne and Richard were separated was in the summer of 1385. The queen remained in London while Richard headed a force into Scotland. The campaign was less memorable than an incident that occurred in the English camp when the short temper of the king's half-brother led to murder. According to Froissart, a quarrel had broken out between an archer in the service of Sir Ralph Stafford, who was protecting a Bohemian knight, and the squire of John Holland, son of Joan of Kent. When the archer killed the squire, Stafford approached Holland to apologise, but Holland barely gave him a chance to speak, killing him at once. On hearing the news, Richard was furious. He confiscated Holland's lands and threatened him with death. Torn between her sons, their mother Joan pleaded on her knees for forgiveness. This was finally granted the following spring, on the promise that Holland would undertake a pilgrimage and found three chantries for Stafford, although it came too late for Joan of Kent. She died just days after the incident, at the age of 56, reputedly of a broken heart.

Queen Anne also attempted to plead for the life of those dear to her family. In 1388, she intervened directly in the events arising from the challenge mounted by the Lords Appellant. When the life of Richard's old tutor and friend Simon Burley was threatened, she spent three hours on her knees, asking for him to be spared. The rebels' refusal to respect her request enraged Richard and added to the festering discontent between him, Arundel, Gloucester, Henry of Derby and others. Burley had been appointed an executor of Joan of Kent's will but neither this nor Anne's words could save him. He was executed as a traitor by the Lords Appellant during the Merciless Parliament that year.

Anne also had to confront a family scandal that had arisen in her own household. It concerned a lady of the bedchamber who had accompanied her to England from Prague, an Agnes de Launcekrona. Richard's cousin Robert de Vere had been married for a decade to Philippa, daughter of Gaunt's sister Isabella, when he embarked on an affair with Agnes, scandalising the court and clashing with Anne and Richard's formal ideals of chivalry and propriety which set the standard for the queen's household. It has also been suggested that Agnes did not give her consent to de Vere; that she was raped or deceived, 'copulated in nefarious marriage', as two of de Vere's followers appear to have abducted her for the purpose. This was not uncommon; double standards were an inherent part of the sexual lives of aristocratic men. Chronicler Walsingham described Agnes as 'ignoble' and 'disgusting', using the Latin term *foeda*, which implies a dirtiness associated with a lower-class woman: according to him, she was a 'cellarer', making her unable to refuse the advances of a man of higher social rank. It is only necessary to give the depositions in the Assize court records a cursory reading to understand just how frequently this power dynamic was exploited by men in a position of power, particularly in the context of master and servant. However, the fact that Agnes was a lady of the bedchamber means her birth cannot have been that lowly and suggests that she was a victim of Walsingham's habitual exaggeration. That it came to the question of divorce signals de Vere's more serious intent. Perhaps Agnes had fallen pregnant, although no child appears to have survived. Perhaps de Vere was genuinely in love.

Despite the inglorious circumstances, Anne was loyal to her fellow countrywoman. In 1387, de Vere successfully petitioned the pope for divorce and took Agnes as his second wife. Victorian biographer Agnes Strickland suggests that Anne even wrote to the pope personally to ask for his support,[18] but whatever her level of involvement, the remarriage proved a deeply unpopular move, alienating the king's mother and uncles. To set aside a woman of royal blood, a granddaughter of Edward III no less, was scandalous, a perceived fouling of the social boundaries by which an unsuitable woman was elevated. It found echoes with the examples of Alice Perrers and Katherine Swynford and challenged concepts of female worth. De Vere's new marriage would not last though, nor would his second wife enjoy the titles that Philippa continued to use. Two years later, a new pope would overturn this match and declare the 1387 divorce to be invalid. But by that time, de Vere was in exile. What happened to Agnes after that is unknown. She may have accompanied her husband to Brabant or returned to her homeland of Bavaria.

In March 1390, Anne played more than a ceremonial role at the jousts Richard organised at Smithfield to honour Gaunt's formal investiture as Duke of Aquitaine. According to Froissart, the occasion lasted two days and was proclaimed across Europe. In line with royal protocol, Anne was responsible for awarding the prizes, arriving with sixty of her ladies riding on palfreys, each leading a knight on a silver chain to the arena through the streets from Westminster to the sound of trumpets. She was also responsible for placing a coronet on the head of Constance, Duchess of Lancaster in recognition of her status in Aquitaine, and hosted a dinner and dancing in the Bishop's Palace at St Paul's.

Anne played a role of even greater significance in 1392 when she pleaded with Richard to have mercy on the people of London after he had fallen out with the bankers and a mob had attacked the Bishop of Salisbury's residence. Richard devolved the administrative courts to York and Nottingham, imposed crippling fines, imprisoned the mayor and his officials, and appointed replacements. London's dignitaries were forced to defer and a reconciliation took place. Richard and Anne made a triumphal return to the city in August (recorded in 'Concordia', a contemporary poem by Richard Maidstone, Gaunt's Carmelite confessor), when the streets were adorned with pageants of towers, descending angels, God and a wilderness of beasts. The celebrations began at Wandsworth with aldermen on their knees, then moved into Bridgegate, where Richard was given gifts of horses and Anne received a palfrey covered in cloth of gold and red and white particoloured cloth, topped by a gold saddle. The queen's devotions were well known: at Ludgate she was presented with a gilt-engraved tablet depicting St Anne and at a Westminster feast the next day, she was given a gold ewer in a case of beryl. The city also contributed towards the royal Christmas celebrations at Eltham that year, paying costs and sending gifts. The following summer, Richard commissioned the warden of London Bridge to pay for statues of himself and Anne to be carved into the stone gate on the bridge.[19] Maidstone depicts Anne's mercy:

They come up to the queen with humble countenance
Beseeching her, and she prays good for them in turn.
Her heart loves them, but grieves that such a famous town

Had earned the royal wrath; but 'hope remains' she said ...
The queen is able to deflect the King's firm rule
So he will show a gentle face to his own folk.
A woman soothes a man by love: God gave him her.
O gentle Anne, let your sweet love be aimed at this![20]

If Anne's marriage had not been welcomed by Londoners in 1381–82, she certainly gained their appreciation over the next ten years. According to Maidstone, her 'pleasing face' was the 'city's friend', promising that 'whatever's in my power ... it will be done'. The 'Concordia' allots her a long, persuasive speech, after which Richard grants her request to look favourably upon the city and Anne's historical reputation as 'the good', was secured. The Westminster Chronicler records that at Epiphany 1393, the grateful city presented its queen with a jewel. Anne was also listed as a recipient in the will made by Isabella of Castile, sister of Constance and wife of Edmund of Langley, Duke of York. On 6 December 1392, Isabella left Richard a jewelled version of his personal symbol, a hart with pearls, while Anne received a gold belt with ivy leaves.[21]

An inventory of Anne's jewels made in 1399 gives some idea of the splendour and symbolism with which she was adorned on ceremonial occasions. The treasury contained five gold collars bearing Anne's badges of ostriches and ferns, set with diamonds, rubies and pearls; five gold and jewelled chaplets and a dozen gold belts, one of which was mounted with a crowned letter A. The most valuable of the chaplets, worth over £500, was set with seventy-two rubies, 150 diamonds and twelve dozen pearls. Three silver gilt basins bore the combined crowns of Richard and the Holy Roman Emperor, a tribute to his union with Anne; on another pair of basins, this same motif was surrounded by the Lancastrian 'SS' collar, suggesting that it was a gift at some point from Gaunt or Henry. There was also a double ostrich egg which opened to reveal Anne's arms, which also appeared on a gold chalice and pax, for the celebration of the Mass.[22] Among their possessions were listed a standing mirror supported on a base fashioned like a tree, which was set with pearls, enamelled with roses and depicted a queen on the reverse. There were fabric belts of different colours, decorated with leaves, jewels and flowers and hung with bells, a fork for green ginger and a pomander.

In the summer of 1394, the plague broke out again across Europe. Richard and Anne were at Sheen when she was suddenly taken ill. Along with Eltham, it was one of her favourite palaces. She had her own apartments and gardens there and, according to Stowe, could seat thousands of people to dine. As Froissart records: 'the Lady Anne, Queen of England, fell ill, to the infinite distress of King Richard and all her household. Her disorder increased so rapidly that she departed this life at the feast of Whitsuntide', which fell on 7 June that year. 'King Richard was inconsolable for her loss,' added Froissart, 'as they mutually loved each other, having been married young.' Richard swore that for a whole year he would never enter any building he had been in with Anne, except for churches, and ordered the royal apartments at Sheen to be torn down.

Three days later, from Westminster, he issued instructions to the magnates to be ready to accompany the body of his 'beloved companion' on its final journey from Sheen. Additional wax candles were ordered from Flanders in time for the procession on 29 July and burial on 3 August. When Joan de Bohun's brother, Richard FitzAlan, the eleventh Earl of Arundel arrived late to the ceremony and asked whether he might leave early, Richard flew into a rage and attacked him with a steward's wand, drawing blood. His brother Thomas Arundel, the Archbishop of Canterbury and an enemy of Wycliffe's Lollards, praised Anne for reading the Bible in English during his eulogy. Soon after the ceremony, Richard departed for Ireland and embassies were dispatched to Scotland, Aragon and Bavaria to begin the search for a new queen of England.

II

Cultured and courtly, it was typical of Richard that he allowed himself to be wooed by a poem. By May 1395, when he approached the English king seeking an alliance, Charles VI of France already had three daughters – Isabelle, Marie and Michelle. In fact, after only ten years of marriage, his wife Isabeau of Bavaria had given birth to seven children and would go on to deliver five more; their fruitfulness offered quite a contrast with Richard and Anne's empty cradle. Yet the daughters of France were scarcely out of their infancy: the oldest, Isabelle, was only 5, Marie was not yet 2 and Michelle only 4 months old. An elder sister, Anne, had died in infancy. Richard was then 28. Even if he took the eldest daughter for a wife, he would not be able to consummate the marriage and produce an heir for at least another decade. So Charles turned to poetry.

Once a soldier, Philip de Mezières was living in the Parisian convent of the Celestines when Charles commissioned him to write an epistle to the King of England. Illuminated and stretching to eighty-two folios, it laid out the reasons why the 'very excellent and very benevolent prince and worthy king' should consider taking Isabelle of Valois as his next bride. Charles hoped the long history of war between England and France would be concluded and urged Richard to join him on a crusade against the Turks; there was also a symmetry in the match, Mezières wrote, in righting the wrongs that had been committed by a previous French bride and the princess' namesake, Isabella of France, who had conspired against her husband Edward II. The French argued that it would be advantageous for Richard to bring up his future wife at his own court, in order to educate her according to his tastes and mould her to his will. The opinions of the 5-year-old girl concerned, so soon to leave her home, siblings and family, were not considered important beside the benefit to France and her future husband's wishes. There was also the question of 800,000 gold francs, 3,000 advanced immediately into English coffers. Richard was convinced.

It was in June 1395 that Froissart visited England and found his stay coinciding with Richard's return from Ireland. He visited the shrine of Thomas Becket and the tomb of the Black Prince in Canterbury Cathedral and awaited the king, who arrived the following day with a 'large retinue of lords and ladies'. Having been presented to the king, Froissart was privy to some of the discussions about the French match, learning that 'if the Duke of Burgundy of the Count of Hainault had had daughters … King Richard would have willingly chosen one of them'. Initially, feeling was against the marriage, it being a 'matter of astonishment in England that the king should be so eager to marry the daughter of his chief enemy', and it did not 'add to his popularity'. Richard, though, remained 'indifferent' to wider opinion and replied to concerns about her age that he was still 'young enough to be able to wait'.

Richard's choice has been interpreted by historians in a number of ways, most interestingly in terms of his sexuality. With Isabelle not quite 7 at the time of the marriage, there was no question of consummation for a number of years. Richard may have been willing to wait to father an heir, or it may have been a deliberate policy to preserve his own chastity. The chronicler Walsingham noted contemporary rumours that suggested Richard's homosexuality and Adam of Usk relates how, in 1399, the charges of 'sodomitical acts' were levelled at Richard by his 'doctors' and bishops, though this is not specifically stated as homosexuality and could refer to sexual acts committed with a woman. It was an emotive term, as sexual irregularity in a monarch could be one too many of a swathe of complaints; it may also have been used to draw a direct parallel between Richard and his deposed and probably murdered great-grandfather Edward II. Yet Anne of Bohemia's letter mentioning her miscarriage implies an active sexual relationship with Richard, so the king was clearly not exclusively homosexual, if he was at all. Richard could have married a woman of reproductive years; as Usk relates, in 1395 he was negotiating with King John I of Aragon for the hand of his daughter Yolande, a woman 'very fair and of marriageable years', but chose Isabelle. Usk calls this 'a matter for wonder' and explains it by arguing that Richard wanted French support to 'pour forth his pent-up venom' and destroy his enemies. It seems more likely that Richard was seeking the most advantageous match, swayed more by immediate questions of political survival and expediency than by any sense of urgency to father an heir. Only hindsight informs us of the untimely end of his reign: as far as he was concerned, he had decades left in which to create a family with Isabelle.

England's new queen had been born in the Louvre on 9 November 1389. It was then a twelfth-century fortress on the western side of Paris with a huge courtyard and a turret at each corner, all surrounded by a moat. Earth ramparts had been built around it during France's conflict with Edward III, but in the 1360s the architect Raymond du Temple had converted the interior into a royal palace, with a central spiral staircase, large windows and extensive decoration, and pleasure gardens laid out to the north. By the time the English delegates arrived in Paris in 1395, led by the Archbishop of Dublin and the Earl of Rutland, Isabelle was living with her mother in the Hôtel Saint-Pol on the Seine, leaving the increasingly mad Charles in the Louvre. Saint-Pol was considered a healthier residence, far from the fumes and pestilence of Paris, and also contained the royal library. It was considered safer for the children to be apart from Charles, whose mental health had begun to deteriorate in 1392, leading to outbreaks of violence and delusion.

On 9 March a truce was signed in Paris, to establish peace for twenty-eight years between England and France. The marriage of Richard and Isabelle was given the blessing of the French Council two days later, followed immediately by a proxy betrothal in the Sainte-Chapelle, where the Earl of Nottingham repeated the vows on Richard's behalf. From England, the king sent his betrothed two rings, one with a diamond and one with a sapphire and a ruby,[23] along with gifts of a jewel, garter robes, a bracelet and devotional tablets. Yet Richard had another aim in mind with this match. One of the clauses agreed early in negotiations was a pledge of French military support in the event of Richard's own subjects rising against him. He had not forgotten the revolt of the Lords Appellant and was anticipating future trouble, although he could not have imagined exactly what lay ahead. Adam of Usk went so far as to suggest that the deciding factor in Richard's marital choice was the support France could offer against the Lords Appellant, and Froissart related a conversation between Richard and the Count of Saint-Pol regarding his fears that Gloucester would rebel again. Unhappily for Richard, this clause was later dropped.

Perhaps it was in response to this clause, or at least a realistic understanding of his relationship with Richard, that led Henry, Earl of Derby, to conclude his own pact of friendship with the French. Signed in Paris on 19 June, it came between Richard's betrothal and Isabelle's departure for England. Henry's ally, though, was not Charles, but his younger brother Louis, Duke of Orléans, who acted as regent during the king's periods of incapacity and was rumoured to be having an affair with the queen. Their agreement excluded the rest of the royal family, including the king's children, but Louis vowed that the 'Duke of Lancaster and myself will always be united in the strictest ties of love and affection, as loyal and true friends should be'. They were to be friends to each other's friends and enemies of their enemies, 'aid and assist' the other in the defence of their person in words and deeds and defend each other in war.[24] This gesture of friendship would last longer than the one forged between Charles and Richard, and was terminated by Louis in 1402 only after Henry had deposed his cousin and taken his throne.

In October, Isabelle left Paris with her father and travelled to Ardres, where the English party was waiting. Richard was lodged at Guisnes (now Guines) Castle, strategically located 6 miles south of Calais and which had been besieged by the English in 1352. The kings met on the morning of 26 October, when the English dukes were presented with gifts of gold collars made by Parisian goldsmith Jean Compère, one of which was seized from Gloucester the following year, according to the treasury accounts for 1399. The young bride was formally handed over four days later, and Richard took his betrothed to Calais in a golden litter, where they were married in the church of St Nicholas on 1 November. The king's gift to his bride was a gold chaplet set with rubies, sapphires and pearls; Gloucester and Gaunt presented her with brooches of white eagles, Gaunt's gift laid out for her to find on a plate of spices and candied fruit after they had dined together. Henry of Derby gave her a golden greyhound.[25] Isabelle had two crowns in her trousseau, both with eight fleurons, four large and four small, decorated with gems and pearls, one featuring the heraldic devices of pimpernel and Plantagenet broom.[26] It was at Calais that the care of the young girl was handed over to the duchesses of Gloucester and Lancaster, Eleanor de Bohun and Katherine Swynford, whom Gaunt had married that January. Two days later the party sailed for Dover and progressed from there through Canterbury, Faversham, Sittingbourne, Rochester and Eltham and on to the Tower. The crowds who gathered on London Bridge to catch a glimpse of her were so large that several people were crushed to death. Isabelle was able to do something for the city in June: the former rights, liberties and privileges of London's officials were restored to them 'at the supplication of [the] queen'.[27]

On 4 December, instructions were issued to the sheriffs of London to attend Isabelle's coronation 'on the Sunday that was the morrow of the epiphany', so 6 January. At New Year, Richard made his wife a gift of a chaplet set with diamonds, rubies and pearls and the city of London presented her with a gold chaplet worth 12,000 francs. She dined with Gaunt and Katherine Swynford at Ely Place, where they presented her with gifts of gold cups and a basin.[28] Reminders of her youth come in the appointment of a French governess, Margaret de Courcy, who received an annual income of £100 from New Year's day 1397,[29] and the details of her trousseau, which included dolls with silver gilt furniture. The treasury accounts for 1399 likewise list a young girl's trinkets. Alongside the silk chaplets – one of white and gold, colours often associated with Isabelle, decorated with a rabbit, one of red and white, and a third with rubies, sapphires and pearls and decorative 'tissues' or ribbon – were mirrors, rings, a rosary with large green enamelled beads, a silk missal, a casket with a gold key sent by her mother and a purse embroidered with pearls. Touchingly, her jewellery was set with clasps to allow adjustment as she grew.[30] She was adorned with many of these items when she rode in procession with her ladies from the Tower along Cheapside to Westminster on 4 January. It is likely that she was crowned in the abbey the following day, the proposed date of 6 January, or on 8 January as one London chronicle mentions, although there is little surviving evidence for the occasion. One historian has even questioned whether the coronation took place at all.[31]

Details of Isabelle's new household survive in the Patent Rolls for 1397. Her chancellor was Thomas Peverell, Bishop of Llandaff, and Master Richard Courcy, Margaret's son, was her secretary, paid 40s a year. The Keeper of Robes was John Elys, John de Merville was master embroiderer, Richard Bluell was master cordwainer and her goldsmiths were Richard Bussh and Christopher Tildeslegh. Her chief tailor was John Waryng, who received 12d a day; Nicolas van Spyre, her yeoman tailor, and a yeoman of the cellar named William Leycestre were paid an annual salary of £10. The silkwoman who was appointed to serve Isabelle, Joan Denardeston, was a well-known and trusted royal employee who 'for seven years past [had] faithfully served the king with silk and … the king's brodery and all other necessaries within his household', and was to 'continue to serve in those respects both the king and Queen Isabel [sic] receiving therefore as shall be agreed upon between the officers of the king and queen and herself'.[32]

Another key early influence on Isabelle was Katherine Swynford, who was referred to by Froissart as the 'little queen's companion' and was the second lady in the land after Isabelle herself. The queen attended the confirmation of the dukedom of Aquitaine on Gaunt on 6 July but, after that, relations between uncle and nephew soured. Froissart relates how Richard was convinced, by gossip relayed to him by Thomas Mowbray, that a plan was afoot to depose him, 'to separate my queen from me and shut her up in some place of confinement'. Protesting their loyalty, Edmund of York, Gaunt and his duchess stayed away from court and in their absence the king seized the opportunity to take aim at his enemies.

That summer, Richard felt confident enough to strike back against the Lords Appellant for their attacks on his favourites a decade before. In July, he ordered the arrests of Gloucester, Richard Arundel and Warwick, riding in person to collect his uncle from Pleshey Castle. Gloucester, his wife Eleanor and their household turned out in surprise to welcome the king, unaware of his intentions. Eleanor would never see her husband again. When the 'Revenge Parliament' sat that September, charges of treason were passed: Warwick was exiled for life to the Isle of Man, Arundel was executed for treason and his brother Thomas, Archbishop of Canterbury fled into exile. An announcement was made that Gloucester had been exiled to Calais, where he had died, although the duke would not actually die, probably on Richard's orders, for another few weeks. An illustration in Froissart's chronicles depicts him being strangled, his hands clasped together in prayer, although other accounts describe him being smothered between two feather beds.

The anonymous author of the poem 'A Political Retrospect' of 1462 described the impact of the event:

> The good duc of gloucestre in the season
> Of the parlement at Bury being
> Was put to deth; and ay sith gret mourning
> Hath ben in England, with many a sharp shower
> Falsehood, mischief, secret sin upholding
> Which hath caused in England endless languor.

An earlier poem of 1450, 'The Death of the Duke of Suffolk', even names his reputed murderers as 'Pulford and Hanley that drownyd ye Duke of Glocestar', and the poem 'On Bishop Booth' also mentions drowning as the method of execution.

Gloucester's supposed 'confession', admitting his treasonous intent, was read aloud in Parliament. His jewels and possessions were seized, including a signet ring with the Lancastrian swan symbol and a white enamelled swan with a chain about the neck, as well as headdresses, sleeves, garters, belts, rings, rosaries, brooches and forks for green ginger.

The impact on Eleanor was devastating, stretching far beyond her personal loss. Only two weeks before, she and Gloucester had celebrated the marriage of their daughter Anne to Edmund Stafford, a younger brother of the Ralph who had killed John Holland, to whom the earldom had passed in 1395. Now legally the widow of a convicted traitor, Eleanor fled to Barking Abbey, where her daughter Isabel was a nun, and paid to recover certain items from Pleshey which were in the hands of the receivers. In February, 'at the king's gift', she had returned to her two carriages containing her 'body garments' and other small items worth around £19 which had been confiscated by the Mayor of London.[33] By 1 March 1398, she had parted with £104 for silver gilt vessels, £160 for two groups of silver, and £440 for the recovery of other items from the castle and London. Gaunt and Edmund, Duke of York reacted with fury and horror to the murder of their brother. However, the treacherous pair Pulford and Hanley named in 'The Death of the Duke of Suffolk' as responsible for Gloucester's death were never brought to justice. Instead, two other reputed murderers, Hall and Serle, formerly in the employ of Thomas Mowbray, Captain of Calais, would be tried and executed for the crime during the reign of Henry IV, Gloucester's nephew and brother-in-law.

Eleanor did not long outlive her husband. Her son Humphrey died on 2 September at the age of 18, which may have hastened her own death on 3 October 1399. Her will was made before Humphrey's demise, as she bequeathed to him a psalter 'well and richly illumined with gold enamelled clasps, with white swans and the arms of my lord and father enamelled on the clasps, and with gold mullets on the binding; this psalter was left to me with remainder to my heirs, and was to pass from heir to heir'. She also left 'a coat of mail with a latten cross on the spot over the heart which belonged to my lord his father' and 'a gold cross hanging by a chain with an image of the crucifix and four pearls round it, with my blessing, as the possession of mine which I loved most'.[34] She was buried in Westminster Abbey, in the chapel of St Edmund, with the de Bohun swan emblem above her head.

But just as Richard struck at his enemies, the wheel of fortune was to turn against him and his young bride Isabelle would not have seen it coming. She was enjoying the position and benefits of queen, though she was too young to exercise real power: her main residences were Eltham and Windsor and, by June 1398, she was also recorded as having a court at Isleworth, on the Thames 8 miles from central London. It was a royal manor house, part of the Duchy of Cornwall, surrounded by extensive grounds that are now part of Twickenham Park, where Henry IV would later found Sion Abbey. The first moated house on the site, with inner courtyard, two bedchambers, tiled roof, outer courtyard and mill, had been burned down in 1264 and may have been rebuilt along similar lines. It was a traditional property of English queens, having been granted to Isabella of France in 1327, Philippa of Hainault in 1330 and held for life by Anne of Bohemia. Much of Isabelle's time was devoted to her education, and she was tutored and prepared for her role by Margaret de Courcy. When the heir to the throne, Roger Mortimer, died at the age of 24 in July, Isabelle was the recipient of all his estates, rents and properties until the majority of his heir, who was then only 7 years old.

Isabelle's reign and marriage had barely begun before it all unravelled. In November 1398, a comet 'burning with extraordinary intensity' was seen in the sky for eight successive nights. It was interpreted by the chronicler of Saint-Denys to herald revolution or the death of a king. Although Richard had taken steps in 1397–98 to remove his rivals and enemies, his position was not secure. Isabelle had only been England's queen for three years when, at the age of 9, her crown was removed.

6

LEGITIMACY, 1394–1403

Old John of Gaunt, time-honour'd Lancaster,
Hast thou, according to thy oath and band,
Brought hither Henry Hereford thy bold son,
Here to make good the boisterous late appeal,
Which then our leisure would not let us hear,
Against the Duke of Norfolk, Thomas Mowbray?[1]

1

In the winter of 1395–96, Katherine Swynford's life was to change forever. Despite her life-long connections with the royal family and her familiarity with courtly ways and manners, her lower birth meant she could hardly have expected to be welcomed by them as an equal. She could never have realistically hoped that Gaunt would make her his wife, his duchess, one of the leading ladies in the land, if not the most senior. Yet, on his return to England, that is exactly what Gaunt did.

Gaunt had been in Aquitaine in 1394–95 but he was already thinking about making Katherine his wife for he applied for a papal dispensation to dissolve the degree of spiritual affinity created by his standing as god-father to her daughter Blanche. A letter written by the pope in September 1396 allows this application to be dated to the period 'when Constance, of blessed memory, had come to the end of her life',[2] so Gaunt must have been considering the match soon after her loss in mid-1394. Gaunt returned to England in December 1395 and made a pilgrimage to the shrine of St Thomas at Canterbury; Henry of Derby sent him a New Year's gift of rolls of velvet there. After that, Gaunt visited the king at Langley, probably to ask his permission to marry Katherine. He must then have ridden north to Lincoln. The wedding took place in the cathedral at once, very soon after the octave of the Epiphany, the week following 6 January, during which no feast or ceremony was permitted. They were thus wed, at the earliest, around the middle of the month.

Unsurprisingly, the majority of Gaunt's peers reacted to the marriage with disapproval, even outrage. The news seems to have hit the royal women particularly hard, who would now be forced to defer to the new Duchess of Lancaster. It was considered an affront to the high-born ladies of the land, especially Eleanor, Duchess of Gloucester, Philippa Mortimer, Countess of Arundel and 'other ladies with royal blood in their veins'[3] over whom the lowly Katherine now took precedence. Froissart makes clear that they 'considered it scandalous' and that Gaunt had 'sadly dis-graced himself by marrying his concubine'. As the marriage fell between the death of Anne of Bohemia and Richard's marriage to Isabelle, it made Katherine, in the brief absence of a queen, the most important woman in the land. Walsingham wrote that everyone was 'amazed at the miracle of this event' because 'such a woman in no way matched a magnate of such exalted rank'. Besides the insult to their rank, it is also possible that people feared Katherine's influence, mindful of the manipulation exerted by Alice Perrers over Edward III in his final years. The Duke of Gloucester in particular was furious and refused to acknowledge the union, although King Richard accepted it, as did Edmund of Langley after an initial period of anger.

So why exactly did Gaunt marry Katherine? He was 55 and not getting any younger, though even at that age he could still have made a useful dynastic marriage, had he been so inclined. Froissart explained that his choice was 'due to affection', but the most likely scenario is that, ever-mindful of family and inheritance, he did it to secure the futures of his Beaufort children. He only had one legitimate son and his boys by Katherine – John, Henry and Thomas – already promised to be assets for the family. Declared legitimate after their parents' wedding, their status was confirmed by a papal bull in February 1397, although they were barred from inheriting the throne. No doubt Gaunt was fond of Katherine, but he is unlikely to have married her for love alone. He was a shrewd political figure in a volatile court and valued the survival of his family.

As Duchess of Lancaster, Katherine chose her new heraldic arms of three gold wheels on a red shield, a reference to her patron, St Katherine. After the wedding in Lincoln, the pair remained in the north, staying at Pontefract on 23 January, travelling to Rothwell Castle from 10 to 31 March, and were also at some point at Coventry, where they were both admitted as members of the Guild of the Holy Trinity, St Mary, John the Baptist and St Katherine. By April, they had returned to London, where Katherine was issued with robes for the St George's day celebrations at Windsor, and the following month they were still living at Ely Place, where arrangements were made for her annual wardrobe income. That August, Gaunt briefly went to France to take part in negotiations for Richard's marriage to Isabelle but was back by the end of the month, after which they went to St Albans, and then on to Hereford Castle.

Katherine played a key role in the reception and early reign of Isabelle of Valois. In the second week of October, she and Gaunt, accompanied by their daughter, the widowed 18-year-old Joan Beaufort, and Henry of Derby, followed the king to Calais. They attended the ceremonies where Richard met Charles VI and the young bride was formally handed over. Katherine and Joan were both given a gold livery collar to wear at the wedding at Calais that November, before travelling back to England with the royal party and witnessing Richard and Isabelle's entry into London. Described by Froissart as the new queen's 'companion', she had taken on a role which was an extension of her previous position as a governess, guiding and caring for royal children.

In 1397, Gaunt and Katherine's newly legitimate daughter Joan made a lucrative marriage. She had already been married once, to Sir Robert Ferrers, Baron Boteler of Wem, and had borne him two daughters whilst in her mid-teens. However, Ferrers had died by the end of November 1396, allowing his young widow to marry again only months later, becoming the wife of Ralph Neville, first Earl of Westmorland in February 1397. The Nevilles' seat was the extensive fortified Raby Castle in County Durham, where Joan would go on to bear fourteen more children, one of whom would be the mother of two English kings. The same month, more lands and estates were settled on Katherine for life, to provide for her in the event of her outliving Gaunt. On her death, they would revert to his heirs, the Lancastrian children of his first marriage to Blanche, keeping the dynastic inheritance intact. That March, the duke and duchess were at Pontefract and in April, they were at Ely Place in London. Then everything changed.

Richard was determined to be revenged upon his enemies. In the opinion of the Kirkstall chronicler, it was as if the king was suddenly 'ruling for the first time' in 1397. At the age of 30, he had found the confidence to move against those Lord Appellants who had opposed him a decade earlier. That July, after Richard had conferred the Duchy of Aquitaine on Gaunt, relations between the king and the Lancastrian family soured dramatically through a series of rumours, plots and double-dealing. Next, Richard moved against Gloucester, explaining to Gaunt and Edmund of Langley, Duke of York that their outspoken brother was plotting against him and asking for their support. Froissart gives further details of this, alleging that Gloucester had attempted to draw in Richard's other heir, Roger Mortimer, Earl of March to depose the king and commit him and Isabelle to lifelong imprisonment, thus allowing Gloucester to take his place on the throne. This sounds unlikely, as Gloucester's two elder brothers, John and Edmund, had stronger claims and would oppose him; they had also declared their loyalty to their nephew. It is difficult now to know exactly who was plotting against whom; it would not have been clear then, either. Gloucester and York did not wish to be drawn into further conflict, so after attempting to pacify the king, both withdrew from court, unaware just how far Richard was willing to go. The arrests of the Arundel brothers, Gloucester and Warwick, were bad enough but worse was to come when Richard took the opportunity to attack his own cousin, Henry of Derby, next in line to the throne by the terms of Edward III's will.

Again, as with Gloucester, the malcontent, or the excuse, was Sir Thomas Mowbray, newly created Duke of Norfolk. Having initially been one of the Appellants of 1387, Mowbray had made a second marriage to Joan de Bohun's sister Elizabeth, and was thus brother-in-law to the Arundels, as well as being a descendent of the first Earl of Lancaster, the son of Henry III. It was he whom Richard named as his informant about the reputed plot of the summer of 1397; in his role as Captain of Calais, he would also have been the conduit for the king's murderous orders against Gloucester.

Now, Mowbray approached Henry, warning him that Gaunt, his sons Henry of Derby and John Beaufort, and his son-in-law John Holland, Earl of Exeter were the intended targets of a plot headed by Gloucester himself, in league with the earls of Kent, Wiltshire and Salisbury. According to Mowbray, Richard had given them his approval and was intending to overturn a ruling against the second Earl of Lancaster made back in the 1320s, whose lands had been restored to his heirs following his execution for treason. Thus, Mowbray was suggesting that the Lancastrian lands would be forfeit to the crown. Something was clearly afoot, as William Bagot, who was previously in Gaunt's service but had transferred to serve Mowbray, was forced to swear two oaths in 1398 that he would not attempt to kill Gaunt or his heirs on pain of death, or be fined if he disinherited them. This strongly suggests that he had been involved in a previous plot, probably this one of 1397, although the details and extent of it are unclear. Henry realised he could not keep such a matter quiet. To remain silent would have been treason. He and Gaunt had been the targets of many plots and attacks so they went straight to the king with what they had been told. Mowbray, unsurprisingly, felt betrayed and denied having spoken. He turned on Henry. The quarrel escalated to a point where Richard decided they must resolve it; he chose the unusually anachronistic method of trial by combat.

The confrontation was scheduled to take place in Coventry on 16 September. In preparation, Henry ordered the finest Italian armour from the Duke of Milan, whose armourers were renowned for their skill, and who offered his assistance by dispatching four of them to England to equip Henry. He arrived at the joust on a white horse draped in blue and green embroidered with gold Lancastrian swans and antelopes, carrying the shield of St George, while Mowbray chose German armour and a horse covered in red velvet. Having presented themselves to the king, both withdrew to await the signal to engage, Henry waiting inside his pavilion decorated with Lancastrian red roses. A huge crowd had gathered on Gosford Green to watch them, including the many supporters of Henry who had cheered him on his arrival into the city the previous day. His popularity with the common people contrasted with the distrust and fear they displayed towards Richard. Gaunt and Katherine were present, as was the young Queen Isabelle. Once the knights were called to the lists, each grasped his lance and prepared to joust. Both were champions in this field, so the outcome was by no means guaranteed. Ironically, it was Gloucester who had determined the rules for the proceeding, the set length, width and height of the lists, and the choice of terrain. Now his nephew faced his would-be murderer. As the final signal was given, they urged their horses forward but then, a sudden cry drew them up short. The king had brought them to the very brink of the fight and then called it off. After a lengthy wait, he summoned the two knights and sentenced them to a decade's banishment. They both had to leave the country by 20 October.

The significance of this was huge. Not only was Henry being denied the right to clear his name, he was being forced to leave his family, his children and ailing father, and live abroad with the stigma of a traitor, which would close many doors to him. His eldest son was only 12 and the baby of the family, Blanche, was only 4. Gaunt pleaded with the king to no effect: Richard visited him and Katherine at Leicester Castle for four days in September, and in October, all were at Eltham Palace, where Henry formally took his leave of the king. Richard gave Henry an assurance that the Lancastrian inheritance would pass to him in the event of his father's death. Mowbray left England on 19 October 1398 and had reached Venice the following February. He would die there of the plague in September 1399. Henry was cheered as a hero through the streets of London as he departed with Gaunt for Dover. There, they made their final farewells on 13 October and Henry headed for the French court. He had arrived there by the end of November, when the appearance of a comet in the skies over eight consecutive days was interpreted by a Parisian monk as a 'harbinger of revolutions' signifying the death of kings.

By the New Year it was clear that Gaunt's health was failing. He and Katherine celebrated together at Leicester Castle, where she presented him with a gold cup, but as their third wedding anniversary approached, she was preparing herself for a future of widowhood. Gaunt drew up his will on 3 February, making provision for his 'very dear wife and companion', which included jewellery, gold cups, clothing, furnishing, sacred images and the contents of a cypress chest, the key to which was to be found in a purse on his body. One item of significance that she received was their bed, with hangings and coverings made of black velvet, embroidered with iron compasses, turtle doves and garters, and matching carpets and cushions. She also received all the property that was hers before her marriage and the jewels and property then in her possession, plus an additional £2,000. Gaunt died later the same day, at the age of 58. He was buried beside his first wife Blanche in St Paul's Cathedral on 15 March.

Gaunt's death and Henry's absence left the Lancastrian inheritance vulnerable. Initially, all his assets were taken by the crown but, on 9 March, Katherine, Duchess of Lancaster was formally given back the estates that were seized from her on the day of Gaunt's death.[4] However, Richard had no intention of keeping the promise he had made to Henry prior to his departure and cancelled the transfer of Gaunt's titles and lands to his son, reverting the Lancastrian rights to the throne as had been threatened. This was exactly what Gaunt and his son had been working for years to prevent, placating the king, navigating through his broken promises and surviving the plots and murder attempts made against them: all for their inheritance to be lost on Richard's whim. From the king's point of view, no doubt the Lancastrians were too powerful, too dangerous a threat to his position, but they had been consistently loyal and Edward III's will named them as his legitimate descendants. Yet Richard's complex personality, his sense of personal vulnerability combined with his despotic exercise of absolute power meant he could no longer tolerate them. Because of who they were, Richard would not feel secure in his kingdom until he had eradicated them. Despite his and his father's years of service, Henry was to be considered a traitor and must never to return to England. He had endured much over the past decades but the injustice of this pushed him too far. Having met with the exiled Thomas Arundel and Thomas FitzAlan, son of the executed Richard, returning to England was exactly what Henry now planned to do.

In the spring of 1399, Richard was planning to invade Ireland, partly to subdue rebels and partly to avenge the death of Roger Mortimer, who had been killed in a skirmish there the previous year. He appointed his uncle Edmund of York as Protector in his absence and drew up his will, which was merely a precautionary measure rather than a sign of some presentiment. Significantly, though, he did not name an heir, and he took the sons of Henry of Derby and Roger Mortimer into his household and on to Ireland, almost as hostages. The Frenchman Jean de Creton, who also went with the king, commented on Richard's 'pure and entire affection' for his young kinsman Henry, dubbing him a knight, which must have reached the ears of his exiled father. Just before his departure, Richard hosted a tournament at Windsor to honour his queen and sent her to live at Windsor during his absence. He visited her there shortly before his departure in May, played with her in the garden and kissed her hand. It was the last time she would ever see him. Another of his last acts was to dismiss her French governess Lady de Courcy, and send her back across the Channel; she and her husband Sir William returned to Charles' court blaming anti-French feeling rather than the large debts they had accrued. Lost in her childhood games, the 11-year-old Isabelle had little idea of the magnitude of the change that would engulf her in the coming months.

¶¶

Henry landed on the English coast at Spurn Head, opposite the port of Grimsby, on 4 July. In the fourteenth century, it was part of the town of Ravenspur, set on the mouth of the River Humber, although all trace of it has since been eroded by the North Sea. Men rallied to support him and his army grew in size as he marched to Pontefract Castle, which he reached ten days later. Richard was still in Ireland, so the figure Henry initially needed to overcome was his uncle Edmund, Duke of York. After meeting his nephew at Berkeley Castle, already at the head of a formidable force, the duke decided not to put up any opposition, judging that this would create a situation of civil war. Even at this stage, Henry was still professing his loyalty, claiming he only wanted to regain the Duchy of Lancaster, but it was a concession of semantics. The oath he swore at

Doncaster, according to the chronicler John Hardyng, was worded in such a way as to allow him to maintain this façade by promising that he was not seeking to seize the throne and would make way for any other more suitable candidate who was next in line. Of course, as it happened, there proved to be none more suitable than Henry.

After meeting York, Henry sent his uncle to take Queen Isabelle into custody, by which act his uncle tacitly accepted the transfer of sovereignty and leadership. Edmund escorted Isabelle from Windsor to Wallingford Castle, a strong and well-fortified defensive residence in Oxfordshire with royal apartments overlooking the Thames. A gift from Edward II to his wife Isabella of France, it had later been used by that queen as her base to overthrow her husband, and thus had sinister connotations for Richard II's future in 1399. If the young queen had questions about her future, it is difficult to imagine how York might have replied, the situation between Richard and Henry being as yet unclear. By many accounts, she had grown fond of her husband, who had always treated her kindly, so she may well have been distressed if she had been informed about the reasons for her move. She had been raised as the daughter of a queen and, despite her years, would have understood the seriousness of the loss of her position. She may also have experienced some shame, disappointment or apprehension about letting her family down, believing herself to be instrumental to Anglo-French peace. In terms of her daily life, how much really changed between Windsor and Wallingford? No doubt there was a contrast in terms of courtly ceremonials and festivities, but even as a queen her domestic life would have been spent among women, fairly closeted and quiet until she came of age. That summer, nothing was yet guaranteed and Isabelle may well have anticipated being restored to her position. Among her ladies at Wallingford, she waited as the days passed for the arrival of news from Westminster.

In Ireland, Richard had learned of Henry's illegal return. Earlier that spring he had sworn that he would never let his cousin return to the country and he saw the danger of this development, so he set sail at once, landing at Milford Haven by July. From there he set out to march to Carmarthen Castle but the residence was not expecting him and, largely unprovisioned and unfurnished, living conditions were basic, far from the luxury Richard was used to. Henry headed west towards Bristol, surrounding the castle and executing Richard's supporters, the Counter Appellants, who had approved Henry's disinheritance and were sheltering inside. With his titles and estates confiscated, his years of service rejected and his name dishonoured, Henry had little left to lose except his life. Perhaps this added to his determination. Initially, he had sought only to pursue his claims to the Duchy of Lancaster, or so he claimed; now Henry decided to stake all he had in a show of force to assert his own rights over those of his cousin.

Even before the two men met, Henry had already assumed the trappings of kingship. At the end of July, he began to use a new seal that bore the title of 'sovereign' and was making appointments that were usually reserved for the king. On hearing this, Richard was outraged, but recognised that, for the moment, his cousin was in the stronger position. For now, he needed to be placated. From his latest place of refuge at Conway Castle, he sent his nephew the Duke of Surrey and his half-brother the Duke of Exeter to visit Henry in Chester Castle. They offered the king's forgiveness and mercy so long as Henry desisted in his abuse of the royal power. Henry had experienced enough of Richard's mercy. He arrested Surrey and Exeter.

Henry also had the safety of his own son to consider. The fifteenth-century chronicler Thomas Otterbourne implied that Richard had berated the young man for his father's actions before accepting that he had little to do with them. According to Walsingham, the sons of Henry and Mortimer had been 'shut away in Trim Castle' and were not released until the end of August. Other sources suggest that young Henry of Monmouth, then aged 12, was ordered by his father to leave the king and rejoin him, which, according to the *Brut* chronicle, he did so only on Richard's prompting. In addition, Henry's eldest half-brother, John Beaufort, had initially remained loyal to the king but now came to beg for forgiveness and Henry saved his life, despite cries from his supporters to put Beaufort to death. It is difficult to know what advice Katherine had given her son, if any, since Gaunt's death: it was probably shrewd of him to remain loyal to Richard II, as Henry and Gaunt had, until it became clear that Henry's challenge was serious. No doubt Katherine would have been relieved to hear of the reconciliation between her son and stepson.

The most critical thing now was for Henry to secure the person of the king. This was effected by a trick, which Henry may or may not have known about. He sent the Earl of Northumberland north to Conway Castle with a large force to arrest Richard, but the earl left most of his forces out of sight and approached the castle with only a handful of men. Those within were lulled into a false sense of security. Once admitted, Northumberland assured Richard that Henry was waiting to ride with him to London to convene a Parliament which would restore Henry's inheritance and titles and Richard would reign with his cousin's guidance. Richard agreed: he had little choice. However, he was determined to play as false as he felt Henry had played him, remarking in secret that there would be no Parliament and that Henry would suffer a 'bitter death' for the 'outrage and injury' done to the king.[5] Then he rode out of the castle, straight into the hands of Northumberland's waiting men, who conducted him to Flint Castle.

The long-anticipated meeting took place at Flint in mid-August. Henry accused Richard of ruling his people badly, creating 'great discontent', and said that he, Henry, would help him rule in the future. From Flint, Richard was taken a day's march south to the red stone Chester Castle, where he was lodged in a tower while Henry dined in the great hall at the high table. The *Brut* chronicle states that it was on this occasion that Worcester, the head of the king's household, broke his staff of office and his attendants were replaced.[6] After making two unsuccessful attempts to escape, Richard was guarded more closely and brought south to London, where he was imprisoned in the Tower. Henry was welcomed by cheering crowds; even the pro-Richard Frenchman Creton admitted that Christ himself would not have been greeted with 'more pleasure', although he could not resist drawing a parallel between Henry and Pontius Pilate. Usk relates that a number of aldermen and citizens of London had already travelled to meet Henry on the way south, to declare their loyalty to him, while others had seized the moment of uncertainty to attack unpopular members of the king's household. Tyrrell's *History of England* stated that the people were 'incessantly crying "Long live the good Duke of Lancaster, our deliverer"'.[7] True to his initial promise at Flint, Henry issued writs for a Parliament to meet on 30 September, but they were in Richard's name.

What happened behind closed doors in the Tower that September is attested by a number of chroniclers. A committee of senior clergy and canon lawyers was established to consider the precedents and possible methods of deposition. Adam of Usk was among them. The panel worked from the assumption of Richard's acquiescence, or perhaps this was no longer considered relevant as his removal was increasingly inevitable to all. They considered him guilty of 'perjuries, sacrileges, sodomitical acts, dispossession of his subjects, the reduction of his people to servitude, lack of reason and incapacity to rule'. Usk was one of many sent to assess the king's mood on 21 September, finding him bewailing the nature of fortune in his 'strange and fickle land'. Eight days later, a deposition of Lords approached him with the question of abdication, reinforced by visits from Henry and Arundel that evening. According to Usk, the cousins spoke together for a while, with 'cheerful countenance'. Richard then agreed to relinquish the throne, expressed his desire for Henry to succeed him and made him the gift of a gold ring from his finger. It all sounded so easy, so smoothly done, almost too good to be true.

Another account paints a different picture. The 'Manner of King Richard's Renunciation' states that Richard refused to resign on any grounds and, only after discussion with Henry, offered to do so on certain conditions. These were rejected. The Dieulacres chronicle described Richard placing his crown on the floor while Walsingham states that the king told the Lords he could not 'renounce his unction or the characters impressed on his soul'. Froissart recorded Richard's 'cheerful mien' and his request that Henry should be a 'good lord' to him, but he cannot have been naïve enough to envision a life of quiet contemplation for himself. John Hardyng believed the king abdicated because he feared for his life. The private conversation between the cousins seems to have been critical. Henry must have impressed upon Richard that there was no other choice, perhaps explicitly stating his failure, his subjects' condemnation or that his life was in danger. Richard signed the articles of deposition on the first day Parliament met. Usk relates how he was referred to now simply as Sir Richard of Bordeaux.

On 13 October, the feast of St Edward the Confessor and the anniversary of the last time he saw his father, Henry was crowned king in Westminster Abbey. Froissart relates how he rode bareheaded, dressed in a jacket of cloth of gold, made in the German fashion, with a blue garter on his leg, mounted on a white horse. Around his neck he wore the order of the king of France. His son Henry of Monmouth, now Prince of Wales, rode with him, along with the dukes, earls and other barons and knights, numbering 800–900, through the London streets, which were decorated with hangings and tapestries. The livery companies processed with him, carrying their banners and the city's fountains ran with wine. The records of the Merchant Taylor's company include a payment of £23 4s for minstrels who played at the king's coronation and over £4 spent on yards of tartarin silk for their costumes. Their accounts also show that windows were cleaned and drinks bought for the bear keepers.[8] At the feast that followed, Henry sat on the first table, 'at the second the Peers of the Realm, at the thyrde the valiant men of London, at the fourth the new made knights' and the day passed with 'great joy and feast'.[9] Of course, one key figure was conspicuous in his absence from these celebrations. A little while later, Richard was sent from the Tower to Pontefract Castle. He died there in February 1400. Examinations of his remains in 1871 showed no signs of violence and starvation, imposed or voluntary, has long been cited as the cause of his death.

As the fortunes of one woman rose, so those of another fell. By early October at the latest, both Katherine, dowager of Lancaster and Isabelle, Queen of England would have received news about the change of regime. Katherine was now referred to as the King's Mother and again, she was the leading lady of the land, but her former charge Queen Isabelle was now merely an inconvenient reminder of the former regime. As Gaunt's duchess and Henry's stepmother, Katherine would have been invited to the coronation, but her age may have prevented her from attending. She spent the remainder of her years living quietly at her house, The Priory, in Lincoln, surrounded by the furnishings, jewels, clothing and other remnants of her life with Gaunt. She may have followed the path of many widows, taking religious vows and following a structure of prayer and contemplation within her own home, as a vowess, as is suggested by her use of the name 'Dame Katherine'. The new king continued to favour her with grants of lands and properties and she retained her position of duchess despite more modern suggestions that she may have remarried. The epitaph on her tomb shows that she retained her title until her death in May 1403. Katherine Swynford was buried in Lincoln Cathedral under a tomb of Purbeck marble decorated with armorial shields and the Lancastrian arms. She had willed a psalter to her daughter Joan, but no other details of the document by which she disposed of her assets survive. She died quietly after a life of notoriety.

Henry's sister, Elizabeth of Lancaster, found her life was to change again as a result of her brother's succession. By then it was thirteen years since John Holland, Duke of Exeter had seduced her and provoked the hasty annulment of her first marriage in order to allow her to wed him at Plymouth, on the way to Castile. She had gone on to bear Holland six children, the youngest arriving as recently as 1399, when her husband was involved in an uprising against her newly crowned brother. That December, Holland met with a core of Lords still loyal to Richard, Salisbury, Kent, Rutland and others, who intended to kill Henry during a tournament and restore Richard. The plan received little wider support; the king soon learned of the plot and did not appear at the jousts at Windsor. Holland was executed along with his co-conspirators in January 1400. That year, Elizabeth fell in love with Sir John Cornwall after watching him joust and the pair were married within months. Cornwall had not asked the king's permission to wed his sister, but after his initial arrest they were forgiven and Elizabeth bore Cornwall two children. The little that is known about Elizabeth suggests that she was impulsive and determined when it came to pursuing matters of the heart, but that her family were willing to overlook her misdemeanours.

In the meantime, there remained the question of Queen Isabelle. An innocent drawn into the political intrigue, the little girl was finally permitted to return home to France only, according to Monstrelet, after pressure was exerted by many French ambassadors. In April 1401, Henry appointed commissioners to treat with France for a new peace and Isabelle's return home; that June, he granted safe conduct for 500 people to accompany the little queen home. He sent orders to the constable of Dover Castle to prepare three balingers, small, square-sailed vessels, for her use from 1 July.[10] Soon after this, Isabelle was escorted across the Channel by Sir Thomas Percy, Constable of England and John Beaufort, who delivered her to the Count of Saint-Pol, husband of Marie Holland, Richard's half-sister, who was waiting at Leulinghen. From there, she travelled to Boulogne and on to Abbeville, where the Duke of Burgundy hosted a banquet to celebrate her return. The Duke of Bourbon then took Isabelle to Paris to be reunited with her parents, who received her 'most kindly' despite her returning without her dowry or revenue from England. This would not be the last Henry heard of it.

Isabelle, though, did not enjoy her freedom for long. On 29 June 1406, at the age of 16, she was married to her cousin Charles, Duke of Orléans, son of Louis, and died in childbirth before reaching her twentieth birthday. She was buried at the Abbey of Saint-Laumer in Blois. Her body was discovered in 1624 and transferred to the church of the Celestines' convent in Paris, near the Hôtel Saint-Pol, where she had lived as a child. An elegy by her husband extols her beauty as 'the fairest thing to mortal eyes' and her purity in living 'so free from taint, so virtuous deemed by all'. Isabelle was too young to establish herself in England as a queen or a key player in the Lancastrian regime. Her departure from England and the arrival of another king's daughter was to mark a new phase in the dynasty's history.

At this point, marking the arrival of the fifteenth century, it is interesting to consider exactly what contributions women had made so far to the Lancastrian dynasty. Many parallels can be drawn between the lives of Blanche of Lancaster and Mary de Bohun. As beloved first wives, they were chosen for affection, from families of strong or comparable status to those of their husbands, with royal pedigrees, bringing titles and inheritances. They appear to have shared common interests with Gaunt and Henry, as patrons or collectors of literature, lovers of music, ideal companions in every respect. Both proved fertile, bearing a number of children at a young age and ultimately losing their lives as a result, making them forever regretted, enshrined in the memory, perhaps even idolised there as a dynastic symbol, a feminine ideal. Both were the 'full package', selected for their charms as well as their blue blood. Blanche and Mary typified what the early Lancastrians looked for in a wife: breeding, culture, dignity and fertility. Yet their lives were essentially domestic. While both filled the public role of duchess, this was little more than a ceremonial role: a figurehead, a hostess, a focus for patronage and piety. Their real sphere of influence lay within the ducal household, as wives and mothers.

Constance of Castile was a desirable addition to the Lancastrian dynasty because of her parentage. Gaunt's second wife differed vastly from Blanche, his first, but the nature of her marriage meant this comparison was never really relevant: it was a mutually useful bargain, by which she allied with Gaunt in order to achieve their joint goals. Despite it not being a love match, it was no doubt a respectful one, her behaviour and piety eliciting her husband's regard. As the daughter of a king, Constance knew how to behave regally and upheld the Lancastrian ideals of loyalty and dignity until her death. Her contribution was of specific significance to Gaunt in terms of his personal ambition in Castile, to which end he even employed the future of the child she bore him. Essentially, she entered the Lancastrian dynasty for a single, specific purpose: she was a stepping stone who accepted her position and fulfilled Gaunt's expectations.

Katherine Swynford's contribution, however, was far more complex and controversial. Her route to power was an unorthodox one, starting as a servant to the family, distinguished by her personal appeal and sexual attractiveness. She was a mother, educator, substitute parent and stepmother to many children in the Lancastrian household and beyond, from her own offspring to the young Queen Isabelle. Her role was initially in the nursery, delivering, rearing, comforting and guiding the next generation, a key formative position which makes her a real matriarch of the dynasty. Over the decades, she proved her patience and loyalty through devoted service to one family through its turns of fortune, sharing in their losses and successes. Her comparatively lowly birth and possible status as a 'foreigner' due to her Hainaulter father was both attractive and problematic, while her beauty allied her with Blanche and Mary, in that she was chosen for her personal charm. She may not have brought Gaunt titles or estates, but her loyalty and personal qualities, as well as her maternity, was rewarded with status and security to the end of her life. Katherine typified some aspects of the ideal Lancastrian woman, but she also demonstrated the ability of the family to recognise exceptional personal worth as a feature that could transcend birth, in certain circumstances. Her marriage to Gaunt was a critical step in the development of Lancastrian fortunes and a measure of her value as a mother of sons, to the extent that the usual laws were bent in her case. At the end of her life, she was referred to as the king's mother, and the descendants of her children with Gaunt would become kings of England.

Yet none of these women became England's queen. The wives of Richard II, though closely related to it, were technically not members of the Lancastrian family, and have been included as foils for their social counterparts – parallels to the women whose line would replace theirs: both Anne of Bohemia and Isabelle of France were chosen, like Constance, for their pedigrees, without even meeting their future husbands. Isabelle was no more than a child and her relations with Richard were respectful; he was a paternal figure for whom she briefly filled a ceremonial role. Anne's position was a more complex one. Although she was not chosen for affection, the love that developed between her and Richard finds parallels in the experiences of Blanche and Mary. Like them, she enjoyed a marriage based in mutual interests and deepening affection against the context of political struggles. She shared her husband's status and took the role of supplicant, patron, the personification of style and acted as a symbol of pious womanhood. Like them, she predeceased her husband and was sincerely mourned, her death leaving a significant void. She differs from Blanche and Mary in her childlessness. This must have been a personal tragedy given her position, and the fecundity of Mary in particular, her direct chronological counterpart and wife of Richard's cousin and rival, must have had a particular sting.

It appears that the ideal Lancastrian woman of the fourteenth century was essentially well bred and beautiful, an adored wife and mother, pious and dignified, devoted and loyal to the dynasty's cause. Yet, as the fifteenth century advanced, women marrying Lancastrian husbands increasingly began to step outside this role, to challenge it and redefine concepts of femininity and rule. It often earned them severe punishment and social censure; sometimes it had great personal cost. Allied with this, though, came a strength of character that could eclipse that of their men and rise to the fore when they were put to the ultimate test. There was one crucial difference too. The Lancastrian women of this century had the status of queens.

PART THREE

PART
THREE

7

JOAN OF NAVARRE, 1403–19

The rose raileth her rode
The leves on light wode
Waxen al with wille.[1]

I

The marriage of the first Lancastrian king was made against the odds. It was a union made between those who should have been enemies, between nations and families who had long been at war. It was a match of equals, initially pursued in secret, then continued in spite of the barriers raised by its opponents to prevent it. In the end, true affection won the day, in a narrative almost worthy of a Shakespearean drama.

Since the death of Mary de Bohun in 1394, Henry had not seriously considered taking another wife. He had not lacked opportunities, however. The daughter of the Duke of Berry was proposed by the French whilst Henry was at King Charles' court in late 1398. She was a similar age to Henry, had borne four children and been widowed twice. In addition, Mary's father was a son of King John II of France, a duke known as 'the Magnificent', a collector and commissioner of illuminated manuscripts, including the *Très Riches Heures de duc de Berri*. However, that Christmas, word of this proposal reached King Richard, who could not allow such a lucrative match for a man he had exiled as a traitor. He intervened and when Henry tried to conclude the terms, he was informed that the union would not be going ahead. Instead, Mary married John of Bourbon in 1401. Fourteen years later, he would be captured at the Battle of Agincourt and spend the remaining nineteen years of his life in English captivity.

Henry was clearly a good catch though. Within a few months, another important European family were considering marrying one of their daughters to the 'traitor'. According to the state papers of Milan, in May 1399, at the end of his exile, Henry had been keen to marry Lucia, daughter of the Duke of Milan. She was unmarried at the age of 26 or 27 and her father had 'agreed that Donna Lucia should have the earl for her husband, if the earl would give one of his daughters to wed one of the duke's sons, these negotiations taking place while the earl's father was alive, and if she will wait until the said Earl of Derby, who is at present out of England by the king's order, is readmitted to the king's favour'.[2] When her father suggested to Lucia that she might have a long wait until Henry was permitted to return to England, she replied that 'if she was certain to have the Earl of Derby for her husband, she would wait for him as long as she could, to the very end of her life, even if she knew that she would die three days after the marriage'.[3] As it happened, Henry would be instrumental in the arrangement of Lucia's marriage to Edmund of Holland, Earl of Kent, and gave her away at her wedding in May 1406.

Perhaps by 1400, the dukes of Berry and Milan regretted not matching their daughters with the King of England, but by then, Henry had another woman in his sights. Now Henry chose a woman he already knew for his second wife; a woman of the same age, who had been married and produced children, and ruled as regent in her own right. Moreover, judging from her warm letters, she was clearly keen to become his wife. An attraction may already have developed between them, before either was in the position to contemplate a new match. Now, Joan, or Joanna, daughter of the king of Navarre, was to join the Lancastrian dynasty.

Joan's history was a mixture of influences from France and what were then independent duchies of Navarre and Brittany. She had been born at Évreux in Normandy in 1368, or possibly 1370, to Charles 'The Bad', King of Navarre and Joan of France, daughter of King John II. As the granddaughter of a French king who had died in exile in England, actually in Gaunt's Savoy Palace in 1364, she already had a complex relationship with the Lancastrian dynasty. Charles of Navarre had a love–hate relationship with France and England, sometimes an ally and sometimes an enemy. The Pyrenean kingdom of Navarre, straddling the mountains of the Basque region, had historically been something of a political football between France and Spain and it was to attack his old enemies that Charles had sided with Edward III. In the 1350s he had supported Parisian rioters against his brother-in-law, then changed sides for money and led the rebels into an English ambush. In the 1380s Charles had allowed Gaunt to use Navarre as a way into Castile but then married one of his sons to Henry of Castile's daughters. At the age of 10 she was betrothed to John, heir of Castile, although this agreement was later broken, and in 1381, she and her brothers were temporarily held hostage in Paris. At 18, Joan was married to John V, Duke of Brittany, with a dowry of 120,000 livres and half that again for an annual pension.[4]

The English also had a recent history of involvement in Brittany, supporting the Montfort heirs in the civil war of succession. Duke John had been twice forced into exile in England, during which he was knighted by Edward III and married one of his daughters, Mary Plantagenet, in 1361. Records describe her wedding dress as made from forty-five ells of cloth of gold, trimmed with forty ermine and 600 minivers. Mary never reached Brittany; she died just weeks after her wedding. John took a second English wife in 1366. This time, his bride was Joan Holland, a daughter of Joan of Kent and half-sister to the future Richard II. They were married for eighteen years but had no surviving children. It was in September or October 1386 that the 47-year-old John married the teenaged Joan at Guérande in southern Brittany, near Nantes. The ceremony may have been held in the Gothic Collegiate church of Saint-Aubin, which still stands in the heart of the medieval town. Within weeks she had fallen pregnant.

Joan gave birth to her first child ten months after her wedding. She was in the medieval city of Nantes on 12 August 1387 when she delivered a daughter whom she named Joan or Jeanne. It is most probable that this took place at the seat of the dukes of Brittany, the central Chateau des Ducs de Bretagne on the bank of the Loire, with its thick granite exterior walls sitting amid a moat and enclosing a central courtyard. The present white Renaissance-style buildings post-date Joan's residence but she would have known the solid thirteenth-century keep and views out across the city.

Barely five months had passed after the delivery before Joan had conceived again. She would have spent the traditional month or so lying in, as prescribed by the Church but also to ensure that her body recovered, before she was churched. The ceremony of churching signified a return to social duties and public appearances, along with a resumption of the marital debt, so, allowing for this period, Joan's second pregnancy actually occurred four months after her return to her husband's bed. It is not impossible that Joan chose to breastfeed her child, given the example of her contemporary Yde or Ida of Boulogne, who fiercely rejected any assistance in feeding her babies,[5] but it would make her another exception rather than the rule. Allowing for a pregnancy that followed the average of forty weeks, Joan would have conceived in January 1388 to bear her second daughter, Isabelle, that October. She was not to be fortunate with her first children: both girls died in December 1388, perhaps from the same illness. Given that a fourth outbreak of plague was sweeping Europe since its arrival in the late 1340s, it is possible that this is what claimed both of Joan's daughters.

Joan repeated the same pattern by falling pregnant again five months after her previous delivery. In March 1389, in the aftermath of her grief for her girls, she conceived again. Late that December, perhaps to celebrate the Christmas season, she was at the newly finished Château de l'Hermine, a vast edifice in Vannes recently completed by her husband. There, on Christmas Eve, she gave birth to a son, whom they named John. The little boy survived and, five months later, in May, Joan was pregnant again. John was joined by a sister, Marie, who was born in Nantes on 18 February 1391. A few years later a plan was mooted to wed Marie to Henry of Monmouth, but this came to nothing and he became her stepbrother. Five more children followed at similar intervals: Marguerite in 1392, Arthur in 1393, Gilles in 1394, Richard in 1395 and Blanche in 1397. All survived to adulthood. Joan had delivered nine children in a decade: an incredible feat of fertility and endurance in an age when pain relief and gynaecological knowledge were limited. Then, with the nursery of Brittany full, her husband John died. Joan found herself a widow at around the age of 30. By a codicil of his will, John demonstrated the extent to which he trusted his wife's capabilities, appointing her an executor of his will and the sole guardian of their children.

Chaucer evokes a powerful image of the coast of Brittany in *The Franklin's Tale*, with its high grassy cliffs overlooking the sea and the 'grisly feendly (fiendish) rokkes blake'. Using the form of a Breton *lai*, a simple narrative of Celtic themes of magic, chivalry and romance, he depicted the faithful Dorigen remaining true to her husband, resisting the suit of Aurelius by insisting she will only submit to him if he can dissolve the black Breton rocks, which he does by the aid of wizardry. This association of Breton culture and magic would prove significant in the future for the loyal Joan in ways Chaucer cannot have imagined. For the time being, this was the land over which Joan ruled as regent for her eldest son John, who was almost 10 at the time of his father's death in November 1399. For a year and a half, until he was able to claim his majority, Joan was in sole charge of Brittany. In March 1401, she accompanied him to Rennes, where he was inaugurated as John VI, the sixth Duke of Brittany.[6] By the time she married into the Lancastrian family, Joan had proved herself in terms of strength, loyalty, pedigree and fecundity.

By 1401, relations between England and France had turned hostile again. Richard II's recent reconciliation with John II's grandson, Charles VI, and his marriage to Isabelle, meant that his deposition led to great indignation. The deposition and subsequent death of a king was to be taken seriously, as was his young bride's return home with her coffers empty. To indicate the new direction of Anglo-French relations, Louis, Duke of Orléans, who had once been close to Henry during his exile, now issued his old friend with a challenge in response to the 'offensive measures' taken against Richard II and 'for having cruelly suffered [Isabelle] to depart from this country in despair for the loss of her lord, and robbed her of her dower'.[7] Henry replied that he had ever shown

Isabelle 'kindness and friendship' and had never acted with 'unkindness or cruelty, towards any lady or damsel'. According to the terms of her dower agreement, claimed Henry, on leaving England, he 'had made her such restitution of jewels and money (much more than she brought hither) that we hold ourselves acquitted'.[8] Henry also received a challenge from the Count of Saint-Pol, Richard II's brother-in-law, 'whose destruction [Henry was] notoriously accused of, and greatly blamed for'.[9] All that summer, stated Adam of Usk, 'the fleets of England and France attacked each other much at sea.' Thus Henry's choice of a wife from within the ranks of the French royal family was bound to cause problems on both sides of the Channel.

When exactly Henry and Joan met is unclear. It may have been in 1396, during the celebrations for the wedding of Richard and Isabelle, when Henry was in France for a month. Descended from the French royal family, she was a cousin once removed from the bride, and as she did not bear a child that year, would have been able to attend. Equally, the meeting may have taken place in England in 1398. That spring, following the birth of her last child, Joan had accompanied her husband on a visit to London, where he requested that Richard II restore to him the title of Duke of Richmond, with its traditional Breton associations. Joan and Henry both attended the Garter ceremonies at Windsor that April and may have met again in France during Henry's exile, which began that autumn. Froissart claims that Henry sailed for England from Brittany, but this is incorrect, as he departed from Boulogne, but it might indicate that he had been a guest at the Breton court at some time earlier in 1399.[10] On all of these occasions, of course, Joan was a married woman, excluded from any plans Henry might be making to select a new wife. However, they clearly developed a liking for each other and once Joan was widowed, they were in a position to act on it. The speed with which Joan moved to secure Henry is testament to the strong mutual attraction between them.

As early as February 1400, Joan was writing to Henry in terms of intimacy and affection. Her address to her 'dear and honoured lord and cousin' was conventional enough but her 'eagerness' to hear of his 'good estate', which she hoped God would make as 'good as your noble heart can desire' and as good as she could wish for him, spoke of a more personal connection. Joan wrote that whenever she heard good news of Henry, her 'heart rejoice[d] exceedingly' and she heard such news to the 'great comfort and gladness of [her] heart'. She urged Henry to let her know if there was anything she might do to help him, and she would 'accomplish it with a very good heart according to [her] power'. The letter was carried by a Joanna de Bavelen, a trusted servant, followed by the Breton envoy Anthony and John Rhys, who bore the letters back and forth across the Channel. At some point later in 1400 or in 1401, the pair reached an agreement to wed. Given Henry's status and Joan's epistolary transparency, it is likely to have been a matter of mutual encouragement concluded by the king's declaration and her acceptance. Affection aside, it was a mutually beneficial match. Both were shrewd enough to recognise the benefits it could bring them: Joan would become Queen of England and Henry may have been hoping to gain a foothold in Brittany.

Henry and Joan were aware theirs would not be a straightforward or popular match. Being related through John of Brittany's first marriage to Henry's aunt Mary, they required a papal dispensation. In addition, the schism in the Catholic Church meant there were currently two popes: the Bretons backed the Antipope Benedict XIII in Avignon, while the English still followed the rule of Rome, under Boniface IX. As well as receiving the dispensation for their affinity, Joan required a second pardon in order to marry and live outside the jurisdiction of Avignon. This was granted in March 1402. Two weeks later, a proxy wedding took place at Eltham Palace, witnessed by John Beaufort and the Rhys brothers. However, the French crown disapproved of the match and the Breton barons forbade Joan from taking her younger sons out of the country. She would eventually depart with her two unmarried daughters, Blanche and Margaret, leaving the boys under the care of their elder brother John VI and the Duke of Burgundy.

Joan was now Henry's wife but she delayed departing for England. In all likelihood, she was making the final arrangements for her sons and winding up her affairs. Henry sent his half-brothers John and Henry Beaufort to collect her and they left Nantes on 26 December. They sailed from Camaret-sur-Mer on 13 January but terrible storms forced them to land on the Cornish coast at Falmouth six days later. The royal party travelled slowly across Bodmin Moor on to Exeter. There, on 30 January, she was reunited with Henry and the pair was royally entertained. From there, they travelled to Bridport and Salisbury, before arriving in Winchester where they were formally married in the cathedral, the ceremony conducted by Henry Beaufort. The king's gift to his bride was a jewelled gold collar decorated with the letter 'S' and Henry's personal motto 'Souveigne', which might be a reference to sovereignty or *souveignez*, which relates to memory, linking to Henry's adoption of the blue forget-me-not as his symbol – a flower that had featured in the accounts of his wardrobe for a decade. Joan also received ten amulets with triangular clasps, featuring diamonds, rubies, sapphires and pearls. The wedding feast was probably held in the great hall of Winchester Castle, which had been a favourite location of Edward III for its Arthurian connections and featured an earlier round table from the reign of Edward I. The centrepiece was a group of crowned panthers made from cake, which breathed real flames, an effect medieval cooks achieved by filling the mouths with camphor and setting light to it. Also on the impressive menu were subtleties of marzipan in the shapes of crowns and eagles, probably coloured or covered with gold leaf.

A week later, Joan made her ceremonial entry into London. She was crowned on 26 January 1403 by the Archbishop of Canterbury, Thomas Arundel, at Westminster. A faint image of the occasion drawn in the Beauchamp pageant, now in the British Library, shows Joan seated alone on a canopied chair atop a dais of six steps. Holding the sceptre and orb, she is the very personification of rule, in an era when queens were rarely afforded both symbols of sovereignty. Another image shows the jousting that followed, with Joan seated beside Henry in an open gallery, watching Richard Beauchamp, Earl of Warwick joust in her honour. Henry granted his new queen an unusually large dowry of 10,000 marks as well as a tower room within the Palace of Westminster for her to use as a council chamber. As well as the majority of the estates and castles traditionally held by English queens, Joan received Lancastrian lands on the death of Katherine Swynford that May. Perhaps the most symbolic of all the new acquisitions of this new royal bride was Leeds Castle, given to her by her husband in the first flush of love after their wedding. She would return there sixteen years later, as a widow, under arrest by her stepson. It seems that the new royal pair experienced a degree of personal happiness. Walsingham wrote that Joan came from 'smaller Brittany to greater Britain, from a dukedom to a kingdom, from a fierce tribe to a peace-loving people'. But the coming years were not to prove as full of peace as Joan may have hoped. One London chronicle, known now as Julius B II, juxtaposed news of Henry's marriage with the appearance of a star, a *stella comata*, a prophetic comet, in the west. Six months after Joan's coronation, her husband was leading a Lancastrian army in defence of their rule.

11

Medieval Shrewsbury, about 10 miles east of the Welsh border, was a flourishing town of around 3,000 residents. It was surrounded by stone walls and housed an abbey, a castle and significant industry in leather, wool, flax and clothing. In the summer of 1403, as the glovers and tanners opened their shops and the Grey Friars knelt in prayer, as the fields around were weeded in anticipation of the harvest and women hung out washing to dry on bushes in the town's gardens, Shrewsbury unexpectedly assumed importance as a strategic location. Riding towards it were two opposing forces; that of Henry's loyal Earl of Stafford and the rebellious Henry 'Hotspur' Percy, who wished to displace him.

It had begun with a letter. Henry IV was at Kennington Palace in Lambeth in late June or early July when he received an ominous letter from the Earl of Northumberland. The first earl and his son Hotspur had been charged by the king with accepting the surrender of Ormiston Castle in Scotland and wrote to request financial assistance, which they felt was long overdue. Having dug deep into the coffers in order to fund his own marriage and find dowries for his two daughters, Henry simply did not have the money to pay them. The letter contained a veiled threat, referencing Mattathias Maccabeus, a biblical kingmaker and questions of chivalry and honour, sufficient to cause Henry alarm and prompt his departure north. The Percys were an established, powerful northern family who had assisted Henry to take the throne in 1399; their connection went way back to his childhood, when Henry Hotspur had been part of the Lancastrian nursery, and the boys were knighted together alongside Richard in April 1377.

Then, a shocking rumour arose. As Henry travelled, reports reached him that Hotspur was claiming that king Richard was still alive, raising an army under the claim of fighting for the deposed king. But Henry had brought his cousin's corpse to London in March 1399, where it was exhibited at St Paul's Cathedral for two days, face exposed. Henry had carried the pall himself. From there, it was taken through the city streets and was on public display for two hours at Cheapside, before masses were conducted for his soul at Westminster. However, the remains of Richard II were not initially placed in the tomb he had prepared for himself in the abbey; they were buried at King's Langley. It was Henry's son, Henry of Monmouth, who would return Richard to Westminster to lie beside Anne of Bohemia. There was no question that Richard was dead. To suggest otherwise was treason.

Henry was no stranger to treason; he had been fighting to retain the crown from the very start. Just two months after his coronation, while Richard II was still alive, Henry's own brother-in-law, John Holland, had joined a group of conspirators planning to depose and kill him during a joust at Windsor. On that occasion, the king was forewarned and the ringleaders were rounded up and executed. Later the same year, Henry had been in Scotland when dissent broke out in Wales as a result of land disputes between friends of Henry and local magnate Owen Glendower. Declaring himself Prince of Wales, Glendower married his daughter Catrin to Edmund, Earl of March, and there had been a cluster of minor skirmishes between him and the king's men. Then, Henry had relied on the powerful Percy family to help quell his enemies, but support for the cause combined with an historic loyalty to Richard II meant that by 1403, Glendower was holding court at Harlech Castle. At some point in 1403, the ambitious Northumberland and Hotspur had decided to back the rebels. They signed a treaty with Mortimer and Glendower, called the Tripartite Indenture, by which they agreed to divide up England and Wales between them once they had ousted Henry.

Around the middle of July, Henry heard that Hotspur and his troops were in Chester and planned to march south to meet with the armies of Glendower and Northumberland. He had to intervene to prevent their forces combining into what would have been a formidable army, so he decided to head Hotspur off at Shrewsbury. Henry knew he had little chance of reaching the town first, so he sent word to the Earl of Stafford, who marched into Shrewsbury and closed the gates against the enemy. When Hotspur arrived, he found himself unable to enter, caught between the town and its river, with the king's troops rapidly advancing from the east. He was unable to call on the support of Glendower or Northumberland, and had little choice but to turn and fight. Waiting to hear news of her husband, Joan's situation was a difficult one. Having only been a wife and queen for six months, she faced the very real possibility that, like her niece Isabelle, she would be returning home a widow to an uncertain future. Richard II's wife had only been a child, but as a mature ex-queen of England, Joan's situation would have been difficult.

Estimates of the size of Hotspur's army have been greatly exaggerated, with chroniclers like Waurin and Dieulacres citing 80,000 and 60,000 men respectively. A more realistic figure, supported by the accounts of Walsingham and John Capgrave, is around a quarter of this. Henry attempted to negotiate and avoid battle, but Hotspur responded with accusations of financial ineptitude and perjury, and that the king had starved Richard to death. His enemy committed and defiant, there was no choice but to fight. Henry led his main army, with Stafford leading the vanguard and archers and the 16-year-old Henry of Monmouth to the south. The site where they met, to the north of the town, is now marked by the church of St Mary Magdalene, which was erected six years later, over one of the mass graves where 1,600 of the fallen were buried. The vanguard of Henry's army was soon destroyed and Stafford was killed. According to Waurin, Henry then 'threw himself into the battle' with many a 'fine feat of arms' and 'slew thirty of his enemies'. Both sides were using the longbow and modern estimates suggest that experienced archers could loose up to fifteen arrows a minute, producing a continual hail down upon the enemy. The 16-year-old Prince of Wales was struck in the face by an arrow when his visor was raised, but he remained on the field to encourage his men with what could have been a mortal wound. Hotspur prepared to launch a charge against the king but was cut down by royal troops as Henry fell back. Seeing the death of his adversary, Henry knew he had won the battle, but there was still work to be done to secure his position. As his son was treated for his wound, and his life saved, Henry rode north to confront Northumberland, who was forced to abase himself in order to avoid execution. Rymer's *Foedera* or *Treaties* claimed that 16,000 men died on that day but exact numbers are difficult to pinpoint. A percentage of the property confiscated from the Percys was given to Joan, including Northumberland's house on St Martin's Lane in Aldgate. Owen Glendower was beaten for the moment but he continued to foment rebellion against Henry, employing guerrilla tactics against his rule and its representatives until he disappeared in 1414.

Yet more resentment was brewing. Despite the defeat at Shrewsbury and the loss of Hotspur, the problem of Northumberland remained. Henry had been lenient in 1403 because the earl had not directly taken part, but he had been stripped of the title of Constable of England, which he had been granted on Henry's succession. In the summer of 1405, Northumberland drew on existing family ties with Richard le Scrope, Archbishop of York, to rebel against Henry again. On this occasion, one of the king's brothers-in-law played a key role in talking Scrope into disbanding his army, allowing him to be arrested. Gaunt and Katherine's daughter Joan had been married to Ralph Neville, Earl of Westmorland, since 1396 and she had already borne him at least four of the fourteen children they would have together. It was Westmorland's negotiations with Scrope that led directly to the failure of his uprising. He was executed on 8 June in a field outside the city and buried in York Minster. Pope Innocent VII, in Rome, excommunicated Henry for this, but two years later the king was pardoned by Innocent's successor, Gregory XII. Again Northumberland escaped justice by fleeing to Scotland. He mounted his final rebellion in 1408, when his army was defeated in Yorkshire and the earl was killed in battle.

Little is known about Joan's life as queen during these difficult years. Her years of experience and her understanding of governance, drawn from her regency in Brittany, qualified her to support Henry through these challenges. It was a period of turmoil during which she cannot have been certain of her future or that of the Lancastrian dynasty. She had chosen to give up the life she had known, close to her children, and to defy her family in the full knowledge that it may not be a smooth ride. Joan and Henry not only shared mutual affection but a shrewd understanding of politics. Given the nature of Henry's journey to the throne, they would have been naïve to anticipate a quiet future. In 1404, between the rebellions, she was visited by her second son, Arthur, who was granted the titular earldom of Richmond in recognition of the fact that the position had been held by his father and had historic links with Brittany, although the actual earldom would be bestowed on Henry's son John. Arthur was only 10 years old and his guardian, the Duke of Burgundy, regent of France would die that April at the age of 62. Arthur may also have brought news of his brother John, who was then in conflict with the French.

The year 1406 marked an important point for both of Joan's stepdaughters. The match of Blanche of England and Louis III, Elector Palatine, had been arranged before that of her father, with a dowry of 40,000 nobeln. Early in 1402, she had departed for Germany and the wedding took place at Cologne Cathedral on 6 July. In her trousseau was the Palatine Crown, now in the treasury of the former residence of the Bavarian royal family, in Munich, but most likely made in Bohemia in the 1370s for Queen Anne. A delicate gold circlet, it features twelve fleurs-de-lys, six large and six small, alternately spaced and decorated with pearls, rubies and sapphires. In 1406, news reached England that the 14-year-old Blanche had borne a son named Rupert; she would fall pregnant again in 1409 but died in childbirth at the age of 17. Blanche's younger sister Philippa, who had been living with her brother John under the care of Hugh de Waterton at Berkhamsted Castle,[11] would have spent more time at court once the queen's household had been established. She was 12 in 1406 when she married Eric of Pomerania at Lund Cathedral dressed in white silk and ermine. The following year, Joan's daughters were provided with husbands: they were married on the same day, 26 June, Margaret marrying Alain IX, Viscount of Rohan and Blanche becoming the wife of John IV, Count of Armagnac.

Further snippets of Joan's life as queen appear in the court rolls. In January 1406, her secretary, John de Boyas, was granted safe conduct to England along with two merchants who were charting a ship containing 'lampreys and other things' for her use.[12] That October, she may have played a role in Henry's promise of security to Breton fishermen in the Channel and the proclamation read in Bristol and other locations in the West Country that no harm was to be done to the Duke of Brittany or his subjects. The same year, safe conduct was provided for Tristan de la Lande, the Governor of Nantes, who was travelling to England to visit the queen, and in July a one-year peace was settled between England and Brittany. On another occasion, Joan was issued with a licence to send six 'fothers' of lead to her son John, Duke of Brittany. Joan was also thinking of the honour of her late husband: a tomb was commissioned for Duke John V in England, made from alabaster by stone merchants Thomas Colyn, Thomas Holewell and Thomas Poppehowe. Early the next year, they were granted safe conduct, along with the merchant John Guychard, to convey the tomb to Nantes, where it was placed in the middle of the choir. A drawing of the tomb from 1700 depicts the duke in generic style, dressed in armour, with a long trailing moustache and hands clasped together in prayer.

As Joan was thinking of a tomb for her first husband, the health of her second was deteriorating. In June 1405, on the same day as Archbishop Scrope was executed, Henry had become ill for the first time, with what appears to have manifested as a skin complaint. Joan was probably not with him when he stayed overnight at Green Hammerton, on his way north from York. He woke screaming in the night, crying treason and believing himself to be on fire. There was no fire but his skin was burning and he presented symptoms described by some as pustules. Henry appears to have recovered from this attack after a week's rest but there were further outbreaks to come, in April 1406 and in the summer and winter of 1408. Some contemporaries described his illness as leprosy, which had emotive connotations of punishment for Scrope's death, but although Henry regularly consulted physicians and experienced outbreaks of skin disease, his symptoms do not appear to conform to the usual progress of the disease.

What exactly the king was suffering from is unclear. The skin condition might suggest psoriasis, but Henry also suffered from seizures or fits, which could indicate the presence of more than one illness. The question is whether these were part of the same condition, or a combination of more than one disease, which modern historians have speculated may have been epilepsy or heart disease. However, the initial suggestion of psoriasis might be sufficient to cover the range of Henry's ailments as, in its most acute form, rapidly developing pustules appear on the body in conjunction with fever, chills, weight loss and fatigue. Erythrodermic psoriasis causes the skin to burn and, through depletion of bodily fluids and proteins, can lead to heart failure. Sufferers experience cycles of attacks, which appears to fit Henry's pattern of illness and Adam of Usk's description of a 'rotting of the flesh, a drying up of the eyes and a rupture of the intestines'. Henry was forced to delay his presence in Parliament in April 1406, as a sudden illness had attacked his leg at Windsor, accompanied by burning skin and a fever, so that his doctors had ruled he was not safe to ride. After these outbursts, Henry's health went into sporadic decline. Increasingly he was forced to delegate many of his duties to the 20-year-old Prince of Wales. This may well have been against his wishes, even against his better judgement.

Prince Henry may also have been giving his father cause to doubt his fitness as a future king. According to the anonymous poem the 'Vita et Gesta Henrici Quinti', the young man was an 'assiduous cultivator of lasciviousness … passing the bounds of modesty he was the fervent soldier of Venus as well as Mars; youthlike he was fired by her torches and in the midst of worthy works of war found leisure for excesses common to ungoverned age'. This implies quite a life of dissipation and in 1406 the Parliamentary Speaker urged the prince to reside more regularly in Wales, in order to keep an overview of the disruption and rebellion there, suggesting that Henry had been neglecting his duties. As he grew older, more serious problems emerged. In 1412, allegations were made that he had appropriated the wages of his garrison at Dover and, according to Walsingham, he was maintaining a household 'larger than any seen before these days'. The chronicler implies that the prince was unhealthy and overweight and that he enjoyed a certain promiscuity, by later comparing his behaviour before and after 1413. Joan must have watched over her stepson with a degree of unease, attempting to smooth out quarrels between him and his father as their relationship became difficult. The prince was angry not to have been chosen to lead an expedition to Aquitaine in 1412 and, given his military prowess and experience, it is interesting that the king opted against this. That summer, rumours circulated that the prince was planning to rebel and overthrow his father, but the letter he wrote in indignation from Coventry in June repudiates this and reaffirms his loyalty. Prince Henry's reputed repentance at his father's deathbed is perhaps the clearest indicator that his behaviour had been less than ideal and that it had put his father, and Joan, under considerable strain.

In the light of this, Henry's ill health must have been an increasing concern for Joan. Having nursed one husband through his final years, she had witnessed the effects of debility and physical decline, which had transferred a degree of power and authority into her own hands. Her first husband's death had made her regent of Brittany, overseeing her son's inheritance and competently managing the financial and administrative aspects of rule. Then, she had still been comparatively young, young enough to remarry, and her widowhood had left her in a position of strength. The illness of Henry IV, however, was a different matter. She could expect no similar authority in the event of his demise; during his periods of incapacity she would have been sensitive to the mood of the court, of councillors looking to the future and preparing to transfer their allegiance to the Prince of Wales. Joan was a foreigner at the English court, no matter that she was also its queen. Power had been vested in her by virtue of her marriage and her personal relationship with Henry. During this uncertain time, she may have wondered about her future in the event of the king's death. No doubt she prayed for him, sought out the best medical advice and soothed him the best she could. Certain events of the winter of 1406 certainly gave her a taste of her own vulnerability, a foreshadowing of things to come.

Henry and Joan spent Christmas at Eltham, but the festivities were overshadowed by cuts and financial restrictions imposed by Parliament, which Henry may have been unable to fight due to his poor health. One of them was aimed at Joan, specifying that she must surrender part of her income whilst living in the king's household, meaning that she did not have to spend money on her own upkeep. When they were apart, she was afforded sufficient income for her household but Parliament was keen to cut the royal budget, perhaps in response to a shortfall in the coffers following the outlay required by her wedding, coronation and income. It was an undignified and restrictive move for a woman of her position. She was probably with Henry at Hertford Castle the following February and March, in an attempt to live more cheaply, and again that summer as he moved between Lancastrian properties.

Early in 1407, Henry's weakened position may have led him to suggest, or at least sanction, the bill introduced by Archbishop Arundel, which confirmed the legitimisation of his Beaufort half-siblings but introduced a clause to bar them from inheriting the throne, to help clarify the future line of succession. However, it did not prove a popular move among his half-siblings, causing a rupture in the family that increasingly pushed the Beauforts to favour Henry, Prince of Wales over his father. The strong Henry of his youth would have dealt with these challenges, but his health was worsening and in June 1408 he fell into a coma. Although he recovered, there had been doubt about whether he was alive or dead, so a new doctor was summoned and his death was anticipated for the remainder of that year. Henry certainly believed that his end was imminent as he made his will in January 1409. He entrusted the archbishop with the payment of Joan's dower when she became a widow. However, against expectations, he gradually improved and by the end of March was writing to Arundel that he was 'in good health'. It must have come as a great relief to Joan.

The Close Rolls for this period give some idea of Joan's business activities. In November 1408 she made arrangements for her properties at Odiam, near Southampton, and the following February she appears again in connection with her properties in and around Bristol. Some of these transactions also help locate Joan at specific times. On 28 May 1409, she was at Hertford Castle, where she arranged the tenancy of her manors in Wooton; and on 9 April 1410, she was at Chertsey Abbey, where the tenancy of her manor at Langley, in Kent, 'by her castle of Ledes', was given to a Thomas Lillebourne and Thomas Gloucester. By February 1411 she was at Langley in person, assigning manors to her esquire Thomas Chaucer, son of the poet, who had died around 1400. Thomas had made a successful marriage and received a large pension in 1399, as well as being chief butler to Henry IV and High Sheriff. That November, she signed grants for the keeping of Nottingham Castle whilst at Westminster Palace and early the following February was conducting business at Eltham.[13]

The Rolls also introduce some of the members of Joan's household. In December 1408, John Fowler, clerk of the queen's closet, was awarded an annual income of 100s, while the following spring William Porter was appointed as the yeoman ranger of her forests for life at a daily pay of 3d, and Robert Tyndale, her yeoman of the bed, was appointed parker of her Devizes estates. On 5 May 1411, Joan's yeoman of the spicery, Richard Botiller, was awarded a robe, his keeping at the privy palace of Westminster and a daily salary of 6*d*, while the following February she made a grant to Henry Maiet, one of the clerks of her almonry. In March 1412, the queen was at Chertsey when she rewarded the steward of her household, Hugh Luttrell, with various offices, including that of Constable, the keeping of two forests and a castle: Sir Hugh was a descendant of Edward I and part of the family that had commissioned the famous Luttrell psalter eighty years before. A close friend of Anne of Bohemia and cousin to both Richard and Henry, he had been Joan's steward since 1410. Joan also remembered those servants who had come with her to England from Brittany, in particular the Perians or Peryans, John and Joan. In December 1411, a grant was made to the Breton-born John Peryan, 'for his services to the King and Queen' and the following year a second grant was made to his wife Joan, 'born in Brittany, one of the damsels' of the queen's household.[14] A grant was also made by Joan to 'her damsel' Pernell Aldrewyche, who may have been another Breton. This belies the tension that had arisen as a result of her large retinue and its expenses: parliamentary demands for the expulsion of foreigners in the queen's household were a regular challenge. In 1404, Joan agreed that 'all French persons, Bretons, Lombards, Italians and Navarrese … be removed out of the palace from the King and Queen, except for the queen's daughters'[15] and also the removal of five key servants, Maria St Parensy, Nicholas Alderwyche and his wife, and John Perian and his wife. This was brought into effect at once, although the Lords permitted her to retain a number of existing staff, including a cook, chambermaids and nurses. It was not enough. The wider sense of distrust in Joan and her foreign favourites would never go away and 'great discontents were engendered in the minds of all classes of men on account of the influx of foreigners which the king's late marriage had introduced into the realm'.[16]

At some point in 1409 or before, Joan's son John, Duke of Burgundy was married to Joan of France, a sister of Richard's queen Isabelle, daughter of Charles VI. This aligned him with Henry's enemies. The long-standing Anglo-French antagonism had reared its head again soon after Joan's arrival in England: there was an attack upon Plymouth in August, merchant ships seized in the Channel that autumn and in December the Count of Saint-Pol, who had been married to Joan of Kent's daughter, Maud Holland, joined with the French to attack the

Isle of Wight. This assault was repelled but it did not prevent the French from continuing to raid the south coast through the spring of 1404. Then, in May, a fleet of around 300 ships from Brittany arrived off the coast near Blackpool Sands, under the command of William du Chastel. In response, the local people gathered by the causeway on the beach and repelled the invaders with arrows and stones; prisoners were taken and du Chastel was killed. A service of thanksgiving was held at Westminster Abbey but this continual sparring only contributed to the existing mood of hostility and resentment towards the French, of which Joan must have been very aware. Having acted as regent for her son in Brittany and then married Henry against the odds, her loyalties must have been torn. In spite of the raids that year, she sent John 76,000 livres raised from her rents in Normandy and her brother, Charles of Navarre. Early in the following year, she influenced Henry 'with mediation and earnest solicitation'[17] to forgive and release the Breton captives held in Dartmouth.

Joan's role was also to oversee and arrange the futures of young people in her care. In 1408 she was granted the marriage of Humphrey, son of the late Earl of Stafford, who was only a year old when his father died at Shrewsbury and was made a royal ward. He would be married in 1424 to Anne Neville, Katherine Swynford's granddaughter and Henry's cousin once removed. Joan was also able to intercede and ask for mercy in specific cases: at her request, a pardon was granted to John Boys of Higham on 24 October 1409 for all his treasons, insurrections, felonies and trespasses 'on account of the sincere affection which the king bears to his lieges'. This may have been the same John Boys who appears as a London mercer in the records for the non-payment of debts. Joan's specific connection with him is unclear.[18]

Another mystery arises in 1412, concerning one of Joan's younger sons. On 20 May 1412, safe conduct was granted for her third son, Gilles, to visit her to 'tarry and return' with twenty men and horses. Gilles was then 18 and would die that July: the cause of his death is unknown and it is unclear whether he was already ill and wanted to be reunited with his mother or if he even arrived in England at all. Wherever he was at the time, the news of Gilles' death would have been a terrible blow to his mother. This was also the year in which Joan sent a gift to her eldest son, Jean: a jewelled tableau depicting the Trinity, which had been part of Anne of Bohemia's trousseau. Four stories tall and made from gold overlaid with white enamel, it included images of Christ and a range of saints set amid sapphires, rubies and pearls.

Further bad news was expected that summer as the king's health took another sharp decline. Having been forced to place power in the hands of his son in Parliament, Henry retreated from public life for a period of recovery through the end of 1410 and first half of 1411. By the summer, he had rallied enough to consider an invasion of France. Ships were even ordered to be ready to sail that September, but Henry's health, or his fears that Parliament might challenge him in his absence, led him to call the venture off. One source suggests that the Prince of Wales asked his father to abdicate in his favour at this juncture, though this cannot be verified, as a second account places this event in 1413. If the prince did request this in 1411, even if the king felt his son capable of it, with the backing of the Beauforts, it would have been reason enough for him to remain in England to preserve his position. A letter the young prince Henry sent the king in June 1412 denied claims that he was 'affected with a bloody desire for the crown' and was planning 'an unbelievably horrible crime and would rise up against my own father', but the fact that he needed to refute this at all might imply that such claims were circulating and that the Prince feared the king would believe them. At the end of the month they were publicly reconciled at Westminster, where the Prince of Wales knelt before his father, who was confined to a chair.

Henry spent Christmas 1412 with Joan at Eltham. In the New Year, he was too ill to attend Parliament and at the end of February he was transported by river to Westminster Abbey to make an offering at the shrine of Edward the Confessor. There, taken ill, he was conducted to the Jerusalem chamber inside the abbot's lodgings. Several chroniclers, including the French Monstrelet and Waurin, along with the English Capgrave, recount that Prince Henry was summoned to his father's side as he lay dying. Joan must either have accompanied her husband on that day, or been close at hand, for as she was at his side when he died on 20 March at the age of 45. Henry's body lay in state in Westminster Abbey before being taken down to Canterbury, where it was buried in the Trinity Chapel on 18 June. Joan's tenure as queen was over, but it was the start of a new chapter of her life.

III

The very day after Henry's death, his son made an ominous move against his stepmother. Back in November 1412, a case had arisen regarding the manor of Halloughton in Nottinghamshire. The house was a narrow two- or three-storey building built by the nearby church in the thirteenth century with a tower and fourteenth-century glass in the window of the great hall. The manor had been granted to Joan by her husband, but this had been disputed by the heirs of one Ralph Harselyn and had gone to court. Joan had been represented by attorney Thomas Smyth, but she had also attended in person in order to state that she had 'the manor by the grant of Henry IV by letters patent'. The matter had been settled in her favour but now, on the first day of Henry V's rule, those letters were revoked.[19] That October, Henry overturned another of his father's rulings, by which Joan lost the rents from the manor of Michelhampton. If Henry took with one hand, though, he gave with another, assigning Joan an income from a number of priories across the country the following January, but it was a sign that her property and estates were no longer securely within her grip.

Joan still had a ceremonial role to perform. Not only was she the 'king's mother' but, in the absence of a new queen, she was still the first lady of the land. On 9 April, amid unprecedented storms and snow, her eldest stepson was crowned Henry V, and his coronation was followed by the usual feasting and jousting. Two years later, he took his formal leave from her before sailing for France and she was part of the celebrations for his return from Agincourt. Her emotions must have been mixed though, as her own son Arthur had been wounded and taken prisoner by the English. No doubt Joan attempted to intercede on his behalf but Arthur would remain in custody for the next five years. The battle had also left her daughter Marie a widow with five small children, with the death of her husband Jean, Duke of Alençon, and claimed the life of Joan's own brother, Charles of Navarre.

Joan did not marry again. To do so would have brought her the protection of a husband but it would also have lowered her status. As a queen dowager, and in her mid-forties, she would have had to find a suitor of royal status in order to maintain her position, yet she was a desirable prospect for an older husband. Eighteenth-century historian and author Horace Walpole identified a set of verses by Joan's contemporary, Edward, Duke of York describing her in the tradition of courtly love. Although the subject of the poem is the Queen of England, York's death date of 1415 make it clear that these must refer to Joan. In alliterative praise, she was a 'bright blossom of benignity, of figure fairest and freshest of days'. He continues:

Your womanly beauty delicious
Hath me all bent unto its chain
But grant to me your love gracious
My heart will melt as snow in rain
If ye but wist my life and knew
Of all the pains that I y-feel
I wis ye would upon me rue
Although your heart were made of steel.[20]

Yet remarriage does not appear to have been a priority for Joan. As was the case with many royal widows, she may have intended to live out her life in quiet devotion, at Hertford, Leicester or the traditional queen's dower property of Havering atte Bowe. It was a wise and dignified move, but, as it happened, her future turned out to be far quieter than she planned.

On 18 October 1414, Joan was at the traditional Lancastrian base of Hertford Castle, a place full of memories of happier times with her husband, but she was not to enjoy the property for long. The following year, she was given the manor of Langley 'in recompense of the castle of Hertford which Henry IV granted her for life and which the king with her assent has taken into his hands'. Joan may have given her assent to the swap but it is difficult to know just how happy she was with it. Clearly, she was expecting a change in her status but, in the absence of a new queen, she had little reason to anticipate that she would be removed from her home so quickly. However, when Henry was preparing to invade France in June 1415, he did give permission for 'the king's mother Joan, queen of England, to dwell with her men, servants and minsters within the castles of Windsor, Wallingford, Berkhamsted and Hertford while the King is on his present voyage beyond the seas'.[21] This implies that

Joan was still able to visit Hertford even though her ownership had been revoked. It is not clear from these entries whether Joan was better or worse off in terms of property, or the circumstances under which she agreed to surrender Hertford Castle, or the reasons Henry gave for it. The action her stepson was to take four years later, though, left no doubt of his hostility or his motivation.

By 1419, Henry V was determined to marry. Negotiations with France for a suitable princess had been dragging out for years and he was now 33. To marry, he required a dowry of 40,000 crowns from an already overstretched treasury, and he turned to underhand methods in order to obtain it. There had been a long literary association between Brittany and witchcraft, in romances and Breton *lais*, and a continuing hostility between the two countries. From rumours that Louis, Duke of Orléans caused Charles VI's madness through sorcery, to the eleventh-century necromancer priest Alberic of Brittany, from Arthurian legends and the *Lais of Marie de France* to the later reputation of Gilles de Rais, Breton culture abounded with tales of magic, werewolves and fairies. The widowed Joan was an easy target. On 25 September, the Archbishop of Canterbury, Henry Chichele, who had been in the position since the death of Arundel in 1414, sent instructions to English priests to pray for the king, who was in danger from the 'suspicious deeds of necromancers'. At the time, Joan was at Havering atte Bowe in Essex, a small but well-situated property that had been part of the queen's dower for the last century and a half. She may well have been in mourning for earlier that year she had received the news of the death of her youngest daughter, Blanche, Countess of Armagnac. Blanche passed away at the age of 23 or 24, some time before her husband remarried that May. The door had also been closed on an earlier generation that spring when Henry IV's first mother-in-law, Joan de Bohun, had died around the age of 72. This breach with the past, coupled with her stepson's callous actions, made this year a turning point for Joan.

Witchcraft was a real and present danger in the fourteenth and fifteenth centuries. Court records show that peopled actually believed that crops and animals could be blighted, infants might fail and die, wars be lost and milk curdle as the result of a witch's curse. Most of the cases from this period deal with the concept of *maleficium*, meaning mischief or evil doing with intent to cause death or harm property. Yet this fear was also a convenient political tool. Powerful women in particular could become the target of witchcraft charges, when there were no other means, moral or legal, with which to attack them. In Joan's case, the deciding factor was that she lacked the support of a powerful husband. No one would have dared level such accusations during the life of the previous king, but now, as a widow far from her home country, speaking with an accent of one of England's enemies, Joan was vulnerable. She may have protested her innocence and loyalty, or decided it was wiser to remain quiet and not antagonise her stepson further, when he was holding all the cards. The 'evidence' against Joan had been given by a friar from her household, a man by the name of John Randolf, who claimed she had imagined the king's death 'in the most high and horrible manner that could be recounted'. This added an accusation of witchcraft to that of treason. The exact form of Joan's supposed betrayal is unclear: whether she was meant to have spoken indiscreetly in the confessional, or hired a necromancer or actively planned against Henry. Tellingly, if these details were specified, they have not survived: it was in Henry's interests to preserve their ambiguity. Two days later, the royal council seized Joan's possessions and dowry properties, estates and lands. On 1 October, troops arrived at Havering and she was arrested.

In the interests of fairness, the possibility of Joan's guilt must be considered. Removing from the equation the anachronistic question of the existence of magic, what is the likelihood that Joan had actually wished for Henry's death, in any real sense, or expressed such in any indiscretion? The use of a friar as witness against her was a clever move for it implied that such secrets might have come out in the confessional, making the charges more likely to stick. It would seem implausible that the widowed Joan was attempting to raise an army against Henry from her dower properties, or speaking openly of her longing for his demise. In a practical sense, it was upon Henry V's goodwill that Joan's present life depended. As the new king, he had her welfare in his hands and, judging from their history, she should have been able to expect fair treatment from him. If she had hoped for his death, who exactly would she have wished to see replace him? Short of a full-scale foreign invasion, the only realistic alternative was Edmund Mortimer, fifth Earl of March, then in his late twenties. Mortimer had already been the figurehead of one plot, just four years earlier, but he had informed Henry of the plans and his co-conspirators in the Southampton Plot had been executed. This may have been the background to Henry's misplaced fear that Joan was plotting against him. Yet what could she have possibly gained from it? It seems more likely that this was a cynical move by the king intended to exploit a widow's position to raise the necessary funds for his marriage.

At the time of her arrest, an inventory of Joan's possessions was made. Its details shed light on the blend of religious and secular wealth in the dowager queen's household, as well as her personal tastes and the potential wealth her stepson may have intended to liquidise for his use. Taken from Joan's possession were a gold tablet bearing the images of virgins, St Katherine and St John the Baptist; tablets for celebrating mass with a crucifix and images of the Virgin Mary and St John; a chalice with the image of the Trinity and a Sarum Missal containing religious texts. She also owned two cameos, or carved stones from Israel, set in gold, with two gold chains and twelve pearls; three pairs of gold beads, coral set in silver, a silver serpent ring, an amber ring, a stone the colour of the sea and another ring with amber and beryl 'knit' together with a thread, a single silver buckle. Two gold spoons in a silk case embroidered with the arms of Brittany spoke of her past life and her ties to her sons. Those possessions with secular symbolism may have been gifts from her first husband, or from Henry, including a gold chain with a florette inscribed with the motto 'amer et servier' [sic] (to love and serve) and a gold brooch in the shape of a heart, inscribed 'à vous me lie' (binds me to you).

Joan's household contained a silver sconce, or candle holder, decorated with pelicans. She kept her pens in a silver and gilt 'penner' attached to her girdle, which bore the motto 'God make us goode men'. She had silver cups with enamelled green lids, or decorated with leaves and acorns, stars and roses; small silver bottles in leather cases lined with silk; a silver tester for rose water; silver forks with dragon's heads; an engraved ivory tablet. The only item of superstitious value was an 'adamant' stone, a very hard stone like a diamond, sometimes used in medieval times to confuse or block magnets.[22]

Joan's wardrobe was sombre, suitable for a widow and suggestive of religious devotion. There was one russet gown and a russet coat of narrow shape lined with polecat fur costing 13s 4d, an ancient russet cloak, two lambskins, a black mantle with lambskin worth 20s and a matching black gown, an ancient kirtle of black russet and a surcoat of black lyre. One splash of colour could be found in the red nightcap made in the Breton style. There was also a mattress and a number of blankets, a bedding set of red worsted with a single canopy, coverlet and two curtains, and another of green worsted with three curtains, two covers and a coverlet. Also listed were a white and red tapestry covering and a green cushion, coffers, table cloths, napkins, linen and towels of Paris work. Finally, the inventory included four quires of paper and various other quires and books on 'art and other sciences'.[23]

Joan was never given a trial. She was imprisoned in turn at Rotherhithe, Dartford, Rochester and Leeds Castle before being moved to Pevensey Castle, a remote moated location on the Sussex coast, where a Roman fort had been constructed on a spit of land. Joan was permitted to live with a degree of luxury as befitted her status as a former queen, with a harp and songbirds, gold girdles for her dresses, rosaries and chains, eating green ginger with silver gilt knives. Her clothing was of silk, fur and good-quality Flanders linen, she drank Gascon and Rhenish wine and she owned at least two books: a thirteenth-century psalter in which she wrote her name, and a Book of Hours now in the Philadelphia Free Library, which has been associated with her.[24] There were probably more in her collection. She was also allowed visitors, entertaining her brother-in-law the Duke of Gloucester, the Archbishop of Canterbury and the wealthy Bishop of Windsor. One guest in particular enjoyed his visit so much that he stayed for nine months. Was this simply because he was Joan's friend, or is there a possibility that the widowed queen indulged in a discreet love affair during her captivity?

Joan's 'close friend', as he is described in the records, was Thomas de Camoys, first Baron Camoys. His connection with the dowager queen went back to the first days of her arrival in the country, and with him she would have been able to recall happier times. Born in the early 1350s, he had served in France and Scotland as a young man before transfer-ring his loyalty to Henry IV, who had trusted him to accompany Joan to England from Brittany. He had fought at Agincourt, commanding the rear of the army and, the following April, was made a Knight of the

Garter in recognition. Camoys had been married twice, his second wife being the widow of Henry Hotspur, and owned estates and property in Oxfordshire and West Sussex. His second wife, Elizabeth, had died in April 1417, so Camoys had been a widower for three years by the time he arrived to stay under Joan's roof on Friday 9 April 1420. He did not leave until Friday 21 January 1421. Five days later he was back for another week's visit. It may well be that Joan was able to derive some comfort from the companionship of Camoys: two old friends, now both bereft of their spouses, enjoying simple pleasures together. If the relationship developed into anything else, the two people involved left no record of it. The only clue to Joan's feelings is her donning of mourning cloths in the wake of Camoys' death on 28 March, just two months after leaving her company. In recognition of the loss of her 'close friend', she was issued with 7yd of black cloth, with satin and fur for her cape and collar. By this time, Camoys would have been aged around 70, but even so, his death may not have been anticipated, for a record from 1422 suggests he died without having made a will.

Joan may have been able to enjoy a little company but she had lost control of her dower and estates, to say nothing of her own personal liberty. The bill for her upkeep in confinement amounted to an annual £1,000, which was nothing in comparison with the revenue Henry now derived from seizing her dower lands. Over the course of the next three years, her former properties appear in the Close Rolls: Cossham, Lugdarsale Manor and the Priory of Clatford, all in Wiltshire, in February 1420; Wedon Pinkeneye, Northampton, in June; the Lincoln Priory of Spalding in July; the Hundred of Ongar in Essex and Hoggeston in Buckinghamshire in November; the Priory of Creting and Everdon in December; and many more, all 'lately assigned in dower to Joan, Queen of England, and now seized into the king's hands for certain causes.' Those 'certain causes' were the wooing of a French princess.

The injustice of this treatment seems obvious to a modern readership. It may have then, too. This was a time when the status of women was so low that the Church was undecided over whether or not they possessed souls; when women were defined by their male relatives, domestic violence was encouraged and male-dominated gynaecological teaching held women up as permanently sexually frustrated. Yet there were many examples of strong women defying the odds, running businesses, leading families and entering traditionally male professions. Women do appear in court records to argue against matters of law, although they are usually represented by a male attorney; they did defy their parents to marry where they chose. Equally, it was common for widows who did not intend to remarry, especially those of noble rank, to accept a quieter life, taking on practical roles of childcare and support, or to adopt a religious path by entering a nunnery or living as a vowess. This sometimes helped the next generation financially, as assets could be transferred and wealth utilised, as in the cases of Elizabeth Wydeville and Cecily Neville a century later. However, the inclusion of the charge of witchcraft against Joan indicates that she would not have gone willingly, or that Henry was looking for a pretext to strip her of her assets.

It is difficult to know just how Joan felt about this process. She had gone from having the status of a queen of England to that of a prisoner, and may have understood that this was purely for financial reasons. It was quite common for widows, even former consorts, to adopt a quiet retirement, but that was a function of, and served to increase, the respect they were held in. It also raises questions about Joan's former relationship with Henry V, which had given every appearance of being harmonious, even warm. Because she never had a trial, Joan was never given the opportunity to defend herself against what was a damaging charge with potentially lethal consequences. The stigma of her imprisonment would be attached to her name forever, a permanent slur on her good name. And in this era, a good name, or good fame, was everything. While the life she led in confinement may not have vastly differed from the frugal life of a widow, Joan's mobility was impaired and she was denied her freedom. Some historians have interpreted the inclusion of stables in her Pevensey household as a sign that she was able to travel, but every household significant enough to reside in a castle would have had horses to enable the delivery of messages or the transportation of supplies. During this period, Joan was denied the opportunity to return to Brittany, had she wished to do so, although she did later elect to spend her remaining years in England. It is also unclear exactly how widely the news of Joan's arrest spread: it would have been the perfect opportunity for her eldest son John V to capitalise on existing Anglo-Breton hostilities, or for her younger sons to object. Perhaps Joan decided, stoically and pragmatically, to sit out the injustice, in the hope that her stepson came to his senses. In reality, she had little choice.

Joan's imprisonment is a stark reminder of the status of women and their complete legal, financial and practical dependence upon men. Medieval society followed an Aristotelian model of thought that explained the female body in terms of imperfect masculinity, so that women were men with certain aspects lacking, relegating them to the rank of inferior beings. Even a queen was defined by her marital status, subject to the authority of her husband, who might choose to exercise physical, sexual or mental cruelty, and controlled every aspect of her life, including her purse strings. A married woman was legally a chattel of her husband, unable to own any possessions and forbidden from making a will. The exceptions in the power struggle were women who had entered the Church or widows, who could exercise considerably more control over their destinies, even enter trade guilds, although widows were still defined by the rank of their late husband. In theory, Joan's former status should have protected her. She could not rise higher up the social scale than queenship and that placed her above every other person in the country. Except one. Her gender still made it impossible for her to defend herself against the attack of a powerful man when that man was a king. In terms of protocol, she was accorded the respect that her position demanded but it was no real protection once Henry had decided to act against her.

At almost every instance in the history of the Lancastrian dynasty to this point, the narrative of the white swan is dominated by that of the red rose. The medieval world, with its male-centric culture, its prescriptive canon and religious law, continually acted to suppress the ability of women to speak, to stand on their own two feet or to challenge inequality. Indeed, since female inferiority was dictated by the Bible, it was the case that women frequently accepted their lot as the only one they knew. Those who did speak up, identified as different or attempted to take male roles were treated with suspicion, even demonised, like Joan of Arc and the visionary Margery Kempe. Yet women can hardly be blamed for not being feminists in advance of the concept, for not stepping outside their time frame or not possessing an anachronistic sense of their own worth. There had been times in Joan's life when she was able to exert her will, to shape her destiny, when the letters she wrote to Henry IV before their marriage briefly forced the female narrative to the fore, and her actions helped direct the course of national history. Nevertheless, she was powerless to speak in her own defence as an imprisoned widow, pointing towards the conclusion that any power exercised by women was something of an illusion, which they enjoyed because their men gave them permission to do so. The female experience was inevitably one of restriction created by a structure catering to the empowerment of men.

But this presents an unnecessarily negative view of women's lives. While the men may have held all the political cards, this interpretation underestimates the abilities of women to make their voices heard in a number of arenas, particularly behind the scenes, in the case of Lancastrian wives and queens. The dynasty is full of examples of powerful partnerships, of strong and successful marriages where each partner adopted the allotted gender role and complimented each other. Where men granted their women the ability to influence them, it was in recognition of their abilities and wisdom, of their personal skills and the different perspective they could offer. While history records the processes of masculine decision-making, of laws and courts, of Parliaments and petitions, coronations and battlefields, it has not retained the nature of the female influence, which has been essentially an oral tradition, through the personal interaction of man and wife, mother and son. Women made their opinions felt at the dinner table, in the chamber, in bed, and the nature of their relationships determined the extent of their influence. Joan's case reveals that for all her status, her power was essentially embodied in her person; the love of her husband placed her in a position of strength which was lost upon his death and the end of their relationship. She had no comparable power over her stepson, whose desire to marry was greater than the respect she elicited in him. And often it was the case that one woman's fortunes fell as another's rose, due to circumstances beyond their control. The arc of the female narrative is a complex one, often delineating solitude rather than solidarity, as was the case with Joan of Navarre and her successor Catherine of Valois, her niece and the next English queen. Joan had to accept that the wheel of fortune had turned for her and her decline was a function of another woman's rise.

8

CATHERINE OF VALOIS, 1420–26

Twixt the Reawmes two England and ffraunce
Pees shal approche rest and unite.[1]

At the end of May 1420, the 30-year-old Henry V met the 18-year-old Catherine of Valois. According to literature and romantic legend, for him it was a case of love at first sight. Shakespeare's princess is light-hearted, teasing and merry, speaking in soft foreign tones as she learns English to please her husband. In the eponymous play, Henry V calls her his angel, declares his love and his ineptitude as a suitor: he might win her love by performing feats of strength and endurance but he could not 'cast out [his] eloquence'. He had no 'cunning in protestation, only downright oaths'; he was a man of 'plain and uncoined constancy' with a face 'not worth sun-burning, that never looks in his glass for love of anything he sees there'. Yet the playwright's fictional king acquits himself well in his speech when asking for her love. The reality was far more prosaic, with a marital bargain struck to secure the marital treaty. What the young French princess thought of the king contemporaries described as looking more like a priest, she did not commit to paper. However, Philip of Burgundy claimed that since first seeing him, Catherine had 'passionately longed to be espoused to King Henry'.

Catherine was born on 27 October 1401 in the Hôtel Saint-Pol. She was the youngest daughter of Charles VI and his wife Isabeau of Bavaria, who had borne six more children in the twelve years following the arrival of her first daughter Isabelle. By the time Catherine arrived, her elder sister had been married, crowned Queen of England, seen her husband deposed and returned home to France. Isabelle would have been back at the Hôtel Saint-Pol in time for Catherine's birth, so one former Queen of England witnessed the arrival of another. Through her childhood, Catherine would have heard talk of the ongoing war with the English, of the terrible defeat at Agincourt and perhaps, from her brother, of the arrogance of their enemy king. Some contemporary accounts suggest that Catherine and her siblings were neglected by their mother, whose union with their uncle Louis d'Orléans only ended with his brutal assassination in the streets of Paris in 1407. With Charles VI behaving increasingly erratically, feuds with the Burgundians and her mother's pursuit of pleasure leaving her children in financial and emotional need, there may be some truth in the story that Catherine was sent to join her sister Marie at a convent in Poissy.

Marie of Valois was eight years older than Catherine and had been destined for the Church since birth. She had entered the convent in September 1397, at the tender age of 4, though she lived in rooms suitable for a princess, at least until she took her vows on 26 May 1408. Her companion was another Marie, the daughter of author Christine de Pizan, and it is possible that during her youth, the younger Catherine spent part of her time there, under the guidance of a sister who would one day become Prioress of Poissy. The royal priory of St Louis, founded in 1304, was a Dominican convent where aristocratic girls were taught to read, write and ply their needles. It was a very wealthy establishment and Pizan described it in the 1400 *Le Livre du Dit de Poissy* with its carved vaulted cloisters around a garden of pines, fresh water piped through all the buildings, airy rooms and a magnificent church with glittering gold icons. The surrounding gardens were well supplied with fruit trees, deer, rabbits, birds and contained two fish ponds to furnish the convent tables. Guests were entertained in a 'fair room', eating meat and drinking wine from vessels of gold, while the talk was of romance. Yet, unlike her sister, the 'fair Catherine' had never been intended for the Church. It was the talk at the dinner table, the tales of love and adventure, to which she would be drawn.

Catherine had first been suggested as a bride for Henry as early as 1408. The idea had resurfaced on his succession but was interrupted by Henry's demands for a large dowry, which had led to the conflict in 1415. Three years later, the king was hoping to pressure the French into making an agreement and, in response, Queen Isabeau wrote encouragingly that she and her husband were 'desirous of preserving peace, amity and concord with you'.[2] A number of meetings had been arranged and called off before November 1419, when Henry's envoys met with Catherine's brother, the Dauphin Charles, at Alençon. Catherine had already lost two brothers, Louis and John, as well as two others who had died in infancy. Such a high rate of mortality meant that the throne of France rested on Charles' young shoulders and his parents were keen to see Catherine settled and providing a potential heir in the event of further tragedy striking the family. One of the conditions suggested by the English for the marriage was that Henry and his heirs should inherit the French throne, bypassing young Charles, who was then in his teens.

In the spring of 1420, all the parties assembled in the Roman city of Troyes. Catherine and her mother lodged 'at the sign of La Couronne',[3] an inn in the market square surrounded by tall, narrow timber-framed buildings. Upon Henry's arrival, they departed for a local Franciscan convent to allow the English troops to occupy the town, although they still spilled out into the villages around. Troyes had once been the centre of the Duchy of Champagne, now annexed to the French throne, but was still prominent in international trade of textiles and spices. Its location made it a convenient middle point for merchants from Italy and the Low Countries, and its bustling marketplace was full to the limit when the annual fair was held around St John's day. It was from there that Henry rode from his lodgings to pay a brief visit to the French royal family in the convent on 20 May. The chronicler Edward Hall, writing retrospectively from the time when Catherine's descendants sat on the throne, cast the couple's feelings in a romantic light. Hall writes that, riding into Troyes, Henry was 'long for the sight of his darling' and there was a 'joyous meeting, honourable receiving and a loving embracing of both parties'. According to the chronicler Chastellain, the king was more restrained, bowing low before the princess and 'kiss[ing] her with great joy'. Thus impressed, he agreed for a formal meeting to ratify the peace and arrange the marriage.

The very next day, the Treaty of Troyes was signed in the cathedral and, although Charles was too unwell to attend, being 'witholden with diverse sickness',[4] he granted the necessary powers to Queen Isabeau and Duke Philip. In Charles' name, they agreed that Henry and his heirs would inherit the French throne and would do all they could to defend his inheritance; in return, the English king agreed to marry Catherine and 'travaille for to put into the obedience of our said father, all manner of cities, towns and castles, countries and persons within the realm of France disobedient and rebels to our said father'. The promises were made before a large assembly, each side followed by a retinue of around 400, including Henry's brother Thomas, Duke of Clarence and his wife. Immediately afterwards, Henry and Catherine were betrothed by the Archbishop of Sens, Henri de Savoisy.

Nor did Henry intend to wait long to claim his bride: just two weeks later they were married. *The First English Life of Henry V*, written a century after the events, relates how 'the sacrament of matrimonie was solemnly sacred betwixt the most victorious Kinge Henrie of England and that excellent glorious Lady, Dame Katheryn'. The exact location of their nuptials is unclear, but it may have been the Gothic Cathedral of St Peter and St Paul at Troyes, as stated by Walsingham, where the treaty was signed, although Henry also made an offering at the church of St John. This was mentioned by French chronicler Jean Juvenal des Ursins, who wrote how Henry 'willed that the ceremony should be carried out entirely according to the custom of France [in] the parish church of St John at Troyes', and placed thirteen nobles (coins) on the book as offering, followed by a gift of 200 nobles. Local knowledge in Troyes also places the wedding at Saint-Jean-au-Marché, a stone church dating from the thirteenth century now replaced by a newer building. Henry brought sixteen singers and thirty-eight musicians to perform at the wedding, who received the payment of a salut d'or each.[5] Hall drew on the writing of three French chroniclers and describes 'such triumphs, pomp and pageants as though the king of all the world had been present'.

Following this, 'there was a feast with wine in the accustomed manner and the blessing of the nuptial couch'. Then Henry and Catherine went to bed. As Prince of Wales, Henry had a few broken diplomatic engagements under his belt and had lived a wild life but, according to Bishop Courtney, since his father's death, Henry 'never had knowledge carnally of women'. If Courtney is to be believed, the king had not taken any mistresses in the last seven years. This would fit the persona he had developed of the ideal pious and chivalric monarch possessed of an abstemiousness pseudo-religious in its exemplary virtue. However, it would have run contrary to some of the medical teaching of the time, which advocated the physical benefits of marital activity among those living secular lives. If Henry had truly refrained from sex for seven long years, he did not intend to linger too long in the bedroom now. The king's passion was more for warfare and it was this which dictated the duration of his honeymoon.

Catherine may have anticipated a period of getting to know the husband she had only set eyes on a few days before. Following the custom of royal weddings, there were plans to hold a joust, but Henry declined because he intended to leave the very next morning, to continue his campaign of warfare. He was taking his commitment to the terms of the Treaty of Troyes seriously. On the morning of 3 June, after rising from the marital bed, he departed to lay siege to Sens, saying 'there we may all tilt and joust and prove our daring and courage, for there is no finer act of courage in the world than to punish evildoers.' The war was against his new brother-in-law, the disinherited Dauphin, and Catherine was present when Sens surrendered on 11 June. After that, she returned to her parents while Henry continued to cut a swathe through the French countryside, laying siege to Melun, which did not fall until November. Exactly how much time she spent with her new husband over the next six months is unclear but in early December, she and Henry, along with her parents, returned to Paris.

The city turned out in welcome to see the two kings riding side by side, to kiss the saints' relics and pray in the Cathedral of Notre Dame; Catherine and her mother entered later, with ermine cloaks carried in front of the royal litter. In his typical self-deprecating style, the chronicler Hall refused to give specific details whilst simultaneously painting a picture of the magnificence of the occasion:

> if I should declare to you the great giftes, the costlie presents, the plenty of vitaile [food] that was given to the King of England, or rehearse how the conduits [fountains] abundantly spouted out wine of divers colours, or describe the costly pageants, the pleasant songs or swete that were shewed, sung and played at divers places of the citie, or shewe the grete gladness, the hearty rejoicing or the grete delight that the common people had at this concord and peace finall, I should rehearse [so] many things that you would be wearied both with the reading and hearing.

Catherine and Henry, along with the king's brothers, set up court at the Louvre, then a twelfth-century castle where now stands an eighteenth-century palace and art museum.

Catherine's new home for the season was palatial in comparison to the penury her parents were living in at Saint-Pol. The Louvre was a square structure of four wings around a courtyard, with ten towers along its outside walls, all surrounded by a moat. An illustration of the castle can be found in the *Très Riches Heures de Duc du Berri*: a white fantasia of turrets in true fairy-tale style, rising many storeys high, topped by tall chimneys and grey-blue roofs. Monstrelet describes 'the feasts and ceremony and luxury of their court' to which French subjects 'came from all parts in the greatest humility to do the king honour'. They also came in recognition that since the Treaty of Troyes, when Henry had been named as Charles' heir, their allegiance was due to the English king. As it happened, the unstable Charles, now in his fifties, was suffering poor physical health and would only live to enjoy one more Christmas. His incapacity and volatile behaviour would have made the martial, competent Henry a far more attractive alternative; he also represented a future concord between the two nations. Not all of Charles' subjects were as welcoming to Henry as Hall might have claimed; Chastellain recorded that the English knights had made Paris into 'a new London, no less by their rude and proud manner of conversation and behaviour as by their language … glorying at the shame and misfortune of the French whose blood they had shed in such quantities'. Memories of Agincourt or the damaging siege of Rouen would not be so easily erased by this marriage.

Nor were Henry's English subjects pleased. In the latest session of Parliament, concerns had been expressed about the absence of their king and his apparent prioritisation of France over England. News of this reached Henry at some point over the Christmas festivities and he departed with Catherine as soon as he could, arriving in Rouen on 27 December. From there, they travelled to Amiens and on to the coast, where they crossed the Channel without incident. According to Walsingham, they arrived at Canterbury on 1 February, and passed a few days there before proceeding to Eltham Palace in what is now southeast London. There, Catherine was allowed to rest in advance of the celebrations, finding herself in Joan of Navarre's old favourite palace, surrounded by a deep moat and drawbridge, with its octagonal hearth set in the great hall, bathroom with tiled floor and glazed windows and garden with vines.

Catherine entered London on 21 February. The accounts in the city's Company of Grocers show that minstrels were sent out to meet her at Blackheath and pageants were prepared. Painters, carvers and joiners worked through the night to construct the giant's head that sat on London Bridge, and two men were set to guard it when it was complete. The mayor and guildsmen met her, dressed in white gowns and hoods. Catherine only just missed being formally welcomed by the famous Dick Whittington, then in his late sixties, whose fourth term of office had come to an end the previous October. His replacement was a grocer, William Cauntbrigge, although it is likely that Whittington was present in some capacity, as an alderman or representative of his guild. Catherine stayed the night in the Tower then, the following day, was escorted by members of the grocers' guild to Westminster. Along the way, she saw the specially made effigy of St Petronella, who had been associated with the French royal family since the days of Charlemagne, and heard the singing angels placed near the giant's head on London Bridge.[6]

Catherine's coronation took place on 23 or 24 February, the latter being identified by Hall as St Matthew's day. According to his account, she was conducted on foot between two bishops under a rich canopy from Westminster's great hall to St Peter's church. As was customary, Henry did not attend, allowing the full glare of public attention to fall on his wife, rather than upstaging her with his greater status. It was also an important political moment. At the banquet that followed, the new queen sat enthroned at a marble table, her diplomatic position reinforced by the food and decorations, with one of the carved marzipan subtleties bearing the banner 'par mariage pur, ce guerre ne dure', emphasising the role of their 'pure marriage' in ending the Anglo-French war. Catherine was a symbol of unity, a reminder of the king's successes on the battlefield and in diplomacy, and representative of the future. With her arrival, the English could look forward to a time when they would rule over France. The expenses and losses of the past and the endeavours at Harfleur and Agincourt, Rouen and Melun were vindicated in the hope that Catherine brought England peace and prosperity.

Catherine was now, literally, centre stage. As a king's daughter, she was no stranger to being the focus of attention but, on the occasion of her coronation and banquet, the focus was upon her alone and her audience were not fellow Frenchmen but the nation by whom they had been defeated. She had been married just days after meeting her husband, who had immediately rushed away to war. It is impossible to know whether she felt confident at this high point of her success, this culmination of her education, or if there were nerves concealed behind the regal façade. The majority of positions in the household with which she had been provided had been filled with English women. Her position as a foreign queen married to a stranger made her unique in the country and there is a sad irony to the fact that the one woman who might have been able to sympathise and support Catherine was her cousin Joan of Navarre. Joan's birth into the Valois family, coupled with her experience of politics and the English people, would have made her an ideal friend and role model for Catherine, had the older queen still been a presence at court. Joan was out of sight, but to what extent was she out of mind? Catherine was aware of her existence, if not the circumstances of her present life, and her absence at key moments of court ceremonials precluded this relationship from developing. For the time being, though, Catherine's position was one of strength. This was the zenith of the Lancastrian dynasty to date: a victorious and powerful king and a newly married queen, of French blood, crowned in Westminster Abbey. As if that were not enough, weeks after her coronation, Catherine fell pregnant.

Then bad news arrived from France. In his absence, Henry had left his younger brother Thomas, Duke of Clarence as lieutenant in his place. The second son of Henry IV and Mary de Bohun, Thomas had married Margaret Holland, his uncle's widow, and had fought against the French under his brother's lead. The wording of the Treaty of Troyes made it clear that in the event of Henry and Catherine failing to produce a child, the French throne would pass to Gaunt's other sons, so Thomas was next in line. At the end of March, he had led a charge against the combined forces of the disinherited Dauphin and the Scots at the Battle of Baugé but may have underestimated the size of his opponents. Despite fighting bravely, he had been unseated from his horse and killed. It was a personal blow but the political significance of his death was huge. With the Dauphin seeking to capitalise on his victory, Henry needed to reassert his position across the Channel as soon as possible but, after his previous campaigns and his wedding, he lacked the necessary funds. Leaving Catherine behind in London, he embarked on a fundraising tour around the country, after which she travelled north to join him at Leicester for Easter. From there, they went on to Nottingham, Pontefract and York, where Catherine remained while Henry went on pilgrimage to Bridlington and Beverley; this may well have been to the shrine of St John at Bridlington, who had died as recently as 1379, a 5ft silver-gilt shrine dedicated to the eighth-century St John located in Beverley Minster. Apart from bearing the same name as his deceased grandfather, the saint at Beverley was already important to Henry for he had fought at Agincourt on the anniversary of John's translation and gave him credit for his victory. Early in June, just as she was beginning to be certain of her pregnancy, Henry sailed for France.

Catherine gave birth at Windsor Castle on 6 December 1421. Her child was a son, whom she named after her husband. Henry himself was not present. He was laying siege to Meaux, which had continued to resist since that October. Terrible epidemics were rife among the English soldiers, even affecting Henry himself with what was probably dysentery, so the news from home came as a boost to their weary morale. While Catherine lay in recovery, the baby was christened with the king's cousin Henry Beaufort and his brother John, Duke of Bedford as godfathers and as godmother Jacqueline, Countess of Hainault, the wife of Henry's other brother, Humphrey, Duke of Gloucester. The baby's nurse was Joan Asteley, whose husband Thomas was in the king's service. For her role in his upbringing she received an annuity of £20, which rose to £40 in 1424. Henry ordered that the women in her service, an unknown Alice, Joanna Belknap, Joanna Courcy and Joanna Troutbeck, were to receive payments of £10 each, while her confessor John Boyers had £20 and a Guillemote, 'damsel of the bedchamber', was given 100s, to be taken out of the dower payment of Joan of Navarre.[7]

Yet Catherine longed for her husband's company. That spring she wrote to him saying that she 'earnestly desire[d] to see him once more',[8] prompting arrangements for her to travel to France. She had not seen Henry for almost a year when she sailed from Southampton in May 1422. Under the protection of John, Duke of Bedford, she was accompanied by a retinue of ladies, some of whom are named in the minutes of a council meeting from 30 March. The first was Lady Margaret Roos or Ros, wife of the sixth Baron Ros, who had been a favourite of Henry IV. They had married in 1394 and had nine children, and in recognition of her status and age, the council awarded her a payment of 100 marks for the trip. There was also Elizabeth FitzHugh, wife of Henry, third Baron FitzHugh, who had served as Chamberlain of the Household to Henry V. Elizabeth had borne fourteen children and was then approaching 60: she was awarded £20 for accompanying the queen, and she and her husband would stay with Catherine when she returned to England sooner than expected. The third woman named was an Elizabeth Chideock, daughter of Baron Fitzpayn, who appears to have been younger than the others. Although her birthdate is unknown, her brother was born in 1401 and her youth and unmarried status are probably reflected in the 40 marks she was offered by the council.[9] If so, she would have been close to Catherine in age and, perhaps, more of a friend and companion than her other motherly guardians.

Catherine and her ladies departed from Southampton and travelled to Rouen, and were welcomed and presented with gifts along the way.

On 29 May, she arrived in the Bois de Vincennes outside Paris to the south-east, where she was reunited with Henry. *The First English Life of King Henry V* describes Catherine being received as joyously by her husband 'as if she had bin an Angell from God'. Again Henry and Catherine were lodged in the Louvre while her parents stayed at Saint-Pol. A mystery play about the passion of St George was staged for their entertainment the following day [10] and Catherine also took the opportunity to visit some of the graves of her ancestors. [11] On the feast of Pentecost, Henry and Catherine 'satt together at there table in the open hall at dynner, marvelouslie glorious, and pompiously crowned with rich and precious diadems'. They dined among dukes and prelates, on food that was 'marvelouslie rich and abundant in sumpteous delicate meats and drinks', the court open to 'all who would come to the feast'. [12] Yet Henry was keen to be off again, making plans with Duke Philip III to lay siege to castles along the Loire Valley. The time the royal couple had spent together as man and wife was brief: in a marriage that lasted only two years, a whole year had been spent apart, raising the question of whether some rift had opened between man and wife, or whether Henry simply prioritised war over his bride. Despite his initial praise of Catherine, neither party was under any illusion that their union had been conducted for anything other than political gain. Quite simply, Henry was embracing the conditions of the Treaty of Troyes, by which he had sworn to defend his father-in-law's inheritance, in order to preserve the kingdom for himself and the Lancastrian line. Until the summer of 1422, Henry could not have anticipated the severity of his illness. As a young, strong and healthy king, he had little reason not to anticipate spending the years ahead with his wife.

It was around this time that Henry experienced an attack of conscience regarding his stepmother. In March 1422, Joan of Navarre had been moved back to Leeds Castle, where she enjoyed better living conditions than she had been at Pevensey. She was able to entertain guests with wine and music from her own minstrel, Nicholas, and was supplied with rosewater, cinnamon, a pot of citrus and nineteen ells of cloth for her 'stewing' clothes, the smocks she would wear in the bath. [13] The wardrobe accounts show that her clothing was predominantly black, as befitted a widow. At Easter 1421, she was provided with 7yd of black cloth at a cost of 7*s* 8*d* a yard and a seamstress was paid 1*s* 6*d* to assemble it into a gown. Joan also had three dozen shoes at *6d* a pair, 400 clasps and a black satin cape with squirrel fur. In July a Walter Fylly was commissioned to bring rabbits to Joan's household and in November, permission was issued to the clerk of her household, Thomas Lilbourne, among others, to supply her with essentials such as food, drink and firewood. Lilbourne was clearly a good servant, as Henry had agreed to uphold the annual £10 Joan had granted him for his service. In June 1421, Lilbourne drew £1,300 from the Exchequer to fund Joan's household until the following summer, making an allowance of around £19 a week.[14] Other rewards that Joan had made – land at Havering to Pernel Androwiche and a pardon for debts to Beatrice, Lady Talbot for 'her good service' – were also honoured by Henry in 1421.[15] Whilst in Paris, something changed Henry's mind about his stepmother. Perhaps it was his illness and a desire to settle the question fairly, or else his position as heir to the kingdom of France guaranteed him sufficient wealth that he no longer required her to live in straightened circumstances. Perhaps his wife had intervened and asked for mercy for her aunt. Henry paid Joan's dower arrears and sent instructions to England that she was to be freed. At last, in July 1422, Joan was given back her liberty.

Across the Channel, Henry was fading fast. He and Catherine remained in Paris until the feast of Corpus Christi, before moving on to Senlis where King Charles and Queen Isabeau were staying. The exact details are unclear, but it seems that Catherine remained there with her parents while Henry attempted to resume his campaign despite his worsening health. He is likely to have contracted dysentery, an inflammation of the intestine, during the siege of Meaux and as he weakened, he had to be carried by litter. Henry was at Vincennes Castle, south-east of Paris and around 50km away from Senlis, when he died on 31 August. Most historians have rejected Monstrelet's suggestion that Catherine and her mother were at Vincennes, or that Henry was at Senlis, in the belief that Henry did not send for his wife, although we cannot be certain. Since he died between two and three in the morning, and allowing for the speed a messenger may travel between the two locations, Henry's queen would have been notified the same day.

Catherine returned to England with Henry's body. Immediately after his death, it had been disembowelled, boiled and spiced and set in a lead casing before a first service was held on 15 September at Saint-Denis, followed by another at Rouen. From there, he progressed slowly towards the Channel, surrounded by the weeping English entourage dressed in white carrying burning torches, and his household all in black. Henry's corpse was pulled on a chariot, surrounded by a boiled leather effigy, wearing a gold crown and holding a sceptre and golden bowl, his face open to the sky.[16] The banners of the Trinity, St George and the Virgin were carried alongside Henry's own arms and those of England and France. Eighteen carts carried his possessions, while Catherine's belongings were piled on to four.[17] According to *The First English Life of King Henry V*, Catherine followed at a distance of two miles, and was 'right honourably accompanied'. As they travelled slowly towards the coast, news reached Catherine of the death of her father Charles VI, which had taken place on 22 October. In two months she had lost her father and husband. The news also meant that her 9-month-old son would now inherit the kingdoms of both England and France.

The exact day when Henry was buried in Westminster Abbey has sometimes been confused; William Worcester places Henry's funeral as early as 7 November, but Monstrelet and *The First English Life* place it on the day before St Martins, which fell on 11 November. However, this confusion may have arisen from the fact that Charles VI's funeral took place on the latter date. The royal party landed at Dover on or around 31 October. From there, it proceeded through Canterbury up to the north Kent coast and Ospringe, Rochester and Dartford, to rest in St Paul's Cathedral. They reached London on 5 November. Waiting in the freshly swept streets, the mayor and aldermen were dressed all in white to accompany the king's body across the bridge to the sound of the hymn 'Venite'. It rested overnight in St Paul's before beginning the procession to Westminster, the coffin draped in black velvet, topped with a white satin cross and cloth of gold. Catherine herself would undertake to pay for the construction of Henry's tomb of Purbeck marble topped with a wooden figure plated in silver with angels and beasts.

As was customary, Catherine did not attend. She may have remained nearby, or else retreated to Windsor to be with her son. Although he had not summoned her to his bedside, Henry had provided for her in his will, to which he had added a final codicil on 22 August. She would receive a number of domestic items, ornaments and jewels, along with the dower payments which would be drawn from their French estates and those of Lancaster. Now though, with the release of Joan of Navarre, the dynasty's budget would have to stretch to meet the needs of two widowed queens. That may have been the least of Catherine's concerns. A widow at the age of 21, her position would now be a largely maternal one as she struggled against opposition to her youth, gender and nationality to participate in the raising of her young son. Along with the guidance of Richard, Earl of Warwick and Henry's two surviving brothers, John, Duke of Bedford and Humphrey, Duke of Gloucester, Catherine oversaw the female half of her son's world to various degrees until his coronation in 1429. Yet her heart yearned for something more. She longed for love and was not afraid to pursue it.

The situation for the young unmarried Catherine differed vastly from that of Joan when she had been widowed in 1413. Catherine was still of childbearing age and the possibility of her remarriage was debated in Parliament for the Lords feared the political power that such a union would give to any husband she might choose. At some point in the mid-1420s, Catherine embarked on an affair with Edmund Beaufort, the grandson of John of Gaunt and Katherine Swynford, who was born in 1406. Just how far this went, or how long it lasted, is unclear, but the danger seemed sufficient to Humphrey, Duke of Gloucester to introduce a statute forbidding dowager queens from remarrying without the permission of the king and Parliament. Although the wording was left open so that Joan of Navarre was also included, Henry IV's widow was then in her late fifties and there seemed to be little doubt about who the change in law was aimed at.

Joan may have raised a wry smile at the new statute, living out her days quietly at Nottingham Castle. It would remain one of her main residences until the end of her life, and she enjoyed reasonable comfort in the solid Norman castle built upon rock. She also lived at Langley before the palace burned down in 1431, after which she used Havering more often. Her larder would have been supplied by the royal forests around and her wardrobe accounts for 1427–28 include ten kirtles and seven gowns, sixteen pairs of hose and trimmings of miniver, sable and ermine.[18] She had endured a period of injustice, false accusations and imprisonment at the hands of a man she should have been able to trust on two counts, as her king and as her stepson, and she had outlived him. Quiet stoicism and endurance had won the day for Joan, whose victory must have been sweet. As was often the case with the narrative of the white swan, it was a matter of patience, of accepting the dominance of the red rose, until such time as the wheel of fortune turned again.

After her release, Joan commissioned a joint tomb to be made for herself and Henry IV in Trinity Chapel, Canterbury Cathedral. Joan may have been thinking of her own mortality, but the mind of her sister queen was fixed on more temporal matters.

9

MRS TUDOR, 1426–37

Well, no matter what quarrel she makes,
she will not loose me from her bond.
Rather I become her servant, surrender to her,
so she can write my name in her contract.
Now don't go thinking I must be drunk
if I love my good lady;
for without her I cannot live …[1]

H istory has cast Catherine of Valois in a predominantly sexual role. Her first marriage was brief and during the small part of her life that she shared with Henry V, he was frequently absent on campaign. She is memorable for her youth and beauty, for capturing the English king, albeit briefly, and for falling pregnant with the next Plantagenet ruler. Her position as a diplomatic pawn, raised to become the wife of an unfamiliar man, a national enemy, did little to establish her identity as a more rounded individual in the eyes of later historians, who latched on to her dynastic significance and her carnal appetites. However, it was her behaviour as a dowager queen that defied the quiet, contemplative ideal that Joan of Kent and Joan of Navarre adopted. Even Katherine Swynford, whose relationship with Gaunt had given rise to gossip, retreated from the public view during his absence and after his death. A key difference is age; the former Lancastrian wives were well advanced in years by the point they were widowed. Each had been married before and borne children. In comparison, Catherine was barely out of childhood. She was not prepared to retire gracefully.

The image we have of Catherine today is also coloured by Shakespeare's depiction of her as a provocative, giddy girl, and his use of puns and wordplay in scenes where she attempts to learn English for her husband. Struggling with the language, she mispronounces 'gown/cown' and 'foot', making them sound like sexual slang, drawing a laugh from the audience and the implication that she would be pleasing Henry in intimate ways. However, this process began before Shakespeare's characterisation, for one contemporary chronicler described her as 'unable to bridle her carnal passions entirely'.[2] Yet this is clearly a one-sided representation of the queen. The emphasis on one aspect of her life is the result of fifteenth-century sexual politics and the masculine monopoly on historical writing. There is also a significant absence of other records which could shed more light on her personality and intimate thoughts. Widowed at the age of 21, lonely and isolated, her situation was a difficult one. It is little wonder that she sought affection where she could. What shines through in Catherine's later life is her warmth and humanity.

A picture emerges of Catherine and her young son in the *London Chronicle* for November 1423, when they left Windsor for the state opening of Parliament and lodged in an inn in Staines, south-west of London. The child's reluctance to leave was recast with a religious dimension: he 'schriked and cryed and sprang and wold nought be caryed forthere, wherefore he was borne ageyne into the inne, and there he bood the Soneday al day'. On the Monday he gave his royal consent to travel, and was borne out to his mother's litter, 'being thanne gladde and merye chered'.[3] From there, they travelled to Kingston and Kennington, arriving in London; later that month, they were at Waltham Palace and spent Christmas at Hertford. Through her son's early years, Catherine's main residence remained Windsor, where musicians were brought to play to Henry and the king's wards were intended to keep him company and share his lessons. She was also granted Baynard's Castle as her central London base, on condition that she kept all the buildings and gardens in good repair until the young Earl of March was old enough to inherit it. In 1425, the 4-year-old Henry was at Parliament again, looking about him 'gravely and sadly' and later rode through the streets on a white horse, to the delight and praise of the citizens. By 1428, when the Earl of Warwick was appointed as his tutor, his time was more formally divided, his summers between Windsor and Berkhamsted and his winters at Wallingford and Hertford. Soon after this though, Catherine left Windsor, perhaps by choice or by the council's command. It may have been to conceal the fact that the dowager queen had fallen pregnant.

Exactly when Catherine met Owen Tudor is unclear. Embroidered retrospectively from the time of their descendants, their story has become a romance in which the handsome Owen falls into the queen's lap after dancing, or has an encounter with an unknown woman whilst bathing in a river and later recognises her as the queen. In reality, it is difficult to pinpoint the moment when the Welsh Squire first caught the young widow's eye, or the steps by which they became lovers, or which of them initiated the relationship. Around Catherine's age and reputedly very handsome, Owen came from an Anglesey family which had played a prominent role in the uprising of his uncle, Owen Glendower, in 1403. It has even been suggested that the young Tudor was named after the rebel leader, who may have acted as his godfather. It is likely that he came to England with his father, in an attempt to restore the family fortunes which had been lost after the Battle of Shrewsbury. One contemporary Welsh chronicler, Elis Gruffydd, stated that Owen found a position working as Catherine's server and sewer, meaning that he poured her drink at table. They became lovers at some point before 1430. Not long after, the dowager queen became his wife. This probably took place between the council's clarification of her marital position in 1427 and the letters affording Owen the status of an Englishman in 1432.

It was illegal for Catherine to remarry. The consequences as outlined by the earlier statute included harsh penalties for any man brave or foolish enough to break Parliament's rule, but perhaps this is exactly why

Catherine chose Owen. He had no land or titles to forfeit and posed no threat to the position of her son; being outside the aristocratic circle at the heart of Westminster and Windsor, he was chosen simply for love. Perhaps the detail that gave most cause for relief among the regency Parliament was that he was not a member of the French aristocracy. Had Catherine chosen to ally herself with a member of the Valois family circle, she would have adopted a position against her son's best interests regarding his joint inheritance. As a result, she may have been pressured to leave England or else bring an influential foreign player into the arena of English politics, which would not have been to the liking of the king's uncles and tutors.

It is difficult to know exactly how discreet Catherine and Owen were. Their liaison is likely to have been an open secret, tolerated by her household and perhaps even by Bedford and Gloucester, given that the dowager queen bore four children over the course of the next seven years. Then again, it is plausible that her marriage was only known to a few intimates and that she used periods of retirement in the country to conceal the later stages of her pregnancies and deliveries. This latter interpretation fits with the locations at which her first two sons were born. In 1430, Catherine retreated to Hadham, or Much Hadham Palace, the home of the Bishop of London in Hertfordshire. The palace stood on the north side of the medieval church, probably dating from a similar era, although today most of it is sixteenth century. The plan shows an H-shaped building, with two wings either side a central hall, and a fifteenth-century beam remains in place in a first floor room, perhaps very the bedroom where Catherine laboured. Her first child by Owen was a son, a half-brother to the king they named Edmund. It has been suggested that the ambiguous time frame might allow for Edmund to have been the offspring of Edmund Beaufort. However, this was never questioned at the time and while Beaufort and Catherine were still close, she appears to have given up the idea of marrying him before embarking on the relationship with Tudor. Owen acknowledged Edmund as his son, as he did Catherine's next child, Jasper, who arrived around a year later at Hatfield Palace. According to a Tudor pedigree chart drawn up in 1500, the couple had at least two more children, although the details about them are unclear. There was a third boy named either Edward or

Owen and a daughter, perhaps called Margaret, who may have entered the Church or died young. Crucially for these children and later generations, the council bill of 1427 regarding the remarriage of queens had specified that any children born to a subsequent husband would be regarded as part of the royal family.

So why exactly did Catherine marry Owen? The simplest answer may be the correct one. She had no need to find a husband for his power or money, as in 1423 her dower payments had been set at 100,000 marks, in line with the Treaty of Troyes, and she was drawing additional income from the Duchy of Lancaster and the properties of Joan de Bohun. Nor did Catherine consider returning to France as her sister Isabelle had done. She remained by the side of her infant son, who was at war with her brother, who was now reigning in contravention of the terms of the Treaty of Troyes as Charles VII of France. To press his joint claim, Henry VI was crowned in England in 1429 and again in Rouen Cathedral in 1431. Catherine may have travelled with him and attended that occasion, if the timing of her pregnancies allowed. The most plausible explanation for her marriage seems to be the romantic one: she was lonely and fell in love, and wanted a husband and family of her own. She had been indiscreet and defied the wishes of Parliament but she had done so in a way that made the least possible impact: she had selected a husband of personal charm and political inconsequence. Having done her duty to the dynasty, she had decided to follow her own inclination when it came to her second marriage. As Holinshed wrote, under the reign of Elizabeth I, 'being yoong and lustie following more hir own wanton appetite than freendlie counsel tooke to husband privilie a galant gentleman and a right beautiful person, indued with many goodly gifts, both of bodie and of mind'. There are some indications that her close circle looked upon her decision with sympathy.

Among Catherine's friends at court were at least two poets. One was the captive King of Scots, James I, author of love lyrics and the autobiographical poem *The Kingis Quair*, who had sat at Catherine's side during her coronation banquet; the other was the monk and prolific poet John Lydgate. While James was something of an honoured guest in the English court since his capture at the age of 12, Lydgate actively pursued the patronage of figures like Catherine, Warwick and Gloucester. In Lydgate's dream sequence poem *The Temple of Glass*, composed in the late 1420s or early '30s, a highborn lady admits to her secret desires for a man she is forbidden to love, although the pair subsequently undergo a sort of marriage service led by Venus and consummate their love after the removal of a symbolic obstacle. The emphasis on secrecy and discretion suggests that this liaison was highly controversial and may well have been inspired by Catherine's predicament. A contemporary copy of the work made by poet John Shirley includes the information that it was a very pleasant dream, 'made at the request of a lover'.

Several suggestions have been made as to the identity of these illicit lovers. The identification of the woman as royal has led to suggestions that it may have been written to celebrate the wedding of Henry IV and Joan of Navarre in 1403, or Henry V and Catherine in 1420, but the secretive nature of the woman's love identifies the poem as a complaint rather than an epithalamium. Lydgate had already written about Catherine in his epic *Troy Book*, composed between 1412 and 1420 at the instigation of Henry V. He celebrated her wedding as bringing peace with 'bright beams shining', and the queen as 'right good and fair … of grace intrepid in her wommanhede'. Catherine was also addressed in the entertainments Lydgate wrote for the court at Easter and Christmas time, such as the Mummings at Eltham in 1425, Hertford in 1427 and Windsor in 1429, in which she was celebrated as a source of the legitimisation of the Lancastrian claim to the French crown, a fleur-de-lys bearing the blood of St Louis, a peacemaker worthy of the love of all people. Lydgate also composed a lament at her bequest on the nature of fortune and changing circumstances, touching on the familiar medieval motif of the *memento mori*, or reminder of mortality. The poem 'That Now is Hay Some-Tyme was Grase' bears the dedication 'John Lydgate the Monke of Bery wrote and made at the commandment of the Quene Kateryn as in here sportes she walkyd by the medowes that were late mowen in the monthe of July.'[4] There was clearly an established tradition of Lydgate writing sympathetically about his queen.

The epic *The Temple of Glas* is also sympathetic to the predicament of a queen, but it is discreet and draws upon literary tradition and metaphor to veil the identities of its lovers. It may be that Catherine or Owen commissioned it, or that Lydgate was hoping to win the queen's patronage with a display of sympathy. One of the most telling details is the discrepancy in status between the lovers, the man believing his lover to be too far above him socially. Into the mouth of this yearning woman, Lydgate puts the words:

> Devoid of joie, of woe I have plenté.
> What I desire, that may I not possede,
> For that I nold is ready aye to me,
> And that I love forto swear I drede:
> To my desire contrarie is my mede.
> And thus I stand departid even on tweyn,
> Of wille and deed laced in a chaine.

Although she felt passionately, she could not speak of her love and was lonely:

> For thoughe I burn with fervence and with heat,
> Within myn hert I mot complein of cold;
> And thurugh myn axcesse thoghe I sweltre and swete,
> Me to complein, God wot, I am not bold
> Unto no wight [person]; nor a woord unfold
> Of al my peyne—allas the harde stond—
> That hatter burn that closed is my wounde.

The narrator gives a description of this lovesick lady, praising her shape, form, deportment and cheer, her 'womanhead' (womanliness) and gentleness, her truth, faith and kindness, 'all virtues each set' in their degree. Her expression was sad but benign. She was 'discrete, prudent, of wisdom sufficience', the 'mirror of wit, ground of governaunce, a world of beauty compassed in her face', which raced through his heart. She is also described as being dressed in green and white, which may be a covert hint at the identity of her lover, given that these were the colours of the Tudor dynasty. In spite of their restrictions, Venus intervenes to join the lovers by a golden chain, after which they kiss to seal their union, offering a decisive but irregular solution to their predicament. The narrator concludes by sending the poem into 'her presence', to await 'her' correction. These textual clues suggest that *The Temple of Glas* was inspired by Catherine's predicament and its importance lies in its timing. This was not a retrospective attempt to defend the marriage, as with Vergil and other Tudor authors: here was a contemporary of the queen, and a religious man, offering sympathy for her lonely and potentially scandalous predicament. For the time being though, Catherine's secret went unnoticed.

Details about Catherine's life and those who served her emerge from entries in the Patent Rolls. In 1430, an annual grant of £20 was made to Joan, the wife of William Troutbeck, for 'her labour and charges in going to the King's mother in foreign parts'. Her treasurer was a William Walysby, whom she later rewarded with a chapel in Hastings. Her cofferer was Thomas Bateman, her chamberlain a Roland Lenthale and her clerk was Robert Bolleston, later keeper of the great wardrobe. Also in her household were Robert Fisshelake and possibly two men appointed to execute the terms of her will, John Merston and Richard Alred. After her death, a grant for life was made to Thomas Hull for fourteen years of service to Catherine at Hertford Castle.[5] Otherwise, the court records indicate she was living quietly during this period. It appears that the secret of her marriage was being tolerated by the council, for whom it may even have come as something of a relief, meaning they no longer needed fear that Catherine might take a more influential second husband. In May 1432, Owen was awarded the same rights and status as an Englishman, suggesting an acknowledgement of his new circumstances. Then, two years later, Catherine assigned some lands and revenues to him, clearly believing him capable and trustworthy, and believing that this move would be considered socially acceptable.

In September 1435, news came from France of the death of Catherine's mother, Isabeau of Bavaria. Having retired to the Hôtel Saint-Pol after Charles' death, she passed away at around the age of 65 and was buried in the royal basilica of Saint-Denis in northern Paris. Not much time elapsed between this event and Catherine's own retirement. At some point in 1436, she entered Bermondsey Abbey, a Benedictine monastery that had been founded in the eleventh century. It sat amid fields on the south bank of the Thames, almost opposite the Tower of London and when the nearby manor house had been granted to the abbey, a condition had been made that the monks should retain 'a residence for the use of the sovereign if he should call for it'. Catherine would have been welcomed by the Abbot John Bromley, who had been in the role since 1432. Yet her status as dowager queen, as welcome guest, may have belied a more sinister truth. It is unclear whether she retired there voluntarily or whether it was at the command of the council, specifically that of Humphrey, Duke of Gloucester. Victorian historian Agnes Strickland was of the opinion that Catherine's marriage remained a secret from the duke until this point and that, upon making the discovery, he separated her from Tudor and her children. It is certainly true that Gloucester treated Owen harshly in the coming years, imprisoning him at Newgate following Catherine's death and then at Windsor, where he stayed until the king intervened. There may be some truth in Strickland's assertion, for Catherine is unlikely to have withdrawn voluntarily from a marriage and her small children. However, there was probably a more plausible reason for her seclusion.

Catherine was already ill when she entered the abbey; her will, made on 31 December 1436, refers to a 'long, grievous malady'.[6] As a New Year's gift, her 16-year-old son sent her a gold tablet decorated with a crucifix, pearls and sapphires commissioned from goldsmith John Pattesby. She died at Bermondsey two days later, having been resident there for less than a year at the most. It may even have been a matter of weeks. She was 35. Her will was supervised by Henry, Cardinal Beaufort, Humphrey, Duke of Gloucester and Bishop Alnwick of Lincoln, with the king as executor.

Catherine's body lay in state in the church of St Katherine by the Tower, before being transported to St Paul's and on to Westminster Abbey. A wooden effigy lay on top for the procession through the streets, thin faced with thin lips and wide brows, which survives in the abbey museum. *Gregory's Chronicle* related how she was given a solemn dirge and a mass before being buried in the old chapel of Our Lady. Her tomb was made of alabaster, inscribed with a poem describing her as a 'perfect flower of modesty', the 'joy of this land and brightness of her own, glory of mothers, to her people dear, a follower sincere of the true faith'. When Westminster Abbey was remodelled by Henry VII, Catherine's tomb was demolished and her coffin opened. Her body was found to be in such a state of preservation that it was put on display, allowing the seventeenth-century diarist Samuel Pepys to indulge a ghoulish passion and snatch a kiss from its mummified lips. Catherine's remains were finally laid to rest during the reign of George III.

Owen Tudor's future was less than peaceful. Shortly after her death, he was charged with violating the law over his marriage to Catherine and, understanding the danger, sought sanctuary in Westminster. Humphrey, Duke of Gloucester promised to guarantee his safety if he left, upon which Owen left the abbey, only to be promptly arrested and thrown into Newgate Prison. Gloucester did not allow his conscience to trouble him over this for long, applying for an indemnity which he was granted in July 1437. Tudor escaped but was recaptured and transferred to the custody of the Duke of Suffolk at Wallingford Castle, then sent to Windsor, under Edmund Beaufort. He was eventually questioned by the council and acquitted of the charges made against him, possibly under the aegis of the young king Henry VI, who showed leniency towards his stepfather. In 1439, he was given a general pardon and his lands and estates were restored, along with an annuity of £40 and the position of Keeper of the Parks in Denbighshire. Owen was then released to live quietly, though his sons were received at court and later ennobled, until such point as national conflict drew him back into the Lancastrian story.

Catherine was outlived by the previous Lancastrian dowager queen, but only just. In her final years, Joan lived at the traditional residence of royal women, Havering atte Bowe, and the palace at Langley, Hertfordshire. Known as King's Langley for its royal connections dating back to the reign of Edward I, the palace stood around three courtyards, with royal apartments, chapel and great hall, extensive kitchens and a hunting lodge. Joan was there in 1425 when she received a visit from her friend Jacqueline of Hainault, a refugee from an unsuccessful marriage, who had recently become the wife of Humphrey, Duke of Gloucester and Joan's sister-in-law. The visit took place on the Exaltation of the Holy Cross, 14 September, when Jacqueline had heard vespers at St Albans and rode on to Langley with an escort of forty horsemen. In February 1427, Joan was at Langley when she granted the office of parker of her estate at Hampstead Marshall to her servant Richard Doncaster. The same year, the Duke of Gloucester visited on his way to St Albans to offer thanks for his recovery from illness, and in 1428 Joan entertained Henry Beaufort, Bishop of Winchester. In 1431, the palace was partially destroyed by fire 'through the negligence and drowsiness of a minstrel and insufficient care of a lighted candle',[7] but Joan still appears to have been in residence after this point, so perhaps part of the lodgings had escaped without too much damage.

At New Year 1437, Joan was at Langley when she received the gift of a gold tablet set with rubies, sapphires and pearls from the young Henry VI, similar to the one he sent to his mother at Bermondsey. Joan was at Havering when she died on 10 June. The cause of her death is unknown and there are no surviving indications that she was suffering from any illness, as exist for Henry IV. However, given that she was aged 66 or 67, a very respectable age for the era, the likelihood is that her demise was considered natural.

Her body was taken to Bermondsey, where it rested briefly in the same location that had witnessed the death of her fellow queen that January. Then it processed on to Canterbury Cathedral, where she joined Henry IV in the enamelled alabaster tomb in the Trinity Chapel on 6 August. The king and queen are depicted lying side by side, their heads resting on red pillows under ornately carved canopies. Joan's effigy is dressed in a cotehardie dress, which is tight and sleeveless, lined with ermine and studded with jewels, with a mantle fastened by brooches and a jewelled band and a collar of the letter 'S', echoing the motif of gifts Henry had made to her at the time of their wedding. A cast of her statue, made in 1875 by Domenico Brucciani, highlights the details of her appearance: her hair gathered in nets on each temple and her eyebrows high and arched; her forehead is broad, her features regular, lips almost pursed and chin strong. The nose of the cast is damaged but on the original, it is pointed and generous without being large. The magnificent tomb, close to the site of the golden shrine of Thomas Becket, emphasises the role Joan played as queen and consort, and serves as a reminder that Henry's life was one of two halves. His first wife, Mary de Bohun, the mother of his children, was the wife of his youth, with whom he had struggled against the trials of Richard II's reign. She continued to lie in Leicester, while the wife with whom Henry had shared the throne, who had advised, supported and comforted him, received the effigy of a queen.

10

QUEEN OF SCOTLAND, 1424–45

By her joy a sick man can recover,
by her wrath one well can die,
a wise man turn to childishness,
a fine man see his beauty change,
the most courtly man become a churl,
and any churl become courtly.[1]

I n the first half of the fifteenth century, the Lancastrian mantle was passed to two women who shared the same name and royal lineage. One made a spectacular marriage, propelling her to a throne of her own amid a turbulent period of Scottish history, while the other lived more quietly in the north of England as a wife and mother, raising children whose lives would be central to the impending Lancastrian crisis. The stories of these two women named Joan Beaufort illustrate the differing directions in which the dynasty was moving a century after the birth of John of Gaunt. The first is remembered primarily for her influence upon one of the literary classics of the era; a figure of beauty, romance and, ultimately, tragedy. Poetry places her in the spring time: in May 1420, amid the fresh blooms of the royal gardens, where her blonde good looks attracted the attention of a prestigious suitor.

The fictional story of the first Joan's marriage was narrated by a young man standing at a window in Windsor Castle. His heart was heavy, filled with unanswered questions as he contemplated the injustice of the past fourteen years, which he had spent in captivity. In true poetic tradition, he gazed down upon the green lawns and pathways below, which were decorated with wand rails and hawthorn hedges, where thick leaves shaded the walks and the sweet scent of juniper berries filled the air. A nightingale sang above a leafy arbour set in a corner by the tower. There, his eyes lighted upon a woman, 'the fairest or the freshest young flower', with golden hair and rich clothes covered in a fretwork of pearls, rubies, emeralds and sapphires, which echoed the colours of the garden flowers. On her head she wore a chaplet of red, white and blue with quaking, bright gold spangles and around her neck a gold chain from which hung a ruby in the shape of a heart. He fell instantly in love.

The scenario described of the young man in the tower conforms exactly to the ideal of courtly love in medieval complaint poetry. Yet although it has been embroidered and rendered into Chaucerian rhyme royal, it is far more than a just story written to entertain the court circle. Despite its literary flourishes and tropes, this tale is autobiographical, recounting the author's history and of one of the most romantic matches of the century. These descriptions appear in 'The Poet is Transported to the Sphere of Love', the third canton of a six-part work called *The Kingis Quair*, or *The King's Book*, written in Middle Scots by King James I of Scotland. Although he had inherited the throne of Scotland from his father in 1406, when he was 12 years old, he had never been able to exercise his power. As a minor, he had been under considerable danger at home, especially following the suspicious death of his elder brother, and plans were made to send him to safety in France. Yet he never arrived. En route, his ship was captured by pirates, who turned him over to the English and Henry IV had kept his enemy king imprisoned ever since. By 1420, Henry IV was dead and the handsome and accomplished James was a young man of 26. He had been educated in England, entertained and treated well; he was afforded the status of an honoured guest at court and in the homes of the royal family, but not at liberty to return to the kingdom he had inherited. It is plausible that James had looked down from his window one day and seen a beautiful young woman walking in the garden, although the chances are that he had already met her at court. Certainly, he would have already known her name and family. The object of his affection was the teenaged Joan, daughter of Katherine Swynford and John of Gaunt's eldest son, John Beaufort.

John Beaufort, first Earl of Somerset had married Margaret Holland, a granddaughter of Joan of Kent. Between 1400 and 1409, they had six children, of whom Joan was the third born, and the elder of the two girls. As a cousin of Richard II, Joan would have been in the court circle into which the captive King of Scots was brought as a young man, at least on ceremonial occasions and perhaps in the household of Joan of Navarre or Catherine of Valois. She was only around 2 years old when James had been imprisoned and was a child during his two-year stay in the Tower and his sojourn in Nottingham Castle before Windsor Castle was settled as his main residence under the governorship of Sir John Pelham, who also oversaw Joan of Navarre's incarceration. It appears that Henry IV took the responsibility for his royal prisoner seriously and James received an education suitable for a king. The young student was described by the Bishop of Inchcomb as 'another Orpheus' for his musical ability, as well as a 'tower, a lion, a light, a jewel, a pillar and a leader', a sportsman, poet and lawgiver.[2] James served in France in 1420–21, when he assisted Henry V by appealing to the Scots troops who had sided with those of the Dauphin. He attended the coronation of Catherine of Valois and sat in the position of honour on her left at the banquet afterwards. Two months later he was knighted by Henry V at Windsor in the annual St George's Day garter ceremonies and from February 1423 to January 1424 received payments from the English treasury totalling £277. At some point around this time, he met the 16-year-old Joan at court. No doubt, as the poem explains, he was struck by her beauty. It was also a shrewd political match, allying the Scottish throne to that of England, which permitted the young king to finally return home. The terms of his release, drawn up in September 1423, specified that he must marry an aristocratic English woman: was this the prompt for his love, or a response to it?

Despite the advantages the marriage brought to both countries, James' poem makes clear the depth of romantic devotion he felt for his young wife as the embodiment of beauty and liberty. Written in late 1423 and early 1424, immediately after his release had been negotiated, *The Kingis Quair* takes pains to establish that his love is genuine. James explains that his incarceration prevented him from wooing Joan because despite his kingship, being a prisoner of the English created a disparity between their statuses. In the words of Venus, the first goddess to whom he appeals:

> It is no match, of thyne unworthiness
> To hir hie birth, estate and beauty bryt
> … as day is to the nyght
> Or sack cloth is unto fine crimson
> … unlike the crow is to the papejay.

He turned to Minerva, who counselled patience and advised him to set aside lustful thoughts for a more noble form of love:

> Be true, and meek, and steadfast in thy thought
> And diligent her mercy to procure
> Not only in thy word, for word is nought …
> Bot there be mony of so brukill sort
> That feign truth in love for a while
> That set all their wits and disport
> The silly innocent woman to beguile
> And so to win their lusts' wit a while.

In response, James assured the goddess that:

> … I declare the kind of my loving
> Truly and good, without variance
> I love that flower above all other things
> … If this be feigned, I can it not repent
> Although my life should forefeit be therefore.[3]

Just as in the fifth canton of the poem, the wheel of fortune turned for James. The drawn-out negotiations with the Scots for his release were finally concluded in December 1423. The wedding took place the following year, on 12 February, at the Augustan priory of St Mary Overie in Southwark, which is now Southwark Cathedral. The building was an ideal place to celebrate the nuptials, having been extensively repaired by architect Henry Yevele on the orders of the bride's uncle, Henry Beaufort, after severe fire damage during the reign of Richard II. Fittingly for the royal poet, it was also the resting place of the poet John Gower. The church had previously witnessed a royal wedding when Henry IV gave away Lucia Visconti to Edmund Holland, Earl of Kent in 1406, followed by a 'sumptuous, pompous feast' in the great hall at Winchester Palace. James and Joan followed this tradition, feasting their guests in the newly repaired hall overlooked by its rose window, the formal residence of Henry Beaufort. The newly-weds departed soon after and arrived in Scotland at the end of March. Joan was crowned jointly with James at Scone on 21 May, with Henry Wardlaw, Bishop of St Andrews officiating. By this point, she was already pregnant.

Joan awaited the arrival of her first child in Scotland's then capital, Perth, a city on the River Tay, 2 miles from Scone. She is likely to have been in the royal apartments at the thirteenth-century Dominican Friary, one of James' key residences, which was used for parliamentary business as well as being the seat of his court. The seasonal festivities would have been well underway as Joan went into labour, delivering her child on Christmas Day itself. It was a girl, whom she named Margaret, after her mother. Over the next nine years, Joan bore seven more children, five more daughters and twin sons, who arrived at Holyrood Palace in October 1430. The older boy, Alexander, died before his first birthday, making his brother James heir to the Scottish throne. According to tradition, the little boy's face was partially covered by a red birthmark, giving him the nickname 'fiery face' and suggesting a hot temper to his contemporaries.[4] By the time she had reached the age of 30, Queen Joan had filled the royal nursery, all her other children surviving to adulthood. The record of her pregnancies, along with James' poetry, suggests the marriage was a harmonious one, but if she had hoped it would smooth relations between Scotland and England, Joan was mistaken.

As a member of the Lancastrian dynasty and a granddaughter of John of Gaunt, Joan would have been deeply conscious of her political standing. Her father and his Beaufort siblings might have been legitimised but they were barred from inheriting the throne, making her marriage and royal status all the more significant. James was not prepared to follow English policy once he had been restored to his position and accepted offers from France to renew their traditional alliance, including a proposal for the marriage of Princess Margaret to the Dauphin. This match took place in the summer of 1436, when Joan's eldest daughter was only 11.

Little is known about Joan's role as queen. Apart from bearing children, she was the focus of her household, in a complementary sense to the king, as his consort, as the figurehead of pageantry and patronage, as a hostess and symbol, a standard of womanhood and behaviour. As with all queens, she was required to be a visible presence at her husband's side when he received visitors, the charitable, compassionate face of royalty, hearing supplicants and pleas for mercy, such as that of Alexander Macdonald, Lord of the Isles, who had indulged in a campaign of violence in the Highlands in 1429 and was treated leniently on Joan's request. She was also an adornment and the animating heart of his court, which James was increasingly inclined to ornament with signs of his new-found freedom and power. He developed Linlithgow Castle into an alternative royal residence and cultural centre for himself and Joan. Following a fire in 1424, he began a large rebuilding programme, transforming the ruin into an elegant pleasure palace set in a park beside a loch. Over the next thirteen years, construction was underway on the present east wing with its original entrance accessed by a drawbridge and flanked by the royal coat of arms and statues of saints. This wing also included a huge great hall on the first floor measuring 30ft by 100ft, its wide stone fireplace and adjoining kitchens making it a central location for the business and celebrations of the court. The nearby church of St Michael's was also transformed for Joan and her family's use, becoming one of the largest churches in Scotland still in use today.

Most of the surviving documentation of Joan's reign relates to her religious activity. What emerges from her life are the papal petitions she made for the advancement of her servants: her treasurer John de Tibbay, her chaplains John Alyeston and Henry Weston and a friar preacher, John

Leveryche. She shared her piety with her husband, and the papal records show the regular grant of indults to her to choose her own confessor. In 1436, Pope Eugene IV wrote to her urging her to assist James in his attempts to reform the Scottish Church.[5] If Joan was filling the role of peacemaker in certain aspects, her husband's foreign policy may have proved more of a challenge. In the same year as Margaret's French marriage, the seven-year truce with England expired, prompting James to lay siege to the English base of Roxborough Castle on the Scottish border. What Joan felt about this conflict is not recorded.

On 21 February 1437, James and Joan were at Perth, in their royal lodgings at the Dominican Friary, following a meeting of the general council which was held in the city. His uncle, Walter Stewart, the Earl of Atholl, was also present, and deeply dissatisfied with the king's handling of the dispute between the Atholl and Albany branches of the Stewart family. Atholl had been a strong supporter of James' ransom and return to Scotland to claim his throne, but for political or religious differences had turned against the king and allowed a group of assassins into the heart of the court. The plot was intended to remove both James and Joan, and the king was pursued through the friary, romantic legend suggesting he may have hidden under the floorboards or become trapped down an escape tunnel that had recently been blocked off. Joan was wounded but managed to escape with her life. Her husband was murdered. Critically, she retained control of her 6-year-old son James, Duke of Rothesay, now Scotland's new king.

Joan retreated with her children to Dunbar Castle to consider her position. As a widowed queen her position was delicate, especially given the manner of her husband's death and the very real threat that dissatisfied nobles still posed for her and her children. The female narrative of subservience, service and quiet duty was no longer appropriate under the circumstances into which fate had thrust the queen. To protect her son and avenge her husband, Joan needed to take a more dominant role, stepping into the political arena to engage with the men of the council, and her enemies, on an equal footing. On 25 March, young James was crowned at Holyrood Palace and the following day Atholl died a traitor's death in Edinburgh after three days of torture. Yet the future was uncertain. Joan's position and her royal Lancastrian blood qualified her to stand as her son's protector and regent of Scotland, yet the prospect of an English woman taking the reins of power proved unpopular. In 1428 and 1435, her husband had insisted on the northern nobility swearing an oath of loyalty to her in the event of his incapacity or death. In reality, this counted for little. Scotland was not ready to be ruled by a woman. Joan's status placed her above all the lords of the land but it was not enough to erase the perceived incapacities of her gender. Instead, she was forced to submit to the council and the next two years of James' regency were overseen by his first cousin Archibald Douglas, while Joan stepped into the more maternal and less politically charged role of his guardian. She spent those two years based at Dunbar, in the imposing castle that stood on the cliff above the harbour. All might have continued smoothly, had Douglas not succumbed to a fever in June 1439. With rivals from the Douglas, Livingstone and Crichton families keen to step into his shoes, Joan was in need of a protector. She turned to one of Douglas' most loyal supporters.

Joan would have come to know James Stewart of Lorne over the previous two years, if he was not already part of the royal circle. He was the son of the Scottish ambassador to England and, at the age of 40, was either still unmarried or had been widowed. Perhaps his appearance or his armour gave rise to the romantic name of the 'black knight of Lorne', by which he is now known. Exactly when his relationship with Joan shifted from the political to the personal is unclear, but it may well have been triggered by seizure and imprisonment of the young king in Stirling Castle by Alexander Livingstone. Perhaps there was an existing affection between the two or a romantic understanding; perhaps simply it was her confidence in Stewart's loyalty that led Joan to trust him enough to unite herself with him legally and bodily, to afford him the status of her son's stepfather, which gave him the authority to act in her interests. Some degree of planning must have been involved, as the pair required a papal dispensation for consanguinity and affinity.

Any happiness the newly-weds might have snatched out of the jaws of the situation was cut short. The marriage was seen as a sufficient threat for Livingstone to capture and imprison Joan and Stewart separately in Linlithgow Castle, lodging the dowager queen in the castle apartments and James in the dungeon. Perhaps as little as a week elapsed between the nuptials in July and their arrest on 3 August. A month later, Joan agreed to sign an agreement to pardon Livingstone, allow him the custodianship of King James and transfer her dowry to him, to pay for his maintenance. These conditions seem very harsh, the financial clause quite untypical, but it is impossible to know what methods were used to convince the dowager queen to relinquish so much or what penalties she feared, being apart from her children and husband. According to the Auchinleck Chronicle, Joan was 'put in ane chalmer and kepit stratlye tharin', meaning she was kept 'straightly' or strictly, while Stewart was put 'in pittis and bollit', or put into pits and boiled.[6] Subsequent events, which saw the murders of the teenaged sons of Archibald Douglas in the presence of the young king, may have justified her fears.

Joan retreated to her daughters at Dunbar Castle. The narratives of men had forced her back into the place prescribed by her gender. Over the next three or four years, she was occupied with bearing three more sons, John, James and Andrew, waiting until her eldest, the young king, reached his majority and could rule on his own. In the meantime, Joan arranged marriages for her daughters: Isabella married Francis I, Duke of Brittany in 1442, and Mary married Wolfert VI of Borselen in the Netherlands in 1444, establishing trading connections. More questions surround the betrothal history of Joan's fourth daughter, who was named after her. Possibly a mute, Princess Joan had been betrothed in 1440 to James Douglas, Earl of Angus, but he died before the match could take place. In 1445, Joan was sent to France, possibly intended as a bride for the Dauphin following the death of her elder sister, though this match was never made and Joan finally returned to Scotland in 1457. It was in 1444, though, that King James turned 14, the age at which he was considered able to rule alone.

Tensions erupted again in the summer of 1445, when James Stewart was arraigned before Parliament for speaking against Livingstone, who retained the king in Edinburgh Castle. Joan retreated to Dunbar, but Livingstone pursued her there and subjected the castle to a violent siege. On 15 July, Joan was killed during the attack and the castle's keeper Adam Hepburn was forced to surrender 'throu trety'.[7] The details of her demise are unclear, whether or not she was attacked directly or her death was the result of the castle walls collapsing. Nor is it clear whether her demise was Livingstone's intention or if he had hoped to urge her to surrender as a result of force. The killing of a queen, and an English woman of the Lancastrian line, appears to have incited little retaliation from her subjects or her family. If it had occurred at any other time, under a different king, there may well have been questions to answer for the Scottish regent, at the very least. Yet it so happened that at the time of her death, England's focus was directed firmly towards Scotland's traditional ally, France. At the end of that May, Henry VI's new French bride, Margaret of Anjou, was crowned in Westminster Abbey. High-ranking Scotsmen had been invited as guests as a goodwill gesture, and if the summer months were something of a honeymoon for Henry, they were also made tense by the financial and territorial concessions he had to make in order to possess her. In addition, Henry may have been reluctant to break the Anglo-Scottish truces agreed in 1438 and 1444. So while England lost a powerful ally on Joan's death, there was little to be achieved by challenging the new regime.

Joan was buried beside James I in the Carthusian Priory at Perth, although their joint tomb, a 'magnificent monument', was destroyed by a Calvinist mob during the Scottish Reformation of 1559. Like that of her first husband, Joan's death was brutal and sudden, serving as a reminder that gender, status and royal blood offered little protection when the political tide turned. Although she experienced more power in her role as queen, Joan's story shared some elements with that of another Lancastrian woman, the grandmother of two future English kings, and Joan's namesake. In a twist of irony, it was the lives of this woman's descendants, all through the line of John of Gaunt, that would provide the greatest challenge to the Lancastrian dynasty.

Katherine Swynford's daughter by John of Gaunt was also named Joan Beaufort. She was a generation older than her young niece, the Scottish queen, having been born in 1379. After being widowed around the age of 17, she was left with two small daughters but her youth and royal blood made her a good prospect for remarriage. Joan accompanied her mother to France to welcome Isabelle of Valois as Richard II's bride before making a second match of her own. Her new husband was Ralph Neville, Earl of Westmorland, who had declared his loyalty to Henry IV during his period of exile and become his trusted supporter and councillor. This proved to be a durable and successful marriage, with

Joan bearing fourteen more children: nine boys and five girls of whom eleven lived to maturity. Their order of birth is unclear, but it is likely that Katherine was the eldest of the girls for she was married in January 1412, which suggests that she was conceived soon after the wedding, with Richard as the eldest boy, born in 1400, and inheriting the title of Earl of Salisbury.

Since around 1398, Joan had been overseeing her increasing nursery at Raby Castle in Northumberland: a magnificent building set beside a lake in parkland, with extensive kitchens and a large hall which once entertained 700 knights at one sitting. Ralph Neville was certainly an important figure under the Lancastrian dynasty, welcoming Henry IV back from exile, opposing the rebellion of the Earl of Northumberland and, at the end of his career, sitting on the regency council of the young Henry VI. Around 1430, Joan and her family were depicted in the Neville Book of Hours, in a miniature by Pol de Limbourg. Kneeling at the head of a train of her daughters, Joan is dressed piously in black and white, although her cloak and cuffs are lined by ermine and the Lancastrian golden livery S-shape collar hangs around her neck, as a reminder of her connection with her half-brother Henry IV. Her features are delicate, her face framed by her white wimple and hennin, or U-shaped headdress, and her beringed hands are clasped together in prayer. One of the young women behind her, adorned with colourful dresses and jewels, is her last daughter, Cecily.

Joan Neville's final child was born at Raby in May 1415, shortly before Henry V's iconic victory at Agincourt. As Cecily and her siblings were growing up, the family maintained connections with their Lancastrian relatives at court: Joan was named in royal grants as 'the King's sister', and awarded certain privileges like the marriage of royal ward John de Clifford,[8] and in 1421 Joan's eldest son by Neville, Richard, attended Catherine of Valois' coronation at Westminster. Like most aristocratic women of her age, Joan was also concerned with religious questions but perhaps went further than most to explore them, inviting the mystic Margery Kempe to visit her at Raby, and later writing a letter to exonerate her from accusations of corruption. One of Ralph Neville's last acts before he died in October 1425 was to approve the marriage between Cecily and Richard Plantagenet, Duke of York. Joan saw the marriage through, and the young couple became man and wife in the chapel at Raby Castle at some point in the spring of 1429. This marriage would later divide Cecily from her Lancastrian roots during the turbulent middle years of the century which pitched one branch of her family against the other.

Joan Beaufort's mind was firmly focused on her dynasty though. In 1437, she was granted a licence to found a 'perpetual chantry of two chaplains to celebrate divine service daily at the altar before which her mother Katherine, late duchess of Lancaster' was buried, the chantry to be named after Katherine.[9] Although little detail survives about her life, she appears to have exemplified the marital ideals of fruitfulness and piety, as well as a commitment to the inheritance of her children that saw the rights of Ralph's children by his first marriage overturned. When Joan died in November 1440, outlived by only one of her Beaufort brothers, Henry, Bishop of Winchester, she was buried beside her mother in a canopied stone tomb in Lincoln Cathedral. With her namesake the Queen of Scots dying five years later, the 1440s marked a shift for the Lancastrian women, a certain sense of closure on the dynasty's initial propagating family, a moving on from that generation fathered by John of Gaunt. It ushered in a new phase of conflict in which women not only stood up for their family's inheritance and status, but were defining their rights against close blood relations. The chief players in this new chapter were to be Cecily Neville, the first woman whose marriage conflicted with her Lancastrian birth, and the dynasty's new queen, Margaret of Anjou. The enemy was now within.

There was another Lancastrian woman whose life would become intimately bound up with the struggles of the fifteenth century. This was Queen Joan's only sister, Margaret, who was around five years her junior. Margaret was born in around 1409 and was married soon after the year 1421 at the age of 12 or 13, much earlier than her royal sister's match, but perhaps because of the additional prestige it generated. Her husband was Thomas Courtenay, Earl of Devon, who was then also a child, having inherited his earldom in 1422 at the age of 8. The family seat was Colcombe Castle, near the town of Colyton, built during the reign of Edward I. Courtenay was awarded an annuity of £100 by Henry VI for his work on local councils in the West Country and was appointed

High Steward of England at the coronation of Margaret of Anjou. The Countess of Devon bore at least eight children, starting from the early 1430s, which represents a fairly late arrival for a first child by contemporary standards but is comparable to the experience of her contemporary, Cecily Neville. Where it is known, the lives of all Margaret's children were to be curtailed by the coming national conflict between the houses of Lancaster and York. Margaret's first child was Thomas, who became his father's heir and the next duke, and married Mary of Anjou, an illegitimate daughter of the Count of Maine. She also had Henry and John, who would briefly inherit the title from Thomas: all three of her sons would fight for the Lancastrian cause and all three would die in the process, Thomas being executed after Towton in 1461, Henry executed for treason in 1469 and John killed in battle leading the rearguard at Tewkesbury in 1471. Less is known about Margaret's five daughters. Joan would marry Sir Thomas Clifford, who would lose his head after Bosworth in 1485, while Elizabeth became the wife of Sir Hugh Conway, a servant of the future Henry VII. Three other girls born to Margaret, Anne, Eleanor and Maude, may have died young.

What emerges from examining these overlapping lives is that it made an important difference for women whether they had been born into a dynasty or joined it as the result of marriage. For those who were born to members of the Lancastrian family, such as Joan Beaufort, Queen of Scotland or Blanche of Lancaster's daughters Elizabeth and Philippa, or Constance of Castile's only child Catherine, the sense of pride in their birthright was clear and determined their social and marital identities. Sometimes it also allowed them some leeway when their behaviour fell short of expectations, like Isabella, daughter of Edward III, or Elizabeth, daughter of John of Gaunt. However, after marriage, the majority of these women transferred their allegiance to the husbands' families, placing their loyalties very firmly with the future of their children. For Margaret Beaufort and her cousin Joan, Countess of Westmorland, that proved to be an easy decision, as their husbands mounted no challenge to the Lancastrian status. However, when it came to spouses who subsequently changed allegiance, such as Cecily Neville's husband the Duke of York, their wives tended to follow their lead. As those women did, it was wives marrying into the dynasty from another family, even perhaps from another country, who were to wield most influence with their characters, fertility and maternity. Whatever the circumstances of their birth, it was the women who bore children with Lancastrian blood in their veins who moulded the dynasty. Nowhere would that be clearer than in the second half of the fifteenth century.

PART FOUR

POTENTIAL QUEENS, 1437–45

Ryche and pore of al this realm
With whole heart and al lowness
Hem recomaunden to that pryncess.[1]

1

The year 1437 was a watershed for Lancastrian women. The deaths of Catherine of Valois and Joan of Navarre left the country without a queen, without the feminine influence that offered shelter, nurture, patronage and intercession at the heart of government. The household of a queen or dowager, whether the king's wife, mother or grandmother, provided a complimentary balance to the male-dominated court and expanded the nature of royal power in a literal and symbolic way. A queen was a model of piety, motherhood and chastity, visible during public ceremonies and enshrined in manuscripts, images, poetry, ritual and effigy. She provided opportunities for the daughters of the nobility to serve the queen, for young nobles to be raised as the king's wards, and the more passive, gentle power wielded by a queen could be just as significant as that of her husband. While an orphaned minor sat on the throne, representations of rule in England were unbalanced: the previous four kings had understood the significance of royal marriage, so the late 1430s and early 1440s were something of a period in limbo, as Henry VI matured and the prospect of his future marriage was still distant.

The young king turned 16 in December 1437 and although this was later than the usual age of majority, he was declared of age and able to rule in his own right. In practice, though, power at his court still resided in the hands of his uncles Henry Beaufort and Humphrey, Duke of Gloucester, who dismissed his tutor Richard Beauchamp, Earl of Warwick, who had been his closest councillor during the past decade. There was little tangible change for Henry in terms of feminine influence, as both Catherine and Joan had lived in retirement in their final years; his mother due to her remarriage and his stepgrandmother as a result of her age and retirement following her imprisonment. Just by virtue of their existence they had filled a symbolic and dynastic role: their deaths in 1437 altered the order of precedence in the country, propelling three new women into the limelight. For the next four years, Henry's controversial aunt, Eleanor Cobham, Duchess of Gloucester was the highest-ranking lady in the land and until he produced a child of his own, she was potentially England's next queen. Initially their relationship appears to have been good but neither this nor her position prevented her from suffering a spectacular public fall from grace that made Joan of Navarre's imprisonment pale in comparison.

Eleanor was born around 1400 at Starborough or Sternborough Castle, in north-east Kent. The original medieval manor house no longer stands, but at its height, it was an imposing quadrangle with corner turrets, surrounded by a moat, similar to that of its near-contemporary Bodiam Castle, just over the border in East Sussex. Reaching her mid-teens, Eleanor would have been a candidate to be placed in the queen's household, but no such household existed until the arrival of Catherine of Valois five years later and if she had been to Joan of Navarre's court

with her parents, that opportunity was lost in 1419. So Eleanor probably stayed at home at Starborough until another opportunity arose. As a
cousin of Mary de Bohun through her grandmother's second marriage,
Eleanor was closely related to the man who would become her husband.
When she first met him though, he was already married to someone else.

In the early 1420s, an opportunity arose for Eleanor to become lady
in waiting to an important woman whose connections would bring the
girl into the heart of English political life. Jacqueline of Hainault was of a
similar age to Eleanor, perhaps a little older, but she was already a twice-
married exile with a colourful history who had fled to England in March
1421. Jacqueline's first husband had been John, Duke of Touraine, an
elder brother of Catherine of Valois. They were married in The Hague
when he was 8 and John was raised by Jacqueline's father until the death
of the Dauphin Louis made John and Jacqueline next in line for the
French throne. For a brief two years, as Dauphine, Jacqueline could anticipate the day when she became queen, but at the age of 16, she was left a
widow when John died unexpectedly, perhaps as the result of an abscess
or poison. At this point in her life she may have met, or become closer to,
John's sister Catherine, who was just a year or so her junior. This would
also explain why Jacqueline chose her sister-in-law's country as a place
of refuge following a disastrous second match. Her second husband was
John, Duke of Brabant and although she was only slightly older than him,
Jacqueline had stood as his godmother, necessitating a papal dispensation for the degree of spiritual affinity.[2] This was granted in December
1418 but was revoked the following January. The marriage went ahead
anyway that March, but it proved to be unpopular, which contributed
to its failure. Lydgate optimistically wrote how 'that Duchye of Holand
by whole affection may be allied with Brutus Albion'. His epithalamium
composed in honour of Gloucester and Jacqueline referred to the union
of Henry V and Catherine of Valois as a perfect example of matrimony:

And as I hope of hert and mening true
The mortal war cesse shal and fine
Betwene tho bothe and pees againe renew
To make love with cleer beemes shine
By meene of her that highte Katherine,

Joined til oon, his deedes can you tell,
Henry the fifte, of knighthood sours and well.

Jacqueline was depicted by Lydgate, who must have known her, as the
flower of womanhood:

… the floure
Thorough-oute the world called of wommanheed,
True ensaumple and well of al goodenesse,
Benign of port, root of goodlihede,
Sothfast mirror of beautee and fairnesse—
I meene of Holand the goodly fresh duchesse
Called Jaques, whos birth for to termine
Is by descent imperial of line.

His praise of her continued, in perhaps one of the best poetical pen portraits of a woman of her era, and is worth quoting at length:

Ther-to she is discreet and wonder sadde
In her apport, whoso list take heede;
Right avisee and wommanly, also gladde;
And dame Prudence doth ay her bridle leede;
Fortune and Grace, and Raisoun also in deed
In all her workes with her ben allied,
That throughout the world, her name is magnified.
To the poor she is also ful merciable,
Ful of pitee and compassioun,
And of nature list not to be vengeable—
Though it so be she have occasioun—
That I suppose nowe in no regioun
Was never a better at alle assayes founden,
So muche vertu doth in her abounden.
A heven it is to ben in her presence,
Who list consider her governaunce at al,
Whos goodely look in verray existence
So aungelik and so celestial,

So feminine; and in especial
Her eyen sayn 'Whoso look weel
Foryiven is oure wrath, every deel.'
And her colurs ben black, white, and rede;
The red in trouthe tokeneth stablenesse,
And the black, whoso taketh heede,
Signifeth parfyt sobernesse;
The white also is token of cleennesse,
And eek her word is in verray sooth
'Ce bien raysoun' al that ever she dooth.

Jacqueline was welcomed to England in spring 1421 by Catherine and Henry. She lodged with the queen at Windsor Castle, possibly as her companion during the months of her pregnancy, and stood as godmother to her son that December. Eleanor probably became part of Jacqueline's household around this time and, by extension, part of the queen's court, enjoying the fine royal apartments, hunting grounds and formal gardens Windsor had to offer. This was a young, exciting world, where the tone was set by the queen and her friends during her husband's absence, and Eleanor would have encountered Henry V's youngest brother, Humphrey, Duke of Gloucester, a cultivated, strong and popular man then in his thirties. The young Eleanor was described by chronicler Waurin as 'beautiful and marvellously pleasant' but Humphrey's initial interest was directed towards Jacqueline and the political advantage of her rich inheritance. Eleanor would have witnessed the process by which he made her mistress his wife two years after her arrival in England.

It proved to be another controversial marriage for Jacqueline. Gloucester's request for a dispensation was rejected by Vatican Pope Martin V, so the duke sought one instead from Benedict XIII, the Antipope of Avignon, for the Church was still divided between France and Italy. Benedict was willing to grant the necessary paperwork and the marriage was solemnised that February or March 1422 or 1423 at Humphrey's possession, the imposing Hadleigh Castle overlooking the Thames estuary. The French writer Cocqueau pins the event down to 'the month of January in this 22nd year' according to the Gregorian Calendar but in 1427, Jacqueline herself claimed that she was not married until after the death of Henry V. This makes a date of early 1423 more likely, with which R.A. Griffiths, the biographer of Henry VI, agrees.[3] John Lydgate wrote celebratory verses in advance of the occasion, in which he extolled the combination of political gain and personal inclination, as the 'Duchye of Holand by hool affeccoun may be allied with Brutus Albyon' and praised the soon-to-be duchess as beautiful and virtuous.[4] Thus Jacqueline and Catherine became sisters-in-law for the second time.

Whatever the feelings of the bride and groom, the marriage was beneficial to both, affording the exiled Jacqueline protection and a home while Gloucester claimed the titles of Count of Holland, Zeeland and Hainault. Two years later, in the wake of a victory won against the French by his elder brother, John, Duke of Bedford, Gloucester and Jacqueline crossed the Channel in an attempt to defend this possession of the titles which were being disputed by the Duke of Brabant. Gloucester captured Mons and established himself for a while in Hainault before returning to England, forced to conclude that the mission had been nothing less than disastrous. Eleanor accompanied her mistress abroad, and may even have been with her in Ghent when the duke laid siege to the town, but Eleanor appears to have remained at liberty while Ghent imprisoned her mistress. It has been suggested by one historian that having secured his wife's titles for himself, Gloucester made no attempt to bring about her release[5] and simply abandoned her. Gloucester did indeed return to England without Jacqueline, but without knowing the circumstances, this may be an unfair reading of the situation. Instead of his wife, he brought Eleanor back with him, who Waurin claims no longer wanted to remain abroad. By this time, the attraction of remaining with Gloucester may have been as strong as her desire to go home.

Eventually Jacqueline managed to escape, and romantic legend describes her dressing in men's clothing and concealing herself among a group of noblemen. However, she did not return to England, but headed through Holland, where she allied with Philip the Good and continued to defend her lands. Philip was her brother-in-law by his sister Anne's marriage to John, Duke of Bedford. That winter, Gloucester sent an English army to assist Jacqueline and Philip at the battle of Brouwershaven but after their defeat he made no further commitment to her. In fact, he was looking to dissolve the commitment he had already made.

Leicester Castle Gateway. Little now remains of the traditional seat of the earls of Lancaster, but this early fourteenth-century gateway serves as a reminder of its royal past. Leicester Castle was the home of Blanche of Lancaster and her parents and she bore her first child there in 1360. It also witnessed the deaths of her parents and sister, of Constance of Castile and John of Gaunt. (Helen Wells)

Dunstable Swan. This jewel was discovered during excavations at Dunstable Priory in 1965 and is thought to be the same one mentioned in the treasure rolls of Richard II. It was made from gold and enamel, probably in Paris for the de Bohun family, who adopted the chained swan as their symbol, featuring it on their books, jewels and tombs. Today the jewel is housed in the British Museum. (Justin Ennis)

De Bohun Window, Ledbury church. The de Bohun chained swan, featured in a window in the church of St Michael and All Angels in Ledbury, Herefordshire. The area had connections with the de Bohun family as a result of their inheritance of the earldom of Hereford in the thirteenth century. Similar to the Dunstable jewel, this swan wears a gold coronet around its neck but is depicted with its wings slightly outstretched. (Isla Newcombe)

Kenilworth Castle. A major Lancastrian stronghold, Kenilworth was transformed into a royal palace through the improvements made by John of Gaunt in the 1370s. Katherine Swynford gave birth to at least one of her sons there, as did Mary de Bohun. Eleanor Cobham was also imprisoned there and Margaret of Anjou fortified the castle further, as a precaution, during the Wars of the Roses. (David Merett)

Rochford Manor. The present manor hall in Rochford, Essex, is later in date than the property the earls of Hertford owned in the fourteenth century. On this site, the older manor would have been well known to Mary de Bohun, who celebrated her marriage here with a feast and music played by minstrels sent by Edward III. (Paul Fairbrass)

Monmouth Castle. Monmouth stands on the southern end of the border between England and Wales, a part of Mary de Bohun's inheritance from the earldom of Hereford. It was here in September 1386 that she gave birth to her eldest child, the future Henry V, tradition has it in a chamber above the gatehouse. (Philip Blayney)

Raby Castle. In 1397, Joan Beaufort, the daughter of John of Gaunt and Katherine Swynford, made a second marriage to Ralph Neville, Earl of Westmorland. She went to live at his family home of Raby Castle in County Durham and bore him fourteen children. The youngest of these was Cecily Neville, whose marriage to the Duke of York forced her into opposition with her Lancastrian roots. (Kristie Davis Dean)

Lincoln Cathedral. John of Gaunt took Katherine Swynford as his third wife in the cathedral in 1396. After his death, she lived out her final days at a property known as The Chancery in the precincts. When she died in May 1403, Katherine was buried under a stone canopy in the cathedral and her daughter Joan was laid to rest beside her in 1437. (David Merrett)

Windsor Castle. In use throughout the period, Windsor Castle was the location of James I of Scotland's poem *The Kingis Quair*, in which he is thought to portray himself catching sight of the Earl of Somerset's daughter, Joan Beaufort, and falling in love with her. The castle was a favourite of Catherine of Valois, who bore Henry VI there in December 1421. Catherine also lived there during the first part of her widowhood, with Jacqueline of Hainault, who became her sister-in-law by her marriage to the Duke of Gloucester. (Khalid B. Al-Ajmi)

Leeds Castle. The beautiful Leeds Castle sitting amid rolling landscape in the Kent countryside was traditionally granted to English queens by their husbands, Anne of Bohemia receiving it from Richard II and Henry IV giving it to Joan of Navarre on their marriage. However, it later became Joan's prison, when she was sent there for three months in 1422. (Amy Licence)

Prince Henry of Wales. The relationship between the prince and his father, Henry IV, had not always been an easy one. The prince became king in 1413 and, for a while, his step-mother the dowager queen was the leading lady in the land. When Henry's focus shifted from his French campaigns to marriage, he required funds in order to welcome his bride to England. This may have prompted his decision to accuse his stepmother of witchcraft and strip her of her assets. Henry repented shortly before his death in 1422 and Joan was released after three years. (Simon Rowe)

Tomb of Henry IV and Joan of Navarre. This tomb, located in the Trinity Chapel of Canterbury Cathedral, was commissioned by Joan of Navarre, probably in the 1420s or '30s. It was made of alabaster, painted and enamelled, emphasising their union and regality. Joan was interred there on 6 August 1437. (Amy Licence)

Raglan Castle. The impressive home of the Earl of Pembroke, Raglan became home to the young Henry Tudor after his custody was granted to the earl. During her second marriage, Margaret Beaufort was able to write to her son and occasionally visit him, although they were not permitted to live together. (Amy Licence)

SI VOUS NE RESPECTEZ UNE REINE PROSCRITE
RESPECTEZ UNE MERE MALHEUREUSE

Margaret of Anjou. For years, Margaret followed the model of contemporary queenship, playing the part of a pious and devoted wife of great energy and character. However, she was not prepared to stand aside in the mid-1450s and watch her husband and son be displaced. She chose to fight for her position, although she was inexperienced and faced formidable opponents. (Deborah Esrick)

Edward IV. Cecily Neville's marriage to the Duke of York placed her in opposition to the Lancastrian regime. In 1460, after Margaret's army was responsible for killing York and his son Edmund at the battle of Wakefield, there could be no reconciliation between Cecily and the woman she had welcomed in Rouen. Early in 1461, Cecily's 18-year-old son returned to avenge his father and, after decisive victories at Mortimer's Cross and Towton, was crowned as Edward IV. (Amy Licence)

Maxstoke Castle. Margaret Beaufort's second marriage to Lancastrian Sir Henry Stafford took place in January 1458, at the beautiful location of Maxstoke Castle in Warwickshire. The chapel was situated to the north of the great hall with a large window in the western wall; the wedding feast would have followed in the hall. (Steve Wilson)

The Union Rose, Canterbury Cathedral. Upon the marriage of Henry Tudor and Elizabeth of York in January 1486, the dynasties of Lancaster and York were united. The symbols of the white rose of York and the red Lancastrian rose were united to create the union rose, examples of which can be found carved into the fabric of buildings and painted on walls and manuscripts. (Paul Fairbrass)

Elizabeth of York. She became the
first Tudor queen, living closely
and in apparent harmony with her
mother-in-law Margaret Beaufort.
She bore seven, perhaps eight,
children before dying after childbirth
in the Tower of London in 1503.
(Amanda Miller)

Their marriage may already have been in trouble, or else the failure of its primary purpose prompted both parties to abandon it and, just at the moment the duke wanted out, the opinion of the papacy turned in his favour. John of Brabant had died in 1425 but Pope Martin now ruled that Jacqueline's second marriage had been valid, meaning that any union she contracted before Brabant's death was not legal, which sounded the death knell of her match with Gloucester. The ruling left Jacqueline in a state of personal and political limbo, especially since, as some historians suggest, she may have experienced a miscarriage or lost a child the year before.[6] There were no surviving children from the union, potential heirs to the English throne, to bind Gloucester to her and it may have been with this factor in mind that he took Eleanor as his lover. Gloucester and Jacqueline did not see each other again.

For Eleanor, the transition from lady in waiting to duchess was considerable. Supplanting her mistress in Gloucester's bed made her complicit in Jacqueline's downfall and, later, her divorce, in a way which is unlikely to have made her popular among the former duchess' peers, or the circle around Queen Catherine. It was not uncommon for a man of the duke's status to take a mistress from among his wife's women, as John of Gaunt had done, or even to make her his wife, but Gaunt had waited until his duchess died before marrying Katherine Swynford. Gloucester's actions, especially his perceived abandonment of Jacqueline, attracted considerable contemporary censure. A petition to Parliament on Jacqueline's behalf in late 1427, carried by the mayor and aldermen, makes clear that the relationship was not only widespread knowledge, but that it was widely condemned. According to Stowe, a group of London women called for Gloucester to set aside 'his wanton paramour … another adultresse, contrary to the law of God and honourable estate of matrimony', in favour of his wife. Having written verses in praise of Jacqueline's marriage, for which he was probably commissioned by Gloucester, Lydgate may be the author of the 1428 poem 'Complaint for my Lady of Gloucester', which describes how the rich and poor of the whole realm 'with whole heart and all lowness', recommended themselves to Jacqueline because 'she is beloved so entierely thorughe all the londe',[7] and widens her support to include more than just the women of London:

Herde in alle citees and alle townes
Howe wymmen made theyre orisons
Desirous that princess to see
And for her coming ransomed to be.[8]

The poem also describes Eleanor and her ladies as 'of courage serpentine' who used 'all their power and their might' to turn Gloucester's heart against 'right' and double his love for his mistress. Such a suggestion might foreshadow the later charges of witchcraft that would be brought against Eleanor. Given this and the later patronage Lydgate enjoyed from Gloucester, these verses may well have been penned by another figure close to the ducal household.

Two illegitimate children have been ascribed to Gloucester during this period and many historians suggest that Eleanor was their mother. The existence of Arthur, known as Arteys de Cursey, and Antigone Plantagenet does not answer many questions about Gloucester's relationship with Eleanor, even though their suggested birthdates of the mid- to late 1420s would fit with the initial phase of their affair. However, in January 1428, when Gloucester finally annulled his marriage to Jacqueline and married Eleanor, it is telling that no attempt was made to legitimise the children. Given Eleanor's later recorded desire to bear Lancastrian heirs who would have been next in line to the throne after Henry VI, it seems unlikely that Gloucester would have passed up the opportunity to do so, especially given the precedent of the Beaufort family's retrospective reinstatement. John of Gaunt had legitimised his children by Katherine Swynford in September 1396 and they had only been barred from the royal succession by Henry IV in 1407, although such bars could be overturned by Parliament. Another possibility is that Antigone and Arthur were borne by another mistress of Gloucester while he was in France during the campaign of 1424–25. It also appears that following their marriage, Eleanor either did not conceive again or did not carry a child to term.

Jacqueline's feelings about being so easily set aside by Gloucester have gone unrecorded. The resulting changes in her status and wealth were significant, though. After Queen Catherine and the dowager queen Joan, she had been the most high-ranking woman in the land but her financial situation descended into desperation after the failure of her marriage to Gloucester. An entry made in the Close Rolls at Westminster on 18 May 1428, referring to Jacqueline by the Dutch name 'Jacoba', grants safe conduct to Arnold de Gent, a merchant who was transporting certain items from England to the ex-countess. She is likely to have been staying at the Binnenhof complex in The Hague at this point, weeks before signing the Treaty of Delft, which allowed her to retain her titles. Among the goods intended for her were 34yd of grey material from Monstrevilliers in France and 13yd of a different shade of grey, 7.5yd of 'moray' or murray cloth, dyed in grain with a kind of red-purple, 10.5yd of red, 22yd of green, 18yd of white, 2.5yd of 'brunet' or brown, 12yd of red satin and what may have been clothing for her servants: two white kerseys, which were made from coarse saye and three mantles furred with rabbit skin, although Jacqueline's status permitted her to wear ermine. The shipment also contained tuns of rye, grain and flour for her kitchens.[9] Jacqueline married for a fourth time in 1434 and died two years later at Teylingen Castle in the Netherlands.

Gloucester had no intention of returning to Jacqueline, and married Eleanor soon after the annulment of his first match. This may have taken place at Hadleigh again, where the couple probably lived before Gloucester began work on transforming his manor of Bella Court at Greenwich, or at Hornsey Manor, then in Middlesex. The following year, Gloucester oversaw arrangements for Henry VI's formal coronation, so it is certain that Eleanor would have attended. Once again, John Lydgate was called upon to record the occasion, producing one of the most detailed accounts of the menu and subtleties served at a royal feast. Seated in Westminster Hall as the new Duchess of Gloucester, Eleanor would have enjoyed boars' heads set in pastry castles of gold, slices of red jelly with white lions carved into them, fritters like suns with fleurs-de-lys set in them, roast peacock in its plumage, pork pies decorated with leopards and gold, and a cold meat pie in the shape of a shield, quartered red and white and set with lozenges, gilt and borage flowers. Adorning the table were three carved subtleties: one of the young king himself, carried by St Edward and St Louis; another of Henry VI kneeling before his father and the Holy Roman Emperor; and a third of the figures of St George and St Denis presenting the king to the Virgin Mary.

Gloucester had recovered some of the respect he had lost as a result of his personal life by 1431, when Lydgate began writing his *Fall of Princes*, which depicted the duke as an able governor and soldier who was pious and cultured. In the same year, Gloucester and Eleanor were received into the confraternity of St Albans. It was a long-standing affiliation for the two, who may have first visited it together back in 1423, when Gloucester celebrated Christmas there with Jacqueline. An illustration from around 1460 depicting their reception at St Albans can be found in the Cotton Nero D. vii manuscript in the British Library, with a generic Eleanor dressed in a long dark robe, what might be an 'S' shaped collar and coronet atop her black headdress. On 6 March 1437, Gloucester and Eleanor were granted a licence to 'impark', or create a park of 200 acres on the north Kent bank of the Thames, to crenellate their manor house and build and crenellate a tower within the park. Their existing Bella Court became a fitting home for two of the most important people in the realm. On the death of his elder brother John in 1435, Humphrey had become heir to the throne, with only the teenaged king standing between Eleanor and queenship. Gloucester was also the sole surviving legitimate adult male member of the Lancastrian dynasty. This made him and his wife easy targets for rivals who hoped to gain control over the young king.

11

In June 1441, a number of members of Eleanor's household were arrested, including her clerk Roger Bolingbroke, her chaplain John Home and her astrologer Thomas Southwell, and accused of using black magic and imagining the king's death. Understanding the danger she was in, Eleanor fled to sanctuary at Westminster. An investigation was begun under the aegis of Gloucester's main rival, Henry VI's steward of the household, William de la Pole, Duke of Suffolk, who was also a close ally of Henry Beaufort. According to Gloucester's biographer K.H. Vickers, Eleanor made an attempt to escape, fleeing downriver perhaps in an attempt to reach the open sea and sanctuary abroad, but was captured and returned to London in order to stand trial.[10] On 23 July, Bolingbroke was questioned and made a public declaration of his guilt at St Paul's Cross, surrounded by the instruments of his art. Two days later, Henry Chichele, Archbishop of Canterbury made a statement in St Stephen's Chapel, Westminster's political centre, regarding 'certain crimes wherein she was detected proceeding', and ordered that Eleanor should be detained 'in the company of persons sworn to keep her' at Leeds Castle. The following day Eleanor was questioned by Chichele, John Kemp, Bishop of London and Henry Beaufort. It was put to her that she and her associates had invoked evil spirits and demons and created a waxen image of the king in an attempt to predict the future; specifically, how long Henry VI would live and whether Eleanor would become queen.[11] She admitted certain charges, but denied treason and insisted she had only turned to sympathetic magic in order to help her conceive a child by Gloucester. A woman named Margery Jourdemayne, the 'witch of Eye', had reputedly furnished her with certain potions for the purpose.

Jourdemayne was a controversial figure whose history exposes the fragility of women's reputations in the field of medicine and its overlap with such ill-defined areas as astrology, ritual and magic. She was married to William, who came from a prosperous yeoman family and was acting as a manorial official on the Westminster Abbey estate in Ebury, or Eye, around the current Bayswater Road and Oxford Street areas of London. Margery had previously come to the attention of the authorities in 1430, when she had been arrested along with other sorcerers and accused of plotting the king's death by magic. She spent the period from November that year until May 1432 in prison, and was then released on condition that she eschew witchcraft and that her future behaviour be good. At some point in the 1430s she was consulted by Edmund Beaufort, to whom she imparted the legend that he would die in a castle. After Jourdemayne's death, the prophecy was fulfilled to a degree when Beaufort met his end on the threshold of the Castle Inn during the first Battle of St Albans.

Two likely explanations emerge for Jourdemayne's association with Eleanor: that of the art of prediction and that of problems associated with women's health. Astrology, horoscopes and other methods of divination were commonly practised at the time, having especial resonance in an era which had witnessed the sudden, devastating effects of plague, as well as the early deaths of two Lancastrian kings from illness. The positions of the planets, astrological symbols, dust, dreams and even the colour of urine were used as diagnostic tools for a range of events from the small-scale to the fall of monarchs. In particular, the phenomena of the natural world were examined, and the appearance of comets, storms, freak weather conditions and eclipses were analysed and interpreted. There was nothing harmful in this. It was believed that divine power was manifest in such ways, so they could be warnings or signs of disapproval which needed to be read correctly. The behaviour of animals could be portentous too and remained within the Church's remit. Thirteenth-century Thomas of Chobham, the subdean of Salisbury Cathedral believed that a dog howling in the house would be soon followed by a death and, a century later, a monk from Chester, Ranulph Higden, believed that the call of a crow indicated the impending arrival of a visitor.[12] This was a far less expensive method of seeking reassurance about the future than consulting with a trained astrologer. However, those who could afford to do so would call upon an elite of university-educated men to draw up specific charts according to the positions of the stars and planets. At her trial Eleanor confessed to having a long association with such men, as well as with Margery: she had also given Gloucester a book of medicinal magic, so he was certainly at the very least aware of her interest.

Margery's reputation was likely to have been built upon medical knowledge. Although the profession would not be formally regulated until the reign of Henry VIII, there was a strong oral tradition of women practitioners: older women who had learned which herbs cured certain complaints and passed this on through the generations, and others who attended births or tended the sick on the battlefield. A proliferation of herbals dating from Anglo-Saxon times through to John Gerard and Nicholas Culpeper shows the strength and accessibility of this tradition, when women would have been able to find ingredients in their gardens and growing in the wild. Often the processes of preparing, consuming and applying such remedies were accompanied by chants, rituals or the wearing of charms. Even this was considered acceptable, as fifteenth-century Benedictine monk Robert Rypon clarified, 'as long as nothing is intended other than the honour of God and the health of the sick person'.[13] No doubt some of their remedies did make a difference, when we consider just how far simple herbs like peppermint and fennel are still in use to cure ailments today, along with ingredients such as willow bark, honey and garlic. It is easy to see how such women, achieving some degree of success, could attract accusations of witchcraft.

In terms of the two charges made against Eleanor, the outcome of Southwell and Bolingbroke's divination was considered treasonous. Eleanor herself may or may not have intended it to be, as drawing up the king's horoscope was not in itself a crime and, had the prediction been for a long and happy life, Eleanor's position may never have been questioned. It was the nature of the future identified by Bolingbroke which caused the problem, coupled with the use of a black mass and the presence of a wax figurine, which was considered a method of causing bodily harm rather like a modern voodoo doll. By illustrating a possible threat to the health of Henry VI through serious illness in the summer of 1441, Bolingbroke and Southwell highlighted Gloucester's status as heir and Eleanor's potential succession as queen. Just how much Eleanor was hoping for this outcome as an indicator of her own rise to power cannot be known.

Eleanor's association with Jourdemayne may have been a completely separate matter. At her trial, the duchess admitted she had used the woman's services for years, having sought assistance in conceiving a child, and that other women in her circle had also sought her advice. Apparently, Jourdemayne had given Eleanor drinks and medicines to make Gloucester fall in love with her and, later, she prescribed Eleanor certain remedies which were intended to help her conceive a child. A number of recipes to aid fertility were included in texts like *Bald's Leechbook*, such as agrimony boiled in ewe's milk, along with other popular methods such as drinking rabbit's blood and mare's milk or boiling chestnuts, pistachios and pine nuts in sugar and ragwort. Jourdemayne may have been supplying Eleanor with these or similar concoctions with a view to her future child inheriting the throne from the then unmarried Henry VI. The 1560 *Mirror of Magistrates* may have exaggerated Margery's powers for dramatic effect when it claimed she could charm fiends and fairies alike, 'and dead corpses from grave she could uprear, such an enchantress as that time had no peer'. If nothing else, Jourdemayne's herbs might have had a placebo effect that allowed Eleanor to believe she was exercising a degree of control over her fertility. Besides Eleanor's proximity to the throne, the pressure on women in general to conceive and bear healthy children was great and the fear of failure must have been profound, especially when Gloucester was the last of Henry IV's surviving sons. The future of the Lancastrian dynasty, which had seemed secure given the large family borne by Mary de Bohun, had only succeeded in producing one grandson, Henry VI. There was much riding on Eleanor's shoulders.

The attack on Eleanor is likely to have been politically motivated, a way of discrediting Gloucester and removing his influence from the throne. It highlights the vulnerability of women even at the top, offering clear parallels to the charges levelled at Joan of Navarre in 1419, with whom Eleanor had enjoyed a friendly relationship. According to Vickers, Gloucester was tainted by association with Joan's case for back then he had defended Friar John Randolf, the man accused of invoking the black arts in Joan's service. This connection would make it all the easier to believe that the duke was guilty or implicit in his wife's guilt. The attack on a woman's character, on the notion of good fame which was central to her reputation, was serious and permanent. Once a good reputation was tarnished, it was lost forever and could have ramifications for her family that affected the line of succession and the careers of those close to her. Some writers of the fifteenth century certainly saw Eleanor's fall, or rather the exploitation of her weakness, to be a cynical attack upon a woman in order to damage a man. The London-based chronicler Robert Fabyan would have still heard stories about Eleanor's disgrace when he was apprenticed to a draper in 1470. When he came to write an account of the city's history, he was certain that the attack on the duchess was part of a larger plan to remove Gloucester's influence over the young king. Some went so far as the point the finger at Gloucester's own family, at his cousins in the Beaufort line. The Beauforts benefitted from the scandal. In the aftermath, Gaunt's grandson and namesake John was awarded an annuity of 600 marks and elevated in precedence over the Duke of Norfolk in acknowledgement of his royal blood, while his younger brother Edmund was made second Duke of Somerset.

Eleanor was sent to Leeds Castle on 11 August, under the guardianship of two valets of the crown, Sir John Stiward and Sir John Stanley.[14] There is no question of her being unaware of the nature of Joan of Navarre's incarceration and, additionally, she may have known that it was Leeds Castle where the former queen had been kept. The parallels were all too clear, but Eleanor was no undefended widow. She was a married woman, the highest-ranking woman in the land, and may have hoped that her position would cushion her and that her husband would come to her defence. Perhaps she thought of Jacqueline abandoned in Mons. Alternatively, she may have understood just how comprehensively her disgrace had robbed Gloucester of his influence. Historian Susanne Saygin suggests that the duke's gift to Oxford University of a number of books on divination, including Appuleius' *De Magia*, was an attempt to save himself and Eleanor by impressing councillors with their scholarly worth, but this was a very indirect effort and had little or no effect.[15] It is just as possible that the gift, which represented a proportion of a very considerable library of English and Italian humanists and was part of a sequence of gifts Gloucester made to the university, had nothing to do with Eleanor's arrest at all.

Eleanor was brought before an ecclesiastical court on 21 October and questioned by the Archbishop of Canterbury. She admitted using astrology and procuring remedies from Margery Jourdemayne in order to conceive, but denied treasonous intent. Bolingbroke admitted that he had practised the art of divination, or attempting to predict the future at Eleanor's request, naming a specific incident which took place at Hornsey Park, where he used certain instruments to foretell the future and Thomas Southwell had recited a black mass.[16] Hornsey Lodge, a residence of the dukes of Gloucester, was no stranger to controversy and potential threats to kings: in 1386, it had been the place where Thomas of Woodstock gathered the Lords Appellant to launch their challenge to Richard II. Norden's *Speculum Britanniae* of 1593 recorded the remains of the Lodge, which appeared to be more like a castle: 'the hill is trenched with two deep ditches, now old and overgrown with bushes; the rubble thereof, as brick, tile, and Cornish slate, are in heaps yet to be seen.' Writing at the end of the eighteenth century, Daniel Lysons identified the remains of the moat in the neighbouring field. This property would no doubt have been Eleanor's home for a significant portion of her married life, alongside La Plesaunce, and no doubt she chose it as the scene of her activities for its convenience and privacy: this is not an indicator that she was guilty of treason, but that she was aware that the use of the black arts involved a 'perversion of holy things'[17] which could damage Gloucester's reputation for piety.

Eleanor's denials fell on deaf ears. On 23 October she was found guilty of all charges levelled against her. Thomas Southwell had died in the Tower, though it is not clear whether this was from natural causes or the result of torture. Historian Michael Miller states that Henry VI had given instructions that Eleanor should be spared torture, which rather implies the men were not.[18] John Home was released but Bolingbroke and Jourdemayne were sentenced to death for their role in the affair. Bolingbroke was hung, drawn and quartered and his head was displayed on London Bridge. Jourdemayne was burned at the stake.

Eleanor had to wait two weeks to learn her fate. On 6 November, in an extraordinary move, she was pronounced formally divorced from Gloucester and, three days later, sentenced to the public penance of walking barefoot through the streets of London accompanied by the mayor and sheriffs. On 13 November 1441, she walked from Temple Stairs to St Paul's 'openly barehede with a Keverchef on her hede', and 'with a meke and a demure countenance', carrying a 2lb taper which she left at the high altar. That Wednesday she performed the same actions from the Swan Stairs in Thames Street to Christchurch in Aldgate and on Friday from Queenhithe to St Michael's in Cornhill.[19] It must have been doubly humiliating for Eleanor to be so publicly punished, especially as she was forced to walk through the crowded streets she may have hoped to one day pass along to her coronation. Shakespeare described the onlookers in *Henry VI, Part Two*: 'Look! how they gaze. See! how the giddy multitude do point, And nod their heads, and throw their eyes on thee.'

One version of the anonymous poem 'The Lament of the Duchess of Gloucester' written in 1441 has Eleanor lamenting her actions, her 'mysgovernance', in a way that absolves Gloucester from any blame and stresses her humble origins. It also turns her into a figure with didactic importance, a warning to womankind in general against the sins of pride and ambition:

As I that was browght up of nowght
A prince has chosen me to his make.
My sofferen [sovereign] lord so to for-sake
Yt was a dulfull destenye
Alas! for to sorow how shuld I slake
All women may be ware by me.

Eleanor Cobhams's trial had an impact upon the treatment of women under English law. In 1442, the existing right for a peer of the realm to be tried by his equals in cases of treason and felony was extended to his wife. For a significant moment, the female narrative punctuated that of the masculine world.

Eleanor was to remain incarcerated for the rest of her life. Like Joan, her private allowance of 100 marks a year was generous enough, but her political significance was far too great to allow her any degree of freedom. She had been sent to Leeds Castle under the guardianship of its constable, Sir John Steward, the King's Master of the Horse, but after her sentencing she was handed over to Sir Thomas Stanley, controller of the royal household. Stanley was then in his late thirties and came from a family with long associations with the governance of Ireland, a tradition which he had continued on his appointment to the lieutenancy between 1431 and 1436. His career would also become particularly bound up with the Lancastrian dynasty as a chief steward of the duchy, and as a result of his birth in Lancashire, he would later represent the county in Parliament.

In June 1442, Stanley moved Eleanor from Leeds to Chester Castle, another property of which he was constable. The original Norman castle had been significantly developed under Henry III and Edward I, but Eleanor was housed in the crypt of the twelfth-century stone gateway to the inner bailey, now known as the Agricola Tower. In October 1443 custody of Eleanor was handed over to Ralph Boteler, Lord Sudeley, constable of the Lancastrian stronghold of Kenilworth Castle. She remained there for almost three years but then rumours arose of a possible rescue bid[20] and she was returned to her former gaoler's custody. In 1446, Stanley took her to the isolation of the Isle of Man in the Irish Sea, of which he had been declared king by Henry IV in 1405. Eleanor was probably lodged in Castle Rushen, an imposing limestone bastion with outer walls 7ft thick. The isle was remote enough to preclude rescue attempts, and had a reputation for witchcraft, folklore and fairies.

Michael Drayton's *England's Heroic Epistles* of 1603 contains a fictional letter written in rhyming couplets by Eleanor to Gloucester during the time of her exile on the Isle of Man. The fictional Eleanor admits using magic in the past but protests that she never won Gloucester's love by foul means, before lamenting her fate:

Where's Greenewich now, thy Elnors Court of late?
where she with Humfrey held a princely state.
That pleasant Kent, when I abroade should ride,
That to my pleasure, layd forth all her pride;
The Thames, by water when I tooke the ayre,
Daunc'd with my Barge in lanching from the stayre,
The anchoring ships, that when I pass'd the roade
were wont to hang their chequered tops abroad;
How could it be, those that were wont to stand,
To see my pompe, so goddesse-like on land,
Should after see mee mayld vp in a sheete,
Doe shamefull penance, three times in the streete?
Rung with a bell, a Taper in my hand,
Bare-foote to trudge before a Beedles wand;
That little babes, not hauing vse of tongue,
Stoode poynting at me as I came along.
Wher's Humfreys power, where was his great command,
Wast thou not Lord-protector of the Land?
Or for thy iustice, who can thee denie,
The title of the good Duke Humfrey?

The equally fictional Gloucester offers consolation in a return letter, promising their union has not been lessened and that they will be reunited after death:

Thou art a Princesse, not a whit the lesse.
Whilst in these breasts we beare about this life,
I am thy husband, and thou art my wife;
Cast not thine eye on such as mounted be,
But looke on those cast downe as low as we;
For some of them which proudly pearch so hie,
Ere long shall come as low as thou or I.
They weepe for ioy, and let vs laugh in woe,
We shall exchange when heauen will haue it so.

But the real duke and duchess were never to have their happy ending and probably did not see each other after 1441. Were they even allowed to write to each other? It seems unlikely. Although at least one later chronicler suggested that Gloucester was plotting to release his wife, there is no contemporary evidence to support this. Less than a year after Eleanor had been taken to the Isle of Man, the tensions underlying her arrest erupted and a plot was launched against Gloucester by the Beauforts. In February 1447, Gloucester was invited to a meeting of Parliament at Bury St Edmunds and, perhaps suspecting a plot, arrived with an armed guard. He was intercepted by Sir Thomas Stanley and placed under arrest in his lodgings at St Salvator's, where he died in his bed five days later, reputedly of natural causes brought about by the shock. No rumours circulated at the time that he had been murdered, and it would have been impolitic to do so in the climate of the moment. Gloucester's body was openly displayed to the public in Bury St Edmunds' Abbey church the day after his death to dispel any rumours that his death had been the result of violence. Within a couple of years though, the myth of the 'Good Duke Humphrey' was being harnessed by enemies of the Lancastrian dynasty who saw Humphrey as the victim of his own family, and the rebels of 1450 accused the unpopular minister William de la Pole, Duke of Suffolk of drowning Gloucester. A Yorkist sympathiser, writing in the 1460s claimed that the duke had fallen victim to a plot of malicious slander[21] orchestrated by Suffolk and Lord Saye, both of whom were killed by the mob during Jack Cade's rebellion in 1450.

It is not known whether Eleanor's guardian, Sir William Beauchamp, informed her of Gloucester's death. Parliament was keen to establish that the duke's marriage to Eleanor Cobham had been fully dissolved in 1441, legislating to ensure that she was unable to claim dower or jointure from her former husband's estates. Two years later, in March 1449, Eleanor was moved to another remote location at Beaumaris Castle, Anglesey, still under the care of Sir William Beauchamp. It was there that she died on 7 July 1452. Unlike her friend Joan of Navarre, she never regained her freedom. By this point, Henry VI had been married for seven years and not produced an heir. The Lancastrian dynasty was threatened with a very real possibility of extinction, especially given the fecundity of their closest rival, Richard, Duke of York, who was preparing to welcome his twelfth child. Between Gloucester's death in February 1447 and the eventual arrival of a prince in December 1453, two main figures vied for the position of king's heir. They were Edmund Beaufort, Duke of Somerset, the eldest of Gaunt's grandchildren, who was reputed to have had an affair with Catherine of Valois, and Richard, Duke of York, who was descended from both Edmund of Langley and Gaunt's older brother, Lionel of Antwerp. The question of birth order, inheritance and precedence would become significant in the coming years. For almost seven years, this made their wives Eleanor, Duchess of Somerset and Cecily, Duchess of York, the most powerful women in the land. A third important woman during this period was the widow of Gloucester's brother John, Duke of Bedford, who had died in 1435. The young and beautiful Jacquetta of Luxembourg quickly remarried to a Lancastrian knight, but she and her children were to find themselves at the heart of the approaching conflict.

12

MARGARET OF ANJOU, 1445–60

Uneasy lies the head that wears a crown.[1]

¶

By 1445, Cecily, Duchess of York was in Rouen. It was a prosperous city of tall, half-timbered buildings clustered around squares and narrow, winding streets, set on the Seine in the heart of Normandy. Following her marriage to Richard, Duke of York and his appointment as Lieutenant of France, Joan Beaufort's youngest daughter had left England in 1441. Life in Rouen cannot always have been easy. It had a long history of warfare with the English, culminating in the terrible seven-month siege of 1418–19, during which Henry V had starved the inhabitants. Many who were expelled from the city were refused permission to leave by the English army, and so they were forced to die in the ditch which was part of the city's defences while those inside resorted to eating vermin. Stories of the atrocities committed by English soldiers were still strong in living memory and negative associations with the Lancastrian dynasty continued. After its fall, the city was placed in the hands of Henry's brother John, Duke of Bedford, who had lived on the outskirts in his pleasure palace, the castle of Joyeux Repos. In 1431, Bedford had been responsible for the trial and execution of Joan of Arc, the young visionary who had burned to death for witchcraft in the market square. Bedford had died just four years later and had been buried in a magnificent tomb in Rouen Cathedral. He was survived by his second wife, Jacquetta, a beautiful young woman of 19. Now Cecily found herself at the heart of the English–French conflict, and also part of its solution.

Cecily and Richard had been resident in Rouen Castle for four years when instructions came from England regarding the king's marriage. At the age of 23, Henry VI was about to take a French wife, who would hopefully bear the children who would ensure the continuation of the Lancastrian dynasty. The duke was to accompany her for part of her journey and the duchess would receive her in Rouen. The city and its castle went into preparation, planning a huge pageant and other events to celebrate the bride's stay. By this point, Cecily already had four children of her own: a girl, Anne, who had been born before they left England and three more who had arrived in France, Edward in 1442, Edmund in 1443 and Elizabeth in 1444. By a twist of fate, it is likely that Bedford's widow Jacquetta was also in the city, as part of Cecily's extended household. When the Yorkists had departed for France back in 1441, *Gregory's Chronicle* records that Jacquetta's second husband, Sir Richard Wydeville, accompanied them, and Henry VI's biographer R.A. Griffiths states that his wife accompanied him.[2] Jacquetta may even have had her children Anthony, Anne, John and Elizabeth with her. Thus the key players of the coming decades were assembled in one place at the same time, including the future Edward IV and his wife Elizabeth, preparing to welcome Margaret of Anjou, the queen they would eventually depose.

The arrival of Queen Margaret was to prove decisive for the Lancastrian dynasty. She was to be a new hope, to represent the rejuvenation and future of the line, to furnish the king with a large family and a strong, reliable consort to protect the Lancastrian inheritance. The feisty and determined Margaret would take these responsibilities seriously, proving herself to be more than capable of sovereignty and defending the positions of her husband and son to the utmost of her abilities against incredible odds. In many ways, it was not a particularly good match for the King of England. The 15-year-old Margaret may have been the niece of Charles VI, but she was the youngest daughter of René, Duke of Anjou, whose impressive array of titles included the kingdoms of Sicily, Naples, Hungary and Jerusalem, but concealed the fact that the family had very little money and scarcely any land outside Anjou. She brought Henry little dowry other than a meaningless claim to Mallorca and Menorca, whilst he had to cede Maine and Anjou to the French and pay for her costs. Henry was prepared to make these concessions in order to reach terms of peace, and initially kept them secret, but they would prove deeply unpopular. What Margaret brought to the Lancastrian dynasty in exchange was a new definition of queenship and womanhood, a queen as warrior and defender, a woman who was not afraid to take a man's role when the situation required it. Ultimately though, she was operating in the masculine arena of politics and warfare, and her very strength proved to be her undoing.

Margaret had been raised to be conscious of her status. Isabelle and Catherine of Valois had been her aunts, and they in turn were Joan of Navarre's nieces, so she was following the precedent of three English queens who had been drawn from the French royal family. Margaret was already 'womanly' by the age of 15, 'exceeding others of her time, as well in beauty as wisdom, imbued with a high courage above the nature of her sex …' with 'great wit, great diligence, great heed and carefulness'.[3] She was a 'most handsome woman … somewhat dark'[4] and described by Barante in his chronicle as renowned 'for her beauty and wit … lofty spirit and courage'. He went so far as to believe that 'there was no princess in Christendom more accomplished than my lady Marguerite of Anjou,'[5] while Hall believed Margaret to excel 'all other as well in beauty and favour, as in wit and policy' and to have the 'stomach and courage more like to a man than a woman'.[6] As early as 1442, Henry had sent artists to paint portraits of all of Duke René's daughters: according to the journal of Thomas Beckington, Bishop of Bath and Wells, who was also Henry's secretary, Margaret and her sisters were to be portrayed 'in their kertelles [kirtles or gowns] simple, and their visages, lyk as you see their stature and their beaulte and color of skynne and their countenances, with al maner of features'.[7] Sadly, none of the portraits appear to have survived. Images of Margaret taken from her prayer roll in the Bodleian Library, and another presented to her on her marriage by John Talbot, depict her with the generic blonde hair that was given to all queens of the period.

Technically, Margaret was already married by the time Cecily encountered her, having gone through a proxy service in Nancy that February, with the Duke of Suffolk standing in for Henry. This ceremony may also have been arranged to coincide with the wedding of her sister Yolande, who became the wife of Frederick, Count of Vaudemont at the same time. From Nancy, Margaret travelled on with the Duke of Suffolk to Paris, where she was presented with holy relics, and then on to Pontoise on 18 March, from where they took barges along the Seine to Rouen, arriving four days later. It may have been travelling on the river that caused Margaret to fall ill, or else exaggerated an existing malaise, but by the time she arrived in Rouen she was feeling unwell. Outside the city, the Duke of York rode to meet her with 600 archers[8] and she was formally handed over to the English. A grand ceremonial entrance had been planned, in which Margaret received a palfrey draped in crimson velvet and embroidered gold roses as a gift from Henry. She was taken by litter to the Hôtel de Ville for a banquet but was too unwell to attend and her place was taken by the Duchess of Suffolk.

Margaret stayed in Rouen for two weeks over Easter, as a guest of Richard and Cecily, Duke and Duchess of York, probably at Rouen Castle. From there, York accompanied her east to Honfleur on the Channel coast, arriving on 9 April. The weather for the crossing was terrible and Margaret's ship was small and suffered much damage: according to her biographer Abbot, it was named *Kiddelaws* and lost both masts[9] before it could safely arrive at the town of Portchester in Hampshire. Margaret was reputedly so unwell by the time it came to disembark, that she had to be carried ashore by Suffolk. However, she had recovered enough to travel the 6 miles west and be married to Henry at Titchfield Abbey, near Fareham in Hampshire, on 23 April. A report in the State Papers of Milan makes the romantic suggestion that Henry disguised himself as a messenger so as to observe her reading a letter before their formal introduction.[10] Her husband was seven years her senior; serious, pious, ascetic, well educated and, quite unlike his own father, keen to embrace peace with France. Envoys sent by Charles VII found him welcoming and giving 'a very good appearance of being well pleased and very joyful'.[11] A papal diplomat visiting England in 1437 stated that the young man 'avoided the sight and conversation of women' and that 'those who knew him intimately said that he had preserved his virginity of mind and body ... and that he was firmly resolved to have intercourse with no woman unless within the bonds of matrimony.'[12]

That wedding night may well have taken place at Portchester Castle, a solid stone building on the cliffs overlooking the Channel, which had been a favourite with the Plantagenet kings as a base for foreign expeditions. The building had been repaired under Edward III and new royal apartments were built for Richard II. However, by 1441, the castle was described as 'ruinous and feeble', so there is a chance that Henry and Margaret remained at Titchfield Abbey. There was another possible location within the walls of Portchester Castle itself, which also housed the Priory of Our Lady at Southwick. How Margaret found her new husband is unknown; this 23-year-old man who had been king as long as he could remember, yet was gentle and pious, and quite unlike the model of royalty she would later espouse. Despite her youth, it was probably clear from the start that she was the stronger character. The character of Henry VI is something of a riddle, and recent reassessment of his reign suggests he may not have been as passive or gentle in the political arena as previously thought, but when it comes to Henry as a lover, it is impossible to know exactly how the pair reacted to each other, or the degree of success they achieved in their personal and sexual relationship. For the first seven years of their marriage, there were no reports of any disharmony and although Margaret did not fall pregnant during this time, it does not necessarily mean there was a lack of intimacy. After their marriage, Margaret and Henry departed for Eltham Palace in Kent and travelled on from there to London, where the new bride was to be crowned queen.

On 28 May, Margaret was met at Blackheath by the mayor and aldermen, along with the sheriffs and guilds, dressed in 'browne blue' with embroidered sleeves and scarlet hoods. The first pageant was set at the foot of London Bridge, an allegorical representation of peace and plenty bearing the motto 'Enter ye and replenish the earth.' Lydgate's verses composed for the occasion described Margaret as a source of wealth, love and abundance. A second pageant, set in the middle of the bridge, represented Noah's ark and praised Margaret for being a bringer of peace to the realm. The sun of comfort would begin to shine as a result of her presence and the flood of vengeance between England and France would retreat. A third pageant was situated at Leadenhall, where a Madame Grace delivered a welcome speech, while other 'sumptuous and costly' performances delighted Margaret with their tales from history. The verses written to be read at the Tonne in Cornhill emphasised parallels between the new queen and the martyr St Margaret:

Conueie of grace. Virgyne moost benigne.
Oo blessid martir holy margarete
Maugre the myght of spirites maligne
To god aboue hire praier pure and swete
Maketh now for Rest pees and quiete
Shewed here pleynly in this storie
Oure queene Margarete to signifie.
The alliance she signified was strong enough to tame nature:
God in heuene comaundynge abstinence
Noo wicked Aungel schall do more greuaunce
Erthe See and Trees shall ben in existence
Obeisaunt to mannes wille and plesaunce
Desired pees bitwixt Englande and ffraunce
This tyme of grace by mene of Magarete
We triste to god to lyuen in quiete.

On 29 May, after investing forty-six Knights of the Bath, she rode from the Tower to be crowned at Westminster. The *Brut* chronicle describes her arriving in a 'horse-bier, with two steeds decorated all in white damask powdered with gold' to match her own clothing: her 'hair was combed down about her shoulders, with a coronel of gold, rich pearls and precious stones'.[13] The following day she was crowned in Westminster Abbey, and a feast was held afterwards at Westminster Palace. It was October when York and Cecily packed up their household in Rouen and returned to England. By this point Queen Margaret had already begun to establish herself as a powerful player on the national scene.

New lodgings were prepared for Margaret at Eltham Palace, under the lead of the clerk of works, William Cleve. Here, at the old palace favoured by Henry IV and Joan of Navarre, a hall, scullery, saucer and serving area were added so that Margaret could entertain as queen, instead of in the apartments at Westminster, which had not been used by a queen since the death of Henry V over two decades earlier. Margaret may have been lauded as a bringer of peace, but the new queen was aware that her primary duty would not be not fulfilled until she could produce an English heir. Two years after her marriage she was still not pregnant. In fact, she was involving herself in the potential marriage of her husband's closest rivals, writing to her uncle Charles VII to urge him to marry one of his daughters to Cecily's eldest son Edward, then aged around 5. This marriage came to nothing but it is an indicator of her willingness at this stage to support the Yorks and her royal position as intermediary. It also supports Margaret's belief in the importance of marriage and duty, which surfaced again in a visit she paid to Norfolk in 1453, which is recorded in a letter from Margaret Paston to her husband, during which the queen encouraged an Elizabeth Clere of Sharynborn to remarry.[14]

In the late 1440s, Margaret wrote an extraordinary letter to Dame Jane Carew. Jane had been married to Sir Nicholas Carew, who died in May 1447, leaving her widowed in her late thirties with a swathe of lands and properties. Margaret approached her on behalf of her squire and sewer, or server at her table, Thomas Burneby, to encourage Jane to accept him as her second husband, for the 'grete zele, love and affeccion that he hath unto your personne, as for the womaly and vertuouse govern-ance that ye be renowned of'. According to Margaret, he 'desireth with all his hert to do yow worship by wey of marriage' and she wished for the match, 'for the increase, furtherance and preferring of oure said squire for his manifold merits and deserts, as for the good service that he hath don unto my lord and us'. She used her position to ask Jane to accept: 'praye you right affectuously that, at reverence of us, ye will have oure said squire … and cause us to have yow both in suche tendernesse and faver of our good grace.' It was an unusually direct request for the 20-year-old queen to make of a mature widow, and the degree of familiarity between Jane and Thomas is unknown. The Patent Rolls attest to Burneby's success at court though. In October 1447, he was granted the position of Sheriff of Merionneth in North Wales, although this does not necessarily imply he had connections with the place, and in November 1450, he became the Serjeant of the king's tents and pavilions.[15] Jane chose not to accept the queen's offer, but instead married Sir Robert Vere, brother of the Earl of Oxford and bore him one son, John.

By 1450, when Margaret reached her twentieth birthday and was still not pregnant, Cecily had already borne ten or eleven children, of whom six had survived. It goes without saying that Margaret could only conceive an heir if her husband was sharing her bed and there may have been a degree of sexual incompatibility between the ardent young woman and the austere king. An account written by Henry's chaplain John Blackman describes the king's shame at the sight of dancing girls with bare chests, averting his eyes and leaving the room; Blackman saw Henry 'like a second Job, a man simple and upright, altogether fearing God and eschewing evil ... a diligent and sincere worshipper ... more given to God and devout prayer than worldly and temporal matters.' He added that the king 'was chaste and pure from the beginning of his days. He eschewed all licentiousness in word and deed' but he kept his marriage vow to Margaret 'wholly and sincerely ... never dealing unchastely with any other woman'.[16] Henry is likely to have strictly observed the days forbidden by the Church for intercourse, routinely donning a hair shirt on those occasions and, according to Blackman, kept 'careful watch through hidden windows' to ensure his servants did not fall prey to lust. Additionally, there is a suggestion that the Bishop of Salisbury was accused of advising Henry not to visit Margaret's bed, but this was not uncommon among devoted Catholics on certain days of the week or times of religious observation and fasting, such as Sundays or Lent.[17]

It is difficult to ascertain what the early years of marriage were like for Henry and Margaret, without being coloured by a certain degree of hindsight. One surviving letter from Henry in 1449 regarding grants of timber from Kenilworth follows the formulaic enough opening of 'right dere and entirely bestbeloved wyf', although such phrasing was not strictly necessary. However, there are no surviving reports of any marital problems, if these would have been articulated by either party, or observed from the outside. Henry may have been prudish around other women by Blackman's standards but he entered marriage with the intention of fulfilling his vows and fathering children. Being an only child, he would have understood the importance of this in order to secure his legacy, but having been king since before he could remember, he may not have felt it to be imperative that it happened quickly. It is impossible to know what happened in the royal bedroom. The only thing that can be stated with certainty is that Margaret did not fall pregnant for seven years.

The new queen found sympathetic friends at court in two veterans of the Hundred Years' War: the Duke of Suffolk and the Earl of Shrewsbury. William de la Pole, Duke of Suffolk had been one of the first members of the English court Margaret encountered and her friendship with him was bound up with the protection and paternal attitude inherent in his role as her deliverer in 1445. In his early fifties, he was the key figure behind the throne, an able minister who had worked his way up through various posts including that of Commander of the English forces at Orléans and Lord High Admiral of England. He was married to Alice, the grand-daughter of the poet Geoffrey Chaucer, and the father of one son, John, born around 1442. On Margaret's arrival in England, Alice, Duchess of Suffolk became one of her ladies in waiting. Suffolk was pro-French in policy and had negotiated the handing over of Maine and Anjou, which proved deeply unpopular. Having played a key part in government, his luck began to turn in the late 1440s. He was reputed to have taken part in a plan for the French to invade, meeting with the Count of Dunois to negotiate the overthrow of Henry VI and wed his son John to Margaret, daughter of Edmund Beaufort. This, along with the losses of further French territories, led to his arrest in 1450. The king commuted the sentence to banishment, but his ship was hijacked on the way to France and after a mock trial on board, Suffolk was executed and his body thrown overboard. It was later found washed up on the beach at Dover. Margaret thus lost a father figure and one of her first allies.

Another leading political figure familiar to Margaret was John Talbot, Earl of Shrewsbury, whose wife, it has been suggested, took the queen's place when she fell ill at the banquet in Rouen. It had been Talbot who commissioned a beautiful Book of Hours in Rouen depicting Margaret's wedding to Henry, which he probably presented to her before they left the city. The manuscript also contained a blend of courtly and political material, with romances and songs as well as treaties on warfare and statutes of the Order of the Garter. Although it has been questioned whether this was a text compiled purely for Margaret, the mixture of the courtly and military suited the young queen well, and was perhaps even a formative influence on her in the early years of her marriage. Shrewsbury had served in France and, after being captured at Rouen, promised not to bear arms against the French again, although he remained a commander. He was playing such a role in July 1453 when he was killed at the Battle of Castillon in Bordeaux. Thus Margaret lost two important advisors from her early years as queen just at the point at which her world was about to change dramatically.

In January 1453, Margaret conceived the child she had been hoping for. Her visits to shrines, pilgrimages, prayers and offerings to the saints had finally borne fruit. She had vindicated her position and silenced those critics who were beginning to wonder whether the marriage was cursed, or that she was infertile; now she had to carry the child to term and deliver what was hopefully a healthy son. Later rumours would question the paternity of Margaret's child, suggesting that she had sought to ensure her position through an illicit liaison and passed off her son as the king's. Yet this should not come as a surprise, given the lengthy period before conception and the way that Margaret's femininity was later represented. Because she would go on to prove herself brave, determined and ambitious, challenging contemporary notions of submissive womanhood, slurs were also directed at her sexuality. Women who chose, or were forced, to defy such conventional gender roles often drew accusations of promiscuity or lewdness to discredit them as enemies. The primary suspect in the minds of the gossips was Edmund Beaufort, Duke of Somerset, whom Margaret named as the boy's godfather.

Somerset was then aged around 40 and had played a significant role in the English occupation of France, lifting the siege of Calais and being appointed as Lieutenant. Reputed to have had an affair with Catherine of Valois in the mid- or late 1420s, he had waited almost a decade to marry, choosing as his wife Eleanor Beauchamp. She was the daughter of Richard, thirteenth Earl of Warwick, who had been tutor to the young Henry VI and bridged the gap in France between the rules of Bedford and York. Eleanor was a widow with three surviving children. By 1445, she had borne around six of the ten children she gave Beaufort. Until the arrival of Margaret's child, Beaufort was the king's closest relative and thus Eleanor was another potential queen in waiting.

Following the deaths of Suffolk and Shrewsbury, Beaufort became Margaret's closest advisor within the Lancastrian family. The theory that he fathered her child has been embraced by historian John Ashdown-Hill,[18] whose explanation includes the statement that Margaret fell pregnant during a period in which Henry was unwell. However, the king's incapacity dated from that summer, specifically during a stay at Clarendon Palace in August, by which time Margaret would have been in her third trimester. Henry still appeared competent and capable during the first session of Parliament that year, which assembled on 6 March, two months after Margaret fell pregnant. He was then planning a progress into the West Country.[19] The rumours of false paternity were contemporary to Edward's birth, as Benet's chronicle records, and apprentice lawyer John Helton suffered a traitor's death for 'producing bills asserting that Prince Edward was not the queen's son'. They were circulated again in the 1460s by the Duke of Warwick, but were far more a political slur designed to discredit the queen than a claim to any inside knowledge of her intimate relations. In fact, Henry had been delighted to learn of Margaret's pregnancy, rewarding the bearer of the news, Richard Tunstall, with an annuity of £40, delighted that 'oure most entirely beloved wyf the Quene was with child, to oure most singuler consolation, and to all oure true liege people grete joy and comfort'.[20]

At first, it appeared that Henry VI was simply unwell. Retiring from public view and taking to his bed, his doctors advised rest and anticipated a full recovery. However, as the days passed, it became clear that a far more serious condition had taken hold of the king, leaving him lying in a catatonic state, unable to speak, recognise friends or feed himself. As Abbot Whethamsted recorded, 'a disease and disorder of such a sort overcame the king that he lost his wits and memory for a time, and nearly all his body was so uncoordinated and out of control that he could neither walk, nor hold his head upright, nor easily move.'[21] It is possible that Henry had inherited something of the instability of his maternal grandfather, Charles VI, who had exhibited paranoia, violence and delusions, believing himself to be made of glass. Whethamsted certainly believed it was Henry's inheritance, or his genes, that were to blame, writing that he was 'his mother's stupid offspring, not his father's, a son greatly degenerated from the father, who did not cultivate the art of war ... a mild-spoken, pious king, but half-witted in affairs of state'. Yet Henry never went to the extremes of his grandfather; his illness manifested itself in a quiet absence, a stillness and retreat from the world. Modern medicine might diagnose a severe breakdown and depression, but contemporary thinkers saw the king's health as correlative with that of the nation. An unwell king was a sign that something was rotten in the political system; a situation that could not be endured for its potential harm to his people.

Illness made the king and his family vulnerable. Margaret arranged for Henry to be moved back to Windsor and the news was initially kept quiet, but the pregnant queen knew that this could not remain the case for long. Her pregnancy was no guarantee that she would deliver a healthy son and survive, so Margaret's position, and that of the Lancastrian dynasty, was precarious. Finally aware of the extent of the problem, the council called an emergency meeting to determine the best way to govern during the king's incapacity. Margaret's closest ally, the Duke of Somerset, attempted to exclude Richard, Duke of York from the meeting but his wishes were overridden. His fears of conflict with his rival were justified though, as York promptly had Somerset committed to the Tower. York had long been agitating for proper recognition as Henry's heir and this action exaggerated the division between him and the queen.

When Margaret went into labour that October, Henry had still not recovered. She delivered a healthy boy and lay in for a month, according to custom, and was churched on 18 November, assisted by Cecily, Duchess of York and the duchesses of Bedford, Norfolk, Buckingham, Exeter, Suffolk and Somerset and the Countess of Warwick. An incredible sum of £554 16s 8d was paid for an embroidered christening mantle for Edward, 540 brown sables to make Margaret's robe and 20yd of russet cloth of gold to decorate the font. Still Henry did not wake. His son, Edward of Lancaster, was presented to him by the Duke of Buckingham at Windsor soon after New Year but Henry was unable to acknowledge the child. Then, according to a servant of the Duke of Norfolk, 'the Queene come in, and toke the Prince in hir armes and presented hym in like forme as the Duke had done, desiring that he shuld blisse it; but alle their labour was in veyne,' as Henry only 'caste doune his eyene agen'. On 3 April, Parliament granted Edward an allowance of 2,000 marks, the same amount his father had received in the first year of his reign, with allowances for other expenses such as learning to ride.[22]

The situation must have been very difficult for Margaret. More than ever, her position and future were uncertain, despite her queenship. There were no guarantees that Henry would recover and his inability to recognise their son could lay her open to slanders about his paternity and, perhaps, even Parliament's refusal to accept him as heir. The alternative was Richard, Duke of York, whom the agitators in Jack Cade's rebellion of 1450 had cited as a suitable king and who had marched against Henry and Somerset in 1452, although the king had regained control after a meeting at Blackheath. York was in his forties, experienced, astute, ambitious and the father of a large family. Moreover, he had repeatedly declared against Margaret's ally and friend, Somerset, and was responsible for his confinement in the Tower. Lacking support, anxious to protect her infant son, Margaret is likely to have viewed York as a threat to the Lancastrian dynasty and baby Edward. In order to protect their rights, she took an extraordinary step.

In January 1454, Margaret set out her bid to become England's sole ruler. In a petition to Parliament, she presented five articles, four of which are listed in a letter of John Stodeley, a servant of the Duke of Norfolk. Firstly, Margaret 'desireth to have the hole reule of this land', as regent for her son until he came of age or Henry recovered his wits. It was a remarkably bold move for a French woman of 23, whose nationality, gender, education, alliances and age would predispose the English Parliament to treat her with suspicion at the very least. Secondly, she requested the right to appoint key figures such as Chancellor, Treasurer, Lord Privy Seal and all officials, which potentially meant a complete shake-up of the existing power base in favour of Margaret's allies. As it was, the Chancellor since 1441, John Fortescue, and Treasurer since 1440, Archbishop John Kemp, were members of Somerset's faction and the Privy Seal was held by Thomas Lisieux, a protégé of Kemp, who in turn had been an ally of the Duke of Suffolk. Thirdly, Margaret wanted power to grant all the spiritual benefices within the realm; and fourthly, she required 'sufficient lyvelode [livelihood] assigned hir for the King and the Prince and hir self'. Stodeley could not recall her fifth demand.

In many ways, Margaret was an unsuitable regent for England. Having been raised in Anjou, which was dominated by French and factional politics, she lacked the subtle understanding of England's history and political composition which veterans such as York did possess. She was a newcomer on the scene whose alliances in the English court easily laid her open to charges of favouritism; she was an unknown quantity with no training or experience in the rule of a country. Worst of all, she was a woman. Even had Parliament considered appointing her as a nominal leader, giving her the final say in a political process which was ultimately the domain of men, it could not willingly put such power into her hands. Her status counted for much, but her gender counted for more. Had the country been enjoying a period of stability, and had the question of a regency arisen as the result of Henry's absence in France, it may have been a different matter entirely. In 1475, Edward IV would appoint his wife as regent during his absence, but he was leaving behind a strong and united realm. The instabilities of the recent years meant that in 1453, the commonwealth was under threat. Margaret's nationality and her gender counted against her when it came to the appointment of someone who needed to be more than a figurehead.

Unsurprisingly, Parliament did not put power in her hands. Perhaps her move was a gesture of defiance against her enemies, or perhaps Margaret felt that it was her duty as queen to rule in the king's absence, but it is difficult to know whether she had really believed her proposals would be accepted. Perhaps she was playing a shrewder game. There is a chance that Margaret made a bold but unlikely request in the full expectation of it being rejected, in order to ensure that her lesser requests were met. She received the necessary funding and retreated with the king and prince to what had been Eleanor Cobham's palace of Bella Court at Greenwich, where she awaited further developments. In March, Parliament appointed the Duke of York as Protector of the Realm. On Kemp's death the same month, the position of treasurer went to Richard Neville, Earl of Warwick, a staunch ally of the Yorkist dynasty. There is little to indicate that Margaret was angered or disappointed at this stage. Her appeal to rule had been rejected, but her focus was firmly on her

husband and son, and her retreat to Greenwich could be read as a conciliatory gesture, stepping aside to allow York to take the reins as she awaited
the king's recovery.

Margaret had good reason to include the request that her household
be properly funded. In the past, finances had been tight as the result
of administrative incompetence, foreign wars, opposition to taxes and
falling foreign revenues. In 1451, the royal credit had run out and the
king and queen had sat down to dine on a meal that never arrived. Part
of the expense had been Margaret's plans to transform the palace at
Greenwich into a residence fit for a queen, to rival that of York's domain
at Westminster. Terracotta tiles bearing her royal monogram were set in
the floors, replacing the previous rush matting; furnishings, walls and
fittings were carved or painted with daisies, or her namesake's *marguerites*;
windows were glazed; a new vestry was created for the crown jewels; and
a new pier was built to give access from the river. Margaret rechristened
the place the Palace of Placentia, or the Palace of Plesaunce.[23] In 1453,
Henry had been granted revenues from the wool industry, so their financial position was comparatively secure again; it was the nature of Henry's
illness that cast his rule in an uncertain light.

Margaret understood that her future and that of her son depended
upon her husband's health. For months, there was little change, then the
condition suddenly lifted as unexpectedly as it had begun. At Christmas
1454, Henry awoke, as if from a deep sleep, and could recall nothing of his
period of illness. On 30 December, Margaret brought Prince Edward to
him, who was then a child of almost fifteen months, 'and when [Henry]
asked what the prince's name was, and the queen told him "Edward" and
then he held up his hands and thanked God thereof'.[24] By the spring of
1455, it appeared that the king was finally in command of his faculties
and when York resigned his position and Somerset was released, Margaret
may have felt relieved that the business of Lancastrian rule could begin
again. However, the conflict was soon to escalate to a level even she could
not have anticipated.

II

In the spring of 1455, Henry planned to hold a council meeting at Leicester for a select group of his supporters. Word soon reached London that York and Warwick, who had both been excluded from this event, were raising an army of rebels to remove the king's 'evil' advisors, whom they believed were planning their arrest. There could have been little doubt in Margaret's mind that this was the culmination of York's long years of rivalry with Somerset and, by extension, an attack upon her own influence over the king. Thomas Gascoigne, a chaplain to Henry VI in the 1430s and '40s, captured this feeling of resentment at the queen's influence: 'almost all the affairs of the realm were conducted according to the queen's will, by fair means or foul, as was said by several people. What will be the result of this, God knows.'[25] Over the last two years Margaret had had little choice but to make decisions for her husband, but it was to be the events of 1455 that catapulted her into an unprecedented style of rule, employing both 'fair means and foul'.

Until this time, Margaret had essentially conformed to the model of demure and quiet queenship offered by consorts like Philippa of Hainault or Joan of Navarre. They had been influential behind the scenes, within the confines of the bedroom or in private discussion with their husbands, complementing the male role and conforming to gendered ideals about the place a woman should occupy, even a queen. Not published until 1474, William Caxton's *A Game of Chesse* typified this view of the quiet queen but drew on influential texts from the fourteenth and early fifteenth century by Christine de Pisan and Jacobus de Cessolis. Advice written by Geoffrey de Tour Landry counselled women to let their husbands be their 'spokesperson and master' but when they were alone, a wife might 'talk to him pleasantly, and advise him to mend his ways if he has done wrong'. This applied to queens too, and Landry gave an example:

> a good woman ought to do this, like Hester the queen of Syria. Her husband the king was fierce and quick tempered, but when he was angry she would say nothing until he had calmed down. When his anger was over, she might rule him as she pleased. This was very clever of her, and so should all women do.

Quick temper was one thing, but there was little to prepare Margaret for dealing with a husband's complete incapacity.

Margaret's response to the political threat of the early 1450s had been passive rather than active. Now she was forced to outstep her former role and take a more active, and therefore more masculine, stance when it came to determining her future and that of her family. The wives of Edward III, Henry IV and, briefly, Henry V, were supportive partners of strong rulers, in terms of policy, power and reputation. Their gentle, conciliatory piety and patronage provided a softer side to the harsher martial masculinity of kings. Margaret's situation was unique. Henry VI's incapacity forced him into the passive role and, in response, Margaret attempted to become the active, militant royal figure to counterbalance him. As highlighted by Joan of Arc's fate at the hands of the Lancastrians in France, the fifteenth century did not readily embrace women who attempted to assume what were perceived to be masculine roles and made themselves 'unfeminine' or a 'perversion' of the norm. This would be a slur from which her reputation would never recover, not even among historians of the twenty-first century.

Despite her offer to rule instead of York, even her friends considered Margaret unfit for the coming conflict. Besides, her person and that of the prince were far too important to place in the line of danger. They were sent to Greenwich for safety while Somerset planned to confront York and, incredibly, Henry himself insisted in taking part in the coming battle, contrary to his hitherto pacifist persona. On 22 May, the two sides met in the little market town of St Albans in Hertfordshire. Henry raised his standard in the marketplace while York and Warwick approached from opposing directions. After about an hour of intense fighting, when the narrow streets reputedly ran with blood,[26] York and Warwick cornered Somerset inside the Castle Inn. This was the moment when the tide turned, when violence overspilled from the antagonisms and rivalries of the past decade to create a climate of vengeance and opposition that escalated the conflict and forced Margaret to redefine her identity as queen.

According to legend, the witch of Eye, Margery Jourdemayne, had made a prophecy back in the 1430s that Somerset would die in a castle. Now, barricaded inside the Castle Inn at St Albans, the duke decided to come out fighting. After a brave show he was killed, effectively ending the battle.

Other loyal Lancastrians, Henry Percy, second Earl of Northumberland and Thomas, Lord Clifford, were also cut down. Henry was wounded in the neck by an arrow and sought refuge in a nearby building but it was not York's intention to harm him. Professing their loyalty to their king, the rebels marched him south to London, where Parliament was called. There, Henry had little choice but to approve the measures York passed and 'declare that none of our cousins ... nor any of the persons who came with them in their fellowship ... be impeached, sued, vexed, grieved, hurt or molested [for] anything supposed or claimed to have been done against our person, crown or dignity'.[27] This Parliament was the first to censure Margaret's involvement in politics, with York's allies stating that government had been managed 'by the Queen, the Duke of Somerset, and their friends ... of late a great oppression and injustice to the people'.[28] When Henry fell ill again at the end of 1455, York again became protector and one of the acts of his Parliament reduced Margaret's household spending. The uneasy truce belied the deep level to which Margaret was vexed, grieved and hurt by York's actions, which had injured her person, crown and dignity. The following year, Benet's chronicle would record that Margaret 'greatly loathed' both York and Warwick.

York's stance in 1455 opened a division among the descendants of Edward III that had implications for the allegiances of Lancastrian women. His wife of twenty-five years, Cecily Neville, had spent the first part of her life as a loyal daughter, a granddaughter of John of Gaunt working to serve the dynasty through the 1430s and '40s, when York was posted to France and Ireland. Although her mother was dead by the time of her husband's breach with the king, many of Cecily's close relatives were still firmly within the Lancastrian camp; in fact, the divisions arising in the extended dynasty caused many to question their allegiance. Cecily's closest sister Anne was the wife of the Duke of Buckingham and, with him, remained loyal to the king. Her elder sister Eleanor had married the Earl of Northumberland, the son of Henry 'Hotspur' Percy, who had been killed fighting for the Lancastrians at St Albans, possibly at the hand of his own uncle. Among Cecily's brothers, William, Baron Fauconberg had fought for the king in 1455 but after the battle had been appointed by York as Constable of Windsor Castle while Edward, Baron Bergavenny had been part of York's Protectorate Council in 1454 and would become a captain in the Yorkist army by 1462. The most ardent of York's supporters were Richard Neville, Earl of Salisbury and his son Warwick, Cecily's brother and nephew. By virtue of her marriage to York and her Lancastrian birth, Cecily could have faced a clash of loyalties once events began to drive the two sides into opposition. However, it does not appear that this caused her much difficulty, as she placed her political loyalties very clearly with her husband and sons. As the matriarch of the York family, the wife and support of the Duke of York, and the guide of her sons Edward, Edmund, George and Richard, Lancaster's most powerful female opponent of the fifteenth century would come from within its own ranks.

A period of shock settled after St Albans. Both sides were stunned by the escalation to violence and the losses of leading figures of the political scene; for a while, both seemed keen to reconcile and overcome their differences. York's second Protectorate ended in February 1456, but even though Henry was able to retake the reins of power, his position was weaker as a result of the York–Warwick faction, whose strength had grown after St Albans. The pardons they had forced through Parliament had made the Lancastrians look weak and eroded their power. There were also reparations to be made to the bereaved families, which indicate just how shocking the outbreak of violence had been. A chivalric code still lingered after St Albans, with apologies, pardons and attempts to reconcile, but it opened the floodgates to a more brutal period which would see enemies beheaded after the fighting had finished, and little mercy shown to those on the opposing side.

One family who perhaps had the right to be the most aggrieved after St Albans were the widow and children of Edmund, Duke of Somerset. Eleanor was 47 when her husband was killed; she had three adult children from her first marriage and ten by Somerset, of whom the eldest son, Henry, had fought alongside his father in the battle and been wounded. At some point in the next two years, her daughter Eleanor would marry another man who had fought for the Lancastrians in 1455 and would remain devoted to the dynasty until his execution for treason by the Yorkists in 1461 – James Butler, Earl of Ormond and Wiltshire. But with ten children born over a period of eighteen years, Eleanor still had young dependents to consider. In 1458, the Duke of York would agree to pay an annuity of 5,000 marks to the widowed duchess and her children as a measure of compensation, but it could not eradicate the antipathy felt by the dead man's family, in particular the three sons who would continue to challenge the Yorkist regime. They were to prove powerful allies of Queen Margaret in the years to come.

After St Albans, Margaret worked to influence her husband in the traditional queenly way: behind the scenes, using location, appointments and alliances. That August, they travelled to the Midlands on the pretext of hunting, but really to establish themselves at Kenilworth Castle, the traditional Lancastrian base, which they fortified with additional cannon. There, Margaret attempted to persuade the king to replace his officials with loyal members of her own household. She gathered around her a new court of young Lancastrians, especially the children of Edmund Beaufort: his eldest son Henry, who had been wounded at St Albans, and his brothers Edmund and John, along with their sister Margaret's husband, Humphrey, Earl of Stafford and his father, the Duke of Buckingham. There was also John Clifford, son of Thomas, who inherited the baronetcy following his father's death in the battle, and now also the Tudor brothers Edmund and Jasper, who had previously been allied with York, but now came out firmly on the side of their half-brother Henry VI. Now in their twenties, the pair were not in line to succeed Henry but had been granted the titles of Earl of Richmond and Earl of Pembroke in 1452, in recognition of their close blood ties. In November 1455, Edmund had married another Margaret Beaufort, not Edmund's daughter, but the child of John Beaufort, son of John the first Earl of Somerset and the grandson of John of Gaunt. Around the time the king and queen were at Kenilworth, Edmund was captured by the Yorkist William Herbert and imprisoned in Carmarthen Castle. He died there that November, leaving his young wife pregnant.

Margaret's queenship during 1456 continued to conform to the traditional model. It was determined and focussed, but largely took place behind the scenes as she worked to re-establish her husband's authority. As John Bocking wrote to Sir John Fastolf that February, 'the quene is a grete and strong labourid woman, for she spareth noo peyne to sue her thinges to an intent and conclusion to her power.'[29] She also worked hard to inspire loyalty in her subjects, making sure Prince Edward was visible to remind people he was the legitimate Lancastrian heir, a role which was echoed in pageantry at Coventry that September. They compared Margaret to the Queen of Heaven and she was presented with silver cups and £100 by the mayor. It may also have been around this time that the large tapestry featuring portraits of the king and queen, now in St Mary's Hall, was created. Dressed in a pearl collar and hood decorated with a fleur-de-lys and topped with a crown, Margaret's hands rest on a missal book as she prays. The following month she and Henry were still at Coventry when James Gresham wrote to John Paston that certain key appointments had changed hands. Thomas Bourchier was dismissed as Chancellor in favour of William Waynflete; the second Lord Shrewsbury, son of Margaret's former advisor, was now Treasurer and John Brown was now Under Treasurer with Laurence Bothe as Privy Seal. The news of these changes soon reached London, prompting York to visit Coventry: John Paston wrote that he had 'departed ageyn in right good conceyt with the Kyng but not in gret conceyt with the Whene [Queen]'. York also 'waited upon' Margaret at Sandal Castle that May, maintaining the official channels of co-operation, although it is likely that his actions in 1455 meant he had already gone too far to ever attain Margaret's forgiveness.

Margaret's focus on Prince Edward was echoed in Lancastrian litera-ture extolling him as, and encouraging him to become, the ideal prince. The anonymous *Knyghthode and Bataile* may have been written by John, Viscount Beaumont, who was appointed chief steward of Edward's lands in 1456. It stresses the divine connection between God and king, refer-ring to the monarch as 'God's son' and the earthly representative of divine order. The chivalric ideal is embodied as a form of worship, moving to the logical conclusion that those who opposed the king were ungodly and did so at the instigation of the devil:

> The premynent is first th'almyghti Lord,
> Emanuel, that every lord is undir
> And good lyver; but bataile and discord
> With him hath Sathanas.[30]

Sir George Ashby's poem to Edward, *On the Active Policy of a Prince*, reminded the prince to continue the legacy of his Lancastrian forebears 'aftur the statues autorised by noble kynges your progenitours', with particular focus on eradicating the threats posed by traitors: 'suppresse youre false conspiratours, aftur the lawe and constitucion, established ayenst opyn traitorous'.[31] The work was dedicated to 'your highnesse Edward by name, trewe son and heir of the high majestie of oure liege lorde Kynge Henry and dame Margarete, the Quene' and drew heavily on the boy's lineage and right to rule. Stating that Edward's Lancastrian predecessors fulfilled this role, the poem offers the child a model of king-ship that would have been complimentary to his mother's respect for the dynasty and active approach to dealing with potential challenges to it. It echoes many of the instructional manuals of the day with its emphasis on finding a middle path, not being too hasty or too slow, too royal or too simple, but to choose clever servants, act wisely, subdue rebellion, heed the lessons of the French wars and to show traitors no mercy 'if th'offence touche the subversion of the realm'. Little survives to give an indication of the boy's character beyond the colourful suggestion that he encour-aged the beheading of his enemies, recounted in a letter by the Milanese ambassador. This lack of evidence has led to fictional portrayals of the prince as little more than a bloodthirsty caricature, barely reflective of the complexity of his and his family's situation. As Edward grew older, in the late 1450s, he became more aware of the deepening hostilities between Lancaster and York. In particular, Margaret and her circle found it dif-ficult to forgive the death of Somerset at St Albans.

In March 1458, both sides took part in a 'Loveday', an elaborate staged performance designed as a public reconciliation and declaration of intent. Margaret and York walked hand in hand to hear a sermon and mass at St Paul's. It was organised by the peace-loving Henry but as York and Warwick were approaching the capital to take part, attempts were made to ambush them. These attacks failed but they underscored the real lin-gering resentment felt by their enemies and may have been instigated, or approved of, by Margaret. Here it is possible that the king and queen were at odds in their purpose and methods. While Henry negotiated with his opponents, using the Archbishop of Canterbury, Thomas Bourchier, as go-between, Margaret may have preferred to remove the danger using unofficial but decisive means. Yet these means were non-confrontational, simply designed to remove the opponent by subterfuge. In this way,

Margaret could actually be seen as a more peaceful figure, attempting to preserve the fragile truce and exert a kind of justice which she felt had been denied by the pardon York had granted himself. In 1457, she had disagreed with Henry when she urged that charges be pressed against William Herbert for causing a disturbance, and had been forced to concede defeat when popular opinion was against her. Margaret's methods could be interpreted as more shrewd and subtle than those of her naïve husband, playing the political game more astutely than his open show of affection, which really fooled nobody but himself. Although Margaret swore the oath of peace that March, she must have been aware that the Loveday highlighted just how far the authority of the Lancastrian regime had been eroded by York's strength.

The Loveday truce did not last long. The following year, Margaret attempted to replace Warwick as Captain of Calais with Henry Beaufort, the young Duke of Somerset. Warwick protested that the position had been granted him by Parliament and a scuffle broke out, which he interpreted as an attack upon his person and fled England. Margaret distributed Lancastrian swan badges and began to gather weapons and an army before summoning Parliament to meet in Leicester. York and his allies anticipated that they would be arrested, probably quite correctly, and refused to attend. Warwick's father, the Earl of Salisbury, was marching south to meet his son when he encountered the king's army under Lord Audley at Blore Heath in Staffordshire. A romantic legend survives which states that Margaret and Prince Edward were close by, staying at the village of Mucklestone, and watched the battle unfold from the local church tower, but this cannot be proven. If she was in the vicinity, Margaret would have soon learned that Salisbury had been victorious, killing Audley and progressing to Ludlow, where he was reunited with York. There, they stood and faced the Lancastrian army, which regrouped under the lead of the Duke of Buckingham. This time, they had Henry as their figurehead. An army headed by the king was an automatic guarantee that those on the opposing side were guilty of treason. As they faced the Yorkists at Ludford Bridge, Henry's presence shook the morale of those enlisted by York and his allies. They deserted in droves before a blow was even exchanged, knowing they could not expect the same leniency and pardons that had followed the unexpected outburst at St Albans. Realising the cause was lost, York fled to Ireland while his son Edward joined Warwick in Calais. The enemy had finally retreated.

Triumphant, Margaret summoned a Parliament at Coventry for that December. It was the first Parliament to meet since York dismissed the session and his Protectorship in 1456. Later described by Margaret's enemies as the 'Parliament of Devils', it was a reassertion of Lancastrian rule and the authority of King Henry away from the pro-Yorkist capital. The new session opened in the chapter house of St Mary's Priory with a speech about peace from Chancellor William Waynflete. York's acts of treason dating back to 1450 were recounted, including a reckoning for St Albans, which had been prompted by the 'moost dyabolique unkyndnesse and wrecched envye'. Parliament then passed a full Act of Attainder against York and his elder sons, Edward and Edmund, along with Warwick and Salisbury, formally making them traitors and stripping them of all titles, properties and lands, and barring their heirs from inheritance. The sixty-six peers assembled swore loyalty to Henry and acknowledged Edward as his son. With her enemies condemned according to the law and in exile, Margaret must have felt vindicated and reassured that the Lancastrian dynasty was secure. Sadly, it was to prove the calm before the storm.

The following June, the royal family were at Coventry when news came that the Earl of Warwick and his cousin Edward of York had landed in Kent and were marching on London. Margaret remained with Prince Edward while Henry headed south. The royal army met the Yorkists at Northampton on 10 July. The Duke of Buckingham and John Talbot, Earl of Shrewsbury were killed along with many other leading Lancastrians, and Henry was taken prisoner. Margaret now decided to flee with her son, calculating that if the king was in custody, at least his heir could remain safe. This was to be a decisive moment and she would follow this course to protect Prince Edward for the remainder of his life. William of Worcester relates how the queen and prince were robbed and perhaps captured as they fled along the road to Chester by a servant of Lord Stanley. Margaret managed to escape and was offered sanctuary by Owen Tudor at Harlech Castle, where she was joined by Henry Beaufort, eldest son of the dead Duke of Somerset.

Meanwhile, York returned from exile in Ireland and his duchess Cecily left her children in London to go and meet him in the West Country. She accompanied him as he marched into London, no doubt learning of his new plans after their lengthy separation. And York did indeed have big plans. Something had shifted in his stance during his exile: the Act of Attainder against him and his heirs now meant he had to gamble all or nothing. On his arrival, he strode into Westminster Hall, put his hands on the throne and claimed it. News reached Margaret that it was York's intention to depose Henry and Prince Edward, and rule England in his own right. It was unorthodox and shocking, but many people saw him as a more reliable ruler than the mentally ill Henry VI or his underage son. When Parliament approved the Act of Accord that October, naming York as Henry's heir and disinheriting Edward, it was the final straw for Margaret.

That December, York was at Sandal Castle near Wakefield when a combined royal and Scottish army led by Henry Beaufort and Henry Percy, Earl of Northumberland surrounded him. Although he was awaiting reinforcements led by his son Edward, York ventured out of the protection of the castle with his second son, Edmund, and the Duke of Salisbury, perhaps to restock after the Christmas season. All three were killed in the fighting that followed, or fleeing in its aftermath, and their heads were placed upon Micklegate Bar in York, the duke's topped by a paper crown. With success close at hand, Margaret marched south, but her army was undisciplined and unpaid, leading to looting and violent behaviour that went unchecked, described by the *Croyland Chronicle* as a whirlwind devoted 'to spoil and rapine without regard for person or place'. This did the most damage to Margaret's cause in the long term, as whatever sympathy the English people had felt for her was replaced by fear as her troops left a trail of destruction.

For Cecily, Duchess of York, the Battle of Wakefield was the cruellest blow. In one stroke, she lost her husband, son, brother and nephew, but not her hope. While Margaret's armies were out of control, Edward met Jasper and Owen Tudor at Mortimer's Cross. His father may have been killed but the 18-year-old Edward of York was now a force to be reckoned with, defeating the Lancastrian army and beheading Owen Tudor in Hereford. Tudor reputedly used his last words to state that the head that had been used to lie in Queen Catherine's lap was now to be struck from his shoulders. He was buried in the Grey Friars' church at Hereford. Shortly afterwards, Cecily's surviving nephew, the Earl of Warwick, met Henry, Duke of Somerset and a second terrible battle raged through the little town of St Albans. There was an element of vengeance about these encounters, with Edward of York and Warwick bent on punishing those responsible for the deaths of their fathers and brothers. Margaret and Prince Edward sheltered in St Albans Abbey awaiting news. This time it was a great victory for the king's forces, with Warwick losing control of Henry, who reputedly sat under a tree during the fighting and then was able to join his wife and son. Now all that remained for them to regain control was to return to London and capitalise on their victory.

Yet, at this moment, the Lancastrians wavered. Rumours of their unruly army had reached the city and, in an unusual step, the mayor sent a delegation to Henry and Margaret expressing the Londoners' fears. What was most extraordinary about this delegation was that it consisted of a triumvirate of Lancastrian women whose mission had a direct impact upon the political future of the country and the dynasty. The first of the three was Emma, Lady Scales, the widow of the unpopular Thomas, who had been killed attempting to hold London against the Yorkists the previous summer. Emma had borne two children but her son had died young, leaving her daughter Elizabeth as sole heir. Within a few years, Elizabeth would pass the title of Lord Scales to her husband Anthony, a son of Jacquetta, once Duchess of Bedford. The second woman was Anne, another daughter of Joan Beaufort, Countess of Westmorland, who had married the Duke of Buckingham and borne him ten children. She is likely to have been the closest sister in age of Cecily Neville, Duchess of York and during the period of York's exile had acted as her sister's guardian, or gaoler. The third woman was none other than Jacquetta herself. She had now been married to Richard Wydeville for over twenty years and had borne him fourteen children. Her eldest daughter, Elizabeth, who may have accompanied her to Rouen in 1441, had been widowed after the death of her husband Sir John Grey at the second battle of St Albans. Together, these three Lancastrian women travelled north to meet Margaret and negotiate the terms of her return to the city, or 'for to entreat for grace for the city', according to the *London Chronicle*. Exactly what the women said is unclear but they succeeded in making Margaret rethink her plans; she withdrew her army to Dunstable.

Margaret's move proved disastrous. She failed to capitalise on the moment of greatest opportunity and left the city open. Without intending it, the delegation of Lancastrian women had paved the way for the Yorkist dynasty but they can hardly be blamed for not anticipating York's next move. Much of the responsibility must lie with the commanders of Margaret's army, and it must be recognised that in recent years she had lost many of the experienced military leaders whose advice may have been beneficial to her at this juncture. The causes extend back into the previous decades, contrasting Henry's inability with York's ability, Henry's limited fecundity with York's fertility and Margaret's lack of passivity with Cecily's conformity to the medieval ideal. Margaret had done her best to be both king and queen when the situation demanded, to hold the Lancastrian empire together but, ultimately, the job was greater than her: only a competent king could hold on to his crown. And Henry VI was not a competent king. In comparison, the 18-year-old Edward of York – tall, athletic, handsome and victorious – was the medieval ideal monarch and his successes appeared to validate his position as an instrument of divine purpose. His father may have been killed, but he had the seasoned commanders Warwick and Salisbury at his side, and benefitted from their cumulative years of experience in England, France and Scotland. In addition, the young Edward had charisma, judgement and a gift for military leadership. He saw his opportunity and seized it. At the start of March, Edward entered London and was declared king. Having mustered his troops in St John's Fields, he gathered a huge crowd of around 5,000 people, according to the Ambassador of Milan, who received him 'joyously'. A delegation of the Great Council visited Cecily's home of Baynard's Castle to formally invite Edward to accept the throne in line with the Act of Accord and, after attending mass at St Paul's with his mother, the new king was sworn in at Westminster. At the end of the month, he decimated the Lancastrian army in the battle of Towton fought in the driving snow, perhaps the bloodiest and most brutal of all the conflicts of this period, during which an estimated 28,000 men died. Towton sealed the Yorkist monarchy. Cecily learned of the victory a few days later, which was read and reported by William Paston: 'oure Soverayn

Lord hath wonne the feld and upon the Munday next ... was resseved
in to York with gret solempnyte and processyons.' On reading the news,
Cecily went into her chapel with two chaplains and ordered Te Deums
to be sung. Paston also reported that 'Kyng Harry, the Qwen, the Prince,
Duke of Somerset, Duke of Exeter ... be fledde in to Scotteland'.[32] After
sixty-two years and three monarchs, the Lancastrians had lost their hold
on England's throne.

13

QUEEN IN EXILE, 1461–82

Where be my gowns of scarlet
Sanguine, murrey and blues sad and light
Greens also, and the fayre violet
Horse and harnys, fresche and lusty in syghte?
My wykked lyf hath put al this to flighte.[1]

Towton was a milestone in the history of the Wars of the Roses and appeared to signal the death knell of the Lancastrian dynasty. The young, handsome Edward IV proved very popular and contemporary poets captured the sense that he was restoring the true lineage of Edward III, which had been usurped by Henry Bolingbroke. Edward may have been the son of Cecily Neville, with her maternal Beaufort blood, but his father, the Duke of York, was descended from Gaunt's elder brother Lionel, Duke of Clarence, albeit through the female line. Edward is cast in the poem 'Edward, Dei Gratia' of 1462 as having had been helped to regain the throne of his forebears by divine intervention: 'God hathe chose thee to be his knight' because of his heritage 'out of the stoke that long lay dead'. The contemporary author of 'A Political Retrospect' also celebrated the Yorkist victory with anti-Lancastrian rhetoric, accusing them of 'gret wrongys of oold antiquity, unrightful heirs by wrong alliance usurping this Realm …' and connecting Edward IV with the reign of Richard II, who was now represented as a paragon:

> Kyng Richard the secounde, high of dignytee
> Whiche of Ingeland was Rightful enheritoure
> In whos tyme ther was habundance with plentee
> Of welthe and erthley joye without languor.

The poet dismissed the Lancastrian kings in turn. Henry IV was a leper who had usurped the crown 'undir the colour of fals perjury', Henry V had been the best of the line but reigned 'unrightfully' and 'by gret folly, all hath retourned unto huge languor' under Henry VI. 'A Political Retrospect' then went further to explicitly blame Margaret for her husband's failings, for her rapacious ambition, meaning she 'ever hath ment to governe all engeland with might and power' and that her troops, her 'wicked affinity', intended to 'utterly … destroye thys regioun, for with theym is but deth and distruction, robbery and vengeance with all rigour'.

This theme continued in the poem 'God Amend Wicked Counsel', written a couple of years later, which had Henry VI lamenting that:

> I wedded a wife at my devyse
> That was the cause of all my moan
> Thyll her intenete seyd I never naye
> Therefore I mourn and no thing and merry.

However much the tide had turned against her, Margaret was not prepared to give up the fight. With Henry and Edward, she fled north, from Newcastle to Alnwick Castle and on to Berwick. Margaret's cousin Louis XI, the new King of France, gave them financial assistance in return for their promise that he would be given Calais once they were restored to power. On 4 April, William Paston wrote to his brother John, describing how Edward had 'wonne the feld' and reporting that 'Kyng Harry, the

Qwen, the Prince, Duke of Somerset, Duke of Exeter and Lord Roos be fledde to Scotteland and they be chased and flowed'.[2] They headed to the Scottish court, where Mary of Guelders was acting as regent to her 10-year-old son James III. James III was the grandson of Joan Beaufort and James I, and reigned from the death of his father James II in 1460, when a cannon he was loading had exploded at the siege of Roxborough Castle. In return for Scottish support, Henry agreed on 25 April 1461 to grant them Berwick and also offered Carlisle, once it had been recaptured. There was also a treaty of marriage arranged between Prince Edward and James III's younger sister Margaret.

Cecily of York was the closest thing to a queen in England. While Edward IV lingered in the north, pursuing his enemies and making enquiries into the rebellions that were led against his father, Cecily was appointed as his representative in London. As the king's mother, she was the most important woman in the land, wielding complete power for a period of weeks, replacing Margaret of Anjou in significance. For the first four years of her son's reign, Cecily was central to English politics in the subtle female role of advisor and supporter. The papal legate Coppini was urged by his doctor to write and congratulate Edward, 'not forgetting on any account, to write to the Duchess of York', because Cecily could 'rule the king as she please[d]'. It was ironic that the woman who replaced the Lancastrian queen was herself a direct descendant of John of Gaunt, with more Lancastrian blood in her veins than the French Margaret.

Through the remainder of 1461, Margaret made plans to unite all her allies in a joint invasion of England to regain the throne. Among the Yorkists, it was feared with good reason that she would enlist the support of the kings of Portugal and Castile, who were descendants of John of Gaunt and welcomed Margaret as a fellow Lancastrian. Rumours reached Edward IV in London that a joint force of French and Spanish soldiers would land at Sandwich, the Duke of Somerset would join with Margaret's brother John of Calabria and land with more Spaniards on the east coast, while Jasper Tudor brought an army to North Wales. Sir Thomas Howes wrote to John Paston that he had learned 'in right secret wyse' that 'kyng Herry and the Quene that was, and by the Dewk Somercete and others, of 120,000 men ... if wynde and weder hadde servyd theym, shuld a'ben here sone upon Candlemasse

… [for] malicious purpose and evyl wylle'.[3] The loyal Lancastrian John de Vere, twelfth Earl of Oxford, was to be the focal point in England.[4] However, these rumours, suggesting an even larger combined invasion, prompted Edward to pre-empt any attack. By this point, Oxford was in his fifties and had been given an exemption from attending Parliament on account of ill health, although this might have been an excuse to avoid involvement with the new Yorkist regime. Edward had his suspicions though, and in February 1462, Oxford and his eldest son Aubrey were arrested for treason and beheaded on Tower Hill.

Margaret knew her best way to help was to enlist foreign support, which was most likely to come from the land of her birth, by appealing to her cousin Charles VII. On 30 August, Lord Hungerford and Robert Whityngham, her 'true subjects and liegemen', wrote to her from Dieppe informing her of Charles' death the previous month, which removed the potential ally from whom she had hoped to find support. The pair tried to offer the exiled queen comfort and a word of warning, urging her to fear not 'but be of gode comfort and beware that ye aventure [risk] not your person, ne my Lord the Prynce by the See till ye have oder word from us, in less that your person cannot be sure there as ye ar [and] that extreme necessite dryfe you thens'. They also advised that the king remain safe, knowing that the future of the Lancastrian dynasty rested in the continuing survival of these three people. The letter concludes with the strange detail that Henry was then at Kirkhowbre with four men and a child, while Margaret and Edward were at Edinburgh with Thomas de Roos, a son of Eleanor Beaufort, Duchess of Somerset by her first marriage. Perhaps it was considered safer to keep the king and prince apart in the event of attacks being made upon them. The letter also included a list of all those loyal Lancastrians who had fled with Margaret, many of whom were part of the extended family by marriage: John Ormonde, William Tailboys, Sir John Fortescue, John Audeley, Sir Henry Roos, John Courtenay and others.[5]

The following April, Margaret travelled to France to meet her father and Louis XI. She left Henry behind in Scotland, but took Prince Edward with her, sailing from Kirkcudbright in a ship financed by Mary of Guelders. She landed on 8 April in Brittany, where Jasper Tudor was attempting to negotiate with Duke Francis to undertake an invasion of England. That summer, Margaret signed an agreement with Louis at

Chinon, by which he loaned her 20,000 livres with Calais as security and a hundred-year peace would follow between the two nations. Margaret returned to Scotland that October. During the winter months, the border castles of Bamburgh, Alnwick and Dunstanburgh were recaptured by the Lancastrians, and Margaret began to feel a degree of optimism, promising lands to the Scottish Regency Council in exchange for their support. Then, for some reason, Louis changed his mind and opened negotiations with Edward IV in June. An attack upon Norham Castle led by Henry, Margaret and Prince Edward failed terribly and Margaret was dispirited by the friendship of Philip of Burgundy with the English king. That August she visited Flanders with her son in an attempt to preserve her alliance with the Burgundians, but could not prevent a truce being signed between England, France, Brittany and Burgundy that October. Margaret's friends had failed her.

Margaret headed back to France with her son. Henry remained behind in England, perhaps to be on hand in the event of a successful invasion; perhaps it was a step too far for the anointed king to leave his country entirely and throw himself upon the mercy of foreigners. Margaret and Edward did not know it at the time, but they would not see him again. Once in France, Margaret established herself at a property owned by her father: Koeur-la-Petite Castle, in Saint-Mihiel-en-Bar, halfway between Verdun and Nancy, and lived on a pension of 2,000 livres.[6] Among her retinue were the dukes of Somerset and Exeter, Sir John Fortescue and a number of other loyal Lancastrians served by a staff of around fifty attendants.[7] In his *De Laudibus Legum Angliae*, Fortescue left a description of the young Prince Edward preparing for his military future, dedicating himself:

> entirely to martial exercises and seated on fierce and half-tamed steeds urged on by his spurs, he often delighted in attacking and assaulting the young companions attending him, sometimes with a lance, sometimes with a sword, sometimes with other weapons, in a warlike manner and in accordance with the rules of military discipline.

Having observed his mother's struggles and their loss of status in England, young Edward was following in the footsteps of Henry IV and Henry V, preparing himself to become the next Lancastrian champion.

Another leading Lancastrian was soon to defect to Margaret's cause. The Yorkists remained wary of members of the Beaufort family, rightly surmising in many cases that shows of loyalty to the new regime did not run very deep. Edward IV sent Edmund Beaufort, son of the Duke of Somerset, to the Tower for two years after Towton. His elder brother Henry had gone to France on Margaret's behalf to negotiate with the ailing Charles VII for an army to invade England and restore Lancastrian fortunes, but Charles' successor, Louis XI, was not willing to undertake such a venture, preferring instead to ally himself with Edward IV. He threw Henry Beaufort in prison. The following year, after being allowed to go free and travelling to Bruges, Henry entered negotiations with Warwick and defected to his army at the end of 1462. The following year, Edward IV restored all Beaufort's lands, 'made full much of him'[8] and invited him to play a role at court, taking part in entertainments and becoming a close companion of the king. Edmund was also freed from prison and his mother Eleanor, Somerset's widow, was granted a pardon and her estates were restored to her. In July 1463, Henry was on progress with King Edward at Northampton when locals attacked him, forcing him to flee to Chirk Castle. From there, he began to reconsider his allegiance and, at the end of the year, fled to Scotland to join Henry VI.

Through the winter of 1463–64, Margaret continued to try to raise support for her cause and Jasper Tudor visited Paris to negotiate again with Louis XI. In the spring of 1464, Somerset, Exeter, Lord Roos and Lord Hungerford made another attempt to regain control of the throne in Henry's name, meeting an army led by the Earl of Warwick's brother, John, Marquess of Montagu, at Hexham. Waiting in France, there was little Margaret could do to influence the outcome. When news came, following the battle on 15 May, it was another terrible blow to her hopes. The Yorkists had won the day. Thirty leading Lancastrian knights were executed after the battle, including Henry Beaufort, aged only 28. Henry VI's support in England collapsed. He had been hidden by friends in various locations in Scotland and the Midlands but the following year, he was captured by his enemies and sent to the Tower.

Another woman briefly emerges into the Lancastrian story at this point. A woman about whom little has been written as barely anything is known, yet she played a part in the continuance of the bloodline from

John of Gaunt, especially after the losses in the Beaufort family and their lack of progeny. When he died, Henry Beaufort left an illegitimate son by a mistress who may have named Joan Hill. Where she came from and who she was remains a mystery, as her name does not appear on any of the court records and was only suggested by a Boston scholar, E.H. Gurney, in 1890. She may have died in childbirth. Henry may have made provision for her, or perhaps Margaret did, because her son received an education that allowed him to take a place at the court of Henry VII and to marry well. Charles Beaufort was legitimised, probably before his first marriage in 1492 to Elizabeth Herbert, daughter of the Lancastrian Earl of Pembroke. She bore him two children before he married again, at least once, and may have fathered three more, establishing the Somerset line with the Beaufort blood. Charles died in 1526 and was buried in St George's Chapel, Windsor, but what happened to his elusive mother is unknown. Joan Hill is probably the most shadowy figure in the history of Lancastrian women, making her single contribution of a child, but she was another link in the chain of survival.

Survival was all that the displaced Queen Margaret could think about after Towton. For five frustrating years, she could do little but scheme, hope and bide her time. However, the political climate in England was changing and the previously solid alliance between Edward IV and his cousin the Duke of Warwick was shifting. The primary cause for this was the rise of the Wydeville family. Warwick had been hoping for a French marriage, proposing Bona of Savoy, Louis XI's sister-in-law, as a bride and queen for Edward, and negotiations took place during 1464. However, when Parliament met at Reading in September, Edward announced that he had already taken a wife, in a secret ceremony earlier that year, probably around 1 May. His bride was none other than Elizabeth, the eldest daughter of Jacquetta Wydeville, a beautiful blonde widow five years the king's senior, formerly married to a Lancastrian knight. Elizabeth was unsuitable as a royal bride on a number of levels, being a widow who had already borne two sons and chosen without consultation with Edward's family and council, and they married in conditions that gave rise to suspicion. The pair had reputedly met when Elizabeth petitioned him for assistance in retrieving her sons' inheritance, but they are likely to have been aware of each other for longer, perhaps meeting at court in the 1450s. At the very least, the marriage removed the possibility of Edward making an advantageous foreign alliance. In 1461, Edward stayed near her family home of Stony Stratford and granted a pardon to Elizabeth's father, Sir Richard Wydeville, for his previous Lancastrian allegiance. The local legend that they met under an oak tree in Whittlewood Forest cannot be substantiated, but it taps into the romance surrounding the match, which may have taken place at the chapel of the Hermitage, on Wydeville's land. Elizabeth was brought to Reading and formally introduced as queen, and her coronation took place in May 1465. The following February, she bore Edward a first child, a daughter also named Elizabeth.

This marriage was the beginning of the rift between Edward and Warwick, who resented the rapid advancement of the new queen's relatives, whom he considered to be social upstarts. By some accounts, Cecily was also greatly displeased that her son had chosen not to confide in her and selected an unsuitable woman to replace her as England's leading lady. In addition, Warwick favoured England's alliance with France but Edward was increasingly siding with Richard Wydeville, who urged that an Anglo-Burgundian friendship would be more beneficial. By 1469, after Elizabeth had borne three daughters but no male heir, Warwick seized the opportunity to marry his elder daughter Isabel to Edward's ambitious brother, George, Duke of Clarence. The match had been forbidden by Edward, causing Warwick to seek a dispensation on his own and retreat to Calais, where the ceremony took place on 11 July. George and Warwick then returned to England in the wake of other risings in the north, declaring against Edward in the hope of deposing him in favour of any male child Isabel might bear. Edward was temporarily captured and held by Warwick, but he stopped short of putting the king to death and found that he needed Edward's presence to rule the country. Licking his wounds, Warwick fled again to France, where he formulated a new plan. The Isabel–Clarence marriage had failed to produce the desired results, when Isabel miscarried a child on board ship. But Warwick had a second daughter. Now he planned to marry Anne Neville to Margaret's son Prince Edward and restore the Lancastrian dynasty. Margaret's bitterest enemy now offered to become her salvation.

It was a bitter pill to swallow but Margaret was a pragmatist and a realist. Her husband was still in the Tower, her closest friends and councillors had been killed and her best efforts to enlist support had failed. A powerful figure like Warwick offered her the only chance to strike again at the English throne, so after a show of strength when she kept the earl on his knees for fifteen minutes, Margaret swallowed her pride and embraced the opportunity. She 'graciously forgave him' for the 'injuries and wrongs done to her in the past' and allowed Warwick to do 'homage and fealty … swearing to be a faithful and loyal subject of the king, queen and prince as his liege lords unto death'.[9] In Angers Cathedral on 25 July, the 16-year-old Prince Edward and the 14-year-old Anne Neville were formally betrothed. Warwick returned to England that September, taking Edward IV by surprise. The king found himself hemmed in by Warwick's allies and fled to the Netherlands while his family and heavily pregnant wife sought sanctuary in Westminster Abbey. That November, the queen bore a son. Warwick then liberated Henry VI from the Tower but the Lancastrian king was overwhelmed and incomprehensible, and had to be led by the hand through the streets on the day of his formal 'readeption' on 3 October. Warwick's success had been spectacular. This was the moment Margaret had waited for. It was time for her to return to England and step back into her former role. Yet she delayed. The poor weather may have been partly to blame, or else she was waiting until Edward and Anne were formally married that December, but Margaret did not land in England until 14 April. That same day, Warwick was killed in battle.

As Margaret's ship docked in Weymouth, and she returned in confidence to her subjects, with Prince Edward and Princess Anne as England's future king and queen, she had no idea of the turn of events that had been played out at Barnet. King Edward had returned from the Netherlands with a vengeance, landing at Ravenspur on 14 March, while Margaret's boats were still waiting for the storm to abate at Harfleur. From the coast, she travelled to Cerne Abbey in Dorset, a large Benedictine house established before the Norman Conquest, and stayed in the newly built guest house with its oriel windows and flint walls. There, they learned the news that Edward IV had defeated Warwick's army after a day of fighting in the mist, and that Earl Richard had been killed in the rout. Margaret could have withdrawn at this point. Warwick had been integral to her plans.

With Henry recaptured, she and her son had the support of a group of loyal nobles, but they lacked a figure of Warwick's mettle to stand against the Yorkists. Margaret was still relatively near the coast and had not yet engaged with the enemy. It would have been easy to turn around and return to France. Instead, she decided to stay and face them in battle.

On 4 May 1471, the Lancastrian troops under Prince Edward and the remaining Beaufort brothers, Edmund and John, met with the Yorkists led by Edward IV and his brothers George, Duke of Clarence and Richard, Duke of Gloucester. Margaret waited for news with her daughter-in-law Anne, in or near Gobes Farmhouse, now Gupshill Manor, which was the centre of the Lancastrian defences, about a mile from the centre of Tewkesbury town, near the abbey and rivers Avon and Severn. Margaret had mustered men from Devon and Cornwall and the final total for her army was around 6,000, outnumbering the Yorkists by about 1,000. The right flank was commanded by Edmund Beaufort, the left by John Courtenay, Earl of Devon and the centre was held by Lord Wenlock and Prince Edward, although the anticipated troops from Jasper Tudor had not yet arrived. There was little Margaret could do except pray and plan. Eventually the news arrived. The Lancastrian forces had been defeated, but the exact nature of their end remains unclear. Some sources claim that Prince Edward and Somerset were killed during the battle, while others describe a series of executions taking place in its aftermath, or state that Somerset and others sought sanctuary in the abbey and were dragged out to be killed two days later. Whatever happened, Margaret's cause was lost. Worse still, her son was dead. She recognised that she could do little now but submit to the Yorkists, sending word to King Edward that she was at his command and submitting to the custody of Sir William Stanley.[10]

On 11 May, Margaret and Anne were brought before King Edward at Coventry. What happened during the meeting is unclear, but three days later, Anne was committed to the guardianship of her sister Isabel and Margaret began the journey south to London. She was kept as a captive, part of the triumphant king's train. Some reports describe her being displayed alongside him in a chariot as a trophy of war. Upon their arrival, Margaret was sent to the Tower, where her husband was still lodged, although she was not permitted to see him. That night, 21 May, Henry VI died.

According to his biographer R.A. Griffiths, 'there can be no reasonable doubt that he died violently'.[11] When his tomb was opened in 1910, the contents were examined at Cambridge University and the conclusion was drawn that his death had not been caused by grief, as circulated by some contemporary Yorkist accounts. His skull was broken shortly before the time of death, his hair matted with blood. The body of the king was displayed to the public at St Paul's Cathedral in order to quell any future rumours of his survival and he was buried in Chertsey Abbey. In 1484, his remains would be moved to St George's Chapel, Windsor. The body of Margaret's son, who would have been the next Lancastrian ruler, was buried in Tewkesbury Abbey. Two other significant casualties of Tewkesbury were the brothers Edmund and John Beaufort, great-grandsons of John of Gaunt and Katherine Swynford. Edmund may have been in his early thirties but unmarried and John was only 16. Both died without heirs and, with their deaths, the Beaufort dynasty came to an end.

The events of May 1471 were a triumph for the Yorkists and Edward IV returned to rule, reunited with his wife and family, including his newborn son, Prince Edward. Just a year after this success, though, his queen was to suffer a personal loss on the death of her mother, Jacquetta, Countess Rivers. The former Lancastrian lady, first wife of John, Duke of Bedford, had experienced mixed fortunes in the intervening years. Her second marriage to Richard Wydeville had been a happy one, even though he was of lower status than her birth and first match had given her, and she had borne him fourteen children, the last arriving in around 1458. Due to Jacquetta's friendship with Margaret of Anjou, to whom she was related, Wydeville had been created Earl Rivers and their loyalty to the Lancastrian dynasty was strong. However, love was to alter all that. Complicit in her daughter's secret marriage six years later, Jacquetta had witnessed the beautiful Elizabeth's sudden power and the birth of her grandchildren, but had also suffered the hostility this brought and proved a target for attack on many levels.

As queen, Elizabeth had promoted her relatives, just as did others who rose to power. In March 1466, her father was created Lord High Treasurer and influential marriages were arranged for her siblings, caus-ing resentment among Edward's former supporters, his brother George and the Earl of Warwick. They took the opportunity to exact revenge when Wydeville fought for the king, his son-in-law, after the battle of Edgecote, capturing the earl and his son John, and executing them at Kenilworth. The bereaved Jacquetta fled to sanctuary with her daughter to wait out the danger but even there, Warwick attempted to discredit them, using the traditional female accusation of witchcraft. The accusation of sorcery is a common thread running through the history of the women of the Lancastrian cause. Coupled with treason, disloyalty, ambition and often sexual irregularity, it blighted the lives of Joan of Navarre and Eleanor Cobham and, after Jacquetta's death, not even the pious Margaret Beaufort would be safe from the charge.

It would not have escaped Warwick's attention that Jacquetta had once been Eleanor Cobham's sister-in-law. Now, twenty years after her lonely death at Beaumaris Castle, Warwick incited one of his servants to make an allegation that Jacquetta had made a leaden effigy of a man, broken in the middle and bound together by wire. This was very similar to the wax image that Eleanor had been supposed to have made in an attempt to harm the young Henry VI. The informant, Thomas Wake, was examined but his evidence relied upon the testimony of a single man, who failed to appear and give account of himself. With Edward IV absent and unable to offer his protection, Jacquetta appealed to the mayor and aldermen, writing them a letter on 31 August, reminding them of the way her intervention had saved the city when it had been threatened by Margaret of Anjou's army. The mayor forwarded her plea to the next most senior royal in Edward's absence, George, Duke of Clarence. Soon though, king, Clarence and earl were reconciled and Jacquetta was formally cleared of the charges in Edward's next Parliament. She may have attended in person to accuse Wake of malice intended to 'hurt and impair her good name and fame, but also purposing the final destruction of her person'. The accusations were to resurface later when it was expedient for Richard III to cast doubt on his brother's marriage.

It isn't clear what Jacquetta died from. She was 56 when she passed away on 30 May 1472, and although the location of her final resting place is unknown, it is likely that she returned to her marital home of Grafton. Elizabeth had only emerged from her fifth confinement, having given birth on 10 April to a daughter, named Margaret, and was probably going through the process of churching around the middle of May. In the last couple of years, she and her mother had been driven together through the uncertainty of the readeption, through birth and death, and seen their fortunes restored. No matter what supernatural powers popular novelists may have ascribed to Jacquetta, she did not have the ability to foresee that the Yorkist dynasty would continue uninterrupted for the next thirteen years, or that there would be a hiatus in 1483. She must have provided considerable support to her daughter and been loath to leave her in uncertain times, just as much as Elizabeth must have grieved her loss.

Just as one queen lost her mother, a former queen and mother was grieving the loss of her child. After Tewkesbury, Margaret of Anjou had nothing left to fight for: she was kept a prisoner in the Tower before being moved to Windsor, Wallingford and Ewelme, where she lived in the custody of Alice, widow of the Duke of Suffolk. Given the long-term friendship between the ex-queen and the Suffolks, this must have been more comfortable for Margaret than remaining in London, in proximity to the new queen, Elizabeth Wydeville. Alice had previously been the custodian of the rebellious Duke of Exeter in 1455, but perhaps the company of her new charge was more to her tastes. With Alice, perhaps Margaret was able to enjoy a little company, gentle pursuits and reminiscences about happier days, recalling when the Duke of Suffolk first accompanied the young princess to England or reading the verses of Alice's protégé John Lydgate. But Alice died in 1475, at around the age of 70, and it may have been this that prompted Edward IV to reconsider Margaret's future. A former deposed queen was a dangerous political commodity, even if she had been brought so low as Margaret. In the same year, Edward led an expedition against the French and in the subsequent treaty of Picardy he offered to ransom his prisoner for the sum of 50,000 crowns as long as she renounced all claims to any English jointure, titles or lands. It was a total defeat for the former queen, a complete annihilation which she had little cause or strength to fight. It may even have come as a relief. Margaret was then in her mid-forties and that November she applied for, and was granted, a papal dispensation to eat dairy products during Lent, as she was of a 'delicate and weak constitution'. Leaving England early the following year, Margaret travelled from Dieppe to Rouen, where she was received by a representative of Louis XI, in a strange, sad reminder of her triumphal entry to the city as a young bride in 1445, when she had been welcomed by King Edward's parents. Margaret signed away her French inheritances too, ceding to Louis the lands she had gained from her brother's death the previous year. Her final years were spent in penury in her father's Castle Reculée but, following his death in 1480, she was dependent upon the charity of one of René's vassals, who took her into his home at Castle Dampierre. Margaret died there in August 1482 at the age of 52.

Margaret's reputation has undergone a range of interpretations during the centuries after her death. As a queen, she made many cultural contributions to the Lancastrian dynasty: as a patron, a focus of piety and as an intercessor. Margaret was the founder of Queens' College, Cambridge, issuing a charter to establish building on 15 April 1448. Her deputy, Lord Wenlock, laid the first stone that very day, which bore the motto 'The Lord shall be a refuge to our sovereign lady, Queen Margaret, and this stone shall be for a token of the same.'[12] Her arms were later removed by Elizabeth Wydeville, who replaced them with her own. Margaret was also the owner of a number of manuscripts, probably including the residue of Gloucester's library from Greenwich. There was the magnificent collection of texts John Talbot had given her on her wedding day, a manuscript containing Lydgate's *Life of our Lady* as well as other lyrics by Lydgate, Chaucer and others, and a Latin life of Gilbert de Semperingham and Georges Chastellain's *Temple de Boccace*, probably written in the 1460s. Margaret commissioned a set of Latin prayers to the Virgin, which included an image of herself and her arms impaled with those of Henry and she owned the manuscript made for Mary de Bohun on her marriage to Henry Bolingbroke, to which she had her own arms added.[13] She may also have commissioned a manuscript of *New Statutes of England* for Edward and other similar texts.[14]

Margaret's letters show that she took the question of royal patronage seriously, frequently writing to advance her servants. In the late 1440s, she wrote to the Master of St Giles in the Fields to request that the 17-year-old chorister Robert Upholme be received into the hospital and given a livelihood, and to the Duke of Exeter, on behalf of her squire Thomas Sharnbourne, whose cousin had been wrongfully dismissed, later also ensuring Thomas had an annual pension drawn from her estates at Waltham Abbey. Margaret wrote to the Abbess of Barking that she might advance Henry's secretary Robert Osborne and his wife, to the City of London on behalf of her tenants and to the Archbishop of Canterbury to right a wrong done to John Reignold, yeoman of the King's Hall. In 1447, two deaths in the royal family prompted her to intervene for the sake of charity. Following the death of the Duke of Gloucester, she wrote to an unknown woman in 1447, perhaps to the wife of the Duke of Suffolk or Somerset, thanking her for the support given to the poet George Ashby and hoping that, despite the duke's death, she would 'continue so forth your benevolence and good dispocioun' towards Ashby. The same April, when Henry, Cardinal Beaufort died, she wrote to executors of his will in the knowledge that a portion of his estate had been bequeathed to the assistance of the needy. Her cause was that of two young people, W. Frutes and Agnes Knoughton, who were 'poure creatures and of vertuous conversacion' who wished to be married if they had the benefit of alms.[15] Margaret had been a particular friend of the cardinal, staying regularly at his house at Waltham Forest, where a chamber had been fitted out in gold damask solely for her use. The hangings were bequeathed to her in his will of 1447.[16]

Verdicts on Margaret's queenship have been mixed and often coloured by issues that have clouded the impressive qualities she possessed and the impossible circumstances in which she found herself. The opinions of many of her contemporaries were dominated by questions of gender, casting her in the role of an unnatural female, a scapegoat for the inability of Henry VI and the failure of his regime, an easy target, as Lisa Hilton notes, of *chercher la femme*.[17] As early as 1462 a pro-Yorkist ballad included the belief that 'it is a great perversion for a woman of a land to be a regent', and Margaret's determination, dedication and bravery have been translated into ambition and an overly militant approach, a charge laid against no man of the period. One part of an anecdotal report of a speech made by Margaret to her army captains cast her in the role of a new Joan of Arc, terror to the English burned as a witch: 'I have mowed down ranks far more stubborn than theirs are now … I will either conquer or be conquered with you.' The anonymous author commented that Margaret's audience 'marvelled at such boldness in a woman, at a man's courage in a woman's breast … they said that the spirit of the Maid who had raised Charles VII to the throne, was renewed in the queen'. The *Davies Chronicle* had Margaret ruling 'the realm as she liked, gathering riches innumerable … the queen was defamed and denounced, that he who was called prince was not her son but a bastard conceived in adultery.'

However, it is disappointing that anachronistic readings of Margaret's abilities in terms of gender appear in later biographies, which portray her as a meddlesome woman, overly ambitious and something of a firebrand or harridan for daring to possess skills for which men of the period are lauded. Some even go so far as to place all the blame at her door. The tone for many of these was set by Victorian historian G.P.R. James, who described her as a woman of 'great virtues … great talents … and high qualities' which were tempered by 'dark and dangerous faults'. She 'was a woman of ambition and intrigue' sharing the throne with a weak prince and was directly responsible for his decline and fall: 'had she joined great virtues to great talents, she might have saved her husband and preserved a crown'. In terms of her marriage, James was also quick to conclude that Henry's character, which he assessed as better suited to the monastery than the throne, meant that Margaret had 'at once … gained the ascendancy over his mind'. Again, the gender boundaries were perceived to have been blurred to Margaret's cost: 'she was a woman of high spirit, strong sense, ready wit and politic habits, desirous of glory, and covetous of fame.' All these qualities were acceptable in Gaunt, Henry IV or Henry V, and the wives who supported them, but not in Margaret, because there was no strong man to offset her ambition, and thus making it visible. Yet Margaret's 'ambition' did not emerge until after St Albans, where it is arguably a defensive mechanism to preserve the inheritance of her son, in the light of her husband's inability to rule. James' estimation of her failure rested on her gender: 'she was not inexpert in business and altogether of a masculine turn of mind. In her political actions, she had one great fault however, which has been frequently attributed to her sex; namely a mutability and unsteadiness of purpose.' In comparison with her husband, Margaret's purpose, either as queen from 1445–55 or attempting to retain power from 1455–61, or in working tirelessly for her son's cause in the following decade, suggests a consistency of service and devotion to the Lancastrian cause, which such authors have downplayed as a negative function of her gender. Instead, she did everything she could within the confines of her circumstances, sometimes defying and exceeding such reductive categorisation.

Equally, her biographer Jacob Abbot blames Margaret's downfall in March 1461 upon a resurgence of national repugnance after the 'shocking cruelties' in which she revelled after the battle of Wakefield. There is no evidence to support his claims that she was 'filled with the wildest exultation and joy' or that Lord Clifford carried Salisbury's head to her on a pike, or that she was 'almost beside herself'. Abbot also cites Edmund, Earl of Rutland as dying in that battle at the age of 12 when, in fact, Cecily's second surviving son was 17. He also paints a vivid picture of Margaret laughing at York's head on the spike at Micklegate Bar, with its paper crown, and exulting over Rutland's death, animated by a 'ferocious hate' and 'furious and vindictive spirit'. Margaret's unruly army no doubt caused considerable alarm but responsibility for the subsequent Yorkist victories at Mortimer's Cross and Towton must lie with the skill and determination of Edward IV.

There is no doubt that Margaret was a militant queen defending her family and dynasty, a great fighter for the Lancastrian cause. She may have made mistakes in the handling of her troops, or in the usual accusation that she relied upon factional politics, which created a fatal division with the house of York, but whatever she lacked in political and military astuteness she made up for in determination and devotion. The worst accusation levelled against women of the fifteenth century appears to be that of ambition, a charge from which the reputations of Elizabeth Wydeville and Margaret Beaufort have also suffered. This anachronism is the residue of stricter gender roles and has little place in modern historical analysis. Margaret and her female contemporaries must finally be allowed to exhibit their admirable strengths without such censure. She may not have conformed to the ideals of queenship as set out by her times, but she was one of the bravest and most loyal advocates of the Lancastrian dynasty and it was fortunate to have her.

Margaret's reputation has also suffered because she was Lancaster's queen, albeit technically deposed, when the dynasty lost the throne. The family fortunes had been building since the time of John of Gaunt, through the trials of the reign of Richard II, to the brave return of Henry IV and the concerted military efforts of Henry V. Each of their wives had contributed to this process, by childbearing, support, dowries, advice and in a myriad other ways but none had been forced to carry the dynasty, to take on leadership, a substitute kingship, in the way Margaret was. And as a result, because the crown was lost in 1471, Margaret's reputation has been associated with failure. It is easy with hindsight to make a judgement about the actions or inactions of the past, about the decisions that were successful, or not, and the circumstances they were made in. It would be easy to say that, had Margaret returned to England that spring before the arrival of Edward IV, circumstances may have been different, but ultimately, these historical cul-de-sacs obscure the very real division of responsibility for the dynasty's failure. Lancaster's nadir of 1471 was the result of a number of factors, but the most significant was Henry VI's mental health and unsuitability to rule, coupled with the strength and vigour of the opposition he faced. It would never have been necessary for Margaret's role to extend beyond that of supportive consort had Henry's kingship been a success. Ultimately, she was operating within the limits that circumstance dictated and she had been dealt a particularly bad hand. While her nationality and gender counted against her, she was not responsible for the dynastic failure that propelled the throne into Yorkist hands. Rather, she did everything in her power and ability to avoid it.

14

TUDOR'S WIDOW, 1471–85

All these lightly should be torned up so downe
Ne were of wommenthe prefight stableness.[1]

I

Lancastrian fortunes reached their nadir in 1471. Not even in the years following Henry VI's deposition a decade earlier had things been so bleak. Then, the king and prince had remained focal points for dynastic hopes: an embodiment of a potential future in which the wheel of fortune would turn again and propel them back into power. With their deaths, there was no clear replacement, no younger Lancastrian son or brother in waiting, with the Beaufort line coming to an end and the Tudors never representing a serious claim due to their parentage. All the male members of the dynasty had died without leaving an heir, or those heirs had themselves been killed. However, there was a woman in whom the blood of John of Gaunt still flowed: his great-granddaughter Margaret Beaufort.

The devastating battle at Barnet in April 1471 which had claimed the life of Warwick also proved to be the last stand of another Lancastrian knight whose death helped shape the dynasty's future. Margaret's third husband, Sir Henry Stafford, had fought on the side of the Yorkists to regain the throne for Edward IV, but had sustained such injuries that he was brought home to die. He lingered for six months but his wounds finally killed him on 4 October. Margaret was then 28. Over her short life thus far she had experienced drama and reversals that had taken her from the heart of the restored Lancastrian court into an uncertain future. However, with a wise marriage, clever negotiation and a degree of good fortune, she was to emerge a woman of resolution and courage, whose determination was to restore the crown to the bruised house of Lancaster.

Margaret's early history had been tainted by tragedy. The daughter of John Beaufort, Gaunt's grandson, she would have had no memories of the father who had fought alongside Henry V in France and replaced the Duke of York as Lieutenant of Normandy. However, his loyalty had not always been returned: between his capture at the battle of the Bauge in 1428 and 1438, he had been imprisoned by the French before being ransomed and allowed to return home. His final campaign in Cherbourg and Gascony proved a disaster and his death in 1444 has long been considered a possible suicide. The official version of his demise charged it to 'an unexpected infirmity' and there were plenty of precedents of such illnesses killing previously healthy adults in their late thirties. By the 1460s though, French chronicler Thomas Basin described Beaufort's 'unexpected infirmity' as brought on by an inability to bear failure and shame, being 'vain and inefficient in his deeds' but his 'proud and presumptuous spirit' made him 'unwilling to bear patiently any sort of disgrace or injury'.[2] By the time the *Croyland Chronicle* was written in the 1470s, Beaufort's pride had escalated into 'extreme indignation' at being accused of treason. Unable to bear the stain, he had 'accelerated his death by putting an end to his existence, it is generally said, preferring to cut short his sorrow, rather than pass a life of misery, labouring under so disgraceful a charge'.[3]

Following her father's death, Henry VI granted Margaret's wardship to Suffolk, even though her mother was still living, which was then fairly usual practice. At Berkhamsted Castle on 31 May 1444 he confirmed that:

> For asmoche as oure Cousine the Duc of Somerset is nowe late passed to
> Goddes mercy, the whiche hath a doughter and heir to succede after hym
> of full tender age called Margarete. We, considering the notable services
> that oure Cousin th'erl of Suffolk hath doon unto us … have graunted
> unto hym to have the warde and marriage of the said Margarete withouten
> anything therefore unto us or oure heires yelding.

Although Suffolk was now her guardian, the girl remained with her
mother at Bletsoe Castle in Bedfordshire, to be brought up in anticipation of a great future.[4]

Margaret's mother, Margaret Beauchamp, had been the heiress
to her only brother, with lands and estates in Wiltshire, Dorset and
Bedfordshire. She was a considerable catch when she first married, in
her teens, to Sir Oliver St John and bore him seven children before being
widowed at the age of 27. Thus Margaret already had a large family of
stepsiblings whose marriages would later create a network of affiliation
with the important Scrope, Pole and Zouche dynasties. Margaret was
raised with the St John children, even embroidering their coat of arms
into a decorative piece that remained on display in the castle until the
reign of James I. Margaret was taught to read French and a little Latin;
later, Bishop Fisher would describe her as 'of singular wisedom ferre
passyng the comyn rate of women. She was good in remembraunce and
of holding memorye … a redy witte she had also to concyve all thyngs …
right studious she was in Bokes, which she had in grete number, both in
Englysh and in Frenshe.'[5] She was also devout, even at a young age, pray-
ing to St Nicholas the helper of all true maidens at four in the morning
'to beseech him to put in her mynde what she were best to do'.[6] Fisher
also identified the intensity of emotion that would show itself on certain
occasions later in her life, writing that Margaret was 'endued with great
towardness of nature'. Later, both she and her mother would be admitted
into the confraternity of the Abbey of Croyland, close to their property of
Deeping, as well as patronising other religious establishments. Mindful
early on of her daughter's position, the potential stigma of suicide coupled with the Beaufort inheritance, her mother agreed to the betrothal of
the young Margaret, aged between 1 and 3, to John de la Pole, eldest son
of William, first Duke of Suffolk. A formal marriage ceremony may have

been undertaken, but it was dissolved after Suffolk's death and Margaret herself never considered them to be legally husband and wife.

Margaret may have been the only daughter born of her parents' marriage, an older brother dying young, but she was not her father's only surviving girl. A woman named Tacine or Tacina or Thomasine of Somerset has sometimes been attached to John, Duke of Somerset, an affair he had whilst on campaign in France. She is traceable through documents relating to her husband, Reginald Grey, seventh Baron Grey of Wilton, who was born on or around 1420. If his wife was a similar age, this would place her father in his late twenties, and their encounter during the period of his service with Henry V. However, some confusion may have arisen between two women of similar name, obscuring the identity of both or perhaps creating two individuals out of one. According to at least one genealogical site, Grey had already been married once, to a Tacinda Tudor, reputedly a daughter of Owen Tudor and Catherine of Valois. If so, this Tacinda died before October 1447, after which point Grey remarried to a Thomasine Beaufort, John's illegitimate daughter by an unknown mother, who went on to bear Grey a son and heir. Tacine's existence is proven by a reference in the Council records for 20 June 1443, when her foreign birth necessitated the award of English nationality: 'the Kyng graunted at the same time and place that Tacyn doughter bastard to my said Lord of Somerset and her heires of her body lawfully begotten.' This was probably in preparation for her marriage because in October she is listed for the first time as Grey's wife; the last reference to her is made in 1469.

It is likely that Margaret was aware of her illegitimate half-sister's existence but with the gap of a generation between them and Tacine already married by the time Margaret was born, they may not have had much to do with each other. Reginald Grey fought with the Yorkists at Mortimer's Cross and lived long enough to see his wife's nephew become the first Tudor King of England. In 1447, Margaret's mother married again, by special licence, to Lionel, or Leon, de Welles, sixth Baron Welles, who had served Henry VI in France and campaigned with Humphrey, Duke of Gloucester in 1435; he had also been Lord Lieutenant of Ireland and joint Deputy of Calais. Welles already had five children from a first marriage, and his new wife bore him a son, John, around 1450. It is not clear whether the young Margaret and the St John children went with their mother to live with him, or where she may have lived if not, but a detail on a tomb in Bletsoe church may shed some light on the question. A Ralph Lannoy was buried there in 1458 and his tomb was formerly engraved with the legend 'Cofferer and Keeper of the Wardrobe to the most noble Margaret, Duchess of Somerset, then married to her third husband, Leo Lord Welles'.[7] The fact that Ralph lies in Bletsoe may be an indicator that it was Welles who moved into Margaret's home, rather than the other way round.

There is no surviving image of Margaret as a young woman. The familiar portraits of her in severe nun-like clothing, head covered and hands together in prayer, which is echoed on her tomb, date either from her final widowhood, during the reign of her son, or from a much later period. Bishop Fisher described her as physically small and historian David Starkey sees a likeness between her picture and that of her grandson Prince Arthur, identifying hooded eyes with bags under them and a hooked nose as common features. It would seem that she was petite and dark-eyed, but looks were of little consequence when it came to the duty of dynastic marriages. More important was pedigree and affiliation, education and character. Fisher also said that Margaret was 'of singular easiness to be spoken unto, and full courteous answer she would make to all that came unto her. Of marvellous gentleness she was unto all folks, but specially unto her own, whom she loved and trusted right tenderly.' She never forgot any kindness or service done to her, 'which is no little part of very nobleness', and she was always ready to forgive and forget an injury.

In 1453, Margaret was summoned to court by Margaret of Anjou. Accompanied by her mother, the 9-year-old arrived in London in the middle of February and was given a generous allowance of 100 marks to purchase suitable clothing. Margaret later recalled that she was at Westminster in May when the Suffolk marriage was dissolved in favour of another match. As she told her confessor, she had prayed to St Nicholas for guidance and he had advised that she repudiate John de la Pole in favour of Edmund Tudor. Her strong sense of personal destiny was not untypical of aristocratic women of the period who had been raised to make dynastic marriages, especially those with royal blood, but her young age underlines the intensity of her focus.

Margaret's wardship was granted to the Tudor brothers and, on 12 August, Henry awarded her a dowry of £111 2s 2d, a third share of 500 marks owing to her father.[8] She married Edmund at Bletsoe Castle on 1 November 1455, conceived his child and was left a widow after his death in captivity the following year. It had been an intense year for a girl barely into her teens, even though she had a strong sense of her destiny and dynasty. Modern sensibilities find the early circumstances of Margaret's life uncomfortable and, even by early modern standards, when consummation was usually delayed until the onset of puberty or the age of consent (at 14 for girls), her married life began when she was very young. Yet, in spite of her age, it cannot be called rape, as some historians and novelists have referred to the marital relations between Edmund and Margaret. 'Rape' is an accusation dependent upon laws of consent, and there is nothing to imply that she did not consent. Her age makes the affair distasteful to twenty-first-century morality, but Edmund was not breaking the law. To describe him as a rapist is anachronistic and unfair.

When it came to delivering the child, Margaret's confessor described her as physically very small, so even though she had begun to menstruate, as her conception of Henry proves, the width of her pelvis must have made for a difficult and traumatic delivery. Henry arrived on 28 January at Pembroke Castle, and Margaret was lucky to survive. She barely had time to recover before her mother was already planning another alliance for the young widow. Three months later, the king settled a third of Edmund's lands upon Margaret, to the value of an annual dowry of £200.[9]

Margaret's second marriage took place in January 1458 at Maxstoke Castle, less than a year after she had given birth and while she was still only 14 or 15. Her husband, Sir Henry Stafford, was her third cousin, eighteen years her senior, the son of the Lancastrian loyalist the Duke of Buckingham. He may also have been a friend of her father. The couple probably spent their early married years at Bourne Castle in Lincolnshire, where a medieval moated site had replaced the Norman motte and bailey and the Saxon Manor that had been home to Hereward the Wake. Indications from correspondence suggest that it was a harmonious match, although no children were born to the couple, perhaps as a result of injuries Margaret had sustained from her first labour at such a young age. After the death of the Duke of Buckingham at Northampton in July 1460, the couple received a bequest of 400 marks annually. The following March, Stafford fought for the Lancastrians at Towton; he was on the losing side, but was pardoned by Edward IV on 25 June.

Stafford was fortunate on that occasion but the escalating struggles between the two factions continued to make a mark on Margaret's personal life. In 1459, her stepfather Lord Welles was captured by the Yorkists after the battle of Blore Heath and later released, but he was less fortunate in 1461. Having served in the army of Margaret of Anjou and been victorious at the second battle of St Albans, he was killed in the terrible slaughter in the snow at Towton and attainted by Parliament that December. Thus none of his properties or effects went to his widow, who survived him by two decades.

The Staffords adjusted to the new Yorkist regime and even prospered. In 1466, Edward granted them an old Beaufort property in recognition of Margaret's descent, the manor of Woking in Surrey. This had once belonged to her grandfather John Beaufort, through his marriage to Margaret Holland, daughter of Joan of Kent from her first marriage. It was an impressive property built on a high spot amid marshy ground encircled by the River Wey, with a large great hall, pantry and buttery, a chapel and private chambers, of which one section of red brick wall remains. Outside the walls lay extensive parklands, fishponds, orchards and gardens. The manor accounts from 1467 show that extra staff were hired to help the new couple settle in, and that roofs and stables were mended and a new larder built.[10] It was from this period that Margaret's friendship with Sir Reginald Bray began: he was resident at Woking as her estate manager and would remain her devoted lifelong servant. In the late 1460s, Stafford worked for the Yorkist dynasty, attending on the king and present at council meetings: once, Margaret accompanied him to London for the opening of Parliament, staying at the Mitre in Cheapside,[11] an inn later known to Samuel Pepys.

In 1468, the Staffords entertained Edward IV at their hunting lodge Brookwood, near Guildford. Margaret would have overseen the arrangements, including the ordering of local produce such as oysters, pike, lampreys, wildfowl, five barrels of ale and 'half a great conger for the king's dinner'. A pewter dinner service of five dozen dishes and four dozen saucers was ordered from London and Margaret selected yards of velvet and Flemish cloth in order to make her dress for the occasion. It was probably a diplomatic move on their part, a gesture of reconciliation that serves as a reminder that the future was by no means guaranteed and, as far as the Staffords knew, King Edward might reign for another thirty years and be succeeded by one of his sons. It was pragmatic to accept the situation and attempt to live as best they could under the Yorkists, no matter what Margaret and her husband might have thought of them.

Another Beaufort marriage took place in the late 1460s to connect the Lancastrian dynasty with one of the most famous families of the century. At some point before 1470, Margaret's niece Anne, the daughter of Edmund Beaufort, Duke of Somerset, married William Paston, a younger son of the Justice of the Peace of the same name. William senior and Margaret, his wife, were the authors and recipients of many of the surviving Paston letters, which paint a vivid picture of life during the period. On 1 March, Anne was referred to in a letter by her nephew John Paston as having recently undergone the process of churching, so she had borne at least one child by this point, although accounts of exactly how many she did deliver are conflicting, sometimes suggesting that she had four girls and sometimes adding four brothers. John mentioned her again in a letter that June, to say that 'myn Lady Anne and myn Onyll Wyllam shall be at London within thes viii or x daiys', so Anne was clearly well enough to travel to Warwick Inn, which was their usual base when visiting the capital. The Pastons were initially Lancastrian sympathisers, especially as Edward IV ruled against John Paston's inheritance of some family land, and they welcomed the readeption of Henry VI, during which William and Anne celebrated their marriage. However, like other families, they were not averse to playing the diplomatic game when necessary and did make efforts to win the favour of the Yorkist king. In 1469, Warwick had laid siege to their property of Caister Castle, but it was restored to the family in 1471 and in the same year the Pastons reciprocated by fighting with the earl at Barnet. Their fortunes fluctuated again with the return of Edward IV but they found a champion in Anthony Wydeville, brother to his wife. The Pastons were proud of their lineage and, like many families of the day, were keen to clarify it and preserve their heritage and rights. It was probably William, identified from his handwriting, who compiled the Paston Book of Arms at some point before 1459, laying out the coats of arms of the family and others related to it by marriage.

In September 1496, Anne's husband made his will, by which point Anne was already dead. He requested that he be buried in the church of the Black Friars in London, at the north end of the high altar, 'by my Lady Anne, late my wife' and that a large stone be placed on top of them both. He also mentions his two daughters Agnes and Elizabeth, between whom his lands and tenements were to be divided, indicating that by this point they were his only two surviving offspring. If Anne had borne sons, to whom the estates would usually have been bequeathed, they had predeceased their father. In fact, this is confirmed by a note by Sir Nicholas Nicolas in his 1826 *Testament Vetusta*,[12] while the couple's third daughter, Anne, married Gilbert Talbot and bore at least two sons. William made provision for his servants and tenants, and for the sale of his properties Warwick Inn, Castre Clere and in Norwich. The church of the Black Friars Priory, where he and Anne lay, was dissolved during the Reformation.

Meanwhile, the wardship of Margaret's son Henry had been given to William Herbert, Earl of Pembroke, who raised the boy at Raglan Castle. Margaret had little say in the matter and, although it was common practice for the sons of the nobility to be raised in the household of a mentor, Henry was her only child. She was able to write to him and visit on occasion, but it cannot have been easy. As the male heir of Lancastrian blood, albeit through his mother's side from John of Gaunt, coupled with his position as half-nephew to Henry VI, Henry's proximity to the throne may not have been as great as the sons of York, but it certainly put him within striking distance. He was an important figure in the Lancastrian picture, whose young life was passed in awareness of the dynastic conflicts that were dividing the country. It was probably with the boy's dynastic heritage in mind that Pembroke included a clause in his will of 1468, stating that he wished his daughter 'Maud be wedded to the Lord Henry of Richmond'. However, this match would never take place. The following year, Pembroke was executed by the Lancastrians following the battle of Edgecoat, when the rebels Warwick and George, Duke of Clarence had taken Edward IV by surprise. The loss of the man who had been a surrogate father was a terrible blow for Henry and, for the time being, he sheltered from the storm with Pembroke's wife, the Countess Anne, to see which way the tide would turn.

The coming year saw more heartbreak for Margaret's family, this time concerning Margaret's stepbrother Richard Welles and his son Robert. At least a decade her senior, Richard had fought alongside his father at St Albans in 1461 and been part of Queen Margaret's army which turned away from London; he had also survived Towton, where his father had lost his life. As was the case with many figures of the time, Richard thought it prudent to ally himself to the new regime, as well as having family ties with the Earl of Warwick. He received a pardon from Edward IV in February 1462 and, after fighting alongside him at Hexham in 1464, where Henry Beaufort was killed, he was awarded his family estates and the title of Lord Welles. In fact, in 1468, Edward favoured Richard's claim in a land dispute that had emerged between him, his half-brother John Welles and his stepmother, Margaret Beauchamp.

However, Richard remained locked in a dispute over land with his neighbour Sir Thomas Burgh, who was Master of the Horse to Edward IV. In February 1470, Richard's son Robert attacked Burgh's house then joined the forces of the Earl of Warwick. The king summoned Richard to London to explain. Initially, Richard claimed to be too unwell to travel, before travelling south and seeking sanctuary at Westminster. He was granted a pardon the following month, but kept in prison whilst Edward dealt with the rebels. When Robert refused to submit to the king, Edward ordered that his father be executed, followed by Robert's own death as a traitor a week later. Robert had borne arms against the king so had little reason to expect mercy, but the death by association of his father, Margaret's stepbrother, after years of loyal service, must have been difficult to accept. When Warwick finally caught up with Edward and the king was forced to flee, Lancastrian fortunes underwent a sudden reversal.

Margaret Beaufort would have heard the news of the restoration of Henry VI with delight, recognising it as the opportunity for her son that she had been waiting for. In October 1470, Margaret, Stafford and the 13-year-old Henry of Richmond travelled by barge to Westminster, where they dined with the king and Jasper Tudor and Henry VI is said to have predicted that his young nephew would heal the divisions of civil war.

Thus, Margaret's son was already being imagined as a future king, a successor to the dynasty given the lack of heirs. It may have been a triumphant moment, but it was brief, as the Lancastrian fortunes were to turn again.

At the end of March 1471, two weeks before the battle of Barnet, Edmund Beaufort paid a visit to Stafford and Margaret at Woking, staying with them for four days. The return of Margaret of Anjou and Prince Edward was imminent and Warwick still held the kingdom for Henry VI, who was something of a puppet with little real understanding of the dramatic events of the past decade. A real Lancastrian restoration was within grasp, with the support of the Tudors and Beauforts, and the Staffords must have been privy to Edmund's discussions and plans, perhaps even his entreaties for support. What happened during Beaufort's visit is unclear, but when Stafford was summoned by Edward IV to fight at Barnet, he obeyed and fought on the side of the Yorkists. Perhaps he considered Edward to be the rightful king or, pragmatically, to be a stronger king: perhaps the thought of treason and reprisals moved him to support a more viable regime. Margaret may have agreed with him, or she may have argued against him. It is impossible now to know her feelings on the matter, but no doubt she considered the position of her son, both as a potential heir to Henry VI and in terms of his personal safety and survival. If she disagreed with Humphrey's decision, she could not prevent him from taking arms against the Lancastrians.

Humphrey's wounds at Barnet claimed his life. He made his wife executor of his will and left a new blue velvet trapping for four horses to his stepson Henry, a 'grizzled horse' to Reginald Bray and £160 for masses to be said for his soul. Other items in his will suggest his piety and local connection to the parish church of Woking for he left money to the high altar and also the church's 'works', a cause which Margaret would have shared. In addition, the witnesses of the will included a Walter Baker, the local vicar and Sir Richard Brigge, 'prior of the Priory of Newark'. Henry left everything else, 'the residue of all my goods, catalogues and debts … I give and bequeath to my entirely beloved wife Margaret, Countess of Richmond, she thereof to dispose her own free will for evermore'.[13]

Henry's final resting place was the de Bohun Castle of Pleshey in Essex, as he was a great-grandson of Eleanor de Bohun and Thomas, Duke of Gloucester. Margaret's son was more fortunate. Jasper Tudor failed to make it to Tewkesbury on time, which may have saved his life as well as that of young Henry. After hearing of the Lancastrian defeat and the surrender of the queen, Jasper Tudor fled to Brittany and took his nephew with him. Both men were included in the Act of Attainder passed by the Yorkists against their enemies shortly thereafter. Margaret Beaufort would not see her son again for fourteen years.

Margaret temporarily left her home at Woking and took a reduced staff of sixteen to live with her widowed mother in her London home of La Ryall in the parish of St Michael. It was a building with strong Lancastrian connections. First named as a tenement in the thirteenth century, it had been granted by Edward III to Philippa of Hainault, who carried out extensive repairs to the property and used it to house her wardrobe. It had also been used as a refuge by Joan of Kent, wife of the Black Prince, during the terrifying Peasants' Revolt;[14] presumably before or after she had been insultingly kissed in the Tower by some of the rebels. By the sixteenth century it was being used as stables but it was probably still a prestigious dwelling in the 1470s. While she was at La Ryall that May, Margaret drew up a will, giving instructions that her body be buried alongside that of her first husband Edmund Tudor, removing him from Carmarthen to Bourne Abbey and preserving an English estate for her son in the event of his return, her vision clearly focused on his future. Just months later, she was left without a husband or son, having lost her Beaufort cousins under a victorious Yorkist regime and facing possibly the most important choice regarding her future.

11

Eight months after Stafford's death, Margaret remarried. Her new husband was Thomas Stanley, a wealthy, shrewd and powerful figure who had served the Lancastrians and made a successful transition to the Yorkist regime. Stanley had been born in 1435, the son of the Stanley to whom Henry IV had granted the Isle of Man and lieutenancy of Ireland, who had acted as gaoler to Eleanor Cobham and broken the news of his arrest to Gloucester at Bury St Edmunds. Thomas had been a squire at the court of the young Henry VI but he had married Eleanor, the daughter of the Earl of Salisbury, who had borne him nine children. When he was called upon by Margaret of Anjou to fight for the king at Blore Heath, Thomas had held his armies back instead of coming into conflict with his father-in-law. Nor had he gone to the assistance of his brother-in-law Warwick in 1470, but had assisted Edward during his return from exile in 1471, and was rewarded with the position of Steward of the King's Household. Eleanor died in 1472, so Thomas' next marriage must have taken place within months. This has been taken as evidence that his union with Margaret was a purely political one, and though the parish registers of half a century later reveal that some marriages did take place within months of bereavement, Margaret probably sought a powerful protector in Stanley and he, in turn, was happy to unite with the Beaufort family with its extensive connections.

Margaret and Stanley were wed at Knowsley Hall in Lancashire, with a contract allowing mutual financial and legal advantage to both. She gained lordships and manors worth an annual £500 while he received similar grants totalling £800. They lived mostly away from the Yorkist court in the north but did return to London for certain occasions, as Stanley was a member of the royal council and Steward of the King's Household. Husband and wife were present in the capital during Edward's preparations for the invasion of France in 1475, when Margaret would have said goodbye to Stanley, who was to command forces for the king. He was also involved in the Scottish campaign of 1482 led by Richard, Duke of Gloucester. On occasions during his absence, Margaret took on some of his administrative and local government duties, hearing disputes between tenants and sitting on panels to resolve property questions. For all intents and purposes, the Stanleys were supporters of Edward IV's regime. They were connected to the Yorkist royal family by marriage, as Thomas' son married Joan le Strange, niece of Queen Elizabeth and such ties were inevitable given the closed world of the aristocracy, but the Yorkists had been responsible for the deaths of Margaret's second husband, stepfather, cousins and stepbrothers.

The nature of the Stanleys' marriage is unclear, but the absence in the initial contract of provision for heirs has been interpreted as evidence that Margaret wished to live chastely, almost like a vowess, under the protection of a husband. Had she simply entered a nunnery, many political avenues would have been barred to her in the service of her son. Whether or not their union was consummated, it provided her with a necessary stability in changing times. She was 29, still not considered too old in this period and still potentially fertile, according to the birth patterns of her direct contemporaries. There is a fair chance that her experience of giving birth at the age of 13, long before her immature body was ready for such an ordeal, created a lasting problem that prevented her from conceiving again or that, as a result, she imposed a ban on sexual activity that arose more from the desire to survive than any sense of piety. Stanley had three sons who lived to adulthood from his first marriage, so did not have much incentive to produce more. Presumably the matter was discussed, but whatever decision they reached, the mutual benefits clearly outweighed any disadvantages.

Stanley was not only gaining a wife with advantageous family connections, he was also marrying a woman of considerable strength of character, piety and intelligence, as well as discretion and an understanding of the political system and just how far her influence might extend. In many ways, she was an ideal wife. Margaret was not about to push the boundaries of gendered behaviour, to challenge authority or respond with a heavy hand, as Margaret of Anjou had done. While the former queen was active and warlike in the defence of her son, Margaret Beaufort adopted a quieter, stealthier method of waiting behind the scenes, building alliances and biding her time. Circumstances dictated their actions but character also played a significant part in their decision-making. Stanley clearly trusted Margaret's abilities, deputising to her in legal matters less than eighteen months after the marriage. In November 1473, he placed her in charge of an arbitration panel established to deal with a property dispute in Liverpool and the following August she oversaw another issue that had arisen between two of her husband's tenants.[15]

In 1476, the Stanleys were present at the reinterment of Richard, Duke of York and his son Edmund, Earl of Rutland. After their deaths at the battle of Wakefield in December 1460, York's and Rutland's heads had been set upon Micklegate Bar in York, while their bodies had been hastily buried, probably in the Priory of St John the Evangelist at Pontefract. Now, the remaining York brothers had them brought home to Fotheringhay, where they would lie in two impressive tombs inside the church. Richard's coffin was topped by a life-size effigy wearing a gown of royal dark blue and ermine, with an angel holding a crown above his head to signify that he was king by right. In the last week of July, a solemn procession including Lord Stanley and Lord Welles accompanied both coffins from Pontefract to Fotheringhay, dressed in black with black hoods. Margaret was probably present in the church when the bodies were reburied on 30 July, with the queen and other leading ladies who offered mass pennies and filed past to show their respect. The Stanleys were among over 1,500 people who were housed in tents on the site afterwards and would have participated in a funeral feast that drew in thousands more. With Edward IV firmly back in control of the country, it did no harm to the Lancastrian cause for Margaret to be seen to be toeing their line.

In 1480, Margaret and Stanley were summoned to attend upon Edward IV and his family. With her own son classed as a traitor and exiled for almost a decade already, it must have been a bittersweet moment when she was asked to take a formal role and welcome the king's youngest daughter. Bridget was born at Eltham Palace on 10 November and her christening followed the next morning, so Margaret must have been invited in advance, and was staying in London or at Eltham itself, awaiting the outcome of the queen's confinement. The service was performed by Edward Storey, Bishop of Chichester, who was the queen's chaplain, accompanied by a procession bearing 100 torches. The girl's godparents were her aunt Elizabeth, Lady Maltravers and her grandmother Cecily Neville, with William Waynflete, Bishop of Winchester as godfather. Margaret was responsible for carrying the baby to the high altar. It was a trusted role, indicative of just how far Lord Stanley's concessions to the Yorkists had been successful. It was also clear that Margaret was judged to be of good character, a pious and respected woman; the legacy of a primer and a book of the Epistles and Gospels from her kinswoman the Duchess of Buckingham confirms this. However, soon after little Bridget reached her third birthday, Margaret's position would again be called into question.

Just before the storm hit, there was an encouraging period of calm. In the first half of 1482, Margaret's mother died and was buried at Wimboune Minster, in Dorset, designated a royal peculiar by Edward II. That June, the Stanleys were at Westminster, where they consulted Edward IV over the disposal of Margaret Beauchamp's extensive properties, accumulated as the widow of three husbands. Margaret and Thomas must have made the case for her son Henry, as Edward agreed to reserve the majority of the legacy for the young man's use, on condition that he return from exile 'to be in the grace and favour of the king's highness'. They may even have discussed a marriage between Henry and Elizabeth of York at this stage, as Lord Stanley later recalled, and Tudor's creation as Earl of Richmond.[16] This proposal predated any intention of Henry to invade England, or assert his claim over that of the Yorkist dynasty, so there is little reason to doubt that it was a genuine offer. Margaret could begin to envision a future where her son lived close by, reconciled with the Yorkist king as she was, playing a part in national or local politics, perhaps even raising a family in the properties inherited from her maternal line. After all, the Beauchamp line had long been connected with royalty, serving Edward III and his wife, when the new line of the present Lancastrian family had been created. But an unexpected event meant that instead of returning home to enjoy his estates peacefully, Henry Tudor would cross the Channel at the head of an invading army.

In April 1483, the 40-year-old Edward IV died after an expedition on the Thames. Having ruled for over twenty years through charisma and strength of character, he had kept a lid on the various factions in his court, from the old nobility to the extended family of his wife, the Wydevilles. His end was unexpected for, though chroniclers like Croyland insisted that he had lived a debauched life, Edward was still active: he had summoned Parliament on 20 January, negotiated a treaty with the Scots and spent much of March at Windsor Castle. Various causes have been suggested for his death, ranging from a stroke, pneumonia, a surfeit of vegetables or an unsubstantiated claim of poison. He had fallen ill by 2 April, but did not die at once. It would have been apparent to his court that his death was imminent. False reports of his death even reached York on 6 April.

The king's eldest son was still underage. Prince Edward had been born in sanctuary during the readeption in November 1470 and he was twelve and a half at the time of his father's death, around eighteen months away from ruling in his own right. He had been raised under a careful programme planned by both his parents, at his own establishment at the traditional Yorkist base of Ludlow Castle on the Welsh Marches. He was in Ludlow with his uncle Anthony Wydeville when the news reached them that the king had died on 9 April. King Edward IV had made a will back in 1475, before he set off to invade France, but at that point his son had been only 4 years old. It is likely that in his dying days, Edward added at least a codicil to his previous will, naming his younger brother Richard as Protector, or establishing a regency council just as Henry V had named his brothers Senior Regent and Protector of the Realm. However, neither of these codicils survived in the coming days, if they were written down at all. This might indicate that they were destroyed by parties whose interests they did not serve.

The news of Edward's death reached Richard, Duke of Gloucester a couple of days after it arrived in Ludlow. He travelled south to intercept the train of the prince, who had set out for London in anticipation of his imminent coronation. What happened during the coming weeks has given rise to much speculation among historians seeking an explanation of the dramatic turnaround in the fortunes of the house of York. With so little primary material surviving to give insight into the motivation of the key players, it is easy to describe the series of events but much harder to interpret them and form any sort of consistent answer or theory. Perhaps this in itself highlights that the transfer of power from Edward's son to his brother was less of a concerted plan than a series of reactions which escalated to an unpredicted level as both sides sensed the necessity to strike against those they distrusted, threats real or imagined. Firstly, Gloucester met with Prince Edward and Anthony Wydeville at Stony Stratford and, after an evening of apparent conviviality, ordered the arrest of Wydeville and two of his associates, and took custody of Edward. The news reached London in advance of Richard, prompting the dowager queen Elizabeth to seek sanctuary at Westminster. Richard requested the presence of her younger son, Richard of Shrewsbury, and then sent both boys to the Tower in order to await the coronation, which had been planned for 4 May, then postponed to 22 June.

However, the coronation of Edward V never took place. On 7 May, the executors of his father's will met at Cecily Neville's London home, Baynard's Castle, a meeting at which Lord Stanley was present. The will of 1475 was rejected and the royal jewels were taken into custody. It is from this period, particularly from this action, that certain historians have extrapolated that the Wydeville family were embezzling the king's coffers: others have taken the view that the Wydevilles were reacting to Richard's return to London with a significant store of weaponry. More meetings were held through the month of May and into June. As the days passed, with costumes being sewn and the nobility being summoned to London to attend, suspicion spiralled out of control at the court. At a council meeting on 13 June, Richard ordered the arrest and immediate execution of King Edward's friend Lord Hastings, on grounds of treason that have never been adequately explained. Stanley was among those arrested that day, reputedly hit on the head by a guard before being thrown into the Tower. The news of his arrest must have reached Margaret amid a climate of uncertainty and fear that escalated through the summer. Luckily, Stanley was released without charge after a couple of weeks; in fact, he was then promoted to be Steward of the Royal Household, such a complete change of fortune at the hands of the same man cannot have encouraged the Stanleys to feel confident in their relations with Richard.

Then, on 22 June, a sermon was preached at the cross outside St Paul's Cathedral by Sir Ralph Shaa, which stated that Edward IV had been conceived in adultery, was 'in every way … unlike the late Duke' and that therefore his sons could not legitimately rule. This was a staggering accusation against Cecily Neville, Duchess of York but worse still was the accusation that Edward's own marriage was not legitimate, having been conducted in secret and pre-dated by a union the king had entered into with Eleanor Butler, née Talbot, daughter of the Earl of Shrewsbury. On 25 June, a delegation from the council arrived at Cecily's home of Baynard's Castle and offered the throne to Richard, Duke of Gloucester. He accepted the following day and was crowned king at Westminster on 6 July. Margaret and Stanley attended this event, as they were duty bound to do; what they made of it has not been recorded. Stanley carried the ceremonial mace and Margaret was in attendance upon Richard's wife and queen, Anne Neville, having been given 10yd of scarlet, 6yd of crimson velvet and 6yd of white cloth of gold for the purpose. After the crowning ceremony, the Duchess of Suffolk sat on one side of Anne and Margaret sat on the other.

The question of what happened to the Princes in the Tower has not yet been resolved. They were last seen playing in the grounds in July before being moved further into the Tower itself, where they were attended by a reduced staff including an Italian, Dr Argentine, who was finally dismissed that summer. At the end of July, an attempt was made to release them by members of Edward IV's old household, while Richard was in the north on progress. The ringleaders were executed. Some have seen this as a critical moment for the boys' survival, Richard realising that they would always be a focus for discontent and plots aimed to overthrow his regime. If the boys were killed, by whatever method, this is a likely moment for it, either at the instigation of Richard III or by someone acting on his behalf or in his perceived interests. However, this is only one theory. Some prefer the solution that the boys survived and were smuggled to the Netherlands, where the younger prince later became the pretender Perkin Warbeck. Another version, fully developed in Josephine Tey's 1951 novel *The Daughter of Time*, favours Margaret Beaufort herself as the killer. Exactly how Margaret became the suspect in this unresolved mystery might be the result of hindsight, the caricatures made of her ambition by later historians and her certain involvement in plots to favour the situation of her son in late 1483.

One of the main issues with Tey's novel, though, is that Detective Grant considers the reading of faces, or physiognomy, as valid evidence. Staring at portraits of Richard, he becomes convinced that his expression is one of gentleness and, therefore, he could not have been guilty of murder, overlooking the examples of Richard's behaviour regarding Anthony Wydeville and William Hastings, and his considerable battle experience. Grant then proceeds to find evidence to support his theory, rather than letting the evidence dictate his conclusions. He also argues that there was no reason for Richard to kill the princes, on account of their illegitimacy, which was confirmed by an Act of Parliament, *Titulus Regis*, passed in January 1484. However, this is a naïve response to the very real danger posed to Richard by the boys, who would have continued to represent an alternative kingship, a focus for rivals, as Henry VI had done to Edward IV, necessitating his death. Acts of Parliament could just as easily be overturned by a later Council, had the princes' line been restored to power. The boys were an immediate threat to Richard in 1483 and their continued existence would always undermine his position. Additionally, there is a lack of surviving evidence from the period: the trail of evidence on the princes goes quiet and their bodies were never displayed, nor were any formal accusations ever made. Yet there may be many reasons for this, and the absence of evidence is not evidence in itself. Since Tey's death, other sources have come to light, such as the account of visiting Italian Domenico Mancini, who provides evidence that there were rumours about the princes' disappearance in 1483, while Tey claims there were none. Notwithstanding these facts, Tey's novel is a wonderful construction of plot, character and suspense, and was voted number one in the top 100 crime novels of all time in 1990. It must be read as a work of fiction which raises engaging questions about the period, but Detective Grant's methods and conclusions must be seen objectively.

For some readers, this emotive story has created a need to search for an alternative villain and the finger of blame has been pointed at Margaret Beaufort, largely for her plans for her son to invade England in the autumn of 1483, although the timing suggests this was in response to the rumours of the princes' demise rather than the reason for their possible dispatch. The sixteenth-century essayist George Cornwallis was among the first to suggest that Margaret may have played a hand in the deaths of the princes in order to advance her own son. Early Ricardian George Buck was quick to follow, describing her as a 'politic and subtle lady' whose influence over her nephew Buckingham was the direct cause of his revolt and who had united with Bishop John Morton to remove the boys from the line of succession. There is also the fact that Stanley was appointed Constable of England, which has been cited by many as evidence that he, and therefore Margaret, had access to the Tower, which was a key component of his role. However, Stanley was appointed to this position in October at the earliest, as a result of the disgrace of the former Constable, the Duke of Buckingham. By this point it was widely believed that the princes were already dead. Nor was he the only Constable, or Lieutenant, for on 17 July 1483, Richard appointed Robert Brackenbury to the position, a man English literature has often charged with the responsibility for the princes' deaths.

It is extremely unlikely that ambition could have overcome Margaret's extreme piety to allow her to commit or order such an act, which would have jeopardised her immortal soul. However, this does not automatically rule her out, given the piety of medieval kings known for their brutality, or the many crusades fought in the name of religion. From her actions, it may seem to a modern reader that Margaret's piety is incompatible with the capacity to murder, but this is merely an academic argument facilitating a theory that lacks detail and substance. No accusation was levelled at Margaret or Stanley during their lifetimes but, after their deaths, such suggestions took a familiar turn. In the absence of evidence, the charge of witchcraft reared its head again. Buck pointed the finger at a Thomas Nandyke, a necromancer from Cambridge in the service of the duke, who was described in the act of attainder against Buckingham in 1483 but was pardoned by Henry Tudor two years later. Fortunately, considering the fates of her predecessors, Margaret and her husband were in a strong enough position that the mud did not stick.

The weapons of choice aimed against aristocratic women were usually slurs against their character, cutting to the heart of the two critical roles of the period: that of wife and mother. For a woman to be discredited, she had to be cast as behaving inappropriately for her position, as being unnatural, or against nature's intent, hence the accusation that Joan of Navarre had conspired against her stepson instead of nurturing him and that Eleanor Cobham had used magic because she was infertile, or ambitious. Likewise, Joan of Arc was burned and Margaret of Anjou was considered an unfeminine woman, a 'she-wolf', because both were prepared to step into martial roles typically filled by men. In the case of the accusations of murder against Margaret Beaufort, soon to become the king's mother, little could damage her more than to be cast as having dangerous impulses towards children, as having been the cause of the death of two little boys. The finger has been pointed at her by subsequent generations as part of a subtle gender campaign to undermine her achievements and her position in the Tudor dynasty. She has been portrayed as overly ambitious, as obsessive and fixated upon her son's position, even though her real efforts to that end only date from the reign of Richard III and were a response to the deaths of the princes.

Margaret was not the only one to suspect that the princes were dead in the autumn following Richard's coronation. The focus of his enemies turned from the boys in the Tower to Henry Tudor, then aged 26 and still in exile with his uncle Jasper at the court of Francis II of Brittany. Several rebellions broke out against Richard across the south-east and Margaret and her family were heavily involved. Her second husband Henry Stafford had a nephew who bore the same name and was now the Duke of Buckingham. He was also related to the royal family: Cecily Neville, Duchess of York was his great aunt and, by virtue of his marriage to Catherine Wydeville, he was uncle to the princes. He had proved a close confidant of Richard III in the days leading to his coronation, and was with Richard when he met Prince Edward at Stony Stratford, who had spent the evening with Anthony Wydeville before his arrest and had proclaimed Richard's right to the throne given the reputed illegitimacy of his nephews. Buckingham had been something of Richard's 'kingmaker' but by October he had turned against the king. It has been suggested that Buckingham had ambitions for the throne or that he had learned that Richard had ordered the boys' deaths. The duke has also been suspected of their murder, though there is little evidence for this. Yet there was also a Lancastrian question at the heart of his dissatisfaction, one that goes right back to the fourteenth century and the de Bohun family.

Buckingham was the great-great-grandson of Mary de Bohun's sister Eleanor and Thomas, Duke of Gloucester. Their eldest daughter Anne married into the Stafford family and their son Humphrey was the father of Duke Henry. Buckingham felt that this connection entitled him to some of the de Bohun lands, and he questioned the fact that they were in the possession of the crown. When Henry IV became king in 1399, his de Bohun inheritance was absorbed into the crown. But in 1461, when the Yorks had deposed Henry VI, they retained the de Bohun possessions, which were part of the Duchy of Lancaster. However, it would appear that Richard had been in the process of granting these lands to his friend, so this may not have been the cause of his dissatisfaction. Just two months after he had smoothed Richard's path to the throne, Buckingham was plotting with Bishop John Morton and Sir Reginald Bray, two close connections of Margaret Beaufort.

Margaret had remained behind in London while Stanley was commanded to accompany Richard on his progress to the north. Although little evidence survives, it seems that from there she was the centre of a network of communication uniting the dowager queen in sanctuary and

Henry Tudor in Brittany. It was Tudor historian Polydore Vergil who described Margaret's role in the plan for Henry to invade England. In his account, she is a wise opportunist who responded to the loss of the Princes in the Tower rather than the instrument of their destruction: 'after the slaughter of King Edward's children was known, [she] began to hope well of her son's fortune' and confided in her physician, Lewis Caerleon, that 'the time was now come that King Edward's eldest daughter might be given in marriage to her son Henry'.[17] She then invited Lewis to be the go-between for herself and Elizabeth Wydeville at Westminster, making the necessary arrangements, while her servant Hugh Conway was the link with Brittany. In fact, Vergil gives Margaret the overall control of the plot instead of Buckingham, stating that she was 'commonly called the head of that conspiracy' and that the duke's dissatisfaction was another facet of a wider swathe of revolts that broke out that autumn.

It was a bold and decisive position for Margaret and she must have been aware of the dangers. After the first uprising in Kent had been quashed by the Duke of Norfolk, the West Country rose and Buckingham attempted to move south and meet with Henry Tudor, who was embarking with an invasion fleet and heading for the Welsh coast. The plan was for their joint army to defeat Richard and for Henry to be married to Elizabeth of York, the eldest daughter of Edward IV and Elizabeth Wydeville. This detail underlines how clear the general belief in the princes' demise had become, because, in their absence, the princess became the heir to her family's dynasty. However, the one thing that Margaret could not plan was the weather. Storms in the Channel beat Henry back and river floods prevented Buckingham from travelling south. He was captured and executed at Salisbury on 2 November. Tudor's ships limped back into harbour but the cause was not forgotten. On Christmas Day at Rennes Cathedral, he swore an oath that he would invade England again and marry Elizabeth.

Another tenet of Josephine Tey's argument that Richard could not have ordered the boys' death rested on the behaviour of the dowager queen Elizabeth. She had remained in sanctuary with her daughters since the summer of 1483 but now that the uprising had failed, she had to reflect on what she might be able to do for the futures of those girls. Elizabeth was not blessed with hindsight, whatever magical powers popular novelists

RED ROSES

have ascribed to her; she had no way of predicting Richard's defeat the following year. As far as she knew, he might occupy the throne for another thirty years. Could she really spend that entire time in sanctuary, watching the youth of her daughters waste away? Whatever malice she may have felt in her heart towards her brother-in-law, balanced with his probable awareness of her liaising with Margaret Beaufort, she put the interests of her living children first and made a deal with him. Elizabeth had no bargaining power; she had nothing left. Parliament had passed the Act of *Titulus Regis* that January, declaring her own marriage to be void and her children illegitimate. Yet the fact that she was able to get Richard to make a public promise to protect her daughters suggests that she at least suspected his guilt in the death of her sons. Her gesture does not demonstrate trust, it highlights the need for clear, public boundaries and an admirable pragmatism. Necessity dictated her actions. She emerged from sanctuary on 1 March, although it was only to enter a kind of semi-confinement in the custody of Sir John Nesfield, living on an annuity of £700 from Richard. Later chroniclers were critical of Elizabeth for taking this route, like Raphael Holinshed, blinded to the political situation by concepts of gender:

> suerlie the inconstancie of this woman were much to be marvelled at, if all women had been found constant, but let men speake, yet women of the very bonde of nature will follow their own sex. But it was no small allure-ment that king Richard used to oversome her for we know by experience that women are of a proud disposition and that the waie to win them is by peomises of preferement and therefore it is the lesse marvell that he by his wilie wit had made conquest of her wavering will.[18]

Having walked a similarly fine and dangerous line through the world of male politics, Margaret was fortunate to survive the events of 1483. She could not, however, escape being attainted as a traitor in the Parliament of December 1483, being condemned for having 'of late conspired, confedered, and committed high treason ayenst oure sovereigne lorde the king Richard the third, in dyvers and sundry ways, and in especiall sending messages, writyngs and tokens to … Henry [Tudor] desiring, procurying and stirryng him, to come into this Roailme and make were ayenst oure said Sovereigne Lorde'. It was due to the intervention of Lord Stanley, whose 'good and faithfull' service to the king was not in doubt, that Richard agreed to pardon her. Like Elizabeth, Margaret was ordered to be kept under house arrest for the remainder of her life, but in Stanley's properties, all of her estates, titles and lands passing to him, a prisoner without access to court or king, to remain in isolation until the end of her days. However, with her husband's assistance, she was able to remain in contact with her son and, with his encouragement, to continue to hope that he would one day restore the dynasty and claim the throne for himself. She did not have long to wait. In August 1485, Lancastrian hopes were to flourish again.

PART FIVE

15

THE KING'S MOTHER, 1485–1509

Myn hert ys set and all myn hole entent
To serve this floure in my most humble wyse
As faithfully as can be thought or ment,
Wyth out feynyg or slouthe in my servyse.[1]

I

On 1 August 1485, Margaret's son Henry and her brother-in-law Jasper Tudor set sail from the Norman port of Harfleur. Henry was 28, intelligent and shrewd, tall and slender with blue eyes and dark hair. Even though he was describing him in later years, when the king's hair was white, Vergil stated that 'his appearance was remarkably attractive and his face was cheerful, especially when speaking'. Furthermore, 'his spirit was distinguished, wise and prudent, his mind was brave and resolute and never, even at moments of greatest danger, deserted him'.

This time, good weather allowed them to cross the Channel safely. Henry's allies within the English court had warned him to stay away from the area around Southampton, where Richard's loyal friend Lord Lovell was awaiting his appearance with an army, so he headed for the Welsh coast, landing at Dale near Milford Haven on 7 August. Margaret certainly knew of his plans and, given her involvement in the uprising of 1483, had probably been encouraging them despite the personal danger to herself. It seems very unlikely that Tudor would have risked a second invasion had he not been confident of some support in England, including that of his stepfather, Thomas Stanley. Stanley had already heard of a plot launched by Richard against Henry in 1484, and sent Margaret's chaplain Christopher Urswick to join Bishop John Morton in Flanders, after which Urswick travelled to France to gain a safe passage for Henry to travel from Brittany into France and escape the danger.

The news reached Richard in Nottingham on 11 August. According to Vergil, he was relying chiefly upon the support of Walter Herbert in Wales, who was married to the Duke of Buckingham's sister, and Rhys ap Thomas, a Welsh magnate who had been in communication with Henry in exile. They declined to engage with Tudor, but joined his forces instead. Another of Margaret's servants was waiting to welcome Henry in Wales that August: his former master of the household under Stafford, Sir Reginald Bray, had continued in her service after her third marriage: now he had gathered an army and a large amount of money to pay 'marines and soldiers', perhaps the 2,000 mercenaries Tudor brought with him. In his entourage were a number of Lancastrians who had served him in exile, including John de Vere, son of the executed Earl of Oxford, Henry's secretary Dr Richard Foxe and the residue of Buckingham's rebellion. As they marched inland, they were joined by other Lancastrians, like Sir Gilbert Talbot, the son-in-law of Margaret's niece Anne Paston, who had an additional 2,000 men. He was 'joyfully' received in Hereford, where his grandfather Owen had been beheaded in 1461. By 20 August, the invading army was 3,000 strong.[2]

Henry's claim was not a particularly strong one, traced through his mother's Beaufort descent, but by this time, with the deaths of so many Lancastrian sons in battle, he was the most plausible dynastic heir. In letters written to muster support, he described his 'rightful claim, due and lineal inheritance of that crown' and the 'just quarrel' he had with the Yorkists. However, he also presented his claim as essential for England, presenting Richard III as a 'homicide and unnatural tyrant, which now unjustly bears dominion' over the realm. Henry was on stronger ground if he could win the country by right of conquest. Richard was prepared for his coming, having anticipated it since the end of 1483 and, when the threat became real in the spring of 1485, had focused on raising funds and building up his navy. He mustered his troops at Nottingham and purchased suits of lightweight Milanese armour and guns. On 23 June, before Tudor even set sail, Richard had issued a proclamation that he had no right to the English throne and was illegitimate through both family lines. If that was not enough, Richard added that Henry was driven by 'ambitious and insatiable covertise', which explained why he 'encroaches and usurps upon him the name and title of royal estate of this Realm'.[3] By all criteria, Richard had the advantage over the invader, with more troops, greater experience, the crown and its resources in his possession and his ability to command loyalty simply by virtue that any opponent to his regime could suffer a traitor's death. It looked as if he would be able to dispatch Tudor easily and return to the business of rule.

At some point in the next few days, Sir William Stanley, Thomas' brother, met with Henry in secret. The brothers had raised around 8,000 men in Cheshire and Lancashire but at that point, although their interactions with Tudor were already treasonous, their ultimate intention may have been undecided. It was also significant that Richard had taken into custody Thomas' son by his first marriage, George, as guarantee for his father's loyalty, a move that must have been made in response to fears that Thomas' allegiance would be torn between his king and his wife. On 20 or 21 August, the Stanley brothers met with Henry at Atherstone in Warwickshire, where he was camped within sight of Richard's army. It is impossible to know exactly what was agreed there; whether or not the Stanleys pledged their support, or if contingency plans were made for the eventuality of Henry's defeat. Polydore Vergil, who may have been writing around twenty years later, but under Henry's guidance, described how Tudor and the Stanleys shook hands with 'mutuall salutation' and their 'myndes wer movyd to great joy'. Although at least one television drama has also placed Margaret at the scene, it is unlikely that she ventured into the camp itself, with all the potential dangers to her person and reputation that could bring. However, she had not seen her son for fourteen years and, as far as she knew, he might have been killed in the upcoming battle, so such a reunion is not impossible.

The armies met on the morning of 22 August about a mile and a half from Ambion Hill, near the small Leicestershire town of Market Bosworth. When Tudor's troops advanced, they were fired upon by the Yorkist cannons, forcing them to regroup on marshy ground. In the initial encounter, Oxford counselled his men to remain together in one mass, instead of dividing them into the traditional three-part attack, the better to face Richard's superior numbers. It proved to be a good decision, for by concentrating their efforts they were able to defeat the troops led by the Duke of Norfolk. Seeing this, Richard attempted to summon the waiting forces of Henry Percy, Earl of Northumberland, but for some reason Northumberland did not engage. It has been suggested by some historians that the terrain made it impossible to do so, but others have believed the earl held back in order to favour Henry Tudor, recalling that his own father had been a loyal Lancastrian, killed by Yorkists at the battle of Towton. In addition, Percy was now married to Maud Herbert, with whom Henry had been raised at Raglan, and who had once been intended as his bride. When Percy let him down, Richard turned to the Stanley brothers, who also hung back and did not commit their troops. The king's response was a brave one. Determined to seize the moment himself, he led a brave charge against Henry as he stood in plain sight near the marshy ground, and he got close enough to kill his standard bearer. This was the point when William Stanley finally engaged, and went to Henry's assistance. Richard's forces were beaten back into the marsh and the king was killed. Against all the odds, the Lancastrians had won the day. The crown is said to have been found in a hawthorn bush by Sir Reginald Grey or by Stanley himself, who either handed it to Henry or crowned him with it. If Margaret's long-awaited reunion with her son had not yet taken place, it would have done so fairly soon afterwards.

For Margaret, the moment must have been euphoric. Having borne Henry at such a young age, been separated from him for most of his life and lived in fear for his safety as well as her own, the almost unthinkable had happened. On a personal level, she could now rejoice that her son was to be king and that she would be guaranteed a position of influence at his court, while on a dynastic level, he had successfully restored the Lancastrian line, the connection of blood going back through Margaret herself, her father and her grandfather, all the way back to John of Gaunt and Edward III. It was a shame that Margaret's namesake, the Lancastrian queen Margaret of Anjou, had not lived to see the family's restoration, having died in 1482, but this did not stop Henry honouring her memory and that of her husband Henry VI and son Prince Edward, via the rather academic exercise of restoring their properties to them and reinstating their positions. Still, it was a mark of posthumous honour and reinforced Henry's own links with the dynasty.

Henry VII went first to Leicester, where he arranged for the burial of the body of Richard III in the church of the Grey Friars. The former king's body was displayed for two days, to prevent future reports of his survival, before being lowered into a grave in the church choir, where it would rest until its rediscovery in 2013 in a car park occupying the site, the priory having been demolished after its dissolution in 1538. Henry then left Leicester and marched to the symbolic location of St Albans, where the first battle of the Wars of the Roses had been fought before his birth, and stayed there overnight. On 27 August he made a triumphal entrance into London, riding in a closed chariot, and was met at Shoreditch by the mayor 'and his brethren' who were dressed in scarlet and other 'worshipful' citizens in violet. From there Henry went to St Paul's, gave thanks for his victory and made offerings. These were accompanied by his three standards from the battle: the image of St George, a Welsh dragon against a backdrop of the Tudor colours of green and white, and a dun cow upon yellow, denoting the Warwick connection that came to him through the Beauchamp line.

From St Paul's, Henry went to private lodgings nearby in the Bishop's Palace. It is likely that Margaret joined him there, or else he saw her in October, when he travelled to Guildford, then on to her home with Stanley at Woking. Their reunion after such a long separation must have been cause for great celebration for them both: the 14-year-old boy who had fled England in fear of his life was now a man of 28. No doubt they had kept in touch by letter, although none of their correspondence from this period survives, but they still had to adjust to each other, and

Margaret needed to get to know the man her son had become. From Woking, Henry gave orders for Coldharbour House to be repaired for her London residence, for 'my lady the Kinges moder', sections rebuilt and painted, windows reglazed and Margaret's arms set on the building so that they were visible from the river. Margaret was also granted the wardships of Edward Stafford, the 5-year-old son of the Duke of Buckingham and Edward Plantagenet, Earl of Warwick, son of George, Duke of Clarence, who was then aged 10. Henry awarded her an annual income of £500 to cover the boys' expenses and the ability to bestow certain gifts to her loyal servants, such as the presentation to Christopher Urswick of the church of All Hallows in the Great, which was 'in the King's gift by reason of the minority of Edward, Earl of Warwick'.[4] Until recently, both had been living at the Yorkist stronghold of Sheriff Hutton, where another Yorkist exile, Elizabeth of York, had awaited the outcome of the battle. Rooms were prepared for both boys at Coldharbour. The coronation was planned for 30 October.

There was no guarantee, though, that the coronation would go ahead. Henry may have overthrown the Yorkist dynasty but there was a potentially more dangerous enemy in the city that he was powerless to defeat. A new disease had hit England. The random savagery of the plague was still part of cultural memory, but Londoners were stunned by the arrival of a completely unknown disease which seemed to strike hard and fast without warning. No one knows exactly how or why the dreaded sweating sickness arrived, but its concurrence with Tudor's invasion was enough to suggest a divine cause in 1485; today it is thought to have been brought by Henry's French mercenaries. Sixteenth-century chronicler Edward Hall describes these forces as comprising 'a sort of vagabonds, rascals and runaways, a scum of Bretagnes, and base lackey peasants', who sound scurvy enough to have been the source of the epidemic. The illness was first noted in the capital on 19 September, claiming the lives of thousands of citizens, including the mayor. Forestier, a contemporary writer who witnessed the outbreak at first-hand, believed that the distant causes were 'the signs or the planets', while a more immediate cause was

the stynkynge of the erthe as it is in many places … and this corrupteth the air, and so our bodies are infect of that corrupt air … specially where the air is changed into great heat and moistness, they induceth putrefaction of humours, and namely in the humours of the heart; and so cometh this pestilence, whose coming is unknown, as to them that die sodenley.[5]

Victims suffered sudden shivers, headaches and giddiness, followed by pains and exhaustion. There was a period of cold, followed by hot sweats, delirium and intense thirst. It did not always prove fatal and survivors might be unfortunate enough to suffer several bouts. By the end of October, though, the disease had claimed a couple of thousand lives.[6]

Prior to the coronation, Henry rewarded those who had been loyal to him: Jasper Tudor became Duke of Bedford; Thomas Stanley, the king's 'right entirely beloved fader', was made Earl of Derby, promoting Margaret to Countess; grants were also given to her essential servants Christopher Urswick and Reginald Bray. Margaret was granted the right to arrange marriages for two of her kinsfolk: she put in motion the arrangements to wed her nephew Richard Pole, son of her half-sister Edith St John, to Margaret, Duchess of Clarence and arranged for her half-brother John Welles to be married to Cecily of York, making him Henry's brother-in-law. From this point onwards, Margaret stopped signing her papers 'M. Richmond' and began to sign simply as 'Margaret R.', which echoed her son's H.R., *Henrici Rex*. She also altered her personal seal to include the Tudor crown and the caption *et mater Henrici septimi regis Anglie et Hibernie* (And mother of Henry VII, King of England and Ireland). Thus Margaret cast off her old identity and stepped into a very different future; she had reached it by being pragmatic, by surviving against the odds, sitting out danger and never ceasing to hope.

From the start, Henry understood the significance of appearances and ceremony, symbols and pomp. On the afternoon of 30 October, he wore a gown of purple velvet, or purple tissue of gold, edged with miniver to walk into Westminster Abbey under a canopy held by four knights, at the head of a long procession. He also had a second outfit made for later, of crimson cloth of gold, designed to impress his majesty upon those assembled, some of whom might still be questioning the legality of his claim. The Abbey and Tower were draped in almost 500yd of fine scarlet and London's streets were swept and cleaned. Among the other expenses for decorations were yards of white cloth of gold embroidered with the red rose of Lancaster, crimson velvet to make Welsh dragons and St George crosses, embroidered falcons, the arms of St Edward and the Welsh hero Cadwallader. Lord Stanley was close at hand, carrying the sword of state, and Jasper was steward at the banquet that followed. Henry was anointed by Cardinal Thomas Bourchier, a grandson of Eleanor de Bohun and Thomas, Earl of Gloucester.

The coronation was a bittersweet moment for Henry's mother. Bishop Fisher later described Margaret's intense emotion on the day: 'when the kynge her son was crowned in alle that grete tryumphe and glorye, she wept mervaylously', for even when she experienced great joy, life had taught Margaret to be wary: 'she let not to saye, that some adversyte would follow.' Only a week followed for celebrations, as Henry's first Parliament met on 7 November. Some historians have questioned why Henry's marriage did not immediately follow, given the pledge he had made at Rennes on Christmas Day 1483, but there was essential business to conduct, not only for the realm, but in order for the wedding ceremony to take place. Parliament had to approve the match and to repeal *Titulus Regis*, by which Elizabeth of York had been declared illegitimate, ordering that all copies should be destroyed. In addition, the close affiliation of the couple meant that a papal dispensation was required, although Henry was thorough enough to request two. It is also likely that he and Elizabeth had not previously met, or that they had done so briefly when she was just 4 or 5, and the intervening months of the winter of 1485 allowed them a chance to get to know each other. This was something of a luxury for monarchs, even at the best of times: Henry VI had married without having met Margaret of Anjou, but there were many precedents for matches of affection and personal choice within the dynasty, such as John of Gaunt and Katherine Swynford and Henry IV and Joan of Navarre, as well as genuine love within politically expedient matches such as Gaunt and Blanche of Lancaster and Henry IV and Mary de Bohun. Nor was it insignificant that Elizabeth's parents had defied the odds to marry for love. Perhaps Henry visited Elizabeth at Coldharbour House and wooed her as a courtesy in expectation of their mutually beneficial match. Perhaps he was making sure of his bride, given the unsavoury rumours that had circulated about her affections in the winter of 1484–85.

Richard III's second and final Christmas as king had been an eventful one. The beautiful 18-year-old Elizabeth had already been at his court, under his protection, for a number of months, while her mother was under the care of Sir John Nesfield. Celebrations were held at Westminster, as recorded by the *Croyland* chronicler, who added that he was 'grieved to speak', that 'far too much attention was given to dancing and gaiety' and hinted at 'things so distasteful, so numerous that they can hardly be reckoned', though he declines to be more specific. This is unlike Robert Fabyan, who was actually in London at the time and in 1486 was auditor of the city's accounts, later becoming sheriff and alderman. He described the events of that season as traditional enough, the 'feast of the nativity kept with due solemnity' and Epiphany celebrated with 'remarkable splendour', Richard appearing in the Great Hall wearing his crown. He does not mention what appears to have offended *Croyland*'s author: the fact that Elizabeth of York appeared in the same dress as Richard's queen, Anne Neville. Given that costumes were often exchanged and fabrics and designs selected in order to compliment and match those of rank, the event might have been interpreted by modern sensibilities as less than the innocent act it may have been. This would not have been sufficient to cause doubt, had rumours not arisen at court.

Anne Neville fell ill in early 1485, possibly never having overcome the loss of her only child the previous spring. She died on 16 March and shortly afterwards Richard issued a declaration that he had no intention of marrying his niece Elizabeth. In fact, he was already organising a joint match for both of them with the royal family of Portugal. Why was Richard required to make this public statement? Either he was actually considering the rumoured marriage, the barriers to which could have been circumvented with a dispensation, or else this gossip had reached a certain level that the story had gained some credibility at court. There was no question that Elizabeth was attractive and had the advantage of being young and fertile. Richard was in his early thirties and now had no heir of his body; a simple remedy to this would have been to marry his niece and ensure the continuance of the dynasty. It may be that genuine affection had developed between them. Perhaps he was also responding to reports that Henry Tudor had pledged to wed her. Yet there must have been a good reason why he did not take this course of action and that is likely to have been the advice of his council, who recognised that it would not be a popular match. A surviving letter reputedly written by Elizabeth to the Duke of Norfolk, known as 'Buck's letter' after the two related seventeenth-century antiquarians who discovered and 'translated' it, remains too full of holes, literally and metaphorically, to be helpful. In all likelihood, it expressed conventional emotions and refers to the impending Portuguese matches, rather than being the love letter described by some historians. That spring, Richard sent Elizabeth away to Sheriff Hutton, where she remained until after Bosworth and never saw her uncle again. Henry cannot have been unaware of these rumours. It is likely that he was taking his time to establish for certain exactly what had happened. A cynic might also suggest that he was waiting to be sure she was not pregnant.

Elizabeth was not pregnant. Not yet, anyhow. The truth of whatever affection she may have felt for her uncle went unrecorded and, over the coming months, Henry became convinced that she was a worthy wife for him. Their courtship may even have become physical. On 18 January, Henry VII married Elizabeth of York at Westminster. It was the marriage Margaret had hoped for back in 1483, and there is no indication that she was anything other than pleased at its culmination. The eldest daughter of Edward IV was just short of her nineteenth birthday and, as the eldest successor of his line, the match united the previously warring sides, though Henry had been very clear to establish that his claim was based on his own birth and his successful conquest. The *Croyland* chronicler appears to have overcome his disdain for Elizabeth's actions at Christmas 1484, writing that in her 'person it appeared that every requisite might be supplied, which was wanting to make good the title of king himself' and that the marriage 'from the first had been hoped for'. Within a couple of months, it became clear that Elizabeth was pregnant. There is a chance she may even have conceived before the wedding.

Henry had a very definite idea about where he wanted his first child to arrive, while Margaret made the necessary practical arrangements. Tudor was keen to capitalise on his Welsh descent and harness his new regime to the story of the legendary King Arthur. He had already used the red dragon symbol on his banners at Bosworth and now planned Elizabeth's lying-in to take place in Winchester, one of the sites associated with

Arthur's court of Camelot. There was a long tradition of such legends in England, which had been gaining in popularity during the fifteenth century. The early twelfth-century chronicler William of Malmesbury had built on existing Welsh legends to suggest that Arthur's return was imminent, which also appeared in the popular romances by Chrétien de Troyes. Geoffrey of Monmouth had located Arthur's coronation at the Roman town of Silchester, 30 miles north of Winchester, but the latter location had been preferred by Edward I, who created a round table which was still in the great hall when Henry Tudor arrived there in the summer of 1486. Edward IV had also been interested in the legends, seeking to trace his descent through Arthur and back to Adam and Eve in a genealogy commissioned in 1470. In 1483, William Caxton had printed John Lydgate's *Fall of Princes*, which predicted that Arthur would return 'out of fayrye', or out of the fairy realm, and among the printer's titles for 1485 was Malory's *Le Morte d'Arthur*, which located Camelot at Winchester. The time was right to harness the myth, with its emphasis on chivalry and a new chance for England, its optimism for the rebirth of a legendary king to unite the country and the union of a Red King and White Queen. Tudor chronicler Edward Hall stated that the name Arthur had a mythical potency for Englishmen, who 'rejoiced' to hear it, while foreign princes 'trembled and quaked' in fear. So Elizabeth was sent from Westminster to Winchester to deliver her first child.

Rooms were prepared for her at St Swithin's Priory, rather than at Winchester Castle, which had seen better days. It was one of the richest monasteries in the land and the new prior, Thomas Silkested, turned over the Prior's Lodgings, now the deanery, for the queen's use. It was a luxurious, three-storey building with an arched portico, set within the Close walls. From that Easter, Margaret had been drawing up a series of ordinances to specify her daughter-in-law's exact requirements, down to the last cushion, which would come to serve as a future standard for the arrival of royal heirs. Under Margaret's direction, the chambers were sealed off and the walls, ceiling and windows were hung with heavy tapestries, chosen for their scenes of romance or chivalry, which would not startle the queen and imprint violence upon the unborn child. Just one window was left uncovered 'so she may have light when it pleases her'. An immense bed measuring 8ft by 10ft was prepared, its crimson satin stuffed with wool and down, on which Elizabeth would labour. Margaret's instructions specified exactly how the furnishings should be arranged, what should be embroidered upon them and what colour they should be: 'two pairs of sheets … every one of them four yards broad and five yards long and square pillows of fustian stuffed with fine down; a scarlet counterpane, furred with ermine and embroidered with crimson velvet or rich cloth of gold'.

What Elizabeth thought of the joint efforts of her husband and mother-in-law has not been recorded. No doubt Margaret was an efficient organiser, but there is no evidence to support the suggestions that she overshadowed Elizabeth; it may well have been that, given her inexperience, the new queen was happy to let others make the necessary arrangements, knowing that she would be well cared for. It may even be that Margaret drew up her ordinances in conjunction with her daughter-in-law. She would have awaited the birth with Elizabeth at Winchester, possibly along with the queen's mother, Elizabeth Wydeville, who may have brought her own favourite midwife Marjory Cobbe to assist. Once the queen's formal withdrawal from society had taken place and the chamber doors were sealed, the birth room was a female-only zone. Elizabeth gave birth to a son on the night of 19–20 September 1486. It was exactly eight months after her wedding, so either the pair consummated their relationship before the ceremony or the boy was born a month early. He was named Arthur. The Tudor dynasty had its first heir. Margaret recorded his birth in her Book of Hours: 'in the morning afore one o'clock after midnight' on St Eustace's day. Her husband, Lord Stanley, was one of the boy's godparents at the formal christening in Winchester Cathedral on 24 September.

11

No sooner had it seemed Henry was secure, than a dangerous threat arose from surviving members of the house of York. John de la Pole was the nephew of Edward IV and Richard III, the eldest son of their sister Elizabeth, who had married the grandson of Geoffrey Chaucer. As a child in 1467, he had been made Earl of Lincoln and had been a strong supporter of his uncle Richard's rule, being appointed by him as head of the Council in the North and the recipient of an annuity of £500. Part of this sum was drawn from the Duchy of Cornwall, which was traditionally awarded to the Prince of Wales. After the death of Richard's son and heir in April 1484, Pole was considered a plausible successor to his estates and crown, although this was never formally clarified and was complicated by the existence of Richard's illegitimate son, John of Pontefract. After Richard was killed at Bosworth, John had little choice but to accept the new regime and took a leading role at the christening of Prince Arthur, although he refused to swear an oath of allegiance. In March 1487, he fled to Burgundy, the home of his aunt, Richard's sister Margaret, who was married to Charles the Bold. Margaret offered to support his attempt to invade England and displace Henry; she equipped him with troops, with which he set sail to Ireland. There, he met a 10-year-old boy by the name of Lambert Simnel, who had been schooled in aristocratic ways and was claiming to be his cousin, the Earl of Warwick, son of the Duke of Clarence. Simnel was crowned Edward VI in Christ Church Cathedral, Dublin on 24 May and coins were issued bearing his image. Whether or not Lincoln believed his claim, he seized it as an ideal opportunity to reinstate the Yorkist dynasty.

When Henry heard of Lincoln's flight, he had assumed that the earl would bring a Burgundian invasion force across the North Sea. He had ridden into Norfolk to patrol the coastline and to make a pilgrimage to the shrine of Our Lady at Walsingham when news reached him in May that Lincoln had actually sailed around to Ireland. Now, Henry feared for his heir and sent Elizabeth to collect him from his nursery at Farnham in Surrey. Then, Henry hurried to Kenilworth Castle and summoned his mother and his 'dearest wife' to join him there. Early in June, he set out in person to meet the invasion force while Margaret and Elizabeth waited in the Lancastrian stronghold. The armies met at Stoke Field in Nottinghamshire on 16 June, the Lancastrian forces led by Henry, Jasper Tudor, Edward Wydeville and John de Vere, Earl of Oxford. After about three hours of fighting, Lincoln was dead and Simnel had been captured, while Richard III's old friend Lord Lovell was missing, presumed dead. The last battle of the Wars of the Roses had been won by the Lancastrians. Only Lincoln's brothers Edmund and Richard remained as the last of the white rose claimants; both thought it prudent to flee the country, but Edmund would be executed by Henry VIII in 1513 while Richard would die at the battle of Pavia in 1525. Lambert Simnel was pardoned and given a job in the royal kitchens, later being promoted to be Henry VIII's falconer. Margaret, who was becoming something of the Tudor dynasty's recorder, listed the event in her Book of Hours: 'the xvith day of June, the year of our lord 1487, King Henry the VIIth had victory upon the rebels in battle of Stoke.' The threat removed, arrangements could finally go ahead for the coronation of Elizabeth of York.

On 25 November 1487, Elizabeth was crowned Queen of England, almost two years after marrying its king. Two days before, Margaret had accompanied Elizabeth in travelling to London from Greenwich and had been met by the mayor and aldermen in splendidly decorated barges, one of which bore the image of a dragon breathing fire. She had been part of the procession when Elizabeth passed through the streets from the Tower to Westminster, her fair hair hanging loose and her person dressed in white cloth of gold of damask, decorated with gold lace and tassels, her train borne by her sister Cecily, who had recently become Margaret's sister-in-law. Margaret rode in a litter, also of white cloth of gold and the streets were hung with 'rich cloth of gold, velvet and silk' or hung with coats of arms. Jasper Tudor rode alongside and behind; in one of the gold chariots was his new wife Catherine Wydeville, sister of the former queen and daughter of Jacquetta. Margaret sat at Elizabeth's right hand in the Parliament Chamber but she and Henry watched the actual proceedings in Westminster Abbey from behind a screen. This allowed Elizabeth to be the focus of attention as their high status would have necessitated reverence being paid to them.

In some ways, Margaret was taking a slightly less hands-on role now that Henry had established himself as king. She retained Coldharbour House on the north bank of the Thames but, from 1487, her and Stanley's main country home was the manor of Collyweston in Northamptonshire, an extensive estate with chapel, library, almshouse and garden, as well as the usual range of private apartments, public and service rooms. It was also a location for business, with a prison and council buildings located near the gates, in order for her councillors to hear the pleas brought by local people. Stanley was rewarded for his loyalty with the earldom of

Derby, a regular place on the royal council and other advantages relating to his estates; his brother William became Henry's Chancellor. Yet whilst dividing her time between court and country, Margaret still had an important role to play. Vergil claimed that Henry 'allotted [her] a share in most of his public and private resources'. Thirteen years after Henry's accession, the Spanish ambassador could confirm that 'the king is much influenced by his mother' but others, including the king's biographer Francis Bacon, thought that Henry listened to his mother but was not unduly influenced. At court, there was also the question of precedence when it came to her and Elizabeth, which opens the further issue of what the relationship was like between the queen and her mother-in-law. It may be an anachronism to even consider the possibility that Elizabeth was oppressed by Margaret's more dominant character, given the familiar mother-in-law meme of modern culture, but the evidence that this applied to Henry's wife and mother is slender.

The evidence that Margaret and Elizabeth worked in unison far outweighs any suggestion of antagonism between them. After all, Margaret had wished the match to take place in 1483 and had overseen the actual courtship, probably inviting Elizabeth into her home, as well as the wedding, the birth of Arthur and the coronation. Margaret also maintained a suite of rooms for Elizabeth at Collyweston and they must have been together frequently, as their names were often conflated into the formula 'the queen and my lady the king's mother'. The two women also wore complimentary clothing to assert their connection, although this has never attracted the sort of negative responses that Elizabeth's similar co-ordination with Anne Neville has done. Such gestures indicated respect and comparable rank. At the Twelfth Night festivities in January 1488, Margaret and Elizabeth appeared in 'like mantle and surcoat' and four months later, on St George's Day, they wore matching red and miniver Garter robes for their shared inauguration at Windsor. They all remained there together for Whitsun, then went to Woodstock for the summer, before returning to Windsor, Westminster and Richmond in a year that typically shows how close the family were. It is perhaps the comment made by the Spanish ambassador that has set the tone for the interpretations of Margaret and Elizabeth's relationship, but this may be misleading. He commented that the queen was 'kept in subjection' by her mother-in-law and that Elizabeth 'did not like' Margaret's influence over Henry, but this was an observation made by an outsider who dismissed the family in generic terms, stating that the queen disliked her mother-in-law 'as is generally the case'. Margaret may well have been controlling, even dominating at times, but she was also an indefatigable and highly competent organiser: exactly the sort of person needed to help the smooth running of things. There is no evidence of Elizabeth ever complaining.

Henry deliberately kept his mother and wife close. In 1487, when the nation was under threat from the invasion force of pretenders to the throne, he awaited them at Kenilworth, requiring that his wife and mother were both at his side. In June 1495, the king and queen embarked on progress into Lancashire, 'there to recreate his spirites and solace himselfe with his mother the lady Margaret wyfe to the erle of Derby, which then lay at Lathome in that country'. Margaret was frequently present when Henry and Elizabeth travelled, especially on other summer royal progresses, including those of the following year, when they all travelled to the Beaufort estates in Dorset and in 1497, when they were all together at Norwich and 1498 at Cambridge. Margaret's rooms were often closely connected with Henry's, too. At Woodstock, her apartments were linked to his by a withdrawing chamber and in the Tower, her rooms adjoined his.

On 11 September 1490, Margaret's own home of Woking Palace was the location for an important international treaty that determined the dynasty's future. Shortly after Arthur's birth, the possibility had arisen of a future match between him and a princess of Spain. The kingdoms of Aragon and Castile had been united in 1469 by the marriage of Ferdinand and Isabella, whose youngest daughter Catherine was nine months older than the Tudor prince. In March 1487, they had approached Henry and suggested a union, which was agreed in the Treaty of Medina del Campo two years later. Now, at Woking, Henry VII and ambassadors for the Holy Roman Emperor Maximilian I made a pact to unite against their common enemy in France, ratifying the arrangements already put in place to marry Prince Arthur to Catherine of Aragon. It was a moment of great significance for Margaret that such an event should have taken place in her home whilst she acted as hostess to the various dignitaries involved. She would also play a role in the later negotiations for her granddaughter and namesake to be wed to James IV of Scotland, although on that occasion she was protective of Princess Margaret, delaying the match until the girl had physically matured, so that she did not undergo the same early labour that Margaret herself had experienced. Shortly after the Scots marriage took place in 1503, Margaret gave up Woking for Henry to extend it into a royal residence and lived increasingly at her other properties of Latham, Hunsdon and Collyweston.

Margaret was clearly an affectionate mother during her absence from court, as all her surviving letters testify. In fact, it is only the correspond-ence between mother and son from after 1485 that survives, although its tone gives a sense of the letters that passed between them during Henry's childhood and exile. In one such letter to Henry from Collyweston on 14 January 1501, Margaret wrote:

My own sweet and dear King and all my worldly joy

In as humble manner as I can think, I recommend me to your grace, and most heartily beseech our Lord to bless you. And, my good heart … I wish my very joy as oft I have shewed, and I fortune to get this, or any part thereof, there shall neither be that or any good I have but it shall be yours, and at your commandment, as surely as with as good a will as any ye have in your coffers ; and would God ye could know it, as verily as I think it … And our Lord give you as long good life, health and joy, as your most noble heart can desire, with as hearty blessings as oure Lord hath given me power to give you.[7]

In response, Henry referred to the 'grete and singularly moderly love and affection' he bore for Margaret. The King's Mother's ordinances were put to good use again with the arrival of more Tudor children: her eldest granddaughter arrived in November 1489 and was named Margaret in her honour, followed by Henry in 1491 and Mary in 1495; two or three other siblings did not survive. Prince Arthur was established in his own household at Ludlow Castle on the Welsh border while the others were raised at Eltham. Margaret took an interest in their education and was a frequent visitor to the palace nursery.

Margaret was a literary and religious patron of the printed word. Since the arrival of William Caxton's printing press at Westminster in 1476, patronised by Edward IV and Anthony Wydeville, the printed word had been gaining momentum in England. Caxton had published editions of Chaucer's *Canterbury Tales*, Ovid's *Metamorphoses*, de la Tour Landry's *The Book of the Knight in the Tower*, de Voragine's *The Golden Legend* and Wydeville's translation of *The Sayings of the Philosophers*. From the 1490s, Margaret sponsored a number of devotional and instructional texts and she and Elizabeth of York presented one of their ladies, Mary Roos, with a copy of Hilton's *Scale of Perfection and Mixed Life*. In addition, she arranged for the printing and circulation of Latin liturgical texts, such as for the celebration of the feast of the Holy Name in 1493. She was the patron of at least three books printed by Wynkyn de Worde, the *Nicodemus Gospel*, a *Life of St Ursula* and the *Parliament of Devils*, and was also the owner of a Sarum Book of Hours and a series of prayers known as the *Fifteen Oes*, among other texts. Margaret also undertook the translation of texts for herself, rendering the fourth book of *The Imitation of Christ* into English in 1504 and the *Mirroure of Gold and the Synfull Soule* in 1506. She surrounded herself with sympathetic clergymen who were engaged in debates, interpretations and translations of religious questions and leading texts, as well as being employed by her in secular roles, creating an intellectual climate of scholarship among the servants of her household. There were also a significant number of university men. Historian Rebecca Krug argues that this community distanced itself from monastic values, while echoing their religious and intellectual activity, creating an elite community that Margaret was able to facilitate with her patronage, time and finances.[8] She was also the founder of Christ's College, Cambridge in 1506 and of the Lady Margaret Professorship of Divinity; and she left instructions in her will for the founding of St John's College. It is not too difficult to see this in the context of the growth of the Renaissance in England, building a community in which her confessor, Bishop Fisher, Bishop Morton and his protégé Thomas More would play a key role, connected with leading European scholars, such as More's correspondence with Erasmus. On a more light-hearted note, in December 1497, a payment was made by Henry of £3 6s 8d to a poet resident in Margaret's household, 'my lady the kings moder poet', presumably for the composition of verses.

The royal accounts also show evidence of Margaret's piety, for which she was granted the right to found chantries and for priests to say daily masses for her soul and those of her family, such as those celebrated in 1496 and 1497 at the Westminster shrine of St Edward, St George's in Windsor and at Wimbourne in Dorset, where both her parents were buried. She also made the arrangements for the burial of her half-brother, John Welles, who died early in February 1498 and directed in his will that he should be laid wherever his sister and wife saw fit. Margaret buried him in the Lady Chapel at Westminster. Shortly afterwards, she stood as godmother to a new grandson, the third son born to Elizabeth of York, whom they named after Henry's father, Edmund Tudor, and who was bestowed with her father's title Duke of Somerset. Sadly, the little boy did not survive.

Margaret's chaplain and confessor, John Fisher, later described her daily routine, in which she rose soon after five in the morning and began her day in prayer, first with her ladies then with her chaplain:

> After that [she] daily heard four or five masses upon her knees, so continuing in her prayers and devotions until the hour of dinner which was … ten of the clock and upon a fasting day, eleven. After dinner full truly she would go her stations to three altars daily [and] daily her dirges and commendations she would say and her evensongs before supper, both of the day and of Our Lady, beside many other prayers and psalters.[9]

It may have been reasons of piety or health, or simple inclination, that led Margaret to make a dramatic personal statement in 1499. With Stanley's permission she swore an oath of chastity before the Bishop of London and made her permanent home at Collyweston in Northamptonshire, while Stanley was based at Lathom. Her husband continued to visit her, but was assigned separate rooms. This raises a number of questions about the Stanleys' marriage, but the public nature of the gesture could imply that it had not always been chaste, necessitating such a redefinition. Her husband's agreement shows that this was probably a mutual agreement, arrived at after a stage of discussion and an acknowledgement that the personal aspect of the marriage was over. It may also have been a recognition that Margaret was no longer in need of the protection that Stanley had given her during the troubled period before Henry's accession: now her son was king and she was the most powerful woman in the land, after the queen.

Those related to Margaret also found her to be a powerful advocate on their behalf. At some point between 1497 and 1503, the king's mother intervened in a land dispute to assist her cousins in the Paston family. Sir John Paston was the nephew of her niece Anne Beaufort, and Margaret wrote to him regarding the inheritance of Anne's heirs, which John retained:

> there was a full agreement made and concluded, and also put in writing, between our trusty and right welbeloved Sir John Savile, knight, and Gilbert Talbot, esquire, on th'one partie and yow on the other, for divers lands which they ought to have in the right of their wives, daughters and heyers to William Paston, esquire, their late fader deceased, which lands ye by mighty power kepe and witholde from them without any just title, as they afferme.

She asked him to remedy the situation without delay. John appears to have acted on her request, as she wrote again to him two months later, enclosing a bill for him to convene so the parties concerned would have 'no cause reasounable to pursue further unto us in that behalve'.[10]

Margaret was also interested in medical matters, particularly when it came to preventing and curing the plague. This may have been because the illness claimed the life of her second husband, Edmund Tudor, though death and sickness had been a constant theme throughout her life, with the outbreak of the Sweat providing the latest example. Bishop Fisher later recalled her horror of the plague, which still broke out sporadically in London and the sea ports, and that horror was not hers alone. The plague is something of a thread uniting the lives of the Lancastrian women; from the dreadful outbreaks in the 1360s through to Edmund's death, it claimed the lives of rich and poor alike, a terrifying reminder of the indiscriminate nature of fate and the fragility of life. It had clearly been on Margaret's mind for years. By 1500, she had acquired a manuscript collection decorated with the Beaufort arms, which contained information on diets, medicines, prayers and chants to saints Anthony and Sebastian, who were traditionally considered to intercede in cases of illness. She may also have been prompted to obtain it by the increasing age of herself and her husband: Stanley was around eight years her elder and turned 65 in 1500, and may have been experiencing ill health before his death four years later.

Other figures from Margaret's past had also been lost in the final years of the fifteenth century. On 8 June 1492, the dowager Yorkist queen Elizabeth Wydeville passed away at Bermondsey Abbey. After having attended her daughter during the birth of Arthur, and been his god-mother, she had retired to the abbey with a scaled down household and expenses, choosing to end her days in quiet contemplation. It has been suggested that this was some form of punishment meted out to Elizabeth by Henry, perhaps for negotiating with Richard III in 1484 or supporting Simnel in 1487, but there is no evidence for this. Henry continued to refer to her in affectionate terms as his 'dear mother-in-law' and even considered arranging a marriage for her to James III of Scotland in 1489, which assumes a relationship of trust between them. Additionally, in 1490, Henry increased her allowance to £400 a year, which was not inconsiderable given that she was not maintaining a household or any degree of finery. Elizabeth was 50 and her life had been turbulent and marred by loss. Just as Margaret Beaufort and Cecily Neville lived the pure lives of vowesses, Elizabeth retired into peace and quiet, perhaps already suffering from illness. She died in June 1492. Her will suggests her humble state of mind, requesting that no pomp or ceremony accompany her burial and that whatever small goods she left behind should be used in the payment of her debts. This is quite in keeping with the choice to enter a holy establishment, and her son-in-law respected her wishes, laying her to rest alongside Edward IV in St George's Chapel, Windsor.

Three years later, treason and tragedy struck at the heart of Margaret's family. After the failed efforts of the Earl of Lincoln and Lambert Simnel, a more serious pretender to the throne had emerged. Perkin Warbeck claimed to be Richard of York, the younger of the two Princes in the Tower, although it is more likely that he was the son of a couple from Tournai who had received an education in Antwerp before being apprenticed to a silk merchant, who took him to Ireland. The young man's good looks and regal manner proved convincing to many of his contemporaries, and later historians have suggested he may have been an illegitimate son of Edward IV, conceived during his exile of 1470–71. Just as Lincoln had done, Warbeck sought the support of Mary of Burgundy, who may have schooled him in the history and ways of the Yorkist court, as well as providing him with funds to invade. Warbeck's attempt to land in

Dover in 1495 failed when he was repelled by locals, forcing him to flee up to Scotland. However, rumours had reached Henry that Margaret's brother-in-law, William Stanley, was feeling ambiguous towards the rebels. Vergil reported that Stanley had stated that if Warbeck proved to be the true son of Edward IV, 'he would never take up arms against him', which was tantamount to treason. He may have sent Sir Robert Clifford to make contact with Warbeck as early as 1493, taking the initiative to discover exactly who the young man was. William was arrested in 1495 and, despite stressing the conditional nature of his support, he was executed in February. Warbeck was eventually arrested and, after a period of imprisonment, died a traitor's death in 1499.

The year 1495 also witnessed the death of Cecily Neville, Duchess of York, whose fortunes had gone full circle and ended up in a far less fortunate place than Margaret. A daughter of the Lancastrian dynasty, Cecily had come to be the mother of their greatest rivals, the Yorkists, and seen two of her sons crowned king. Having lost them both, she had spent the last ten years in retirement, living like a vowess at Berkhamsted Castle in Hertfordshire, but had witnessed the rise of her granddaughter Elizabeth to become England's queen. In her will, dictated at Berkhamsted on 4 April, she left a bequest to Henry VII of two gold cups and any customs money owing to her, while Elizabeth received a small diamond cross, a psalter covered in green cloth of gold with silver clasps and a pyx, a reliquary containing the flesh of St Christopher. To her great-grandson Arthur, she left an arras hanging for a bed, and a tester and counterpane embroidered with the motif of a wheel of fortune; to his brother Henry, she left three wall hangings depicting biblical scenes. Margaret was also a beneficiary of her will, receiving a service book covered with black cloth of gold with gold clasps. Cecily died at the end of May and was buried alongside her husband the Duke of York at Fotheringhay church.

Another disaster followed in 1497, which could have had far more serious implications for the dynasty. Margaret and her family had been celebrating Christmas at Richmond Palace on the Thames when a fire broke out overnight. According to an eyewitness account, it began about nine o'clock at night, on the feast day of St Thomas, 29 December: 'a great fire within the King's lodging and so continued until twelve of the night and more … a great part of the old building was burned and much harm done in hangings, as in rich beds, curtains and other appertaining to such a noble court'. The Venetian ambassador believed that the fire had started when a beam in the queen's apartments caught fire, presumably from a taper on the wall below. Although there have been suggestions it was deliberately started by Perkin Warbeck, who was a prisoner in the palace at the time, this location seems to suggest it was accidental, and the ambassador noted that it was 'not due to malice'. Margaret, Henry, Elizabeth and their children escaped unharmed and the king saw it as an opportunity to rebuild Richmond into a splendid Renaissance palace in the Burgundian style. Out of the disaster came something magnificent: the old manor was transformed into a fantasia of three storeys with pepper pot domes and oriel windows, a chapel decorated with roses and portcullises, sophisticated plumbing, a great hall of carved statues and a library full of illuminated manuscripts. One contemporary visitor described 'wyndowes full lightsome and commodious', courtyards paved with 'marbill in whose mydill there is a conducte [fountain]', galleries 'pavyed, glasid and poyntid, besett with bagges of gold' as well as 'pleasaunt dauncyng chambers … most richely enhanged'. There were orchards, vines and gardens encircled by a two-storey walkway overlooking topiary mythical beasts: 'lyons, dragons and such other diver kynde … properly fachyoned and carved'. The new palace was a fitting location to play host to an important national event.

The marriage of Catherine of Aragon and Prince Arthur finally took place in 1501. After years of treaties and discussion, Catherine's ship limped into Portsmouth harbour after a terrible storm on 16 October and was given a warm impromptu welcome by the locals. She and Arthur met at Dogmersfield in Hampshire after an impatient Henry rode down from London and insisted upon the meeting against the usual protocol. The young pair conversed a little in Latin, assisted by bishops as their pronunciation likely differed, and Catherine summoned her minstrels and watched Arthur dance. She was given a splendid welcome to London, where pageants and decorations had been assembled in the streets, overlooked by giant figures of St Katherine and St Ursula, featuring the imagery of the Tudor dynasty: Arthur's three ostrich feathers as Prince of Wales, Lancastrian red roses and the Beaufort portcullis. There were suns and moons, virgins and saints, heraldic beasts and mythical creatures, while the fountains ran with wine and musicians played and sang. It was probably on this procession that Margaret first saw the girl who was to marry both her grandsons, watching her pass by from a house hired in Cheapside at 13s 4d from a merchant called Whiting, probably the same location from which she had watched Elizabeth back in 1487. Perhaps Margaret agreed with Thomas More when he observed that by English standards of beauty, the Spanish princess 'possessed all the qualities that make for beauty in a very charming young girl', even if her foreign clothing drew some criticism. Catherine was conducted to lodgings in the Bishop's Palace and later visited Baynard's Castle, where she was introduced to Elizabeth of York. Margaret acted as hostess to members of the Spanish delegation at Coldharbour House, just along the river.

Aged 15 and 16, Catherine and Arthur were married in Westminster Abbey on Sunday 14 November. Margaret sat behind a screen with Henry and Elizabeth to watch them process along a specially built platform covered in red worsted that extended the entire length of the cathedral, culminating in a round stage. Arthur was wearing a suit of white velvet and gold, matching that of his younger brother Henry, Duke of York, who was to give the bride away, while Catherine was dressed in a white silk dress and farthingale, with a silk veil to her waist embroidered with pearls, gold and precious stones. The wedding feast was held in the Bishop's Palace, followed by disguisings and interludes, before the bride and groom were formally put to bed back at Baynard's Castle. Further celebrations stretched on until the end of the month, the Spanish entertained at Henry's splendid new palace at Richmond until their departure on 29 November. Catherine and Arthur remained at the English court for a further month before departing to their own establishment at Ludlow.

The spring had barely arrived the following year when bad news reached London. The prince and princess had both been taken ill, perhaps with some form of the sweating sickness that had broken out in the area. While Catherine recovered, the illness may have exacerbated an existing condition in Arthur, or else simply coincided with it, as the young prince died on 2 April 1502. His parents were devastated and the news can only have exaggerated Margaret's existing fears of pestilence and belief in the inevitability of misfortune. Elizabeth had borne another son in February 1499, named Edmund, but he had died of unknown causes at the age of 16 months. For a brief period, Henry had enjoyed the security of having three sons but these losses focused all the dynastic imperative upon the shoulders of young Henry, Duke of York, who was only 10 when news of Arthur's death arrived and made him heir to the throne. It was these events and this vulnerability which led Henry and Elizabeth to conceive another child for by the summer of 1502 the queen was pregnant again for the seventh time.

There was also a new royal marriage to be arranged, in which Margaret had played a key role. On 25 January 1503, the proxy wedding of James IV of Scotland and Princess Margaret took place in the queen's great chamber at Richmond Palace. The Earl of Bothwell represented the Scottish king, dressed in cloth of gold, standing beside the diminutive 13 year old, which must have brought back memories for her grandmother of her own marriage at the same age. Margaret had requested that the princess not be sent to Scotland at once, as she did not trust the King of Scots to wait to consummate the match – he was then almost 30 and had a number of illegitimate offspring. A feast followed the ceremony, with jousts, pageantry and dancing, and items were prepared for Margaret's anticipated departure, including a pair of crimson state bed curtains embroidered with Lancastrian roses. The match would be celebrated in verse by the Scottish poet William Dunbar, using the iconography of the thistle and the rose.

The surviving accounts of Elizabeth's household from February 1502 to March 1503 give a flavour of life at the court at which Margaret and Stanley would have been frequent visitors. Piety is a regular feature, defined by the calendar year but also by specific, personal acts of charity; these include payments to old servants, those seeking alms and offerings on saints' days, alms to a hermit and to a poor man for guiding the queen. Elizabeth rewarded those who brought gifts to her various palaces, largely local items, often homemade, to supplement the royal diet: she was given carp, almond butter and game, cushions, rabbits and quails; a poor man brought her apples and oranges, a poor woman brought chickens, a servant brought pears, an abbess sent rose water, a servant of the Archbishop of Canterbury brought cheese, the wife of William Greenweye brought peasecods. Elizabeth looked after her servants, paying 20s for the upkeep of the queen's fool while he was ill and 6*d* for a pair of shoes for him, and gave money for the care and keep of the queen's woman Anne Saye during a period of sickness. Edmund Burton was given 6*s* 8*d* for keeping the little garden at Windsor and 4*s* 8*d* was paid to two men for building a little arbour there; 5*s* was paid to grooms and pages for making bonfires on the eves of St John the Baptist and St Peter; 5*s* 8*d* was paid to a servant of the Mayor of London for bringing chairs for the queen; and a London tailor was rewarded for covering chairs in crimson cloth, crimson satin, blue cloth of gold, purple velvet and cushions of cloth of gold.

Elizabeth's wardrobe accounts, her costumes overlapping with Margaret's on occasion, indicate the kind of splendour that Henry's family enjoyed: she purchased gold Venice lace, Venice silk and gold damask for making lace and buttons at 50*s*, yards of black tinsel satin to edge a black velvet gown, yards of green satin, crimson satin and 4yd of russet and tawny green sarcenet; 56*s* 8*d* was paid to a coppersmith for silver and gold spangles in the shapes of stars, squares and points to be sewn on to jackets for a disguising and 13*s* 4*d* to the royal embroiderer; at the other end of the scale, 12*d* was paid for a night bonnet. The accounts expose some of the business of court life, which would have been familiar to Margaret; there were preparations for a visit to Richmond of the Hungarian ambassadors, the hiring of boats and rowing of possessions and people up and down the Thames, payments for ropes and repairs to the royal barges and rowers required to collect certain items that were needed from other residences. The prosaic aspects of daily life appear too, with the expenses for 'hir hors meat' of the queen's laundress Agnes, strings bought for the lute of Margaret's eldest granddaughter and 5*s* 4*d* for four rolls of white wax and the same again for ten rolls of yellow wax.

One particular payment stands out in the accounts: 6*s* 4*d* was paid in December to a monk who brought the girdle of Our Lady from Westminster to the queen. This was a relic commonly used by women in childbirth as the focal point of prayer, and serves as a reminder that by the Christmas of 1502, Elizabeth was in her final trimester of pregnancy. She planned to lie in at Richmond but her labour pains began at the end of January, while she was staying at the Tower. Perhaps Elizabeth miscalculated or the baby was premature, but something was clearly wrong when she delivered a daughter on 3 February. The child was named

Katherine but she and her mother both died, Elizabeth on 11 February. The gap of eight days between delivery and death suggests that the cause of the queen's death was puerperal fever as some postpartum infection set in, although the delivery may have proved difficult and caused injury. Margaret responded to the death in the way she knew best: by organising and remaining busy. She drew up a series of mourning ordinances, describing in detail the correct protocol and clothing for all those involved, including the size and shape of hoods worn and the length of trains. Elizabeth was buried in Westminster Abbey, her coffin draped in black and white, topped by a gold cross and a life-like wax effigy of the queen in robes of state, which survives in the museum at the abbey today. From that point onwards, with the disbanding of the queen's household, Margaret became the principal lady of the land, the most senior and authoritative feminine face of English royalty.

And Margaret was soon to suffer more personal losses of her own. In December 1503, her stepson, Stanley's heir George, Lord Strange, died in unusual circumstances after a banquet at Derby House on the Strand. He had gone from being the hostage for his father's loyalty at Bosworth to a father of seven children and died as the result of what was considered to be food poisoning. He was in his early forties when he was laid to rest in the nearby church of St James Garlickhythe. Perhaps George's premature death hastened that of his father. Stanley was at Lathom when he died on 20 July 1504, at the age of 69. He was laid to rest in the Stanley family chapel at Burscough Priory in Lancashire. Over the remaining five years of her widowhood, Margaret continued her pious works, her patronage and charity, taking a place at her son's side, each supporting the other in their solitude and overseeing the education of the children in the royal nursery.

16

ROYAL GRANDMOTHER, 1509

all Englonde for her dethe had cause of wepynge.[1]

In April 1509, Henry VII lay dying at his Renaissance fantasia Richmond Palace. His health had been poor in the last two or three years, as he suffered with lingering throat afflictions, fever, failing eyesight and diseases of the joints. He had suffered a serious bout of illness in 1503–4, when he required lotions for his eyes, again in 1504 and had a regular cough every spring, suggesting a tubercular lung infection. By 1507 he was suffering from gout and 'wasted' lungs causing him to experience 'great fits and labours', but recovered sufficiently to go hunting that October in 'perfect health'.[2] Margaret would have been with him when he passed Christmas 1508 at Greenwich and Richmond, before Henry travelled to his house at Hanworth, Middlesex, where he was overcome by an impending sense of mortality. Henry was seen less and less before retreating to his state apartments at Richmond and shutting himself in to await the end, calling for his confessor on 21 February. False reports had been given out of his death as early as 24 March and he made his will a week later, but in fact, he was to linger for another month, with his son at his side.

Prince Henry was now 17. He had been raised at Eltham Palace, carefully tutored by a range of talented thinkers, including Margaret's protégé, the poet laureate John Skelton who composed *Speculum Principis*, *The Mirror for Princes*, a book of conduct to guide his young charge. Margaret had taken an interest in both her grandsons' education and development, giving them books such as the copy of Cicero's *De Officiis* which included illustrations of Tudor dynastic symbols. In 1506, she had bought Henry a horse costing £6 13*s* 4*d*, with a saddle and harness covered in black velvet decorated with gilt flowers. Despite all Margaret's piety though, she also shared a love of fun with Henry; he enjoyed dancing and playing at dice and she liked to make a wager on a game of chess, listen to her minstrels or watch her jesters Skip and Reginald the Idiot perform their tricks. Her relationship with the young Henry must have been a blend of fun and the formidable intellectual endeavour for which Margaret had come to be known. She would also become his guide through the dramatic weeks ahead, witnessing the transition from one monarch to another and ensuring that the right decisions were taken for a smooth handover of power.

Henry VII died on 21 April. At once, the machinery of government sprang into action, beginning the next reign with a subterfuge designed to ensure that key decisions were made before the news was announced. Henry lay dead in his bed for almost two days, and his son remained in his private apartments, speaking in hushed voices to maintain the appearance that the king was still alive. Meals were brought for Henry and masses were said for his recovery. Behind the scenes, though, the chief members of the Privy Council were handing over their offices and instructions to their successors and time was being bought for certain individuals to arrive at Richmond. Margaret had certainly been summoned from Coldharbour House to see her son before his death and was now placed to take a central part in the discussions. It was agreed that until Henry reached his eighteenth birthday on 28 June, Margaret would act as regent. Clearly there were differences between this situation and the offer made by Margaret of Anjou in 1453, but it illustrates just how much Margaret

Beaufort's abilities were trusted. Late on St George's Day, 23 April, after the new king had eaten supper and attended evensong, still addressed as the Prince of Wales, the news was finally broken to the court. Only then was his son proclaimed as Henry VIII and left Richmond for the Tower, to await his coronation. Margaret joined him there shortly afterwards.

The two months of Margaret's regency witnessed a number of important decisions. Henry VII's unpopular councillors Edmund Dudley and Richard Empson were arrested at once, scapegoated for some of their former king's more unpopular financial policies, and taken to the Tower. They would be executed that August. Another arrest hit closer to home. A warrant was issued for Henry Stafford, younger brother of the Duke of Buckingham, the ambitious sons of the Buckingham who rose against Richard III, and a great nephew of Margaret's former husband, who was also taken to the Tower. This may have been intended to send a warning sign to the Staffords, whose claim to the throne was also a strong one, an attempt to impress upon them the authority of the new regime. Henry Stafford would be released after the coronation. A general pardon was also issued, other prisoners were released and the new king promised to right wrongs suffered under his father's regime, although the remaining Yorkists, the de la Poles, were exempted from it. Negotiations were also made with Ferdinand of Aragon and, after the long-awaited arrival of the second half of his daughter's dowry, a marriage between Henry and Catherine was now arranged.

Margaret oversaw the arrangements for her son's funeral. On 11 May, she signed the warrants for approval of payments for black mourning cloth, wages for the torchbearers and chariot to bear his body to Westminster. Her ordinances, drawn up in the wake of Queen Elizabeth's death, no doubt were the foundation for the process by which Henry's body was embalmed and revered during a 24-hour vigil during which masses were said over his coffin, before being set on the chariot covered in black cloth and topped with his life-size effigy, 'richly apparelled' in his Parliamentary robes and adorned with jewels and the ball and sceptre of state. The funeral procession travelled from Richmond to Southwark, on to Tower Bridge and into St Paul's Cathedral, accompanied by solemn mourners and witnessed by a great crowd. The following afternoon, Henry undertook his final journey to Westminster and his coffin was lowered into the vault alongside that of his wife. John Fisher, Bishop of Rochester delivered a long homily which so greatly moved and impressed Margaret that she ordered it to be printed by Wynkyn de Worde and distributed.

It must have been a time of mixed emotions for Margaret. On one hand, she was burying her beloved son, whose journey she had witnessed from exile to England's conqueror and king; on the other, she had the opportunity to act as midwife to a new regime, to deliver the realm into the hands of her grandson. Henry clearly appreciated her steadying hand and her interest. On 19 May, he granted her her old property of Woking Palace, which she had surrendered in 1503 to her son, who had renovated and used it as one of his favourite residences.

On 11 June, Henry married Catherine of Aragon at the church of the Friar Observants at Greenwich. The match had been approved by his council but it would appear that only a few witnesses were present, rather in contrast to the bride's first state wedding in white silken finery at St Paul's Cathedral. Henry's Lord Steward, George Talbot, Earl of Shrewsbury and Privy Chamberer William Thomas were named in the documentation but it is not clear whether Margaret was there too. It would seem likely that she was, but this cannot be proven and there may be unknown reasons for her absence. Henry appears to have wished to conclude the ceremony in advance of his coronation, which was scheduled for two weeks later, to allow himself and his new spouse to be crowned together. Yet there was much planning to do, with pageants and decorations, banquets and feasts planned, arrangements made, verses written and clothing sewn. The standard was set by the *Ryalle Book*, partly written during the reign of Edward IV, along whose formal Burgundian lines the stage was set for the coronation of Henry VIII, the heir to the dynasties of both York and Lancaster.

Saturday 23 June dawned bright and sunny. Henry and Catherine set out from the Tower at around 4 p.m., following a day and night of celebrations and the ceremony of the Knights of the Bath. Henry was first, dressed in robes of crimson velvet and ermine over a gold jacket and collar of rubies. He rode under a gold canopy, his horse trapped in ermine and damask gold, flanked by knights in red velvet and children dressed in blue and gold. Catherine's litter followed, pulled by six white palfreys draped in white cloth of gold. She wore a dress of white satin and a gold coronet on her long loose red hair. Margaret probably watched them from the position of a house on Cheapside, as she had witnessed other important events in recent years. Even a sharp shower of rain could not dampen the mood as Catherine was forced to shelter briefly under a draper's stall in Cornhill. They arrived at Westminster, where they were to dine and rest for the night, being received 'with much joy and honour'.[3] Henry and Catherine were crowned the next day in the abbey, where Margaret took her place in the choir. The next few days were spent in feasting, dancing and jousting.

Observing everything was Margaret Beaufort, the king's grandmother, the last member of the old Lancastrian dynasty. Amid all the Tudor pomp and ceremony, mingled with her grief and apprehension for the future, she could feel secure that her regency had been successful. Embodied in Henry VIII, the figure who united the dynasties of Lancaster and York, was the future Margaret had long fought for, the security that had seemed at times in her life to have been out of reach. She had been born before the Wars of the Roses, even before Henry VI had fallen ill or Margaret of Anjou had set foot on English soil. She was the great-granddaughter of John of Gaunt, her bloodline stretched back to Edward III and Philippa of Hainault, the product of an illicit love affair between a royal prince and the governess of his children. Her lifetime had witnessed the out-break of violence, the shedding of blood from the noblest houses of the country, by their own brothers and cousins, in an unpredictable tussle for the throne. She had been married too young, borne a child when she was only a child herself; there had been years when she was parted from her boy, when she feared for his life and perhaps her own, until the final moment of triumph at Bosworth Field. Now she had outlived her child, but she had spent those terrible weeks of grief busily, negotiating to ensure his son was in full possession of his inheritance. On 28 June, the court celebrated Henry VIII's eighteenth birthday. With this rite of passage, Margaret's regency formally came to an end. The following day, she died peacefully at Cheneygates, the Deanery at Westminster Abbey. The cause of her death is unknown.

Margaret's body was moved to Westminster Abbey refectory on 3 July, where candle-lit vigils were held and masses were said for her soul. Six days later she was buried in the Lady Chapel, in a black marble tomb topped with a golden effigy designed by Pietro Torrigiano, who also created the nearby tomb of Henry VII and his queen. She was depicted in her widow's weeds, with a hood and long mantle, her head resting on two pillows depicting her symbols of the portcullis and Tudor rose, while at her feet is the mythical yale, another Beaufort device. The tomb is also adorned with the arms of the Staffords, Stanleys, Henry V and Catherine of Valois, Henry VIII and Catherine of Aragon and those of Margaret's parents. The inscription on the tomb, written by the Humanist scholar Erasmus, reads:

> Margaret of Richmond, mother of Henry VII, grandmother of Henry VIII, who gave a salary to three monks of this convent and founded a grammar school at Wimborne, and to a preacher throughout England, and to two interpreters of Scripture, one at Oxford, the other at Cambridge, where she likewise founded two colleges, one to Christ, and the other to St John, his disciple. Died A.D. 1509, III Kalends of July (29 June).

Margaret's chaplain Bishop John Fisher delivered a laudatory sermon which has helped to shape a sense of the king's mother's character for later historians. He compared her to the biblical Martha in four senses: in their nobleness of person, in the disciplining of their bodies, in the ordering of their souls to God and in the keeping of hospitals and giving charity to their neighbours. Fisher praised Margaret as a true daughter of Lancaster, honouring her parents in being 'bounteous and liberal to every person of her knowledge and acquaintance' and loathing 'avarice and covetousness'. He gave further descriptions of her character:

> She was also of syngular Easyness to be spoken unto, and full curtayse answere she would make to all that came unto her. Of mervayllous gentylenesse she was unto all folks, but specially unto her owne whom she trusted and loved ryghte tenderly. Unkynde she wolde not be unto no creature, ne forgetfull of any kindness or service done to her before, which is no lytel part of veray nobleness. She was not venegable ne cruell but ready anone to forgete and to forgyve injuryes done unto her, at the leest desire or mocyon … mercyfull also and pyteous she was unto such as were grevyed and wrongfully troubled and to them that were in poverty, or sekeness or any other mysery.

She possessed:

> awareness of her self she had always to eschew every thyng that myght dishonest ony noble woman or distayne her honour in ony condycyon. Tryfelous thyngs that were lytell to be regarded, she wold let pass by, but the other that were of weyght and substance wherein she myght proufyte, she wolde not let for ony payne or labour to take upon hande. These and many other such noble condycyons left unto her by her Auncetres.

Margaret also lived soberly, restricting her dietary intake for personal and religious reasons:

> Her sober temperance in metes and drynkes was known to all them that were conversant with her ... kepying alway her strayte mesure and offen-dynge as lytell as ony creature myghte: eschewing banketts, reresoupers, joncryes betwixt meles. As for fastynge, for aege and feebleness albeit she were not bounde, yet those days that by the Chirche were appointed, she kept them diligently and seriously and in especyall the holy Lent; through-out that, she restrayned her appetyte tyl one meal and tyl one Fyshe on the day besydes her other peculer fastes of devocyon as St Anthony, St Mary Maudelyn, St Katherine, with other theroweout all the Yere, the Friday and Saturday she full truly observed.

According to Fisher, Margaret also wore a hair shirt beneath her cloth-ing, made according to the traditional Catholic method of animal hair or coarse sackcloth, sometimes woven with twigs or thin wire to mortify the skin as a means of penance and repentance:

> As to harde clothes wearyne, she had her shertes and grydyls of here, which when she was in helthe, everi week she fayled not certain days to weare, sometimes the one, sometimes the other, that full often her skynne, as I heerd her say, was perced therewith.

And when she made her confession, every third day, she would weep copiously:

Her mervaylous wepyng they can bere wytness of, which here before have herde her confession, which be divers and many at many times of the yere … what flodes of teeres there yssued forth of her eyes!

These devotions were conducted despite considerable pain in her joints, for which the remedies were kept in her closet:

All this long time her knelynge was to her paynful, and so paynful that many tymes it cause in her back payne and disease. And yet nevertheless dayly, when she was in helthe, she fayled not to say the Crowne of Our Lady, which, after the maner of Rome, conteyneth sixty and three Aves; and at every Ave to make a kneylynge.

She also suffered great pain in her hands, probably rheumatic:

These mercyfull and lyberall hands to endure the moost paynful cramps, so greveously vexynge her compellynge her to crye O Blessyd Jhesu help me! O Blessyd Lady socoure me! It was a mater of grete pyte.

Fisher also praised the organisation of her household, which was run 'with mervaylous dylygence and wysedom', writing ordinances quarterly to be read aloud by her officers, whom she would 'lovingly' encourage to do well, although she was prepared to deal with any dissent or factions within her house 'with great discretion'. She was a thoughtful and sensitive hostess:

… what payn, what labour, she of her veray gentleness wolde take with them, to bere them maner and Company and intrete every person, and entertayne them, according to their degree and haviour [behaviour] and provyde, by her own commandment, that nothynge sholde lack that might be convenient for them, wherein she had a wonderful redy remembraunce and perfyte knowledge.

And took care of those suitors and the poor who came to petition her for justice and help:

… of her own charges provyded men lerned for the same purpose, evenly and indyfferently to here all causes and admynyster right and justyce to every party, which were in no small nombre and yet mete and drynke was denyed to none of them … Poore folks to the nombre of twelve she dayly and nyghtly kepte in her House, gyvynge them lodginge, mete and drynke and clothynge … and in their sykenesse visytyng them and comfortynge them and mynystrynge unto them with her owne hands: and when it pleased God to call ony of them out of this wretched worlde, she wolde be present, to see them departe … Suppose not ye, that yf she myghte have gotten our Savyour Jhesu in his owne Persone, but she wolde as desyrously and as fervently have mynystered unto hym?

Despite, or perhaps as a result of, her piety and suffering, there was a fatalistic streak to Margaret:

She never was yet in that prosperity, but the greter it was, the more alwaye she dreded the austerity. For when the King her son was crowned, in all that grete tryumphe and glorye she wept mervaylously; and lykewyse at the grete tryumphe of Prynce Arthur, and at the last coronacyon, whereyn she had full grete joy, she let not to say that some advertise wolde followe. So that eyther she was in sorowe by reason of the present adversytes or else whan se was in prosperyte, she was in drede of the adversyte for to come.

She was a treasure, concluded Fisher, and 'all Englonde for her dethe had cause of wepynge'.

An inventory taken of the closet beside Margaret's chamber reveals a combination of her personal preferences and functional items, its detail creating a sense of rifling through her cupboards. Locked away were piles of her papers, including annuities, bonds and indentures for her wards and dependents, as well as the jointure settled upon her by Thomas Stanley. There were service books, bound in velvet and wrapped in linen; two pairs of gold spectacles and ivory combs, a gold purse containing true love knots and another with rings thought to prevent cramp. Margaret had at least one significant Beaufort item, a goblet made of gold with a cover in the shape of a portcullis, as well as silver candlesticks and spoons. Inside a little black coffer were silver pots used to hold medicinal powders and a number of remedies prepared to ease the stiffness in her joints. She also had a small portable shrine gilt and glazed, containing relics, as well as a little bag containing a 'heart of relics' and a silver-gilt plate bearing the image of the Virgin Mary.[4]

The executors of Margaret's will grouped her items under the headings plate and great jewels, small jewels, chapel stuff, wardrobe of beds, wardrobe of robes, silks and napery, certain wines, kitchen stuff, certain stuff in storehouses, standards and chests, certain spices, palfreys and chariots, small trash with glasses and pewter basins. Further inventories of her bedroom equipment describe the furnishings including beds of fine arras or red saye, counterpoints of tapestry, gold and silk, down pillows, gold cushions, carpets, canvases, coverings for chairs and litters. Major bequests were made to Christ Church College and St John's College, Cambridge, to Westminster Abbey and other places that had enjoyed her patronage, like Burne Abbey, or had family connections, like Wimbourne. Margaret's will also rewarded a painter named Wolff for his 'warkemanshipp' in 'the making ii pyctures of my lady's personage', and a Maynerd Wayweke 'for makyng an ymage for Crystex College'. Payments were also made for painted books made for the college, for the writing and sealing of the books, and to Lady Scrope in recompense for a ring which Prince Henry had from her and to Master Fisher of Hatfield for an old pair of 'dydrygurders' or hurdy-gurdies that were left behind by the Lord of Misrule. Thus the separate pieces of her life were assigned or returned until the material traces of Margaret Beaufort were all dispersed.

Margaret's reputation among later writers has been mixed. Poet and tutor to Henry VIII, Bernard Andre described her as 'steadfast and more stable than the weakness in women suggests', which springs straight from contemporary gender conceptions but allows Margaret to be strong and constant as an exception to the stereotype. Her nineteenth-century biographer Charles Henry Cooper saw her as 'the brightest example of the strong devotional feeling and active charity of the age in which she lived', who 'stepped widely … out of the usual sphere of her sex to encourage literature by her patronage and her bounty' and was 'united to the strictest piety the practice of all the moral virtues and … chastened, while she properly cherished, the grandeur of royalty by the indulgence of domestic affections and the retired exercise of a mind at once philosophic and humble'.[5] Cooper's contemporary Caroline Amelia Halsted echoed his view of Margaret as a role model to whom 'the females of Britain look with duty and affection, with pride as women, with devotion as subjects' considering her the 'brightest ornament of her sex'.[6] By contrast, David Starkey's assessment typifies a more critical modern reaction to Margaret's talents, referring to her as 'imperious' and 'tight-fisted'. As Helen M. Jewell summarises, Margaret's most recent biographers have taken a 'shrewder perspective, crediting her with a calculating temperament and natural astuteness, "a veteran of bruising political battles" whose life and work show "a constant blend of the practical and the pious, which argues at least an active and disciplined will"'.

There is little doubt that Margaret was a dynamic and influential figure, a survivor whose strength and resilience increased as a result of the dangerous circumstances to which she was a witness. She was also an opportunist, biding her time until she could seize whatever chance might arise to further the fortunes of her family. In this, she was no different from the men of her era, although her sphere of influence differed greatly and the power she exercised was largely in the gift of the men in her life, her husbands and son, even at the height of her influence. As the final link in the chain of the Lancastrian women, her qualities and success underscore the journey the dynasty had taken since the marriage of John of Gaunt and Katherine Swynford, her great-grandparents.

17

WHITE SWANS, RED ROSES

Now may the housband in the south dwell in his own place
His wif and eke his faire doughter and all the goode he has
Suche menys hath the rose made by vertu and grace.[1]

Τhis book has traced the interfaces of two narratives, those of
the red rose and the white swan, symbols of the masculine
and feminine experiences of history. Traditionally, the dominant version of events comprises the lives and works of great
men, the story of possession of the throne, which follows the transfer of
political, religious and military power. Thus only a small percentage of
the lives of the people of the past find representation, those of the kings
and bishops, generals and traitors, whose births and deaths have been
inscribed in school curricula along with the names of the battles they
fought at Poitiers, Agincourt, St Albans, Towton, Tewkesbury, Bosworth

and Stoke. Even so, the names most of the thousands of casualties who gave their lives in the cause of England, or Lancaster, or York, or just in the course of survival, have now been lost. The story of the red rose of Lancaster is one of victory and defeat, of unexpected reversals of fortune and the consequences of character and circumstance. Yet, all the while, this dominating metanarrative has been underscored by swathes of alternative accounts, overlapping, colliding and separating, sometimes merging; each a function of the other, sometimes breaking through and derailing another historical path, and each just as valid as the first.

When it comes to the story of the white swan, the narrative tracing the contributions of women to the Lancastrian dynasty, the surviving evidence is more limited, more transient. The lives of women in the fourteenth and fifteenth centuries are often illuminated by history only where they come into contact with men, when the light of the red rose casts them into relief or draws out a long shadow behind them. Although many of these women were fortunate enough to be literate, they did not keep diaries and few of the letters they wrote have survived. They were perceived as daughters, wives and mothers, and their challenges to these labels came at a cost. The limitations of women's lives in a personal and legal sense has also meant that the narrative of the white swan has suffered as a result of the dominance of the red rose, being distorted or curtailed by louder historical voices. Their contributions to dynastic success have been less measurable beyond the traditional yardstick of fertility, and more confined to the personal sphere of private human relations. Yet they have also been guides, confidantes, educators, queens, regents, role models and much more.

The narrative of the white swan falls into four distinct phases. Firstly, there were the women who helped build the dynasty, who were close to the throne but never saw it as within reach; the beloved wives Blanche of Lancaster, Mary de Bohun and Katherine Swynford of the late fourteenth century whose fertility established the family line. They were English-born or, in the case of Katherine, spent the majority of their life in England as members of the nobility, with close family ties to the court. Secondly, there were the women of the early fifteenth century who rode the crest of Lancaster's new-found success as queens to strong men at the height of dynastic good fortune, such as Joan of Navarre and Catherine of Valois. From around the middle of the century though, the family's luck went into decline, starting with the charges against Eleanor Cobham, through to the circumstances of Margaret of Anjou's queenship and the Lancastrian nadir of Tewkesbury. The final phase was heralded in 1485, with the final radiant victory of Lancastrian patience and determination that was Margaret Beaufort. Yet they were not the only ones. Many other women contributed, whose lives reflect the complexities of the era and whose allegiances may have changed as a result of marriage, which frequently proved to be a far more determining factor than their birth.

It is difficult to determine an ideal Lancastrian woman. So far as the models of the time go, the medieval definition of feminine perfection could be contradictory, but was largely focused on submission and fertility, piety and duty. Certainly many of them conformed to this ideal, as far as was possible, while questions of marital harmony and fecundity left others falling short of the popular standard by circumstances beyond their control. By understanding the expectations of the age, it may be possible to approach the feelings of the women involved when they fell short of those standards, as at the time it would take an exceptional individual to reject conformity and the security it conferred. Clearly motherhood mattered and around it turned the opportunities of the Lancastrian dynasty. Had Anne of Bohemia borne a live child in the 1380s, the future may have been very different for Henry Bolingbroke. Equally different could have been the path taken towards civil war if Eleanor Cobham had succeeded in falling pregnant instead of Margaret of Anjou. On such questions of biology have the narratives of red roses and white swans turned.

There were certain specific qualities shared by the wives, mothers and daughters of Lancaster: loyalty and dedication to their cause. However, this was not always straightforward as allegiances were challenged by new bonds, causing women such as Jacquetta and Elizabeth Wydeville and Cecily Neville to follow the fortunes of their men when they were led into conflict with the dynasty of the red rose. All were Lancastrians early on, by marriage, such as Jacquetta's to John, Duke of Bedford and Elizabeth's to John Grey, or by birth in Cecily's case. Loyalty and determination remained their key qualities but marriage witnessed their transfer to the house of York, although they would have perceived this as a duty to the continuance of their bloodline and no disloyalty at all. Certainly ambition was a frequent part of the make-up of the Lancastrian woman, perhaps more so after the dynasty's crowning success of 1399. It may have played a part in convincing Joan of Navarre to act on her preference for Henry IV and independently arrange her own marriage. However, when it came to marriages like that of Joan Beaufort to the King of Scots or her cousin Joan Beaufort to Ralph Neville, Earl of Westmorland, it is impossible to establish just where the impetus of ambition lay, divided as it was among the bride and her relatives. On the verge of making their matches, these young women were likely to have been just as keen to marry well as the families whose values had shaped their social outlook.

What resonates through many of these women's stories is the theme of love. In an era when marriages among the aristocracy were arranged for mutual advancement, a surprising number of love stories emerge. Mistresses became wives in the cases of Katherine Swynford and Eleanor Cobham, while the majority of those marrying into the dynasty became cherished companions. It is possible to see the warmth between Edward III and Philippa of Hainault replicated down the years in the marriages of their descendants, resulting in the remarkable matches of the Black Prince and Joan of Kent, Henry IV and Joan of Navarre, Richard II and Anne of Bohemia. Then there was the unusual match borne of out affection between Catherine of Valois and Owen Tudor, forbidden and scandalous as it was, but which created the bloodline that allowed the Lancastrians their final comeback in 1485. Romantic love certainly played its part in the story, but it was perhaps not as decisive as the maternal love that drove Margaret of Anjou and Margaret Beaufort, with very different results.

The theme of witchcraft also appears with surprising consistency through the narrative as part of the social and sexual history of violence against women. The close connection between John, Duke of Bedford and the fate of Joan of Arc in Rouen in 1431 established a theme for the middle years of the century that was adopted by these women's allies and enemies alike, with the imprisonment of Joan of Navarre, the condemnation of Eleanor Cobham and the accusations made against Jacquetta Wydeville. One of the most powerful weapons available against a woman of any rank, the accusation of witchcraft, exposes just how fragile their positions were, and how dependent upon the goodwill of men for their survival.

This book is an attempt to trace an alternative narrative of English history during the period 1345–1509, to complement the dominant male version of events with one of female experience and influence. Of course, the two are inseparable in terms of understanding the era and at times they collide and merge, but the lives of women of the period are rarely highlighted at the expense of accepted masculine truths, of well-trodden paths that may present their world as a continuous series of dates. Instead, this female history is fragmentary; a mosaic or jigsaw of overlapping lives, some of which only appear in the spotlight briefly, before their trails go cold in the margins. I have attempted to look beyond the continuum to where these women came from and where they went. This has involved a degree of necessary diversion that has only made their stories the richer, by helping uncover the many similarities between their situations and the interconnectedness of their key moments. The span has been vast. From Blanche of Lancaster's brief life and exhaustive maternity to Margaret Beaufort's spell as regent, the women of the dynasty have undergone an arc of redefinition, as part of the constant struggle that has been the universal truth of women's lives throughout history.

Just as the narratives of male and female experience were closely woven, the blood of the combative red and white roses was mingled upon the wedding of Henry VII and Elizabeth of York, and embodied in their surviving son, Henry VIII. It seems fitting to end this study with a song dating from the early years of their marriage, perhaps to celebrate the arrival of Arthur in 1486, using the symbolism of the roses to anticipate peace:

> I love the rose both red and white
> Is that your pure perfite appetite?
> To here talke of them is my delite
> Joyed may we be
> Our Prince to see
> And Roses three.

NOTES

PART ONE

Introduction: Time Honour'd Lancaster

1 http://www.history.ac.uk/richardII/dunst_swan.html
2 Planché.

1: Blanche of Lancaster, 1345–68

1 Armitage-Smith, *John of Gaunt*.
2 Horrox.
3 Ibid.
4 Ibid.
5 Ibid.
6 Ibid.
7 *Ordinances*.
8 Calendar of Close Rolls (CCR), Edward III, 6 May, 1348.
9 Ibid.
10 Horrox.
11 Ibid.
12 Ibid.
13 Ibid.

14 Crane.

15 Richardson, *Plantagenet Ancestry*.

16 CCR, Edward III, 10 March 1348.

17 Horrox.

18 Shrewsbury.

19 Ibid.

20 CCR, Edward III, March 1351.

21 This quotation comes from a text written slightly after the event; Grosmont was still Earl, not Duke, at this point.

22 Froissart.

23 Treasure.

24 Richardson.

25 Lancelott.

26 Froissart.

27 Mortimer.

28 www.queens.ox.ac.uk/about-queens/history/

29 Mortimer.

30 Calendar of Patent Rolls, Edward III, 1353.

31 Ibid.

32 Ibid.

33 Mortimer.

34 Richardson.

35 Ibid.

36 Chaucer.

37 Ibid.

38 Ibid.

39 Froissart.

40 Weir.

41 Close Roll, Edward III, 26 October 1360.

42 Goodman.

43 Armitage-Smith, *John of Gaunt*.

44 Holinshed.

45 Goodman.

46 Ibid.

47 Lawrance.

48 Crawford.

49 Mortimer.

50 Shrewsbury.

51 Rymer.

52 Richardson.

53 The surname is Holland, the Baronetcy Holand.

54 Saul, Nigel, *Richard II.*

55 Shrewsbury.

56 Ibid.

2: The Girls' Governess, 1368–71

1 Chaucer.

2 Weir.

3 Fine Rolls, Edward III, November 1361, January 1362.

4 Given-Wilson.

5 Mortimer.

6 Weir.

7 Walsingham.

3: Constance of Castile, 1371–94

1 Gower.

2 Mortimer.

3 Goodman.

4 Papworth.

5 Ibid.

6 Ibid.

7 Emery.

8 Goodman.

9 Armitage-Smith, *John of Gaunt's Register.*

10 Now in Oxfordshire, it was in Berkshire until the redrawing of the county boundary in 1974.

11 Armitage-Smith, *John of Gaunt's Register, Volume 1.*

12 Quotation attributed to John Locke.

13 Walsingham.

14 Fletcher.

15 Ibid.

16 Weir.

17 Emery.

18 Walsingham.

19 Ibid.

20 Froissart.

21 Goodman.

22 Ibid.

23 Ibid.

PART TWO

4: Mary de Bohun, 1380–94

1 Carruthers.

2 Ibid.

3 CCR, Richard II, May/June 1380.

4 Green.

5 CCR, Richard II, October 1380.

6 Ibid.

7 The 1381 manifesto of the Peasants' Revolt.

8 Amt.

9 CCR, Richard II, December 1384.

10 Hearne's Fragment. Published in Various, *The Chronicles of the White Rose of York*.

11 Labarge.

12 Cockayne.

13 Forceps had not yet been invented for general use.

14 Hall.

15 See Licence, Amy, *In Bed with the Tudors: The Sex Lives of a Dynasty from Elizabeth of York to Elizabeth I* (Stroud: Amberley, 2012) for more information about childbirth customs, infant and maternal mortality.

16 Allmand.

17 Thompson.

18 Radcot Bridge is now in the county of Oxfordshire, but was previously in Berkshire.

19 Thompson.

20 Saul, *Richard II*.

21 Green.
22 Mortimer in Shakespeare's *Henry IV.*
23 Ibid.
24 Allmand.

5: Richard II's Queens, 1382–97

1   Hector.
2   Thomas.
3   Costain.
4   Thompson.
5   Parliament Rolls, Richard II, May 1381.
6   Jefferson.
7   Lancashire.
8   Cherry.
9   Hilton.
10 Stratford.
11 Maidstone.
12 Froissart.
13 See Westminster Abbey's webpage.
14 Bennett.
15 Gillespie.
16 Geaman.
17 Ibid.
18 Strickland.
19 Carlson.
20 Maidstone.
21 Stratford.
22 Ibid.
23 Ibid.
24 Monstrelet.
25 Stratford.
26 Ibid.
27 Calendar of Patent Rolls (CPR), Richard II, December 1396.
28 Weir.
29 Hilton.
30 Stratford.

31 Weir.
32 CPR, Richard II, October 1398.
33 CRP, Richard II, February 1398.
34 Ward.

6: Legitimacy, 1394–1403
1   Shakespeare, *Richard II*.
2   Weir.
3   Walsingham.
4   CPR, Richard II, March 1399.
5   Mortimer.
6   Bennett.
7   Tyrrell.
8   Gillespie.
9   Ibid.
10 Rymer.

PART THREE

7: Joan of Navarre, 1403–19
1   Poem attributed to John Lydgate.
2   CSP, Milan, 1399.
3   Ibid.
4   Hilton.
5   Gathorne-Hardy.
6   Lawrance.
7   Monstrelet.
8   Ibid.
9   Ibid.
10 Mortimer.
11 Rymer.
12 Ibid.
13 CCR, Henry IV, 1408–11.
14 Ibid.
15 Strickland.

16 Ibid.

17 Rymer.

18 CCR, Henry IV, October 1409.

19 Ibid., 1412.

20 Strickland.

21 Patent Rolls, Henry IV, 1414, 1415.

22 Myers.

23 Ibid.

24 Ibid.

8: Catherine of Valois, 1420–26

1   Poem attributed to John Lydgate.

2   Dockray.

3   Allmand.

4   From the 'Treaty of Troyes', 1420, reproduced in Rymer's *Foedera*.

5   Hall.

6   Allemand.

7   Strickland.

8   Ibid.

9   Nicolas.

10 Allemand.

11 Hilton.

12 Anon.

13 Woolgar.

14 Myers.

15 CPR, Henry V, 1421.

16 Monstrelet.

17 Allemand.

18 Woolgar.

9: Mrs Tudor, 1426–37

1   Poem attributed to William of Aquitaine.

2   Mitchell.

3   Cockburn.

4   Mitchell.

5   Patent Rolls, Henry VI, 1430.

6   Strickland.
7   Ibid.

10: Queen of Scotland, 1424–45

1   Brown.
2   Brown.
3   James I.
4   *Calendar of Papal Registers.*
5   Ibid.
6   Anon.
7   John Stuart, *Rotuli Scaccarii Regum Scotorum.*
8   Close Rolls, Henry VI, May 1428.
9   Close Rolls, Henry VI, May 1428.

PART FOUR

11: Potential Queens, 1437–45

1   Craik.
2   Ibid.
3   Griffiths.
4   Scattergood.
5   Nijsten.
6   Weir.
7   Scattergood.
8   Ibid.
9   Close Rolls, Henry VI, May 1428.
10 Vickers.
11 Saygin.
12 Rider.
13 Ibid.
14 Vickers.
15 Saygin.
16 Newall.
17 Ibid.
18 Miller.

19 Vickers.
20 Griffiths.
21 Ibid.

12: Margaret of Anjou, 1445–60
1 Shakespeare, *Henry IV, Part II*.
2 Griffiths.
3 Hay.
4 CSP, Milan, October 1458.
5 Strickland.
6 Beckington.
7 Ibid.
8 Hilton.
9 Abbot.
10 CSP, Milan, October 1458.
11 Griffiths.
12 Ibid.
13 Dockray.
14 Gairdner, *The Paston Letters*.
15 Patent Rolls, Henry VI, 1447–50.
16 Dockray.
17 Ibid.
18 Ashdown-Hill.
19 Griffiths.
20 Ibid.
21 Dockray.
22 Strickland.
23 www.british-history.ac.uk/survey-london/bk14/pp16-24
24 Paston letters.
25 Dockray.
26 Whethamsted's Chronicle published in Various, *The Chronicles of the White Rose of York*.
27 Rotuli Parliamentorum.
28 Strickland.
29 Paston letters.
30 McGerr.

31 Ibid.

32 Paston letters.

13: Queen in Exile, 1461–82

1 Paston letters.

2 Ibid.

3 Ibid.

4 Griffiths.

5 Paston letters.

6 Hilton.

7 Griffiths.

8 Gregory, Baldwin and Jones.

9 Griffiths.

10 Ibid.

11 Ibid.

12 Strickland.

13 McGerr.

14 Ibid.

15 Strickland.

16 Ibid.

17 Hilton.

14: Tudor's Widow, 1471–85

1 Murray.

2 Ibid.

3 Ibid.

4 CSP, Henry VI, May 1444.

5 Cooper.

6 Ibid.

7 Halsted.

8 Patent Rolls, Henry VI, August 1453.

9 Ibid.

10 Gregory.

11 Ibid.

12 Nicolas, *Testament Vetusta*.

13 Halsted.

14 White.

15 Gregory.

16 Ibid.

17 Vergil.

18 Holinshed.

PART FIVE

15: The King's Mother, 1485–1509

1 Ridley.

2 Ridley.

3 de Lisle.

4 CPR, March 1487.

5 Creighton.

6 Ibid.

7 Norton.

8 Krug.

9 Hymers.

10 Norton.

16: Royal Grandmother, 1509

1 Taken from the sermon preached at Margaret Beaufort's funeral by Bishop John Fisher.

2 Comment made by the Spanish Ambassador, cited in Bacon, *The History of the Reign of King Henry VII and Selected Works*.

3 Hall.

4 Underwood and Jones.

5 Cooper.

6 Halsted.

17: White Swans, Red Roses

1 Anon.

BIBLIOGRAPHY

Calendar of Close Rolls Edward III, ed. H.C. Maxwell Lyte, Volumes 1–14 (HMSO 1896–1913)

Calendar of Close Rolls Richard II, ed. H.C. Maxwell Lyte and A.E Stamp, Volumes 1–6 (HMSO 1914–27)

Calendar of Close Rolls Henry IV, ed. A.E. Stamp, Volumes 1–4 (HMSO 1927–34)

Calendar of Close Rolls Henry V, ed. A.E. Stamp, Volumes 1–2 (HMSO 1929, 1932)

Calendar of Close Rolls Henry VI, ed. A.E. Stamp, Volumes 1–6 (HMSO 1933–47)

Calendar of Close Rolls Edward IV, Edward V, Richard III, ed. W.H.B. Bird and K.H. Ledward, Volumes 1–3 (HMSO 1949, 1953, 1954)

Calendar of Close Rolls Henry VII, ed. K.H. Ledward, Volumes 1–2 (HMSO 1955, 1963)

Calendar of Entries in the Papal Registers Relating to Great Britain and Ireland, ed. W.H. Bliss et al. Volumes 3–9 (HMSO, 1897–1912)

Calendar of Fine Rolls Edward III, ed. A.E. Bland, Volumes 5–19 (HMSO 1915–39)

Calendar of Patent Rolls Edward III, Volumes 1–16 (HMSO 1891–1916)

Calendar of Patent Rolls Richard II, Volumes 1–6 (HMSO 1895–1909)

Calendar of Patent Rolls Henry IV, Volumes 1–4 (HMSO 1903–09)

Calendar of Patent Rolls Henry V, Volumes 1–2 (HMSO 1910, 1911)

Calendar of Patent Rolls Henry VI, Volumes 1–6 (HMSO 1901–10)

Calendar of Patent Rolls Edward IV, 1 Volume (HMSO 1897)

Calendar of State Papers and Manuscripts in the Archives and Collections of Milan 1385–1618, ed. Allen B. Hinds (HMSO, 1912)

Abbot, Jacob, *Margaret of Anjou* (New York: Harper and Brothers, 1902)

Allmand, Christopher, *The Hundred Years' War: England and France c.1300–1450* (Cambridge Medieval Textbooks, 2008)

Amt, Emilie, *Women's Lives in Medieval Europe: A Sourcebook* (Routledge, 2010)

Anon., *The Auchinleck Chronicle: Ane Schort Memoriale of the Scottis Corniklis for Addicioun* (Edinburgh: Thomas Thomson, 1819)

Armitage-Smith, Sydney, *John of Gaunt* (Constable, 1904)

Armitage-Smith, Sydney, *John of Gaunt's Register, Volume 1*. Camden Third Series 20, 21 (Royal Historical Society, 1911)

Ashdown-Hill, John, *Royal Marriage Secrets* (Stroud: The History Press, 2013)

Bacon, Francis, *The History of the Reign of King Henry VII and Selected Works* (Cambridge University Press, 1902)

Beckington, Thomas, *A Journal by one of the suite of T. Beckingham … during an embacy to negotiate a marriage between Henry VI and a daughter of the Count of Armagnac*, ed. Nicholas Harries Nicolas (William Pickering, 1828)

Bennett, Michael, *Richard II and the Revolution of 1399* (Stroud: Sutton, 1999)

Brewer, Derek S., *The World of Chaucer* (Woodbridge: Boydell & Brewer, 1978)

Brown, Michael, *James I* (East Linton: Tuckwell Press, 1994)

Carlson, David, R. (ed.) with William Maidstone, *Concordia* (Middle English Texts, 2003)

Carruthers, Mary (ed.), *Rhetoric beyond Words: Delight and Persuasion in the Arts of the Middle Ages* (Cambridge: Cambridge University Press, 2010)

Chaucer, Geoffrey, *Book of the Duchess*, ed. Larry Benson (Oxford: Oxford University Press, 1988)

Cherry, John F., *Goldsmiths* (Toronto: University of Toronto Press, 1992)

Clode, Charles M., *The Early History of the Merchant Tailor's Guild* (Harrison and Sons, 1888)

Cockayne, Thomas Oswald (ed.), *Hali Meidenhad* (Early English Texts Society, 1866)

Cockburn, J.S., H.P.F. King and K.G.T. McDonnell (eds), *A History of the County of Middlesex*, Vols 1–12 (Constable, 1969)

Cooper, Charles Henry, *Memoir of Margaret (Beaufort), Countess of Richmond and Derby* (Cambridge: Cambridge University Press, 1874)

Costain, Thomas B., *The Last Plantagenet: The Pageant of England, Volume 4* (Doubleday, 2012)

Craik, George Lillie, Hans Charles Hamilton and Charles Mcfarlane, *The Pictorial History of England Volume V* (Charles Knight, 1839)

Crane, Susan, *The Performance of Self: Ritual, Clothing and Identity during the Hundred Years' War* (Philadelphia, PA: University of Pennsylvania Press, 2011)

Crawford, Anne, *Letters of Medieval Women* (Stroud: Sutton, 2002)

Creighton, Charles, *A History of Epidemics in Britain* (Cambridge: Cambridge University Press, 1891)

de Lisle, Leanda, *Tudor* (Chatto & Windus, 2013)

Ditchfield, P.H. and William Page (eds), *Victoria County History of Berkshire, Volume 3* (London, 1923)

Dockray, Keith, *Warrior King: The Life of Henry V* (Stroud: Tempus, 2004)

Emery, Anthony, *Greater Medieval Houses of England and Wales 1300–1500, Volume Three: Southern England* (Cambridge: Cambridge University Press, 2006)

Fletcher, Christopher David, *Richard II: Manhood, Youth and Politics 1377–99* (Oxford Historical Monographs, 2008)

Froissart, Jean, *Chroniques*, trans. Geoffrey Brereton (Penguin, 1978)

Gairdner, James (ed.), *Gregory's Chronicle 1461–9* (London, 1876)

Gairdner, James, *Henry VII* (Oxford: Oxford University Press, 1899)

Gairdner, James, *The Paston Letters*, 6 vols (Oxford University Press, 1904)

Gairdner, James (ed.), *Three Fifteenth Century Chronicles* (London: J. Cambden Society, 1880)

Gathorne-Hardy, Jonathan, *The Rise and Fall of the British Nanny* (Faber & Faber, 1972)

Geaman, Kristen L., 'A Personal Letter written by Anne of Bohemia', *English Historical Review* 128.534 (2013), 1086–94.

Geaman, Kristen L., *Anne of Bohemia and her Struggle to Conceive* (Oxford: Oxford University Press, 2014)

Gillespie, James L., *The Age of Richard II* (Stroud: Sutton, 1997)

Given-Wilson, Chris, *Chronicles of the Revolution 1397–1400: The Reign of Richard II* (Manchester: Manchester University Press, 1993)

Given-Wilson, Chris, *Fourteenth-Century England, Volume 2* (Boydell Press, 2002)

Goodman, Anthony, *John of Gaunt: The Exercise of Princely Power in Fourteenth-Century Europe* (Routledge, 1993)

Gower, John, *Confessio Amantis*

Green, Mary Anne Everett, *Lives of the Princesses of England from the Norman Conquest, Volume 3* (Henry Colburn, 1851)

Gregory, Philippa, David Baldwin and Michael Jones, *The Women of the Cousins' War: The Duchess, the Queen and the King's Mother* (New York: Touchstone, 2011)

Griffiths, R.A., *The Reign of King Henry VI: The Exercise of Royal Authority, 1422–1461* (Ernest Benn, 1981)

Gurney, E.H., *Reference Handbook: For Readers, Students and Teachers of English History* (1890)

Hall, Edward, *Hall's Chronicle* (J. Johnson, 1809)

Halsted, Caroline Amelia, *Life of Margaret Beaufort, Countess of Richmond and Derby, Mother of King Henry VII* (Smith, Elder & Co., 1845)

Hamilton, J.S., *The Plantagenets: History of a Dynasty* (A. and C. Black, 2010)

Hardy, B.C., *Philippa of Hainault and Her Times* (J. Long, 1910)

Hay, D. (ed), *The Anglia Historia of Polydore Vergil* (Camden Society, 1950)

Hearne, T. (ed.), *Titi Livii Foro-Juliensis Vita Henrici Quinti Regis Angliae* (Oxford, 1716)

Hector, L.C. and Barbara F. Harvey (eds and trans) *Westminster Chronicle* (Oxford: Clarendon, 1982)

Hilton, Lisa, *Queens Consort: England's Medieval Queens* (Weidenfeld and Nicolson, 2008)

Holinshed, Raphael, *Holinshed's Chronicles of England, Scotland and Ireland* (J. Johnson, 1808)

Horrox, Rosemary, *The Black Death* (Manchester: Manchester University Press, 1994)

Hymers, J., *The Funeral Sermon of Margaret Beaufort, Countess of Richmond and Derby* (Cambridge: Cambridge University Press, 1811)

James I, King, *The Poetical Remains of James I* (Edinburgh: J. and E. Balfour, 1793)

James, G.P.R., *Memoirs of Celebrated Women Volume I* (Philadelphia, PA: Carey and Hart, 1839)

Jefferson, Lisa, 'The Language and Vocabulary of the Fourteenth- and Early Fifteenth-Century Records of the Goldsmiths Company', in *Multilingualism in Later Medieval Britain*, ed. D.A. Trotter (Woodbridge: Boydell and Brewer, 2000)

Jewell, Helen M., *Women in Medieval England* (Manchester: Manchester University Press, 1996)

Jones, Michael K. and Malcolm G. Underwood, *The King's Mother: Lady Margaret Beaufort, Countess of Richmond and Derby* (Cambridge: Cambridge University Press, 1993)

Krug, Rebecca, *Reading Families: Women's Literate Practice in Late Medieval England* (Ithaca, NY: Cornell University Press, 2011)

Labarge, Margaret Wade, *Women in Medieval Life* (Penguin, 1986)

Lancashire, Anne, 'Early London Pageantry and Theatre History Firsts', *Shakespeare Studies*, 30 (2002), 84–92

Lancelott, Francis, *The Queens of England and their Times, Volume 1* (New York: Appleton, 1858)

Lawrance, Hannah, *Historical Memories of the Queens of England* (Edward Moxon, 1838)

Lucraft, Jeanette, *Katherine Swynford: The History of a Medieval Mistress* (Stroud: Sutton, 2006)

McGerr, Rosemarie Pottz, *A Lancastrian Mirror for Princes* (Bloomington and Indianapolis: Indiana University Press, 2011)

Maidstone, Richard, *Concordia (The Reconciliation of Richard II with London)*, ed. David R. Carlson, trans. A.G. Rigg, Middle English Texts Series (Kalamazoo: Medieval Institute Publications, 2003)

Miller, Michael D., 'Wars of the Roses', www.warsoftheroses.co.uk/index.htm

Mitchell, J. Allen, 'Queen Katherine and the Secret of Lydgate's The Temple of Glass', *Medium Aevum*, 77 (2008), 53–76

Monstrelet, Enguerrand de, *The Chronicles of Enguerrand de Monstrelet*, ed. Thomas Johnes (Longman, 1810)

Mortimer, Ian, *The Perfect King: The Life of Edward III, Father of the English Nation* (Vintage, 2008)

Murray, Alexander, *Suicide in the Middle Ages: The Violent against Themselves* (Oxford: Oxford University Press, 1999)

Myers, A.R., *Crown, Household and Parliament in Fifteenth-Century England* (A. and C. Black, 1985)

Newall, Venetia, *The Witch Figure: Folklore Essays by a group of scholars in England Honouring the 75th Birthday of Katharine M. Briggs* (Routledge, 2013)

Nicolas, Nicholas Harris, *Proceedings and Ordinances of the Privy Council of England, Volume II* (Eyre and Spottiswoode, 1834)

Nicolas, Nicholas Harris, *Testament Vetusta* (Nichols and Son, 1826)

Nicolas, Nicholas Harris, *Purse Expenses of Elizabeth of York* (London: W. Pickering, 1830)

Nijsten, Gerard, *Jacoba of Bavaria*, Online Dictionary of the Netherlands

Norton, Elizabeth, *Margaret Beaufort, Mother of the Tudor Dynasty* (Amberley Publishing, 2012)

Papworth, Martin, 'Uncovering the Home of John of Gaunt', *British Archaeology*, 46 (1999)

Pegge, Samuel (ed.), *The Forme of Cury* (J. Nicols, 1780)

Planché, J.R., 'On the Badges of the House of Lancaster', *The Journal of the British Archaeological Association*, 6 p.374–92 (1851),

Power, Eileen Edna, *Medieval English Nunneries* (Cambridge: Cambridge University Press, 1922)

Richardson, Douglas, *Plantagenet Ancestry: A Study in Colonial and Medieval Families* 2nd ed. (Salt Lake City, UT: Richardson, 2011)

Richardson, Glenn (ed.), *The Contending Kingdoms: France and England 1420–1700* (Aldershot: Ashgate Publishing, 2008)

Rider, Catherine, *Magic and Religion in Medieval England* (Reaktion Books, 2012)

Ridley, Jasper, *A Brief History of the Tudor Age* (Robinson, 2002)

Rotuli Parliamentorum, Volume 5, 1439–72 (1783)

Routh, E.M.G., *Lady Margaret: A Memoir of Lady Margaret Beaufort, Countess of Richmond and Derby, Mother of Henry VII* (Oxford University Press, 1924)

Rubin, Miri, *The Hollow Crown: A History of Britain in the Late Middle Ages* (Allen Lane, 2005)

Rymer, Thomas, *Foedera, conventiones, literae et cuijuscunque generis acta publica inter reges angliae* (J. Tonson, 1739–45)

Saul, Nigel, 'Richard II, York and the Evidence of the King's Itinerary' in *The Age of Richard II*, ed. James L. Gillespie (Stroud: Sutton, 1997)

Saul, Nigel, *Richard II* (New Haven, CT: Yale University Press, 1999)

Saul, Nigel, *St George's Chapel Windsor in the Fourteenth Century* (Woodbridge: Boydell Press, 2005)

Saygin, Susanne, *Humphrey, Duke of Gloucester (1390–1447) and the Italian Humanists* (Leiden: Brill, 2001)

Scattergood, V.J., *Politics and Poetry in the Fifteenth Century* (Blandford Press, 1971)

Shrewsbury, J.F.D., *A History of the Bubonic Plague in the British Isles* (Cambridge: Cambridge University Press, 2005)

St Leger, Francis Barry B., *Froissart and his Times* (Ulan Press, 2012)

Stratford, Jenny, *Richard II and the English Royal Treasure* (Woodbridge: Boydell Press, 2012)

Strickland, Agnes, *Lives of the Queens of England from the Norman Conquest, Volume 2* (Philadelphia, PA: Lea and Blanchard, 1848)

Stuart, John (ed.) *Rotuli Scaccarii Regum Scotorum, Volume 5* (Public Record Office, 1878)

Taylor, J., W.R. Childs and L. Watkiss (eds) *The Chronica Maiora of Thomas Walsingham* (Oxford Medieval Texts, 2003)

Thomas, Alfred, *Anne's Bohemia: Czech Literature and Society 1310–1420* (Minneapolis, MN: University of Minnesota, 1998)

Thompson, Edward Maunde (ed.), *Chronicon Adae de Usk 1377–1421* (Oxford: Oxford University Press, 1904)

Thomson, Richard, *Chronicles of London Bridge* (Smith, Elder & Co., 1827)

Treasure, Geoffrey Russell Richards, *Who's Who in British History A–H* (Taylor & Francis, 1998)

Tyrrell, Henry, *Henry Tyrrell's History of England* (London: London Printing and Publishing Co. Ltd, 1860)

Various, *A Collection of Ordinances and Regulations for the Governance of the Royal Household, made in divers reigns from King Edward III to King William and Queen Mary* (London: Society of Antiquities, 1790)

Various, *The Chronicles of the White Rose of York* (London: James Bohn, 1845)

Vickers, K.H., *Humphrey, Duke of Gloucester* (Archibald Constable and Co., 1907)

Waugh, Scott L., *England in the Time of Edward III* (Cambridge: Cambridge University Press, 1991)

Ward, Jennifer C., *Women of the English Gentry and Nobility 1066–1500* (Manchester: Manchester University Press, 1995)

Weir, Alison, *Katherine Swynford* (Jonathan Cape, 2007)

White, William, *Notes and Queries, Volume 1: November 1849–May 1850* (George Bell, 1850)

Woolgar, C.M., *The Sense in Late Medieval England* (New Haven, CT: Yale University Press, 2006)

INDEX